284 THINGS A BRI(
ILLINOIS BOY CAN DO

A BOY'S ADVENTURE BOOK (AGES 8-16)

By Bill Nunes © 2010

[signature: Bill Nunes]

Printed in the USA by McNaughton & Gunn ISBN 9780978799472

OTHER NUNES BOOKS THAT CAN BE ORDERED BY MAIL

Illinois in the Roaring Twenties sale price $5.00 - 300 pages, 625 illustrations (no state roared louder)
Illinois in World War II sale price $5.00 -328 pages, 650 illustrations (has a history of the <u>entire war</u> plus interviews with veterans)
Incredible Illinois sale $5.00 – 600 illustrations (sorry, sold out)
Big Book of St. Louis Nostalgia $19.95; 328 pages, 650 illustrations (the only book of its kind - really cool info) 2008
Big Book of St. Louis & Southern Illinois Crime $20.95; 344 pages, 650 illustrations - massive book, 2009
Send check to Bill Nunes, 3029 Mark Trail, Glen Carbon, IL 62034
$3.25 postage for each book ordered
Send $22.95 for additional signed copies of this book!
Satisfaction guaranteed – 65,000 copies sold

bnunesbook@aol.com   billnunesnostalgia.com   618-288-5185

Dedicated to my grandchildren, Evan Eure and Carlie Reneé Jones

Thanks to Arleigh Jones and Wanda Watson for proofreading sections of this book. Special kudos to Bill Jacobus of Belleville, Illinois who helps in so many ways once the book is printed and ready for distribution. Illustrations are by Marion Strohman of Edwardsville and St. Louisan Lonnie Tettaton. Thanks also to Wikipedia for providing information and pictures.

Table of Contents

INTRODUCTION

PARENTS: Once your son has this book you should keep an eye on him since it contains instructions for numerous robust activities that might need to be supervised, depending upon the boy's age and maturity level. This volume can transform your son from a lethargic video game couch potato into an energetic, inquisitive mass of protoplasm anxious to learn how to make things and do things.

There have long been books in existence similar in format to this one. And I can still remember Mr. Wizard (Don Herbert) demonstrating on his television show some of the neat science tricks in this book. Currently, there are a number of "how to" books for boys on the market but, disappointingly, they are full of Bart-Simpson-like vignettes that will guide youngsters who read them into lifestyles that most parents want their children to avoid. One such book suggests various ways to judge a woman's bra size. (The next thing you know Johnny will be getting suspended from school for snapping bra straps.) Another one, purportedly written for older boys and men, gives tips to young adults on how to win money by gambling at a casino and how to have fun participating in drinking games. Some other topics in these books include: Tips on Belching, Fun Barfing Facts, Snot Department, and Fun Ways to Pass Gas.

I bought one of these books on E-bay (having only the title to go by) with the intention of giving it to my grandson for Christmas. After thumbing through the book when it arrived, I showed him how to do several things it described, but then decided it just wasn't an appropriate gift because of other dubious activities. My goal is to do a wholesome book that not only will give a young man a wealth of interesting activities, but one that is also full of information that will show him that learning is fun. Any young man who takes the time to learn the informational items in the book – presidents, weather, the body human, authors, dinosaurs, inventions, world capitals, artists, stars and planets, mythology, geography – will be a leg up on most of his classmates. With the possible exception of the dinosaurs, few young people will graduate from high school mastering the aforementioned topics in this volume.

I also have avoided including practical jokes because most boys who get into doing these invariably go too far and end up hurting someone's feelings. If it isn't that it leads them to getting into trouble at school, and what parent needs that grief. If your son is into these kinds of things, then the *Jackass* movies are right up his alley. Yes, this wholesome book might prevent your son from becoming a stand-up comedian, but if you watch Letterman or Leno, a good number of their nightly jokes have crude innuendo. Give me the good old days when we arrested filthy mouthed comedians such as Lenny Bruce.

I might be sort of a prude, but if you read through a handful of topics in this book I think you'll agree that they encourage youngsters to use their imagination and build self-esteem by showing them how to make interesting things, deal successfully with life's problems, and carry out fun activities.

1

It has been said there is nothing new under the sun, and almost everything in this book has appeared in a different form in dozens of books, magazine articles, in *Popular Science,* Boy Scout books, or on the Internet.

Some of the things herein are more appropriate for older boys in the 13-16 range instead of younger ones. **Parents might want to decide in advance which things are age appropriate for their particular boy(s).**

I wanted this to be a book that boys will treasure, read and re-read. Unlike other "how to" books, I decided to sprinkle it with inspirational stories and tales of derring-do. This is the book I hope they read late at night, under the covers, with a flashlight. This is the book that might motivate them to become the best student and the best person they can possibly be. I am hoping it will be a book that parents and grandparents will buy and realize that, by working on some of the projects with their young man, they will share in fun and adventure that will last a lifetime. At a time in our history when so many young people go astray because they are looking for kicks, perhaps this book will help teach them the importance of God, family, country, and values we hold dear.

One of the best supply houses for science materials and chemicals is Science Stuff, on the Internet at www.sciencestuff.com or 1-800-795-7315.

If some of the experiments and models described in this book don't work for you, please don't contact me, call the FBI or the President. Or, you can just grit your teeth and move on to the next item in the table of contents. You should find enough of them to work to still make this book very much worth your while. If you find a really, really serious mistake, you can E-mail me and I'll check it out and make a revision in the reprint. My E-mail is bnunesbook@aol.com. My Website is billnunesnostalgia.com.

NOTE: This author cannot be responsible for kids who might fall and injure themselves during a described activity, cut themselves with a knife, or swallow some chemical. Life is full of risks and parents should not

Bill Nunes and Johnny Rabbitt of WRTH Radio

allow their sons (or daughters) to do these things if they can't assume responsibility for what might happen. That would be roughly equal to letting people sue car makers every time they have an accident that is their fault. That is why we have insurance. I, therefore, disclaim any liability for accidents that may occur as a result of information given in this book. If you think it's too dangerous, don't let your son try it.

When I was in grade school there were "monkey bars" on our playground. If you fell and hurt yourself, your parents didn't sue. You

2

learned a valuable lesson to be more careful next time. Sadly, because of goofy lawsuits, you don't see these on playgrounds anymore.

Young people using this book should make sure they get permission from their parents (in advance) before doing any of the physical activities described.

To use this volume properly, you will need to use good common sense at all times: always wear appropriate safety gear, stay within the legal limits of the law, ask an adult for assistance when necessary, and be kind and considerate to others. Finally, don't use this book to become a showoff!

HOW TO SPIT POLISH A SHOE

In 1957, when this author went to high school, gym shoes weren't allowed to be worn in the classroom. Everyone back then wore polished leather shoes to school. At that time, and through most of the 1960s, male teachers wore suits and ties in the classroom. Currently it is fashionable to not only wear Nike-type sport shoes to school, you can even see grown men dressing down and wearing this type of a shoe to church.

If you want to look sharp, persuade your parents to buy you a black pair of polished leather shoes. This is what people wear to proms, weddings, funerals, and nice restaurants. This is what lawyers and other professionals wear, along with a classy suit. Remember, you don't dress up to show off. Research shows that the better people dress **the better they feel about themselves** and the better they tend to behave.

Hard leather shoes need to be polished frequently to restore the original shine and to hide scuff marks. You will need a polish rag, a buffing cloth and a can of shoe wax to begin. My preferred brand is Kiwi. First, take a slightly damp cloth and wipe off all dirt and grime from the shoe. Allow to completely dry before you continue. Polishing does not clean the shoe. It merely helps to waterproof it and restore the shine. Use your polish rag to apply the wax to the shoe. Don't get too much wax on the rag at one time and be careful not to get the wax on anything else because it will cause a permanent stain. By the time you finish the second shoe you can go back to the first one and use the buffing rag to bring out the shine.

After buffing both shoes, you are ready for the spit shine. Military personnel use this technique to bring the polish to a mirror-like finish. Spit on the toe of the shoe and mix the spit in with the wax. Continue to apply a second coat of wax over the rest of the shoe. Traditionally, the spit shine is only used on the front of the shoe. Do the same thing to the second shoe and then go back and re-buff.

HOW TO PLAY CHINESE PING PONG

Does playing the same old ping pong game occasionally get boring? Is your backhand your biggest weakness in ping pong? Here is a great variation of the game. When you read the rules it sounds like this is going to end up being a slow contest, but in some ways it's actually faster than the traditional game.

Under the traditional rules of ping pong, the ball bounces once on your side of the table and then you must return the ball to your opponent's side of the table by hitting it over the net. In Chinese ping pong there is only one important difference. Instead of hitting the ball back over the net you must **bounce it over the net** by hitting the ball on your side of the table first.

When players first experiment with this rule change there is a tendency to bounce the ball very high. This results in a slow, tedious game. Keep practicing and the object is to keep the ball low as it bounces over the net, just like a fast serve which you bounce over the net. If both players do this, the result is a very fast-paced game. The best way to make your opponent miss his shot is to try and angle the ball so it lands on the other side of the net and bounces off the SIDE of the table rather than the end. That way your opponent doesn't have much table left to bounce it back over the net. You will also discover that

Table Tennis/ ping pong

your backhand weakness is minimized by this style of play. When I was a teen, there were a lot of good players that could beat me at ping pong, but very few could best me at the Chinese version. Like any sport, the more you practice it the better you will become.

HOW TO DEAL WITH A BULLY

If you have two or more cats around the house, you'll notice that they quickly establish a "who's in charge" pecking order. We have a female cat that occasionally picks on another female and, when confronted, the other cat turns tail and hides under the bed. We also have a male cat that is slightly overweight and is scared to death of thunder. However, when our dominant female tries to buffalo him, he just holds up his paw as if to say, "Forget it! I'm the top cat around here." It works every time and I have never seen any cat get the best of him. He stops the nonsense dead in its tracks without fighting. The other cats always back down.

I was fortunate as a youth in that I never really had to deal with a bully. I was a bit skinny but I was fairly athletic and taller than average. It was my experience that those who were picked on lacked athletic skills and were usually a bit chubby.

In the movies and in novels, quite often one of the characters advises to challenge a bully physically because "most of them are cowards." The classic bully, complete with scowl and yellowed teeth, is Scut Farkus in the cult film,

A Christmas Story. Most bullies I knew as a youth were fairly big and strong and I certainly had no desire to confront them physically. One of the best ways to deal with bullies is to avoid them. Take a different route if you have to. Most schools will no longer tolerate bullying so another way to handle the problem, especially if they start picking on you, is to report them to an assistant principal. Not only will the administrator give the bully a good talking to, he will notify the parents and let them know about what is going on.

What do you do if this guy is hard core and continues to go after you? If you stand your ground and fight, most likely both of you will get suspended. Yes, he might have been the aggressor, but you could have walked or run away from it. I was an assistant principal at a high school for four years and that was my rule of thumb. Running away might seem cowardly, but remember the quote: "He who fights and runs away, lives to fight another day." Running away before the fight begins quite often prevents you from getting pummeled. Use your head. Will fighting him really solve the problem?

I have seen several movies where the bullying problem is solved thusly. The victim finds a bigger and stronger classmate than the bully. Then he somehow makes friends with this potential bodyguard. Maybe he introduces him to his cute older sister. Or he might help him with his math homework. Perhaps he does him some big favor. On the surface this approach doesn't seem very realistic, but they say that sometimes life imitates art.

In the animal kingdom the hunters, such as lions or hyenas, often pick out the young or the weak as their victims. Since bullies also frequently do this, one way to avoid being picked on is to stand tall and show confidence and self-esteem. You can also improve your physical appearance through daily exercise and light workouts. Even the lowly pick pocket targets people who act like airheads and look like victims.

MUSICAL GRASS

Find a large blade of grass – wider and longer is better. Place the blade of grass vertically between your knuckles and press your knuckles together so the grass doesn't slip away. Your thumbnails should be facing toward you. The strip of grass should be dangling in the gap between your knuckles and where your thumbs are attached to your hands. Blow against the blade through that gap and you should hear a whistling sound. If this doesn't work, adjust your lips and the space between the grass and continue the effort.

WHY DO DIMES AND QUARTERS HAVE RIDGES?

When the government was minting dimes, quarters, and half dollars (in the days of my youth) they had silver content. This was to prove they had worth and value. Thieves came up with a device to trim some of the edge off the coin and steal some of the metal with silver content. It should be remembered that this was before inflation when you could buy a whole loaf of bread for a nickel. Thus the small amount of silver stolen had real value. The thieves would do this to hundreds of coins and thus steal a significant amount of money.

However, the amount they trimmed from each coin was small enough so most people didn't notice the difference. The value of pennies and nickels was too small to alloy their metal with silver. Their edges have always been smooth.

To discourage this thievery, the government began minting coins that contained silver with ridges on the edges. Any effort to trim the edges of these coins would be quite noticeable. In 1963, the government discontinued placing silver content in coins. The metal that is used in stamping out coins is produced by the **Olin Company of East Alton, Illinois**. If you look at the edge of a modern quarter you'll notice that there is a variation in color. That's because it is a "sandwich coin" – two separate pieces of metal pressed together. Olin ships the metal in huge rolls to the mint and the coins are stamped from the sheet roll. The offal, metal that is

1938 dime with silver content

left over after the roll is used up, is sent back to Olin where it is melted down and reused.

WHY WAS THE STOCK MARKET FIGURED IN EIGHTHS?

The origin of the New York Stock Exchange in NYC dates back to 1790 when George Washington was president. It is located on Wall Street. New York was originally settled by the Dutch who named it New Amsterdam. To protect their thriving colony on Manhattan Island, they built a wall as a defense against invasion – hence Wall Street. In 1664 the English captured New Amsterdam with a force of four frigates and the name was changed to New York in honor of the king's brother (the Duke of York) who eventually became King James II.

Spanish Pieces of Eight

Spain, which had become rich as a result of its territorial conquests, had minted a lot of gold and silver coins and these coins were accepted in trade by other nations due to their precious metals content. One particular coin that was widely circulated in use was the Spanish "pieces of eight." This silver coin was actually scored so that

6

you could use it to pay smaller amounts by breaking off a bit.

At the time the stock market was founded the American dollar was a bit unstable in value and the Spanish coin was in wide use. The Spanish "pieces of eight" remained legal tender in the USA until 1857. The organizers of the Stock Exchange decided that they would figure amounts smaller than a dollar in eighths instead of tenths. A tenth of a dollar was ten cents. One bit from a Spanish pieces of eight equaled twelve and a half cents. When a person read the newspaper to check how a stock he had bought was doing, it was reported something like this: ATT (American Telephone and Telegraph) + 3/8. This meant that since the day before, one share of this particular stock had gone up in value 37 and ½ cents. This tradition was continued for over 200 years until a few years ago the stock exchange finally switched to digital units of dollars and cents.

It used to be quite common during my youth for people to speak in eighths when it came to monetary terms. The adult admission price to a movie used to be two bits – 25 cents. A shave and a haircut at the barber shop was six bits or 75 cents. In high school, one of our cheers at a football game went something like this: Two bits, four bits, six bits a dollar/ All for East Side stand up and holler/ Yaayy, East Side!

BLOODLETTING BARBERS

In George Washington's time barbers had three skills. They cut hair and shaved faces with a straight razor, but they were also blood letters. The practice of medicine wasn't very far advanced in Washington's time. Doctors lacked modern skills and modern treatments and often resorted to sawing off legs and arms that became infected. Penicillin was over 100 years away from being discovered. Doctors were often referred to by the nickname "Sawbones." During war-time, soldiers injured on the battlefield had their infected limbs sawed off without any benefit of anesthesia. They would be given a twig or a lead bullet to bite down on so they wouldn't scream in agony. This gave 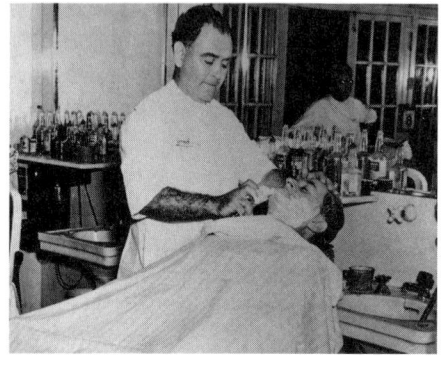 rise to the expression "bite the bullet" when someone had to do something that was unpleasant.

People back then didn't know about germs and disinfectants. If someone fell ill and it lingered on, **a barber was called in to cut a vein and drain a pint or more of "bad" blood from the body**. Thus barbers began to place a red and white striped pole in front of their office. The red stood for the blood and the white represented the bandages. Some barbers even went into the practice of performing abortions, although abortions were largely illegal in this country until 1973.

When George Washington fell ill and was on his deathbed, a barber was called in to drain off some of his "bad" blood. Some medical experts believe this practice may have actually hastened his death.

In modern times, as barbers stuck to giving shaves and cutting hair, the idea of a bloody red and white pole didn't seem like such a good idea. A blue stripe was added to give the pole a patriotic touch.

HOW TO PAINT A DOOR WITH RECESSED PANELS

Around the house you'll probably notice that there is a time-honored division of labor between men and women. Men traditionally take care of the cars, mow the grass, paint the house, take out the trash and barbeque meat. Women cook, clean, iron, do dishes and hang wallpaper. (Men may work from sun to sun but women's work is never done.) This doesn't mean that a man can't cook or that a woman can't paint, but these are exceptions to the rule. And mowing or taking out the trash is often a chore assigned to an older son in the family.

When you go to a restaurant or a place like Kentucky Fried Chicken, the division of labor is still there. Older boys and young men tend to be the cooks while the women deal with customers and are waitresses.

Many men love to do carpentry but hate to paint because sometimes it gets tedious. Painting flat surfaces is relatively easy but the task gets a bit more difficult when there are recessed panels.

Always use a drop cloth when painting anything inside the house so you don't get anything on the floor. For this task let's assume you will be painting the front door which opens out to the stoop or porch. Quite often homeowners paint the inside panels one color while the rest of the door is yet another color. In some cases you need to mask off certain areas and for this hardware and paint stores sell painter's tape. However, for this task that shouldn't be necessary. If there is any loose paint, scrape it off with a putty knife. If the old paint surface is rough, smooth it down with pumice stone. Next you should wipe the door down with a very weak solution of soapy water. When finished, wipe it down again with just water. Allow 24 hours for the door to dry.

Disassemble the lock assembly with a screwdriver so you don't get paint on the knob or escutcheon (cover plate). Use a two inch brush to paint the recessed panels. Stir the paint well with a paint stick and stir again during the painting process. Be sure you get all the nooks and crannies and haven't used an excess amount of paint that will leave globs of paint called drip marks. Drip marks are the sign of an amateur. Wipe off any excess paint that gets on the wood that surrounds the panels. Don't worry about slight paint stains on this part of the door because they will be covered up when you paint the rest of the door in a different color. After the recessed panels are completely dry apply the paint to the rest of the door but stop about 3/8 of an inch before you get to the recessed panels already painted. The final step is to paint those molding areas around the recessed panels. Dip your brush only a half inch deep into the paint

8

and then rub most of it off on the inside lip of the can where the lid goes on. Excess paint will drip back into the can. With the tip of the bristles facing away from the recessed panel you are working on, drag the brush toward the recessed edge to paint the rest of the door. As long as you don't have too much paint on the brush you can paint this strip without any of it running over the edge and down into the recessed panel.

If you are using an older brush where the bristles aren't neat and tight, you can slip a rubber band around them to hold them tight. If you get interrupted for any length of time while painting, place the brush in a Ziplock bag to keep it from drying out. When the job is finished, clean the semi-dried paint from the outside of the brush. Hold it under a stream of warm water and scrub it with a wire brush or Brillo pad. Then hold the brush upside down and let the water run until no more paint color is coming out of the brush. Allow the brush to dry for 24 hours before you return it to the storage area.

Note: If you use oil-based paint instead of latex, the brush will need to be cleaned with a solvent recommended by the paint store. Make sure you put the lid back on the paint can tightly and store it upside down to prevent air from seeping in.

Replace the lock assembly and you should have a door that looks as if it were painted by a pro.

HOW TO BUILD A GOOD CAMPFIRE

126

A group sitting around a blazing fire is a good setting for roasting marshmallows, telling scary stories, or singing religious choruses. Depending on your age, you might ask an adult to help you with this. Select an open space away from trees, houses, cars, etc. Don't be tempted to build a bonfire as these can easily get out of hand and endanger life and property. Select some medium sized stones to mark the perimeter. Place two logs about five or six inches in diameter in the middle of the circle with about a foot of space between them. Place two crumpled sheets of newspaper between the two large logs. Now go find some kindling in the form of smaller branches about the thickness of a pencil. Make sure they are dry enough to readily burn. If they can easily be snapped in two they are probably suitable. Lay these small twigs on top of the paper between the two logs. Next place some logs about three inches in diameter across the two large bottom logs at right angles in criss-cross fashion. Then pile on another layer of smaller twigs, again in a criss-cross pattern. Now place a larger log on top of this. Finally, take some logs that are about 8 inches in diameter and place them on end around the circumference of your pile in wigwam style. There should be sufficient airspace between the kindling and the wigwam fuel logs. Light the newspaper on two different sides and before long you'll have a comfy fire that will impress everyone.

When you have finished and the fire has died out, use a long stick to separate the embers and pour water on the ashes to make sure no strong wind will bring back a flame and rekindle the fire. Careful, those rocks you used will still be hot. Don't leave the fire until there are no more glowing embers. **Remember, once you build a fire you must never leave it unattended.**

P.S. If you feel that using a newspaper isn't in keeping with the spirit of Daniel Boone, you can use very small twigs or dry grass instead. Lint from your mother's clothes dryer is another good start up material. Belly button lint is also excellent but it takes six months to collect enough to get a fire going.

HOW TO TIE A KNOT IN A DRESS TIE

All young men should learn how to properly tie a dress tie. If you watch old Three Stooges movies, you'll notice that ties back in the 1940s tended to be wide and short. Ties nowadays are a bit narrower and should just about touch your belt when you are finished forming the knot. After you learn this basic knot, you can Google "Windsor knot" for instructions on a fancier knot.

Select the tie you want to wear and then lift up your shirt collar. Place the tie around 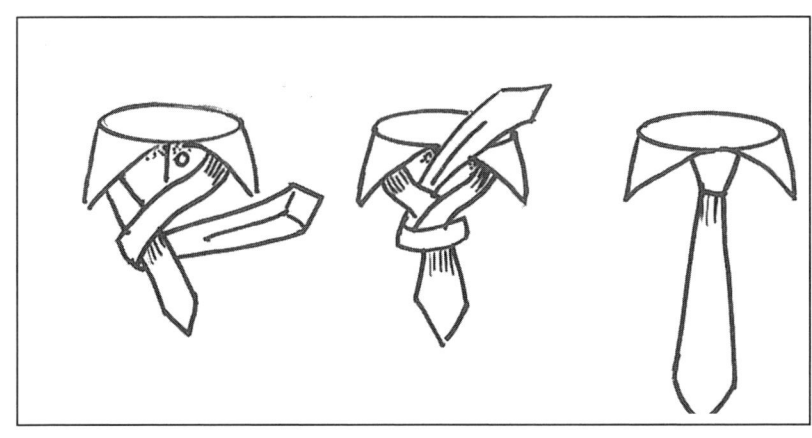 your neck and then pull your collar back down. If you are right handed, you want the narrow end of the tie on your left and the wide end on your right. Reverse this if you are left handed. The wide end should be hanging about twelve inches longer than the short end. Take the wide end over the narrow end and then take it under and around. Bring the wide part across the narrow part once more and then pull it up behind the loose knot you have just formed toward your Adam's apple. Now bring the wide end down through the front loop of the knot. To complete the knot, take hold of the narrow end with your left hand and slide the knot up to your neck. Pull on each end of the tie until the knot is firm but not too tight. If the wide part of the tie is too short, start over again and start with the wide part being 14 inches longer than the narrow part. It may take some experimenting on your part but eventually you'll figure out what lengths to start with at the beginning of the procedure.

THE MAGICAL SPINNING PING PONG BALL

You can perform this trick with either a hair blower or a leaf blower. If you use a leaf blower have someone else hold the blower wand in a vertical upright position and then turn the machine on. Then take a ping pong ball and place it in the middle of the air stream one or two feet from the nozzle. Incredibly, the ball should stay up in the air indefinitely as long as the machine stays on. This can also be done with a hair blow dryer, as long as the nozzle stays vertical. You can always use something like bookends to hold the dryer nozzle in the upright position. The reason this works is that gravity pulls the ball downward but the airflow pushes it back up. If you can't get it to work, try placing the ball in the air stream at a higher or lower level and determine what works best.

As a youth I can remember going to the Sears Store and vacuum cleaner salesmen had a ball magically spinning in the air to attract a crowd of potential buyers. The hose was hooked up to their air outlet port on the machine to get the blower action.

SYMBOLS ON THE DOLLAR BILL

Most of us spend our money without giving it much thought except we generally know that Washington is on the dollar, Lincoln is on the $5, Hamilton is on the $10, Jackson is on the $20, Grant is on the $50 and Ben Franklin is on the one hundred dollar bill. The hundred dollar bill is the largest denomination currently printed, but until 1947 there was a $10,000 bill with the picture of Salmon P. Chase on it. Careful! **Money is considered one of the dirtiest and most germ-infested things we routinely handle** because it has passed through the hands of so many people.

Great Seal of the United States

The obverse, or front, was originally issued in 1963 when our government switched from silver (backed) certificates to a promissory note format. Instead of gold and silver backing our currency, as it did back in 1930, our currency is backed by our nation's reputation and past performance.

In the center of the dollar bill is a portrait of George Washington, taken from a famous painting of him by Gilbert Stuart. His mouth looks a bit grim because he is wearing a set of ivory (not wooden) dentures. His hair cut may also look unusual because he was wearing a white wig which was fashionable for men in 1790. To Washington's left is the black seal of the Federal Reserve, created during Woodrow Wilson's administration. Under this seal is the bill's serial number, which is printed in green. There are twelve Federal Re-serve districts throughout America. The letter J on the front indicates that it belongs to the Federal Reserve Bank in Kansas City. A letter B represents the New York branch. The four black numbers in the rectangular white space also indicate the relevant Federal Reserve Bank.

The other seal belongs to the U.S. Treasury Department. In its center is a carpenter's square, a symbol of the group known as the Masons. Below the emblem is a mortise key, representing the key to the U.S. Treasury. Above the seal is a pair of scales.

Below the Treasury seal is the signature of the Secretary of the Treasury. That person doesn't actually sign each bill. That would be very tiring. That person's signature is mechanically reproduced. Directly below the serial number is the signature of the Treasurer of the U.S. To the left of the secretary's signature is the series year date.

On the reverse side of the bill is the Great Seal of the United States. The main focus is on a bald eagle with splayed wings. (Ben Franklin proposed a turkey instead of a bald eagle for our national symbol.) In the eagle's beak is a scroll with the Latin words *E Pluribus Unum*, which means "one out of many" (50 states, one country). Over his head the stars represent the 13 original colonies "a new constellation in the firmament of nations." There are 13 stripes on the shield, again representing the 13 colonies. In his talons the eagle holds 13 olive branches, symbolizing a willingness for peace. In the other talon are 13 arrows, showing our determination to defend our nation.

To the left is another Masonic symbol – a pyramid, representing strength and permanence. The pointed capstone has not yet been placed on the pyramid, indicating that the work of the nation is yet unfinished. The eye in the triangle represents the all-seeing Deity who guides our progress. Above the pyramid is the motto: *Annuit Caeptis* which translates: "He (God) hath smiled upon our undertakings." At the foot of the pyramid it says *Novo Ordo Seclorum* – A new order of the centuries. The date in Roman numerals is 1776, the year of our independence from the British.

I might add that there are a number of groups in America that see the symbols of the secretive Masons as sinister and evil. They say the stars above the eagle are in the shape of a hexagram, the symbol of witchcraft. In actuality, a number of the Founding Fathers were Masons, including George Washington.

These critics also point to the year 1776 as the year that another secretive group, the Illuminati, was founded. The Illuminati is purportedly a conspiratorial organization which acts as a shadowy "power behind the throne", allegedly controlling world affairs through present day governments and corporations, seeking to establish a New World Order.

In 1900, it was common for workers to earn wages of a dollar a day.

HOW TO MAKE YOUR OWN DIAMOND KITE

Kites were first invented by the Chinese and they were used as signal devices by the military. You can pretend your kite is a military signal by painting it a certain color. To confuse the enemy a red kite can be an all clear or a go signal. Conversely, a green kite can mean stop or caution.

Secure the following materials: A roll of light twine, a sharp pocket knife, a tape measurer, some glue, a piece of brown wrapping paper about 40 inches square, brown shipping tape, two 3/16 inch diameter dowel rods – one 34 inches long and the other 40 inches. Finally, you'll need some ribbon strips for the tail.

Cut a notch in the center ends of the dowels ¼ inch deep, to accommodate the string. Careful with that knife! Don't cut your finger off and get blood on your mother's freshly mopped kitchen floor. Form a cross by placing the short dowel (the spar) over the long one (the spine), about ¼ the way down from the top of the long one. Making sure the notches are parallel to the table, tie the two pieces together. Make sure the left and right arms of the cross are equal in length. Once you determine where this spot is, mark it with a pencil or pen. You can place cereal boxes next to the short dowel to make sure your right angles are true. Place a dab of glue on the joint after it has been tied in place.

Tie a knot at the end of your twine. Place this end of the twine in the notch on top of the cross and go all the way around the kite in clockwise fashion, making sure the twine goes in each of the notches. When you get back to the top wrap the string around the top and tie another knot. When finished, the string everywhere should be taut but not so tight as to warp or bend the dowels.

Place the frame on top of the paper. Cut around it in the customary diamond shape leaving a border overlap of about an inch and a half. Fold the edges over the twine and glue them down. Use the brown tape to strengthen areas that might tear or look a bit weak. Use sparingly because the less you apply the lighter your kite.

Next you make what is technically called a bridle. This

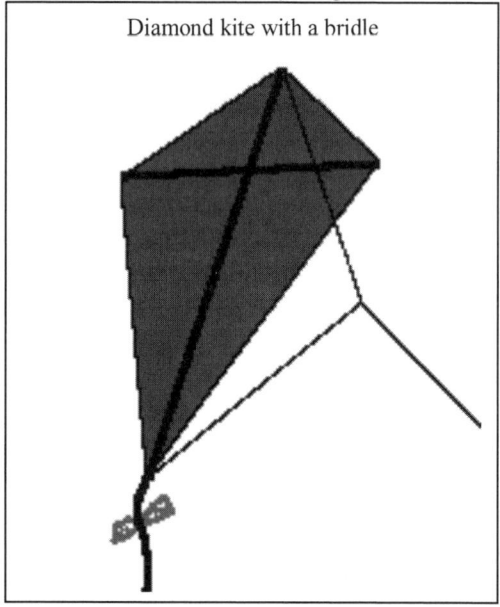

Diamond kite with a bridle

length of twine is what you will tie your ball of string to. Cut a four foot length and attach one end to the top of the kite dowel and the other to the bottom. Make sure the bridle is on the bottom or finished side of your kite. Take a small piece of twine and tie a loop in the twine of the bridle just above the point where the dowels cross. This is where your control line will be attached.

Tie a piece of string to the bottom of the spine to give your kite a tail. The tail should be about four or five times the length of the kite. Tie a ribbon bow around the twine about every ten inches. You can experiment when you first fly the kite. Extra ribbons will give more stability but also add more weight.

Try this! Tie a piece of twine on the left side of the horizontal spar and pull it over to the right side. Before you fasten it, make a bow by bending the crosspiece and then tying it tight. There should now, in the middle of the kite, be a distance of about four inches from your cross string to your stick. As a kid we used to call this a bendy bow. This additional feature allows you to fly the kite with a shorter tail, thus less total weight and easier for lift off.

Dangle your kite and if one side seems heavier than the other add stickers or tape to the light side.

Cotton twine can be used for your control string but it tends to be a bit heavy. A fine nylon or polyester line will be strong enough and will be lighter.

FLYING YOUR AIRFOIL

Take your kite to an open field or a park away from the trees. Kites fly best in an 8-16 mph wind. As you run with your kite to get it airborne, it is the line holding it down that makes it fly. The wind will push against the bottom of the kite. Since the wind cannot push the kite any farther than the string will allow, the wind gets deflected downward producing lift, in accordance with Newton's Law. It took the Wright brothers a while to discover that it was the wind, rushing upward and over the rounded edge of a wing, that was responsible for producing lift which enabled their *Flyer* to become airborne.

Stay away from power lines, airports, trees and large birds. And for heaven's sake, don't attach a key to your line and fly the kite in a thunderstorm to mimic Ben Franklin. You don't want to be the lead story on the evening news.

ABOUT THAT DANDRUFF PROBLEM

Dandruff is simply dead skin. Much of the dust around your house comes from dead skin. Scientists estimate that everyone sheds about a half pound of dead skin every year. There are tiny creatures in your bed called dust mites. These creatures exist by feeding on your dead skin. For this reason you should either have your mom place a plastic fitted sheet over your mattress or turn it completely over about three times a year.

Dandruff is embarrassing because it is so noticeable. It causes low self-esteem and forces those afflicted not to wear dark clothing so it won't be so noticeable. Everyone sheds dead skin but if you have overactive oil glands around your hair roots this speeds up the shedding process. If your oil glands get plugged up, this results in dry-looking hair and dry dead flakes of skin.

Most of the time the problem can be solved by shampooing every other day with a dandruff shampoo such as Selsun Blue or Denorex. You might want to try a shampoo that contains coal tar, especially if you find your hair becoming too dry. Another way to fight dryness is to alternate your medicated dandruff shampoo with regular shampoo. While shampooing, thoroughly massage the scalp with your fingers (not your fingernails which will damage the skin). Be persistent. Occasionally it takes several weeks before you begin to notice a difference. Try several different shampoos and if none of them work go see a dermatologist who can prescribe a medicated shampoo.

A side effect of dandruff can be an itchy scalp. Avoid shampoos that contain alcohol. If the problem persists, the dermatologist can prescribe a separate medication that can be applied to the scalp to treat the itch problem.

DRUGS, CIGARETTES, AND ALCOHOL

This author's mother was a smoker and social drinker from her late teen years until she was about thirty. She attended a Church of God service and responded to the altar call by becoming a born again Christian. From that point on she never once had any desire to smoke or drink again because our church preached against those two things. My father didn't drink but he did smoke. He tried to give it up but couldn't kick the habit. He even bought a drug store aid called Nick-o-Ban but that, too, was unsuccessful. He didn't give up smoking until years later when he started going to church and became a Christian. He laid his pack of ciggys on the altar and never touched them again.

There is the story about a father who wanted to teach his son about the dangers of drinking alcohol. He took his son into the kitchen and placed two glasses on the table. He filled one with water and another with vodka. He took an earth worm from his pocket and plopped it in the water. The worm wiggled and swam around, happy as a lark. Then he placed the worm in the vodka and it shriveled up and died.

"What lesson can you take from this demonstration?" the father asked. The son thought and thought and finally responded with, "I think I know. If you drink, you won't get worms."

Smoking has recently fallen into disfavor due to government pressure, but millions of teenagers start smoking every year because their friends do it or because it's something grown-ups do. Thousands and thousands of Americans still die annually from throat or lung cancer. Unfortunately, there isn't much public pressure against drinking, although it also causes many, many deaths from cirrhosis of the liver or fatal car crashes. Alcohol reduces inhibitions and researchers estimate that nearly one-third of all pregnancies occur after the consumption of alcohol.

Most teens drink large quantities of soda, perhaps two or three a day. The acid in soda eats away at the enamel of your teeth so try to limit your consumption to no more than one a day. It helps to rinse your mouth with water after drinking a soda. Make an effort to drink more fruit juices and plain old tap water. If you are stranded in the middle of a desert, you'll die of thirst before you starve to death. About 70 percent of the human body is water. Try to drink about four or five glasses of water a day.

It may sound silly but when it comes to drugs, follow Nancy Reagan's advice and "Just Say No." Smoking pot occasionally might seem harmless but most people addicted to hard drugs started out by smoking marijuana. Just look at the number of drug-related deaths suffered by rock stars and Hollywood personalities. Actor Robert Downey Jr. (*Ironman*) nearly ruined his acting career because he couldn't kick the drug habit.

The friends you keep often determine whether you get involved in these three bad habits. If the crowd you run around with drinks, smokes, and takes drugs, it is very likely you will not want to stand out from the rest and be different. Choose your friends wisely.

KNOW YOUR ROMAN NUMERALS

Roman numerals are an interesting numeral system of ancient Rome based on letters of the alphabet, which are combined to signify the sum (or in some cases, the difference) of their values. The first ten Roman numerals are:

I, II, III, IV, V, VI, VII, VIII, IX, X

The Roman numeral system does not include a zero. It is a cousin of the Etruscan numerals, and the letters derive from earlier non-alphabetical symbols; over time the Romans came to identify the symbols with letters of the Latin alphabet. The system was modified slightly during the Middle Ages to produce the system used today. Roman numerals are commonly used in numbered lists (such as the outline format of an article), clock faces, pages preceding the main body of a book, chord triads in music analysis, dated notices of copyright, months of the year, successive political leaders or children with identical names, and the numbering of annual events. The year that a particular motion picture was made is often listed in the credits at the end in Roman numerals.

The number 50 is represented by the letter L; the number 100 by the letter C; the number 500 by the letter D, and M represents 1,000. Thus 15 would be XV, 19 is XIX (X = 10 and IX = 10 minus 1), and thirty two is XXXII. Forty can be written as either XXXX or XL. In the case of XL a subtraction system is used with X being subtracted from L. Thus 90 can be either LXXXX or XC. Four hundred is either CCCC or CD. Nine hundred could be either DCCCC or CM. A good way to practice your Roman numerals is to write them out from one to 1,000. Our current year of 2010 is written as MMX. A movie made in 1984 would be written in the credits as MCMLXXXIV. This system is easy to learn and it is another one of those useful bits of knowledge you can store away in your brain.

If you are ever at the board in math class and the teacher tells you to write a number on the board, you can startle your class by writing the number in Roman numerals. Remember to do this in good humor. You don't want to come off sounding like a smart alec.

THE BODY HUMAN

Genes are basic units of heredity of which the body has many. **Eye color** is a visible characteristic of a gene.
A **chromosome** is a single piece of DNA containing many genes. **Males have one X and one Y** chromosome and females have two X chromosomes.

DNA - A nucleic acid that contains the genetic instructions used in the development of all living organisms.

The adult human has 206 bones in the body. The hyoid bone is one of the smallest as it is in the throat and supports the tongue

The smallest bones in the body are in the middle ear; they are the **hammer, anvil and stirrup** or stapes: The tympanic membrane is your eardrum.

Your tongue has four tastes – sweet, sour, salty, bitter.

Cranium = skull, **mandible** = jawbone, **sternum** = breastbone, **vertebrae** = backbone, **patella** = kneecap, clavicle = collarbone, **scapula** = shoulder blade, **coccyx** = tailbone, men and women each have **12 pair of ribs** in the ribcage totaling 24, **pelvis** = hip, **phalanges** are ends of fingers and toes, **carpals** = wrist bone, **femur** is thighbone, **tibia** is shinbone

Kidneys - 2 bean-shaped body organs that produce urine; sometimes called renal glands; they have tubes that lead to the **bladder** which stores urine.

Endocrine glands in the body secrete substances; **adrenal glands** are located above the bean glands and they produce **adrenaline**; **pituitary gland** is at the base of the brain and it **regulates growth**; the **thyroid gland** is a butterfly-shaped gland in the neck just below the **Adam's Apple** and it regulates metabolism; women have **ovaries** which produce an egg once a month and men have testicles which secrete **sperm**. When a sperm unites with an egg a baby is formed.

Metabolism is the rate at which your body breaks down digested food into protein, acids and enzymes.

Pancreas - located on the right side of the abdomen and this gland produces hormones and insulin.

Hormones are chemicals released by cells that affect cells in other parts of the body. Testicles produce the hormone testosterone which gives men more muscle mass than females and greater bone density. Female ovaries produce estrogen which helps regulate the menstrual cycle and breast development. Men have small amounts of estrogen and females have small amounts of testosterone. Because of testosterone, a steroid, men are about 30 percent stronger than women.

Menstrual cycle – women produce one egg a month and if it is not fertilized the body gets rid of it by blood flow out the vagina. Young girls start menstruating at puberty around age 12 or 13.

Insulin is a hormone produced in the pancreas that affects metabolism and other body functions. Sugar in food stimulates pancreas to produce insulin. People with the disease diabetes (too much sugar in the blood) must take insulin shots.

Cartilage is dense tissue in the ears and nose; sharks have no bones but have cartilage instead.

The skin contains sweat pores, pigment cells, hair follicles, blood vessels and nerve cells. **Dermatologists** are skin doctors. Excessive exposure to the sun causes skin cancer.

The average adult human has **8-10 pints of blood**. You can donate a pint to the Red Cross and your body will quickly replace it. Every human has a **blood**

type. You are either A, B, AB, or O. If you are type A and need more blood you must get it from someone who is either type A or O. Type O blood can be used by anyone, no matter what their blood type. Type O people are called universal donors. My blood type is O negative.

Veins carry blood to the heart and an **artery carries blood away** from the heart. The heart is part of the circulatory system and it has **four chambers**. The heart's **aorta** is the largest blood vessel in the body and it sends oxygenated blood to all parts of the body. The **pulmonary veins** bring oxygenated blood from the lungs to the heart.

Lungs come in pairs and when you breathe in they take in oxygen and when you breathe out (exhale) they get rid of carbon dioxide. Trees are important to the environment because they take in carbon dioxide and give off oxygen.

Liver produces bile which aids in digestion. The size of a football in adults, it is the body's largest internal organ. Too much drinking of alcohol can cause liver disease and death. Adults can donate part of their liver to children who need liver transplants.

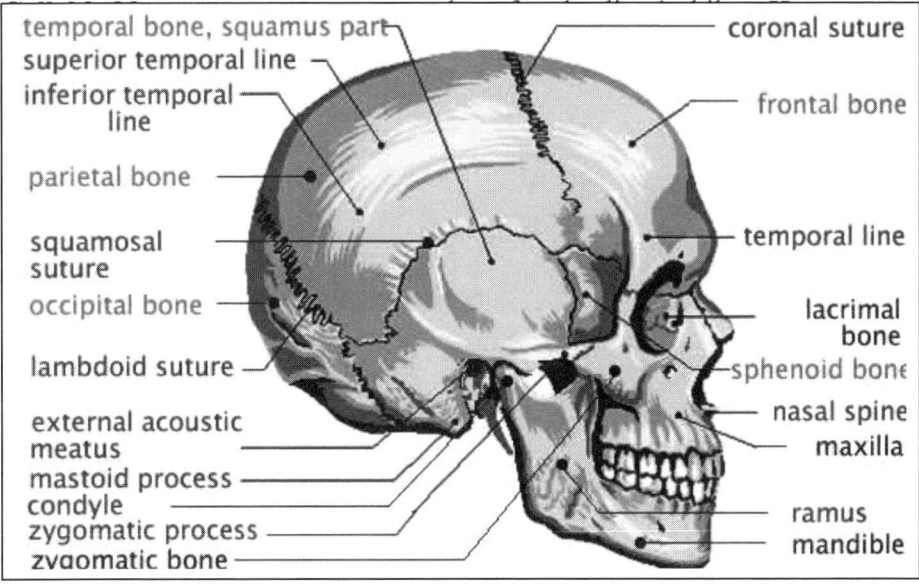

You have four molars on each side or eight total; next to bicuspids are the **cuspids** – one on each side or four altogether. These have a bit of a point at the end. In the front are your **incisors**, four on top and four on bottom.

Trachea – Also known as the windpipe. It is breathing tube in the throat that takes air to the lungs; consists of twenty rings of cartilage.

Pharynx –rear part of mouth that connects to the esophagus

Esophagus – muscular tube which takes food from pharynx to the stomach

Palate – roof of the mouth

Epiglottis – cartilage attached to rear of tongue that directs food into the esophagus instead of the windpipe

Uvula – Conic projection of tissue coming down from soft palate in rear of mouth

18

Tonsils – Tissue on each side of the uvula in the back of the upper part of the mouth; repeated inflammation causes doctors to perform minor surgery to remove them.

Three parts of the brain: **cerebrum** (front) **cerebellum** (middle), **medulla** (rear)

Alimentary canal - your entire digestive system

Your bean-shaped **kidneys** excrete waste into the urinary bladder.

U.S. PRESIDENTS

1788-1796 – George Washington – a Federalist; Father of our Country; our first president; established the two term precedent

1796-1800 – John Adams – the last Federalist, avoided war with France; first to live in the White House

1800-1808 – Thomas Jefferson – Democratic Republican – Louisiana Purchase, Barbary pirates war; wrote Declaration of Independence

1808-1816 – James Madison – Democratic Republican – War of 1812 against British, White House burned – our shortest president at 5-4

1816-1824- James Monroe – Era of Good Feelings, Monroe Doctrine, Illinois statehood

1824-1828 – John Quincy Adams – Accused of stealing the election; authored the Monroe Doctrine as Secretary of State

1828-1836 - Andrew Jackson – Democrat – first president west of Appalachian Mountains; Jacksonian Democracy

1836-1840 – Martin Van Buren – Democrat – Hurt politically by the 1837 depression; Indian removal to the West; first president born in the new United States

1840-1841 – William Henry Harrison - Whig – died a month after giving his inaugural speech; his vice-president Tyler took over

1841-1844 – John Tyler – originally a Whig but became a Democrat

1844-1848 - James Polk – Democrat – conducted successful war against Mexico; annexed Texas

1848-1852 – Zachary Taylor –Whig hero of the Mexican War; died 16 months later and succeeded by Millard Fillmore

1852-56 – Franklin Pierce – A northern Democrat with southern sympathies; supported Kansas-Nebraska Act

1856-1860 – James Buchanan – only bachelor President; Dred Scott Case and John Brown's Raid during his term

1860-1865 – Abe Lincoln of Illinois– our first Republican; our tallest and greatest president; prosecuted the Civil War; murdered by J.W. Booth; Gettysburg Address

1865-1868 – Andrew Johnson- Democrat – was easy on southern rebels after the Civil War; impeached but not removed from office

1868-1876 – U.S. Grant - Republican – Oversaw harsh reconstruction of South; Thanksgiving an official U.S. holiday

1876-1880 – Sam Tilden won popular vote but Republican Rutherford Hayes won 20 disputed electoral votes; South yelled foul so Compromise of 1877 – Hayes allowed to become president while federal troops withdrawn from South

1880-1884 – James Garfield, a Republican; our first left-handed president; was assassinated in 6 months; succeeded by Chester A. Arthur

1884-1888 – Grover Cleveland a Democrat; only President married in a White House ceremony

1888-1892 – Benjamin Harrison – Republican; the Centennial President (100 years) massive labor strikes caused his defeat in 1892

1892-1896 – Grover Cleveland - Democrat- only president to serve two non-consecutive terms

1896-1900 – William McKinley - Republican – Spanish-American War against Spain; annexed Hawaii; "Remember the Maine"

1900-1901 – William McKinley - Assassinated Sept. 1901; succeeded by Vice-president Teddy Roosevelt

1901-1908 – Teddy Roosevelt - Republican – gave us national parks and broke up big corporations and businesses; the "Trust Buster"

1908-1912 – William H. Taft – Republican – Our heaviest president at 326 pounds – had to have new bath tub in White House. When he left a baseball game after 7 innings everyone stood up; became a tradition called 7th inning stretch. Also broke up big business

1912-1920 – Woodrow Wilson – Democrat; first income tax, World War I against Germany; League of Nations

1920-1923 – Warren Harding – Republican; many of his appointees were crooks; died of a heart attack/stroke

1923-1928 – Calvin Coolidge – Republican – Business prosperity in 1920s

1928-32 – Herbert Hoover – Republican – blamed for stock market crash and Depression; Hoover/Boulder Dam named for him; first president born west of the Mississippi

Ronald Reagan of Illinois

1932-45 – Franklin Roosevelt – Democrat; New Deal, World War 2, Social Security; he was crippled by a disease called polio- died in office from a stroke

1945-1952 Harry Truman – Democrat who was Roosevelt's vice-president; dropped A – bomb on Japan, fought Cold War, Korean War; Berlin Airlift

1952-1960 - War hero Dwight Eisenhower - Republican; Interstate highways, Senator Joe McCarthy looked for communists in USA; Fidel Castro comes to power in Cuba

1960-63 John F. Kennedy - Democrat; Bay of Pigs; Cuban missile crisis; assassinated by Lee Harvey Oswald in Dallas; first president born in the 20th Century

1963-1968 Lyndon Johnson - Democrat; Kennedy's vice-president; War on Poverty; Civil Rights Act of 1964; Martin Luther King Jr. and Bobby Kennedy assassinated 1968; Vietnam War

1968-1973 Richard Nixon Republican; ended Vietnam War; visited Communist China; started EPA – Environmental Protection Agency; only president to resign from office because he lied about what happened at Watergate

1973-1976 Gerald Ford – Nixon's Republican vice-president; Communists violate terms of peace treaty and take over Vietnam in 1975

1976-1980 Jimmy Carter - Democrat – Americans taken hostage in Iran; Stagflation – (stagnant economy, high prices); first president born in a hospital

1980-1988 Ronald Reagan - Republican; former movie actor; rebuilt America's defenses, credited with winning Cold War when Soviet Union collapsed in 1989; oldest president to leave office at age 77

1988-1992 George H.W. Bush – Reagan's Republican vice president; won the Iraq War (Desert Storm) against Saddam Hussein

1992-2000 - Bill Clinton - Democrat – impeached after lying about having an affair with Monica Lewinski; his wife Hillary is Secretary of State under President Obama; economic boom thanks to the dot com bubble

2000-2008 George W. Bush - Republican, son of George H.W. Bush; terrorists crashed airplanes into twin towers of World Trade Center; Bush declared war on terrorism; Second Iraq War resulted in execution of dictator Saddam Hussein; also invaded Afghanistan to drive out the Taliban, a group of terrorists; U.S. economy collapses in September of 2008

2008-present; Barack Obama - Democrat; triples the country's debt with bailout packages and stimulus plan; health care plan passes despite strong opposition

FAMOUS ARTISTS

Marc Chagall – Russian Jew, died 1985 – left Russia for France 1930s because they disliked Jews and he didn't do political art. Fled to USA during WW 2. He did painting, stained glass, tapestries, theater sets and advertising labels. His wife Bella was the model in numerous paintings.

Thomas Hart Benton – Active in leftist politics, an enemy of modern art, regional muralist, did murals at Jefferson City, Missouri (state capital), died 1975; *Persephone* painting

Vincent Van Gogh (Dutch) friend of Gauguin, works did not sell; cut off his ear; died in poverty – *Starry Night, Self-portrait, Crows in Wheat Field, The Potato Eaters, Sunflowers* – used bold strokes – died 1890

Paul Gauguin – Lived a while with Van Gogh in Paris – went to Martinique and then to Tahiti and painted Tahitian women; French impressionist; died from syphilis and alcoholism in 1903; he was broke at the time.

Pablo Picasso – Lived in Barcelona and Madrid, Spain; Gertrude Stein bought his paintings and displayed them in her house; though married he had numerous affairs; painted *Guernica* – depicting destruction of a town in Spain during Spanish Civil War 1937; 1944 joined French communist party; sat out two world wars and called a coward. Chicago has a famous Picasso sculpture. He had a blue period and a rose period; died 1973. Picasso and George Braque founded **Cubism** which had geometric shapes

Albrecht Durer – *Praying Hands* – founder of etchings

Roy Lichtenstein – founder of pop art – died 1997 – paintings looked like panels from a comic book – his painting *Torpedo. los* sold for $5.5 million in 1987 at Christies; *Varoom* and *Hot Dog*

Andy Warhol – Marilyn Monroe painting and *Campbell's Soup Can*; comic book type art; died 1997

Prado Museum is in Madrid, British Museum is in London, Hermitage is in Moscow, Louvre is in Paris, Smithsonian is in Washington, D.C., MOMA – Modern Museum of Art is in NYC.

Jasper Johns - made people mad with his disrespectful *Orange American Flag.*

Jackson Pollack - threw paint on a canvas and called it art – the drip artist – died 1956 in a car wreck

Edward Munch - the *Scream* is his most famous painting

Georgia O'Keeffe – painted American Southwest desert scenes and large flowers

Rembrandt van Ryn (of the Rhine)1606-1669 - Self portraits, *Man in Gold Helmet, Night Watch, Anatomy Lesson of Dr. Tulip;* Dutch painter

Henri Taulouse-Lautrec- 1864-1901 French; broken leg and disease made him cripple; painted *Life at Montmarte Café*; designed poster for Moulin Rouge (red mill)

Painter Thomas Hart Benton

Jacques David- Napoleon's court Painter; *Death of Marat*...he supported radical Robespierre   Hated Louis 16 and Marie Antoinette; *Coronation of Napoleon;* fled to Brussels after Napoleon's defeat at Waterloo

William Hogarth - British; *Marriage a la mode*; the Father of Caricature, a fancy word for cartoons with exaggerations

Winslow Homer-1836-1910 – born in Boston but lived in Maine;-painted seascapes- *The Gulf Stream, 8 Bells*

John Trumbull – American artist – *The Declaration of Independence*

Gilbert Stuart – American – did portrait of Washington that was reproduced and placed in most elementary school rooms

Emmanuel Luetze - *Washington Crossing the Delaware* 1851 - by German-American artist

Auguste Rodin –French - 1840-1917- Sculptor- *Adam,   Eve, The Kiss, Headless Man* at SIUE, *The Thinker*; Rodin Museum in Philadelphia

Andrew Wyeth – American painter; *Christina's World* and Helga nudes

Ansel Adams- American – famous black & white photographer 1902-1984

Alexander Caulder famous for mobiles – art objects hanging from strings or wires

Thomas Gainsborough –British landscape and portrait artist - famous for *Blue Boy* and *Pinkie*

Hans Holbein - Court painter for Henry 8th of England – *Portrait of Henry 8th*

Diego Velasquez- 1599-1660; Lived in Madrid, Spain, visited by Reubens; court painter for King Phillip IV and Pope Innocent X, The *Toilet (bath) of Venus*

Peter Reubens – Flemish (Belgian); Reubenesque women are slightly plump; his most famous pupil was Anthony van **Dyck**; did many works with religious themes for the Catholic counter-Reformation. A Van Dyck is a short pointed beard or goatee.

Botticelli – Italian – *The Birth of Venus*

Salvador Dali - born in Catalonia, Spain; *Persistence of memory*; *Giraffe on fire*; moved to Paris 1929, 1940 came to America; Surrealism (having an odd dreamlike quality – not quite real); designed jewelry; wore a long, thin moustache

James McNeil Whistler-1834-1903; Dismissed from West Point; Joanna Hefferman his model; *Portrait of Thomas Carlyle*; *Portrait of Artist's Mother* (Whistler's Mother); *Study in Gray and Black*- lived in London and compared art to music, *Nocturne in Black, Gold*

Frans Hals – Dutch painter - *The Laughing Cavalier*

Leonardo da Vinci-1452-1519; Self portrait - old with beard; *Universal Man* drawing; fresco of *The Last Supper* (Jesus and his disciples) in Milan; *Mona Lisa* in Louvre; *Virgin of the Rocks*

Michelangelo-Bunarroti - Florence, Italy; Frescoes (painting in plaster) on Sistine chapel ceiling; sculptures - *The Pieta, David* ; worked for Pope Julius II; *Last Judgment*- frescoes on altar wall of Sistine Chapel; *Moses,* Tomb of Lorenzo de Medici; *Creation of Adam*-on Sistine Chapel ceiling at the Vatican where the Pope lives

Claude Monet - 1840-1926; founder of French impressionism; good friend of Renoir; wore heavy beard, often confused with Manet; married Camille-fled to London to escape the Franco-Prussian War, series of paintings on haystacks and poplar trees; *Rouen Cathedral, Camille, Water Lilies;* his *Impression Sunrise* gave the name to impressionism where paintings are not very clear

Pierre Renoir -French 1841-1919; painted Forest of Fontainbleu scenes; good friend of Monet, *Gabrielle in an open Blouse*; Gabrielle, his wife's cousin was his favorite; model. *The Bathers* - the girls are slightly big; *Les Grandes Baigneuses* (bathers); he was also an impressionist; *The Swing*; *Girls at the Piano*

Gutzon Borghum – chiseled Mount Rushmore in South Dakota

Louis Eiffel – Eiffel Tower and framework for Statue of Liberty; Frederic Bartholdi did the copper sculpture

El Greco 1541-1614 Born Domenikos Theotopolous in Crete - His name means "the Greek One;" student of Italian painters Titian and Tintoretto; married a woman in Toledo, Spain; he never spoke Spanish; *Philip II at the*

Escorial; some thought his paintings were too loud; had a tendency to stretch or elongate people   (Google these paintings to see what they look like.)

GREEK GODS AND GODDESSES

Zeus – the king of the gods and the ruler of Mount Olympus; son of Cronos and married to Hera; Roman equivalent is Jupiter (married to Juno), the Queen of the gods

Apollo - the god of the sun; son of Zeus and had a sister, the huntress Diana – the Romans also called him Apollo

Poseidon – god of the sea, often depicted holding a three-pronged trident – Romans called him Neptune

Ares – Greek god of war; Romans called him Mars – son of Jupiter and lover of Venus

Aphrodite – goddess of love and beauty; Roman equivalent was Venus

Hephaestus – Greek god of fire and patron saint of metalworkers and blacksmiths; Vulcan is Roman equivalent god of volcanoes; Hephaestus was lame as he was thrown off Mount Olympus.

Athena – armed warrior goddess and goddess of wisdom – City of Athens named for her

Dionysus was Greek god of wine and drunkenness; Roman equivalent was Bacchus.

Hermes – Greek god of trade and commerce – the wings on foot messenger; Mercury was his Roman equivalent

Artemis – goddess of the hunt; Diana was her Roman equivalent

Daphne – turned into a laurel tree; Apollo was in love with her; made himself a laurel wreath to wear on his head.

Cupid – shot arrows from bow to make people fall in love; Eros, god of lust was Roman counterpart

Hymen – god of marriage; he was celebrated during marriage ceremony and the song was called a hymn

Narcissus – looked into a pool of water, saw his reflection and fell in love with his own image

Sisyphus - betrayed some secrets of Zeus so he was condemned to forever push a large boulder up a hill, only to have it roll back, and he had to repeatedly do it again

Cronos – a Greek deity said to be the personification of time – a chronometer is a watch

Atlas shouldering the world

Atlas – Greek strongman god who carries whole world on his shoulders

Titans – there were 12 titans who ruled Greece during a golden age, but they

24

were eventually overthrown by their offspring

Elysian Fields – paradise for the Greeks in afterlife

Tartarus – Souls were judged after death and bad ones were sent to Tartarus (hell) as punishment.

Hades was the god of the underworld and his Roman counterpart was Pluto.

Cerberus – Three headed dog that guards the gates of Hades (hell)

Medusa – A gorgon monster – looking at her directly would turn one into stone; her hair consisted of dozens of snakes; Perseus slew her by looking at her with a mirror, then cutting off her head; from her blood sprang the winged horse **Pegasus**

Prometheus – Stole fire from the gods and gave it to humans. Punished by Zeus who had him chained to a cliff and every day an eagle came and ate his liver; every day he grew a new liver and every day the eagle came and ate it for the rest of eternity

Amazons – a nation of all female warriors; cut off one of their breasts to make it easier to use their bows and arrows

Griffin – Mythical creature with the body of a lion and the head and wings of an eagle

Centaur – Mythical race with head and chest of a human and the body of a horse

Homer's *The Odyssey* (journey) - Odysseus (called Ulysses by Romans) King of Ithaca and hero of Homer's poem. He was punished by the gods for his disobedience and it took him ten years to get home after the Trojan War. It was his idea to build Trojan horse which enabled Greeks to win the war. During his wandering sea voyage he encounters **Polyphemus – a one eyed Cyclops** who eats his men until Odysseus blinds him; at another place they encounter **Circe, a witch** who turns his men into swine (pigs); then they sail past a huge whirlpool and face **Scylla and Charybdis (two sea monsters** guarding the straits of Messina); next they sail past island of sirens, 3 female creatures who sing songs that lure men to shipwreck on the rocks; they foil the sirens by putting beeswax in their ears. Odysseus wants to hear them so he doesn't use wax and tells his men to tie him to main mast until they are safely past. The sirens' songs nearly drive him mad. Odysseus finally returns home to find suitors trying to woo his wife, **Penelope**. She wove a tapestry and she told suitors that when she was finished she would choose one of them to marry. Meanwhile, they ate her food, drank her wine and chased her maidservants. Every night she secretly undid her day's work so she never finished the tapestry. Odysseus disguises himself as a beggar and his faithful dog is the only one who recognizes him. He locks the suitors inside the great hall and kills all of them.

Homer's *Iliad* - story of 10-year long Trojan War. Helen, beautiful wife of the King of Sparta, is kidnapped by Paris and taken back to Troy. Odysseus was sent to King Priam of Troy to get her sent back, but he refused. This led to war with many Greeks participating. Agamemnon was leader of Greek army and Ajax was a great warrior and cousin to Achilles. Ajax has two big battles with Hector. Achilles was the Greek's greatest warrior. His mother had made him invincible in battle by dipping him in the river Styx when he was born. Unfortunately, she held him by his heel and this left him vulnerable. The Trojans are led by Hector. Achilles dies in battle when struck in the heel by a poisoned arrow, shot by Paris. Achilles almost ended the war by getting permission from king Priam to marry his daughter, who was also Paris's sister. Paris would have to give up Helen if this happened so he hid in bushes and shot Achilles in the heel. Odysseus rescues his shield and dead body. Achilles previously killed Hector and dragged his body behind his chariot. Paris was also killed later in the war. The Greeks act like they are going to quit the war and build a big wooden horse and leave it in front of the walled city. The Trojans take it inside the gates but Greek soldiers are hidden inside. That night they open the city gates to let their army in; they win the war and Helen finally returns home.

FAMOUS AMERICAN AUTHORS

Laura Ingalls Wilder

Mark Twain – Samuel Clemens - Riverboat pilot and humorist. *Tom Sawyer* (talks others into whitewashing fence for him) *Huck Finn, Jumping Frog of Calaveras County, Roughing it, Life on the Mississippi Walt Whitman – Leaves of Grass and Song of Myself*
Emily Dickinson – *poet – Because I could not stop for Death*
Stephen Crane – *The Red Badge of Courage* (a war wound)
Robert Frost – Poet – *Stopping by the Woods on a Snowy Evening* – he read a poem at John Kennedy's inauguration; *The Mending Wall* is a poem about a stone wall – "good fences make good neighbors" is a famous line

James Fenimore Cooper

Carl Sandburg of Illinois – Abe Lincoln biographer; poem ***Chicago***: Hog butcher of the world, a player with railroads
Sinclair Lewis – *Main Street*
T.S. Eliot – Poet born in St. Louis but moved to England – *The Waste Land*
O. Henry – *The Gift of the Magi*
William Faulkner of Mississippi – *The Sound and the Fury*
John Steinbeck – *The Red Pony, The Grapes of Wrath, East of Eden*
Robert Penn Warren – *All the King's Men* is the story of Louisiana governor Huey Long

26

Theodore Dreiser – *Sister Carrie*
Nathaniel Hawthorne – *The Scarlet Letter, The House of the 7 Gables*
James Fenimore Cooper - *The Last of the Mohicans*
Henry David Thoreau – *On Walden Pond*; went to jail for refusing to pay taxes to support the Mexican War
Ralph Waldo Emerson – Founded Transcendental Club – wrote *A Concord Hymn, Essay on Self Reliance*, friend of Transcendentalists were radicals who believed God did not have to reveal truth, it could be found by studying nature.
Washington Irving – *The Legend of Sleepy Hollow*
Edna Ferber – *Giant, Ice Palace, Cimarron, Showboat*
Laura Ingalls Wilder – *Little House on the Prairie*
Henry Wadsworth Longfellow – *Evangeline, Song of Hiawatha, Paul Revere's Ride*
Frank Baum – *The Wizard of Oz* – Dorothy and dog Toto live in Kansas
Margaret Mitchell - *Gone With the Wind* – Scarlet O'Hara, Rhett Butler, "Tomorrow is another day!"
Wila Cather – *Oh, Pioneers*
Herman Melville - *Moby Dick; Billy Budd* is executed for mutiny on the ship *Pequod, Moby Dick* - Captain Ahab chases great White Whale.
Harriet Beecher Stowe – *Uncle Tom's Cabin* – a book about the evils of slavery
Louisa May Alcott – *Little Women* – Meg, Jo, Beth and Amy March; 1868 Concord Massachusetts, *Little Men* 1871
Ernest Hemmingway – *Old Man and the Sea* – fishing near Cuba, *Sun Also Rises* – Jake Barnes a WW I veteran and American expatriates, living in Europe, go to Pamplona, Spain to see the running of the bulls *A Farewell to Arms* – WW I novel; Hemmingway committed suicide in Idaho in 1963
F. Scott Fitzgerald - *The Great Gatsby* – Nick Carraway, a Midwesterner, goes to live among the rich on Long Island 1925 – Set during Prohibition, Gatsby is a rich bootlegger; Daisey Buchanan is main attractive female; *Tender is the Night, The Jazz Age*

AVOIDING LIFE ALTERING MISTAKES

When teens act irresponsibly in movies or on TV, it gets shrugged off as, "Oh, that's just Jim going through a rebellious stage. That's normal for teenagers." I certainly didn't go through a rebellious stage and neither did my sister. Nor did my son or daughter. In their later years, nearly all teens who cause their parents needless grief and worry regret this past behavior. Don't do it.

Part of the process of growing up is learning to make your own decisions and mistakes. The key is to minimize these mistakes in judgment and learn from them. More important, be careful to avoid those situations that could be life altering or fatal.

Try to save part of what you earn. The average credit card debt in America is roughly $8,000. Learn to pay off credit cards every month and if this doesn't work switch to debit cards. **Arguments over money and debt are a leading**

cause of divorce.

Don't get involved in drugs, liquor or cigarettes which can kill you or shorten your life span. Don't engage in irresponsible sex that could result in HIV or another sexually transmitted disease. The Bible makes it clear that sex should be engaged in only by married couples.

Don't be tempted to try some of the **stupid stunts depicted in *Jackass* movies**. After seeing a movie similar to *Jackass*, one young man decided to emulate what he saw in the film. He went to a busy road and lay down on the stripe that separated the two lanes. He was subsequently struck by a car and severely injured. **Don't engage in binge drinking**. **Don't drive without seatbelts**. Don't ride a bike or motorcycle (donorcycle) without wearing a helmet. Life offers so many other ways to "get high;" don't become a thrill seeker who needs to push the envelope with sky diving, mountain climbing, racing cars, or flying in one-seat experimental planes. **Never drive recklessly or get in a car with a driver who has been drinking.**

HOW TO ADMINISTER ARTIFICIAL RESPIRATION

Artificial respiration is sometimes referred to as mouth-to-mouth resuscitation. It should be administered to people with a beating heart but who are not breathing. Knowing how to do this might someday save a person's life. Once the brain is deprived of oxygen for about 5 minutes, brain damage or death can be the result. First check to see if there is anything blocking the air passage. If there is, go ahead and remove it with your fingers. Immediately call 911 for an ambulance. Now check to see if removing the obstruction restarted the breathing process. If not, place the person on their back. Use your hand to tilt their head slightly backwards. Use your other hand to pinch the nose shut with your thumb and index finger. Inhale deeply and place your mouth over the victim's forming a seal. Then exhale and blow into that person's mouth. Sometimes this is called the **kiss of life**. This force of air should cause their chest to rise or expand. If it doesn't, check again for an obstruction. Remove your mouth and their chest should go down once more. Repeat the process by holding their nose and blowing into their mouth again. Repeat this process four or five times and then check to see if the victim has a pulse. This can be done by placing two fingers on the underside of the wrist in line with their thumb. Another way to check for pulse is to use two fingers to check the carotid artery in the neck. If the person doesn't start breathing on his/her own continue the process until the ambulance arrives.

If the person starts breathing on their own, place the closest arm parallel to their body. Take the other arm, bend it at the elbow and place the hand against their cheek. Reach for his/her far knee and bend it. Using one hand to protect the head, roll the person toward you and keep them on their side. Stay with them until the paramedics arrive.

ADMINISTERING CPR

Cardiopulmonary resuscitation is administered to people whose heart has stopped beating. As in the case of artificial respiration, time is essential because brain damage or death can occur if the heart is stopped longer than five minutes. If the heart stops in a child roughly twelve years old or younger, only one hand is placed on the chest. For those thirteen or older, both hands are used in the process. This procedure is unlikely to restart the heart. Its main function is to keep some blood flowing to other parts of the body, especially the heart, until a paramedic can take over. Most likely, that trained person will then administer electrical shock to the patient in an effort to restart the heart.

A person's heart can stop beating due to drowning, a heart attack, being struck by lightning, or from some kind of trauma. CPR should only be performed on someone who is unconscious, has no heartbeat and isn't breathing.

Be sure to call 911 or have someone else do it before you begin. The first thing to do is use your index and middle finger to lift the chin while you assist this process by gently tilting the victim's head back a bit. Use your thumb and index finger to pinch the nose closed. Inhale deeply and place your mouth over the victim's forming a seal. Then exhale and blow into that person's mouth. This force of air should cause their chest to rise or expand. If it doesn't, check again for an obstruction. Remove your mouth and their chest should go down once more. Repeat the process by holding their nose and blowing into their mouth again.

Using the heel of your hand, place it right in the center of the person's upper stomach, just below the ribs. Cover your hand with the heel of your other hand, and lean your body forward; place your hands on the person's upper stomach. Quickly and firmly press your hands into the lower chest until it sinks about two inches. Perform 30 fast compressions, stop, perform two more breath procedures, and then repeat: 30 compressions followed by two breaths. Check for breathing. Continue alternating compression and breath procedures until help arrives.

You should not try CPR on the upper chest (sternum and ribcage) because you might break a rib and puncture a lung. This technique should be used only after becoming certified by going through a Red Cross (or similar training program). CPR should also not be used on drowning victims or someone suffering from a drug overdose. **Also, don't attempt CPR if you do not witness the heart stoppage**. Most classes last about three hours and the technique is practiced on a mannequin. There are studies that indicate the compression of the lower abdomen pushes almost as much blood to the heart as ribcage compression.

Most people think artificial respiration and CPR are more successful than they actually are. This is due to an unrealistic high success rate as described in novels and shown on television dramas and in films.

GETTING RID OF AN UNWANTED NICKNAME

Do you know anyone whose nickname is "Tubby," "Fats," "Freckles," "Pootsie," or something roughly equivalent? My full name is Herbert William

Nunes. I went through 12 embarrassing school years of being called Herbert by my classmates and teachers. Now in the 1950s, Herbert ranked right up there with old fashioned names such as Clarence or Beulah. How I wished my name would have been Steve or Brad. It wasn't until after I graduated that I hit upon the solution. For legal documents, such as a driver's license, I simply wrote H. William Nunes. I also told my friends that I was going to start using my middle name William, and from then on I wanted them to simply call me Bill.

But what do you do if your friends all call you "Pootsie?" The quicker you get rid of such an embarrassing nickname the better off you'll be. The first thing you do is inform your parents and siblings (brothers and sisters) that you do not appreciate that put-down of sorts, and from now on EXPECT to be called simply John, Evan, Doug, or whatever your actual name is. You might run into some resistance at first, but if you are firm about it and keep reminding people, the change you seek will soon take place.

What do you do about the person who, just to be mean, insists on using the old nickname? You put a hand on their shoulder and look them square in the eye. Then you tell them that you are dead serious about the name and that if they wish to remain your friend, they will stop using the unwanted nickname. If they still don't get it, ask them how they would feel if you started calling them Dumbhead. "Hey Dumbhead, do you want to go roller skating with the youth group tonight?" Trust me; that will do the trick. If they are one of those one in a hundred who just won't stop, tell them that friends don't say hurtful things to their buddies and that if they continue this behavior you won't consider them a friend anymore.

CHOOSING A LIFE PARTNER

The Bible says that a man and woman should not be unequally yoked in marriage. What this means is that it isn't a good idea for a Christian to be married to a non-Christian. As a teen who attended church regularly, I saw numerous women bring their children to Sunday school and church every week, while their husbands stayed at home and watched television or went fishing. I felt sorry for these women because none of their husbands ever changed and became Christians.

When couples get married they are facing an uphill battle because statistically about 46 % of all marriages end in divorce. Christian divorce rates are much lower because each partner generally tries to include God in their life plan. If a problem develops, they are more likely to resolve it through prayer and discussion.

It is often said that you don't get to choose who you fall in love with, but that isn't quite true. If you don't go bar hopping you are less likely to end up marrying a drunk. If you go to college you increase your chances of marrying someone who also has a college degree and is your intellectual equal. When it comes to marriage, rich people usually don't marry poor people. White people tend to marry other whites. Good looking people usually end up marrying someone else who is equally attractive.

Before my wife and I were married we went to the same church, but we attended different colleges our freshman year. I was in love with her but she wasn't sure and had been used to playing the field. At the University of Illinois, she dated several young fraternity men who smoked, drank, and had values far different from hers. Their behavior and mannerisms were a turn off, and that summer she fell in love with me. We've been married 50 years and our similar church upbringing had a lot to do with our marriage's success.

When you are young and date someone the first thing your friends want to know is how cute is that person. Judging a person solely on their looks is a shallow and immature way to determine a relationship. Naturally you want to marry someone you're physically attracted to, but pay attention while you are dating. Does the person you are thinking about marrying share your beliefs, goals and values? Do they have a temper? Are they trustworthy and reliable? Do they mix well with others socially or are they "loners?" What bad habits do they have? Are they reckless drivers? By the time a person reaches maturity their personality has pretty much already been formed. Many people enter into a marriage thinking they can change that person or cure them of their bad habits. About the only time that happens is if and when that person becomes a born again Christian.

If you marry the wrong girl, she might be a spendthrift and leave you with a large debt. In a divorce proceeding, the wife almost always gets the house if there are children. The husband is usually required to pay monthly alimony to the wife and child support for the children. Also, the wife usually gets custody of the children and the ex-husband is limited to seeing them on weekends or during the summer. Divorces can be very bitter, quite expensive, and emotionally draining. **Marry the right girl!**

KEEPING PHYSICALLY FIT

Statistics tell us that nearly one-third of all young people are overweight and physically unfit. Ideally, young people should get 60 minutes of play and exercise every day. Those who are physically fit are more alert, lead healthier lives, and are less likely to get diseases such as heart problems or diabetes. Good health is one of your most prized possessions. It is true that the genes you inherit from your parents also play an important part in longevity and health, but exercise can go a long way in giving you a longer and happier life.

Don't get caught in the trap of a diet that consists mainly of burgers, fries, tacos and pizza. Yes, those are all tempting foods, but make sure you also include plenty of fruits and vegetables in your diet. Scientists aren't quite sure why, but two of the best things you can eat are apples and tomatoes. "An apple a day keeps the doctor away."

Eating lots of fried foods can lead to high cholesterol problems and this, in turn, can lead to heart attacks, clogged arteries that require the insertion of stents, and sometimes open heart surgery that consists of a triple or quadruple bypass.

Most young people are picky eaters. Not a good idea. As a teen I was somewhat picky, but over the years I widened my tastes and now I can eat practically anything – corn, spinach, squash, pumpkin, zucchini, tomatoes, beets, turnips, rice, lima beans, sauerkraut, slaw, potato salad, yogurt, quiche – you name it.

Whole milk has a lot of artery clogging fat and that is why you see many older people drinking 2 percent or skim milk. As a youngster I never thought I could drink skim milk, but as my cholesterol levels went up that motivated me to make the switch.

GOOD GROOMING

When I was a teen I remember hearing adults saying something like this: "Sally is going out with that Hammond boy from church. He seems like a nice, clean-cut young man." Notice that the commentator didn't know much about the boy but gave her approval based on his appearance. Clean-cut meant he was neatly dressed and neatly groomed. Currently, you hear young people say all the time that they don't care what others think, but that isn't true. That is why the vast majority of teens go along with the fashion of the day. In my time if I would have gone to school wearing my baseball cap backwards my friends would have thought I was nuts.

At some point in life, teens need to show maturity with their appearance. When Tony Romo first became the starting quarterback for the Dallas Cowboys, he was frequently seen on the sidelines wearing his ball cap backwards. After a few years he decided this was a mark of immaturity. He wanted to be a mature team leader so he started wearing his cap with the bill forward.

Another fashionable item nowadays is the tattoo. These are also seen as signs of immaturity. Not too long ago, for this very reason, police departments were reluctant to hire men on the force who had visible tattoos. During my teen years about the only people you saw with tattoos were sailors who got drunk on shore leave and were talked into it by their buddies. An easy way to avoid tattoos is to view them as defacing your body. On girls they're called "tramp stamps." Dermatologists can readily attest that large numbers of people in society regret getting tattoos and later go through a painful and expensive process of getting them removed.

It's ok to follow harmless fashion fads. I once wore pegged Levis to school and in the 1970's I wore those outrageous plaid leisure suits. Go ahead and sport shaggy hair, wear pants without a belt, leave your shirt hanging out, and have holes in the knees of your jeans (the urchin look), but when you go to church or to a restaurant, learn to dress up a bit. And when you enter the world of work it won't hurt to "dress for success." Studies have shown that when people are dressed up they behave better and feel more confident about themselves. It's like the old U.S. Army motto: "**Be All That You Can Be**." Remember, it was the apostle Paul who said that when he was a child he did childish things, but when he became a man he put away childish things.

HOW TO CLIMB A ROPE

There will probably come a time in gym class when the teacher gets out a thick natural fiber rope and announces that everyone in class will attempt to climb it. Rope climbing used to be an Olympic event until it was discontinued after the 1932 Olympics. In modern rope climbing competitions you are not allowed to grip the rope with your feet. You must only use your arms to pull yourself up. You never know; one day you might find yourself in a reality survival show where rope climbing in some snake-infested jungle might come in handy. In any event, you don't want to be one of those in class that futilely grabs the rope and then slides back to the floor in ignominious defeat. Here's how to do it.

1. Grab the rope with both hands extended above the head. 2. Pull hard on the rope and jump up at the same time and you will be lifted off your feet. 3. Twist your left leg to wrap the rope around it and then use both your feet to pinch the rope. 4. Reach up as high as the top of your head and grab hold of the rope. Release the rope from your feet and, using your abdominal muscles, bend your knees up to your chest. Quickly re-secure your feet higher up the rope. 5. Straighten your legs and reach up as high as you can on the rope. Continue the previous steps until you reach the top. 6. When coming down, loosen your grip on the rope with your feet and lower yourself in a hand over hand technique.

Rope or pole climbing is something you should practice at home in your backyard. You can tie a sturdy rope to the overhanging branch of a large tree. Lacking a tree, persuade your dad to erect a 15 foot high pole made of inch and a half diameter galvanized pipe and set in concrete. Climbing this pole regularly is one of those recommended ways to get physical exercise, build your arm strength, and to stay fit.

FAMOUS PEOPLE IN THE OLD TESTAMENT

Abraham – Founding patriarch of the Israelites; married to Sarah; father of Isaac

Adam – the first man, husband of Eve; his son Cain murdered his brother Abel; had no navel

Ahab – King of Israel; married to Jezebel; stole Naboth's vineyard; killed in battle

Daniel – Survived after being placed in a den of lions

David – Slew the Philistine giant Goliath; became King of Israel

Deborah – The only female judge of pre-monarch Israel

Esther – Jewish queen of Persia who foiled a plot to commit genocide on the

Israelites

Eve – The first woman; yielded to temptation in the Garden of Eden; wife of Adam; also had no navel

Gideon – Defeated the Midianites at the battle of Jericho; one of the judges

Isaiah – Old Testament prophet who was killed by being sawn in two with a wooden saw

Jacob – Stole his brother Esau's inheritance, wrestled with an angel; son of Isaac

Jeremiah – Known as the Weeping Prophet because Israelites often disobeyed God

Job – God allowed his loyalty to be sorely tested by the devil but he held steadfast

Jonah – Was swallowed by a great fish after he refused to obey God

Joseph – Eleventh of twelve sons of Jacob; other sons jealous of his coat of many colors

David and the severed head of Goliath

Moses – Led his people out of Egyptian slavery; given 10 Commandments on Mt. Sinai

Noah – He and his family survived the Great Flood by building the Ark

Rachel – Wife of Jacob who worked for her father 7 years to earn her; mother of Joseph

Ruth – A widowed woman, married Boaz; Ruth is a fore-mother of Christ by lineage

Sampson – Hebrew strong man who slew the Philistines but was tempted by Delilah

Saul – Hebrew king who committed suicide in battle; son Jonathan was a friend of David

Solomon – Son of David and Bathsheba and wise king of Israel

HOW TO MAKE AND READ A COMPASS

Before any serious voyages of discovery and exploration could take place several things had to be invented – printing, the astrolabe (to determine a ship's latitude), a seaworthy type of ship (caravel) and the compass, which gives direction.

You will need the following equipment to make a crude, but workable, compass: A sewing needle about two inches long, a small bar magnet or refrigerator magnet, a small piece of cork, and a small bowl of water to float the cork and needle. Needles are sharp, so be careful.

34

First run a magnet over the needle a few times, always in the same direction. This will magnetize the needle. Carefully shove the needle through a piece of cork. Cut off a small circle from the large end of the cork, and drive the needle through it, from one end of the circle to the other, instead of through the exact middle. Be careful not to poke yourself! Next float the cork and needle in your bowl of water so the floating needle lies nearly parallel to the surface of the water. Place the compass on a table and watch what happens next. The needle should rotate and point towards the nearest magnetic pole - north or south whatever the case may be.

The mass of the earth produces a magnetic field and the needle will align itself with that field. Whenever you read a map the north direction printed on it is called True North. However, magnetic north will be slightly to the right (east) of true north. Advanced compasses have a base plate or a bezel housing which slightly rotates and corrects this problem.

The reason for magnetic north being a bit different from true north is due to the tilt of the earth on its axis. This occurred after there was a big ruckus between a bunch of Greek Titans and the ensuing commotion caused the earth to tilt about 23 degrees.

Once you determine where north is then south will be in the complete opposite direction, east will be to the right and west will be to the left. Out in the woods it helps to remember that the sun rises in the east and sets in the west, and that moss grows on the north side of trees.

To use the compass to find your way to a distant mountain, turn the base plate of the compass so that the direction-of-travel line points at the mountain. Now turn the compass housing (called the bezel) until the orienting mark is beneath the north end of the compass needle. Check once more to make sure the direction-of-travel line still points at the mountain. This gives you your bearings. Follow the direction-of-travel line while keeping the needle over the orienting mark and you will make it to the mountain without any trouble.

PERFORMING A ROPE TRICK

Here is something you can do that will amaze your friends. Hand them a piece of clothesline rope a little less than three feet long. After performing the trick you can adjust the rope length to what works best for you. Hand the rope to a friend and **challenge them to tie a knot in the rope without letting go of either end**. When they can't figure it out hand the rope to the next person in the group and challenge them. When they give up in frustration ask if anyone in the group thinks he or she can do it. At this point no one is likely to come forward. Tell them you can do it.

Stand in front of a card table and lay out the rope in front of you. Now cross your arms so that your right hand is near your left armpit and your left hand is touching your right bicep (muscle). Keep your hands and arms in this position and bend over and pick up the rope ends. While keeping your grip on the rope ends, slowly unfold your arms and everyone will be astonished to see a knot form in the middle of the rope.

35

Be sure you practice this trick in advance until you have it down pat so you don't goof up during your performance.

HOW TO PROPERLY MOW A LAWN

When I was a youngster, almost nobody in the neighborhood worried about clover or dandelions in their yard. They also mowed with one of those old fashioned push mowers that had rotary blades that "ate grass" as you pushed the machine forward. And the idea of spreading fertilizer on the grass so you would have to mow it more often just seemed insane. Most home owners today are much more demanding and sophisticated.

Hundreds of people every year are injured using a power mower. Remember these safety tips. 1. Always make a quick tour of the lawn before you begin to remove paper, limbs, rocks, or other obstacles such as toys. 2. Always wear safety goggles 3. Always keep your hands and feet away from the mower deck 4. Never mow wet grass, especially if there is significant slope to your yard. 5. Always check oil and gas levels before starting. 6. Wash dirt and grass from the mower after every second use. 7 Change the oil at least twice a season using heavy 30 W oil. 8. Leave the grass a bit longer during the hot summer months and a bit shorter heading into winter. Most people like their grass to be about an inch and a half long after cutting. 9. Blades should be sharpened a minimum of at least twice a season. 10. You can avoid the washboard or ripple effect by changing the direction of the cuts by 90 degrees every second time around – up and down, north to south, followed by back and forth, east to west.

Catching your clippings can be a bit expensive when you have to pay for waste removal, but you end up with a nicer looking lawn and it isn't necessary to de-thatch the lawn every year. Discharging the clippings back on the lawn isn't too bad if you have mulching blades. If you discharge the clippings don't throw them onto your driveway or on the street. This is unsightly. Go the other direction for at least two turns around the yard so this doesn't happen.

You can make your yard look a bit more interesting by cutting it at an angle instead of horizontally. If you want to leave stripes on your lawn the way you see it done at ballparks, your mower must have a roller on it. It is healthier for your lawn if you change the direction of the cut every other time you mow. When you irrigate, soak the lawn with **an inch of water** to promote deep root growth.

Cutting the lawn has traditionally been a man's job so learning how to do this when you are about nine or ten is good training. It is also a good way for a bright and energetic young man to help out around the house and to learn how to take pride in accomplishing something. Mowing lawns in the neighborhood is also a good way to earn money during the summer. The pay is usually around $20 to $32 per lawn, depending on the size.

LEARNING HOW TO JUGGLE THREE BALLS

Critics say the most accomplished juggler of all time was Enrico Rastelli. He was an Italian born into a circus family and practiced for hours and hours until he perfected a routine. He became the first person to juggle seven balls at once, a feat thought to be impossible.

Remember how you learned how to use a skateboard or ride a bicycle? You kept trying and trying and trying and then practicing and practicing and practicing until it became easy. Almost anyone can learn how to juggle three balls in the same manner. You must be determined.

Start off by practicing with just one ball. Make sure the ball is not too large for your hand. Toss the ball up in the air to a height just above eye level and catch it at waist level with the left hand. The path of the ball should be parabolic (the shape of the St. Louis Gateway Arch). Keep practicing this until you can do it pretty routinely without dropping the ball.

When you think you are ready for two balls place one in each hand. Throw ball A in the air as previously described. As soon as you throw ball A, move ball B from the other hand to your throwing hand. Wait until A reaches its apex (high point) and then throw ball B in the air. Catch ball A, quickly transfer it to your throwing hand and toss it up as ball B reaches its apex. If you find you can't react quickly enough try throwing the balls a little higher. Keep up this routine for as long as you can. When you've mastered it you are ready for three balls. In your right hand hold two balls and have the other ball in your left hand. Throw ball A up and before it reaches its apex toss up ball B. Before you catch ball A with the left hand transfer ball C to your right hand. Throw up ball C just before ball B reaches its apex. In order to keep three balls in the air at once, you might have to toss them a bit higher. With this circular motion you keep all three balls going at one time. Keep practicing until you have perfected it. When you show your juggling ability to your friends they will be impressed.

HOW TO WAX A CAR

There is a famous scene in the *Karate Kid* film where the teacher instructs the young pupil to wax his car before any actual karate lessons begin. The young man becomes very frustrated because he doesn't see any relationship between the two things. For most people, buying a car is one of the most expensive expenditures in their budget. New cars cost, on average, anywhere from $16,000 to $32,000 and represent an investment that should be taken care of.

Purchase a good quality pre-softened paste product such as Turtle Wax or Meguiars. Don't trust waxes that you spray on with a hose. Do not wash or wax the car in direct sunlight. Find a shady spot for this project. First, remove any road tar. Next, wash, rinse and dry the car thoroughly before waxing. Don't ever use kitchen soap when you wash a car because it will dissolve the wax. Buy a specially formulated cleaner at the store for this chore. Dampen the applicator cloth/sponge and use it to scoop out some wax. Do the top of the car first and then work your way down. Start in the middle of a section such as a roof, door, or hood and then work your way to the edges. When you get to a seam, make sure there is no glob of wax on your applicator. The glob will go in the crack and make the job of wiping off the hardened wax more difficult. When the wax dries to a haze you can remove excess wax and polish it to a bright shine by rubbing in a circular pattern. When it rains the drops will form beads of water on the hood, roof, and trunk of the car. When the rainwater stops beading it is time to re-wax.

Waxing a car is something a young man can learn to do around age 11 or 12. Waxing the family car at this age is a good way to start assuming some family responsibil-ities. It is also a good way to demonstrate that when you reach 16 you will be mature enough to take good care of your own car.

HOW YOUR WATCH CAN BE A COMPASS

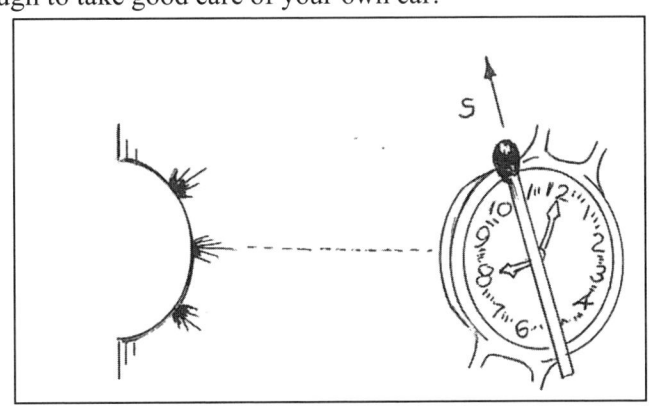

Back in the 1970s digital watches that had readouts, instead of hour and minute hands, became very popular. Nearly every man and youth put their old-style watch in a dresser drawer and bought a slick, modern watch. Well, that lasted about fifteen years and then, inexplicably, nearly everyone went back to the old style watch. That is still what is popular.

The digital watch with the led readout was absolutely useless when it came to using it as a compass if you got lost in the desert, jungle, or wilderness. I know the chances of this actually happening to you are pretty slim, but it's still kind of neat just knowing how to do this. Just think, if Moses had had a watch, he and the Israelites wouldn't have needed to wander around lost in the desert for 40 years. Here's how it's done.

Slip your watch from your wrist and point the small hour hand toward the sun. (If it's dark, just be patient until the sun comes up.) Now lay something like a match or a toothpick across the radius of the dial halfway between the hour hand and 12 o'clock. The match will always be pointing south. If you're in the southern hemisphere (Australia, South America, etc.), the match, toothpick or blade of grass will be pointing north. If you face south, north will be directly to your back. East will be on your left and west will be on the right.

And what if you're wearing one of those useless digital watches? Take that match or toothpick and spit on one end of it. Push the wet end in some dirt and then use the muddy end to draw an imaginary watch with hands on your palm. You can then follow the aforementioned steps and still determine north or south.

BASIC KNOWLEDGE ABOUT DINOSAURS

During my school years, dinosaurs had been discovered but they weren't studied in school the way they are today. This was also before the Flintstones were on television and made these amazing creatures popular. The closest thing we had to a dinosaur in popular culture was Godzilla, that Japanese fire breathing monster. Of course, the other thing that brought these creatures to the forefront in modern times were the films *Jurassic Park* and *The Lost World*.

Hold on. I just thought of something else from yesteryear. In the 1933 *King Kong* film, that big ape lived on Skull Island, a place infested with dinosaurs. There is a famous episode in the film where King Kong gets challenged by a Tyrannosaurus Rex and the two engage in a deadly fight. (T Rex is good but Kong, a superior being with opposable thumbs, triumphs.)

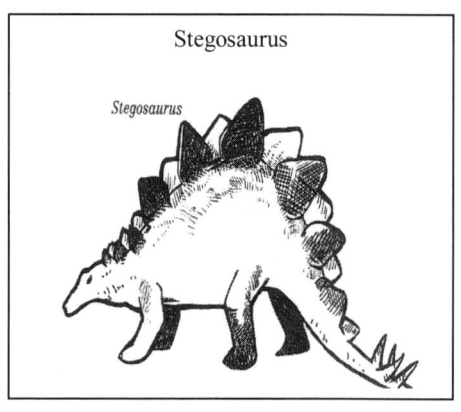

A – The word **di-no-saur** means terrible lizard; they lived during the Mesozoic Era, the Jurassic Era was one part of the Mesozoic Era and that is the origin of the movie title *Jurassic Park*.

B - Dinosaurs were extinct by the time mankind finally arrived on earth. The Age of Reptiles was 200 million-140 million years ago; man did not appear until a million years ago.

C – A **Paleontologist** is someone who studies fossils and dinosaur bones.

D - **Fossils** are dinosaur bones that have turned to stone over millions of years.

E - Much of western America consisted of inland seas and heavy vegetation back then – there were no Rocky Mountains. Much of the world had a warm climate and jungle-like vegetation was extensive.

F - The existence of dinosaurs was unknown until the first skeleton was found in England (1811).

G - Flesh-eating dinosaurs were **carnivorous**; plant eating dinosaurs were **herbivorous.**

H - **Tyrannosaurus Rex** (King of Tyrants) was the greatest of the flesh eaters.

I - **Brontosaurus** (Thunder Lizard) was about 65 feet long and weighed 80,000 pounds. It lived around swamps and lakes and had to eat constantly to stay alive.

J - **Stegosaurus** – (Armored Reptile) had a small head and bony plates along his spine for protection. His tail, used as a weapon, had four spikes on the end of it.

K - **Ankylosaurus** had an armored body and he could swing his bony tail club for protection.

L - **Triceratops** had three spikes on his head and a bony frill protruding from the rear of his head.

M - **Plesiosaur** had a body like a turtle and a long neck, what some would think a sea serpent would look like; lived entirely in the water.

N - **Velociraptor** (or Raptor) weighed about 30 pounds and had feathers. In *Jurassic Park* it was erroneously depicted as being much larger and it was without feathers. Each hind leg had a curved killing claw. Its tail provided balance and stability, particularly at fast speeds. Many scientists think dinosaurs were more like birds than reptiles.

O - The world's largest T-Rex skeleton is named **Sue** (for its discoverer, Sue Hendrickson) and it is on display at the Field Museum of Natural History in Chicago.

P - Dinosaurs suddenly died out about 65 million years ago. The earth began to cool and perhaps they couldn't adapt. Oxygen levels dropped and carbon dioxide levels increased. A large asteroid or meteor struck the earth at Mexico's Yucatan peninsula and created clouds of dust that blocked the sun's rays and caused cooling. Some scientists blame this for their demise.

STAR GAZING

Learning about the stars and planets in outer space not only can be fun and informative, it can be very useful when you are old enough to start dating. Instead of going to a movie or the zoo or an amusement park, a trip to the local planetarium is different and quite interesting. If you don't live near a city with a planetarium, you can still ask Mom and Dad for a telescope as a birthday or Christmas present and this will suffice. Not many of your guy dating rivals will know much about space, the stars and the planets, so this will give you a bit of an edge.

You can learn all about celestial bodies in the sky by watching science programs on TV, by checking out library books, and by Googling things on your computer.

Try to learn a bit about each planet. There are **9 planets** – Mercury, Mars, Venus, Earth, Saturn, Neptune, Uranus, Jupiter and Pluto. In 2008 scientists decided Pluto was just a mass of gases and was not really a planet.

The **planets are named for Roman gods**: Mercury is the winged messenger; Mars is the god of war; Venus the goddess of love; Neptune the god of the sea, Saturn, the god of the harvest; Uranus the god of the heavens; Pluto the god of the underworld.

The **earth orbits around the sun** once a year and the moon orbits around the earth every 27.3 days, giving us different phases such as a full moon, half moon and crescent moon.

All planets orbit around the sun in an **elliptical path**. The gravitational pull of the sun keeps them in place.

Comets are made of rocks, ice, and gases. They orbit the sun in an elliptical path taking from 6 to 200 years. Halley's Comet visits the earth every 76 years. It was last seen in 1986. To the naked eye, it looks as if comets have a tail.

Asteroids are small planets that also orbit the sun.

Meteors are large rocks that occasionally hit the planets. On earth, the smaller ones disintegrate due to friction of our atmosphere. The moon has no atmosphere and its craters are visible meteor strikes. A meteor that burns up as it enters the earth's atmosphere is called a **shooting star**. Since **70 percent of earth is water**; most meteors fall into the ocean.

The **earth's atmosphere is 78 % nitrogen, 21% oxygen and 1 % argon**.

The moon probably tore away from the earth when it was in its gaseous formative stage. The moon produces no light. The light we see is sunlight striking the moon's surface because it has no atmosphere.

Constellations are patterns of stars in the sky named for signs of the

The Moon

zodiac. **There are 88** of them and they were named by the ancients. The number 88 is easy to remember because there are also 88 keys on a piano. Some of the more famous constellations: **Orion** the Hunter, **Pegasus** the winged horse, **Aires** the Ram, **Taurus** the bull, **Lupus** the wolf, **Hydra** the serpent with 9 heads, **Draco** the dragon, **Pisces** the fish, **Scorpius** the scorpion, **Leo** the Lion, **Sirius** the dog and **Hercules** the strong man. There is also a **Big Dipper** in Ursa Major, the bear constellation, and the **Little Dipper** known as Ursa Minor. The brightest star in the little dipper is **Polaris**, called the North Star. To locate Polaris at night look northward. I live in Glen Carbon, IL (near St. Louis) which is about 39 degrees north latitude. If I look north at night about 39 degrees above the horizon, Polaris is easy to find because it is the brightest object. If you live about 10 degrees south of Glen Carbon, look about 29 degrees above the horizon. Ten degrees farther north of G.C. and you look 49 degrees above the horizon.

The stars in the sky are actually suns, like our sun, but they are very far away. **Alpha Centauri** is our closest star.

The gravitational pull of the moon and sun causes earth's crust to bulge slightly. The oceans bulge even more and these are called tides – high tide and low or neap tide. The **Bay of Fundy**, between New Brunswick and Nova Scotia (New Scotland), near the state of Maine, has the biggest tides in the world.

There are many, many galaxies in the universe. Earth is part of the galaxy known as the Milky Way.

Mercury is the closest planet to the sun and the smallest in our universe (unless you consider Pluto a planet). The surface of Mercury looks like our moon – pockmarked with craters. Mercury has an iron core. Like Mars, the planet was volcanically active in its formative years. The surface temperature of Mercury is the hottest in our solar system. Mercury rotates around the sun every 88 days. There is almost no axial tilt. Ancient B.C. Greeks knew about Mercury. Mercury and Venus arc the only two planets with no moons.

Venus is the second planet from the sun and is called the morning and evening star because that is when it is most easily seen with the naked eye. It is called earth's twin because it is so similar in size and gravity. It has clouds but they might be dust clouds. About 96.5 percent of its atmosphere is carbon dioxide. Most physical features on Venus are named after mythical women. Venus rotates very slowly on its axis. **Venus is always brighter than any star in the sky**.

Earth, the most dense planet, is the third planet from the sun**.**

Mars, the 4th planet from the sun, half the size of earth, has a thin atmosphere and polar ice caps. It has two moons, probably captured asteroids, and has the highest mountain (Olympus) and biggest Grand Canyon in the universe. Only Venus shines brighter. Mars is sometimes called the **Red Planet** because it looks a bit reddish to the naked eye. Mars has four seasons, due to its tilt on its axis, but its year is twice as long as Earth's. An early scientist who studied Mars thought the long lines on it were water **canals**. The surface temperature of Mars is 100 degrees below zero.

Jupiter, the 5th planet from the sun, is the **largest planet;** it is huge and one of its moons, named Europa, is as big as a planet and it is covered with ice. It is a **gas planet** along with Saturn, Uranus and Neptune. It is the third brightest object in the sky after the moon and Venus. It is about ¾ hydrogen and ¼ helium. The **great red spot** is a giant storm. It has 63 moons and the largest, Ganymede, is bigger than Mercury. Jupiter is bigger than all other planets combined.

Saturn is the 6th planet from the sun and the 2nd largest planet. It was named for a Roman god that is the namesake of Saturday. The planet is composed mostly of hydrogen and is famous for the rings that encircle it. It has an interior core of rock and ice. It has a substantial gravitational force and high surface winds. Sixty-one moons orbit the planet. Titan, one of its moons, is larger than Mercury. It has a prominent hot spot at its south pole and the planet is a bit flat at the poles and bulges at the equator. Saturn's rings are mostly ice. It is the most distant planet visible to the naked eye.

Uranus – Named after the Greek deity of the sky it is the 7th planet from the sun. It was the first planet discovered with a telescope (1781 by William Herschel). Uranus and Neptune are called the ice giants. Uranus has the coldest planetary atmosphere. Both Uranus and Neptune have small rings around them. Uranus lies on its side due to a huge axial tilt with its rings looking vertical rather than horizontal. Uranus has 27 satellites or moons. Titania is its largest moon.

Neptune, the 8th planet from the sun, was named for the Roman god of the sea. It was found in 1846 by mathematical prediction. A scientist guessed correctly that something was affecting the orbit of Uranus. It has 13 moons and its largest is Triton, named for Neptune's trident. Its southern hemisphere has a **great dark spot**. The only planet farther out from the sun is Pluto. It is a gaseous planet, similar to its twin, Uranus. Its atmosphere is 80 percent hydrogen and 20 percent helium. Neptune is not visible to the naked eye.

Many fans (myself included) of the universe reject those scientists that recently declassified Pluto as a planet. Pluto, the **smallest planet**, is the **9th planet from the sun**. It was discovered in 1930. Scientists decided to declassify it as a planet (for a very technical reason), and it is now referred to as a dwarf planet. The name Pluto, after the Roman god of the underworld, was suggested by an 11 year-old school girl from England. Walt Disney's cartoon dog, Pluto, first introduced in 1930, was so named in honor of the planet. Its largest moon is Charon. Pluto is mostly nitrogen ice with traces of methane and carbon monoxide. It is so distant from earth we don't know much about it. The general U.S. population rejects the downgrade and still refers to Pluto as a planet. Clyde Tombaugh, the discoverer of Pluto, was an Illinoisan so the state legislature designated March 13 as Pluto Planet Day. Pluto is the only

planet discovered by an American. USA! USA! USA!

HOW TO TURN A CARTWHEEL

This is another one of those athletic things that looks pretty cool when you can do it properly. When you watch other youth do it the cartwheel is usually in modified form and isn't as impressive. Also, this is another one of those things that is good outdoor fun and exercise. Grass stains are sometimes difficult to get out of jeans so be sure to wear shorts, cutoffs, or old jeans.

Make sure your performance area is clear of obstacles and there is plenty of room to complete the maneuver. Begin with your arms extended completely and your left leg should be slightly bent. Reach down with your left arm (palm open), throwing up your right leg at the same time. Your right arm will quickly follow so be sure your palm is open. For a brief moment, when both hands are on the ground, you will be in a handstand position. Your momentum will carry your body over in circular fashion and your right leg will be the first to land. Push off with your hands and bring your left leg down and end up in a standing position.

During the cartwheel your body should be straight and your arms and legs looking like the spokes in a wheel. If your legs are bent in perpendicular fashion you are doing it improperly, like most teens. One way to maintain the correct position is to practice your cartwheel against a wall.

HOW TO STAND ON YOUR HEAD

The more of these athletic maneuvers you can do the easier the next one is to perform. Many young people try something like this and if they don't master it after a couple of tries they give up. It always takes more repetitions than this to master the skill. Think about it. Most young people aren't ready to drive a car after only three lessons. It is a good lesson in life to learn patience and acquire determination when it comes to doing something and doing it well. It's like the young violinist who asked a concert master, "How do you get to Carnegie Hall?" Her answer? "Practice, practice, practice!"

Standing on your head actually is a bit easier than some of the other athletic stunts in this book. If it's all right with your parents, find a vacant spot on a wall in your house to practice on. Until you master this technique you should make sure that if you fall to either side there isn't a table or other furniture where you could break something or injure yourself. It is also a good idea to have someone assist you until you master the procedure.

Begin by removing your shoes and getting on your hands and feet and placing your head on the carpeted floor (or a throw rug). Your hands and arms should be apart at approximately the width of your shoulders. You should be about a foot from the wall. Put your right knee in the crook of your right elbow. If you are left handed (footed?), it might work better for you to place your left knee in the crook of your left elbow. Push off with your toes and straighten your left leg to shift your weight forward. Now bring your right leg up and straighten both of them with your heel resting against the wall. Getting both legs up in the vertical position is the most difficult part and an assist from the person helping you might be needed at first.

You will now notice a throbbing sensation in your head. This seems odd because when you are inverted and standing on your feet you don't notice throbbing in your lower extremities. Don't worry! The throbbing sensation you feel is due to the heart being closer to your head, and it is now easier to pump blood into your brain.

After you master standing on your head against the wall you might want to do it outside on the lawn with nothing to support your body. This is a bit more difficult for when you bring your legs up you will need to keep your legs slightly bent until you have your balance.

There are some people who claim that standing on your head isn't good for you but medical studies seem to indicate this is nonsense. Standing on your head strengthens your abdominals (abs) and triceps (muscle on the bottom of your arm from your elbow to shoulder). Standing on your head also turns your organs upside down which can relieve pockets of compressed tissue which may improve digestion.

HOW TO DO A BACK FLIP

Of all the athletic moves described in this book, *this is by far the most dangerous. Serious injury, permanent paralysis or death could result from doing a back flip improperly. This should only be done with professional instruction and only after first getting written permission from your parents*.

Most male cheerleaders at college football games know how to do the back flip and it is quite an impressive maneuver. Cardinal shortstop and **Hall of Famer Ozzie Smith** was noted for running to his position (in the first inning of a home game) and then doing a back flip.

You should be in a well padded area with two people alongside to catch you if you do the flip improperly and fall. Start with your right foot slightly forward to achieve a firm sense of balance. Then bring your right foot even with your left. Now swing your arms forward and bend your knees as if you were going to sit in a chair. This actually lets you build up the energy needed to perform the flip. Jump straight up to gain height. Do not jump backward, as you might have expected, or else you will not gain the necessary height. Now use your abs to tuck your knees up to your chest and begin to rotate your body into a backwards turn. As you near your landing position, extend (straighten) your back. As your feet hit the pad, bend your knees again to lessen the shock and help maintain balance.

For some people it is easier to learn the back flip on a trampoline. If that is the case make sure you have four spotters appropriately spaced. Another way to learn to do a back flip is to take a class and learn from a professional gymnast. You might also inquire about the possibility of learning how to do this by taking a diving class at a swimming pool. Swimmers learn how to do back dives off the board or platform by being placed in a harness that is designed to allow a person to do a back flip while still in the harness. The safety device allows a trainer to hold on to the trainee as he completes the back flip procedure.

MAKING A HOMEMADE VOLCANO

I have to admit that a baking soda volcano is not as spectacular as the real thing but, nevertheless, it is a lot of fun. You can make a more impressive volcano out of papier maché (strips of paper and white paste), but for this little activity modeling clay will be quite suitable. The other things needed before you begin are some liquid dish detergent, a 35 mm roll film canister, cardboard, scissors, vinegar, baking soda, and red and yellow food coloring.

Make your volcano cone about 10 inches tall. Form your cone out of flexible cardboard and use the glue to hold the two ends together. Trim with scissors to suit your personal taste. The opening at the top should be big enough to accommodate the film container. Place a thin layer of gray or brown modeling clay over the cardboard to make your volcano more realistic. If everything collapses, find a large funnel and turn it upside down to place the cardboard and clay around. The film container should sit on top of the narrow end of the funnel but should be far enough down from the mouth of the volcano to be realistic.

When the structure is completed you can start placing the ingredients inside the canister. Add two teaspoons of baking soda, one spoonful of dish soap, about 6 drops each of the food coloring (to simulate fire and hot lava). Now that you are ready for Mt. Vesuvius to explode you can add a spoonful of vinegar and get ready for the fireworks. When the vinegar is added to the concoction you get a chemical reaction. If you think the lava flow is too fast, try some experiments to determine what will slow down its flow. Here's another thing to consider. Try doing this experiment without the dish soap. What happens? Another thing you can do is variably increase or decrease the amounts of the other ingredients to see if you get a better or worse chemical reaction.

Homemade volcano

Mt. Vesuvius, near the bay of the present city of Naples, Italy, erupted in 79 A.D. and destroyed the Roman cities of Pompey and Herculaneum. It was estimated that about 20,000 people were killed in this cataclysmic event.

SHOULD YOU GET INVOLVED IN SCHOOL SPORTS?

Some of the best years of your life should be your high school years. It is a good idea to get involved in school activities but be careful so they do not interfere with your commitment to your church or your youth group at church. These are the years when you begin to mature as a person and make the transformation from being a child or teenager to a responsible adult.

Numerous recent studies indicate that young people who are physically fit develop higher IQs. Physically fit people get more blood flow to the brain and hence more oxygen. The term IQ refers to an intelligence quotient test that measures a person's ability to learn. Generally speaking, if your IQ is 100 that puts you right in the middle of the population. About 50 percent are below you while another 50 percent are ahead of you.

Physically fit people are less prone to disease, are more mentally alert, are stronger, and, as noted above, tend to have higher IQs. These factors combined seem to indicate that being involved in school sports is a good idea.

Young people involved in sports also learn about team concepts, working toward goals, and building self-esteem. Being a member of a team often results in the formation of friendships that can last a lifetime.

If you just aren't adept at sports or simply aren't interested, most schools have a host of other extra-curricular activities that are worthwhile. Consider joining one or more of the following: band, cheerleading, chess club, science club, stamp club, Model U.N. debate, foreign language club, drama club, math club, student council, photography club, etc.

A word of caution about drama club. Acting is a heady experience and often it can lead to a professional career with a very rewarding salary. Unfortunately, many of the roles offered will call for the actor to speak lines with curse words or to violate the Third Commandment by taking the Lord's name in vain. And increasingly there are scenes that call for nudity. Once your career progresses to that point it becomes quite easy to rationalize and accept these degrading roles. Hollywood values are not Christian values. Read Pat Boone's autobiography because he relates how he went from being a popular singer to an actor who was asked to perform roles that nearly led him astray. Another Pat Boone book, *Twixt Twelve and Twenty*, though dated, still has good advice for teens and can be bought cheaply on eBay.

HOW TO DRIVE AND TAKE CARE OF A CAR

Once you turn 16 it is almost axiomatic that you will start driving a car. Few teenagers comprehend the awesome responsibility this entails. Statistically, the leading cause of death among young people is automobile accidents, followed by suicides. You will be in charge of operating a lethal machine that weighs more than a ton, going at a speed of 60 MPH or more. When young people take drivers ed courses in school, they are warned about this and are shown horrific pictures of fatal teen crashes. Lack of maturity causes these warnings not to "sink in." Psychiatrists attribute this to an **"aura of invincibility" syndrome that most teenager have.** Despite warnings about HIV, they continue in large numbers to have unprotected sex. Teens are the largest age group committing suicide because they don't quite understand the finality of their act. And many continue to drive irresponsibly because they think they are going to live forever. They also rationalize, as do many adults, that these things happen to others but not to them. The insurance industry tells us that, despite young people having superior response reflexes, they collectively have the worst driving record of any age group when it comes to accidents. Yes, part of this is due to inexperience but all the more reason to drive defensively.

Here are some tried and true Dos and Don'ts: As soon as you get in your car, buckle up – it's the law. Start the engine and while it warms up, adjust your seat and mirrors. Obey speed limits and follow the rules of the road. If others are in the car with you, don't get distracted. Keep your eyes on the road. Don't text while driving. This is an absolute no, no. Keep cell phone use to a minimum. If possible, try to set up a system where you can use your stereo speakers and a car mike to talk without having to reach for your phone.

If you drive in a suburban area on interstates, spend most of your time in the center lane. If you stay in the left lane someone will always be honking their horn to pass you. If you stay in the right hand lane you repeatedly have to worry about merging traffic coming in from a side road. In case of a traffic problem, being in the middle lane also gives you a choice of going left or right to avoid that potential problem. Do not tailgate. Despite knowing better, most drivers still tailgate and this is why you frequently hear of twenty car pile-ups when there is an accident. Do not make the mistake of trying to keep up with the traffic flow. If you do you will be boxed in by someone in front, someone behind, and a vehicle on either side of you. Simply drive the speed limit. You'll notice that practically everyone else on the highway will be passing you because they are speeding. Instead of being boxed in, most traffic will be ahead of you and moving away from you which is a much safer proposition.

How do you take care of a car? Use synthetic oil. It reduces friction, gives you better gas mileage, and allows you to go longer between oil changes. Check fluid levels and tire pressure at least once a month. Change air and oil filters per manufacturer's specifications. Protect the finish by waxing your car once in the spring and again in the fall. Wash the car regularly and clean out all litter and clutter. Vacuum and wipe down the interior at least every two weeks. Check the owner's manual and make sure specified services arc performed at the mileage levels that are recommended.

Famous people who have been killed in car accidents: James Dean, Jane Mansfield, Tom Mix, Eddie Cochran, Jackson Pollack, General George Patton, Steve Allen, Herb Brooks, Princess Diana, Princess Grace of Monaco, Ernie Kovacs, Billy Martin, Margaret Mitchell, Mel Ott, Steve Prefontaine, Buford Pusser, Jessica Savitch, Karen Silkwood, Bessie Smith, N.C. Wyeth, and baseball Cardinals' pitcher Josh Hancock in 2007.

WHAT IT MEANS TO BE A CHRISTIAN

Christians believe that sin separates man from God and that God sent his Son Jesus as the Redeemer to take man's sin upon himself. Jesus was crucified on the cross, was buried, and after three days was resurrected and later ascended into heaven. The Holy Spirit is the third leg of the Holy Trinity that brings people under conviction for the guilt of their sins. Those who repent of their sins and accept Jesus Christ through faith as their Savior are promised an eternal afterlife in heaven. The Bible is the word of God and it was written by men under the guidance of the Heavenly Father. Christians should be well enough grounded in their beliefs that they can lead others to Christ or be able to intelligently and courteously justify those beliefs to those who might try to convert them to a false religion or cult.

The Bible teaches that mankind is saved by grace alone and not through acts of kindness or philanthropy. However, Christians are taught to lead exemplary law-abiding lives of truthfulness, kindness, and generosity.

Christianity was not meant to be exclusively for one particular country or ethnic group. Christianity is for all mankind. The Bible warns about false prophets (cult leaders) and false religions. While Christians are tolerant of those who profess belief in Buddhism, Islam, Mormonism, Judaism, etc, they do not accept these on an equal basis with Christianity. There is only one true faith. That is why Christians believe in missionaries and follow the dictates of the New Testament – "Go, make disciples."

A Christian's hierarchy of allegiance is God, family, and then country. Christians should study the Word of God and follow the Ten Commandments. Christian boys should not be mean-spirited, selfish, or spiteful. They should learn how to get along with their brothers and sisters. They should honor their mother and father by being respectful at all times and not do back-talking. If you find that you are fighting at school, misbehaving in class, or being grounded by your parents, these are not the earmarks of a Christian life and you should reconsider and alter your behavior.

Neither are Christians lazy. They should strive to be physically fit, mentally alert and self-motivated. They should make a concerted effort to get good marks in school so that they have a better chance of graduating from school with enough educational skills and tools to succeed in college or vocational training programs.

Do you have to belong to an organized religion to be a Christian? The answer is no, but Biblical truths and social and emotional support come largely from attending an organized church on a regular basis. The number of people who successfully lead Christian lives without going to church is probably very small, except for those who are physically handicapped or who are shut-ins due to advancing age. The Bible admonishes us not to hide our lights under a bushel.

UNDERSTANDING YOUR GRANDPA

Your grandpa grew up in an earlier time when America was far different than it is today. His was a safer world relatively free of drugs, serial killers and predators. Sociologists estimate that the distance your parents allow you to play away from home is 1/10 of the freedom that your grandpa had. Prayers used to be allowed in schools and the Pledge of Allegiance was a daily ritual. Curse words weren't allowed in the movies or on television. Teen pregnancies were a rarity and when they did occur the girl almost always gave the baby up for adoption instead of keeping it. Gramps most likely walked miles to get to and from school – uphill both ways – instead of riding in a bus. People in his time had crank-operated wall phones and the ice man delivered ice on a daily basis because people had ice boxes instead of an electric refrigerator.

Also, keep in mind that as one gets older the body begins to deteriorate. This might come in the form of a bad back, high blood pressure, diabetes, sore joints, frozen shoulders, shingles, weaker muscles, arthritis, cataract eye operations and knee or hip replacements. Grandpa isn't looking for sympathy. He's learning to live with life's aches and pains, and it will help if you understand that someday you most likely will have to deal with those things. ….Your grandpa quite likely had only radio – no television to watch when he was young. His family's first television set had no color and was a mere 7 inches in diameter; no such thing as big screens. He grew up listening to big band sounds and singers such as Bing Crosby, Frank Sinatra, Doris Day or Dinah Shore. The electric guitar wasn't invented until about 1953 and the first rock and roll song wasn't recorded until 1954. He probably considers contemporary music as white noise and will probably warn you that listening to such loud music will cause deafness at an early age. (He is right about that.)

James Dean, Marilyn Monroe and Elvis Presley were pop idols during his high school years. He probably detests long hair because in his youth most teen boys wore crew cuts. He was taught to respect authority and hated it when long haired hippies burned flags and draft cards to protest the Vietnam War.

In his time children didn't dare backtalk their parents or a good whipping with a leather belt was sure to follow. At the dinner table, children were to be seen – not heard. He was also taught to eat everything on his plate – waste not, want not. And his parents made sure he knew that leaving food on his plate was somehow being unfair to all those starving kids in Africa and China.

The iceman

If grandpa seems to be too critical of you or seems a bit grumpy most of the time, it will help if you remember his different upbringing. And don't be too surprised if he shows no interest in owning or using a computer. In his day people wrote letters to each other and have them bundled and tied with ribbons while they are being stored in the attic.

Most likely you can change all of this by occasionally asking him to tell you about the "good old days" and giving him a chance to relive his glory years. You might also find some of the things he tells you to be quite interesting. You can start off by asking him what kind of games he played as a youngster. If he tries to say his life was all work and no play, ask him about mumblety peg, marbles, horse shoes, and yo-yos.

Keep at it and you might end up with a new "best friend."

WHO INVENTED WHAT

Somewhere along the line in school you'll learn about scientific advances and achievements. Wouldn't it be pretty cool to learn these things in advance and be ahead of the game? What follows is a list of some of the more important and interesting inventions.

Steel Plow – John Deere	Bifocals – Ben Franklin
Safety Razor – King Gillette	Fountain Pen – Louis Waterman

Airplane – Orville & Wilbur Wright
Light Bulb – Thomas Edison
Mechanical Reaper – Cyrus McCormick
Pullman Sleeper Car – George Pullman
Vulcanized Rubber – Charles Goodyear
Automobile – G. Daimler and Carl Benz
Adding Machine – William Burroughs
Air Brake – George Westinghouse
Cotton Gin – Eli Whitney
Telephone – Alexander Graham Bell
Revolver – Samuel Colt
Roll Film – George Eastman
Steamboat – Robert Fulton
Flaked Cereal – John Kellogg
Telegraph – Samuel Morse
Typewriter – Christopher Sholes
Printing – Johann Guttenberg
Frozen Foods – Clarence Birdseye
Electric Guitar – Les Paul
Battery - Alessandro Volta
Air Conditioning – Willis Carrier

The Coil - Alessandro Tesla
Phonograph – Thomas Edison
Elevator – Elisha Otis
Sewing Machine – Elias Howe
Steam Engine – James Watt
Scissors – Leonardo da Vinci

Samuel Colt

Clarence Birdseye

HOW TO LOSE WEIGHT

Studies show that over one-fourth of American teenagers are overweight. Overweight people tend to face more discrimination, have shorter life spans, and are more prone to disease. Americans also spend millions of dollars annually getting into various dieting schemes or buying weight loss pills. The sad news is that about **94 percent of all diets fail**. Another key reason you don't want to diet as a teen is this is a time when your body is growing and developing. **Teen dieting can lead to low bone density**, which causes problems in later life.

Overweight people tend to be sedate. That means they don't get much physical activity that burns calories. Instead they sleep, watch television, read magazines or books, or become addicted to their computers. To lose weight you need physical activity every day. This means you need to get out and run a mile or so a day. If you can't run, ride a bike. If you're too large to ride a bike start walking.

Swimming is another excellent way to stay fit and burn calories. If you don't know how to swim, join the YMCA and take an instructional class.

51

The next thing you do is start eating less. Don't drink more than one soda a day because each twelve ounces has over 100 calories. If possible, switch to diet soda with zero calories. Learn to drink water with your meals instead of soda. This is far healthier.

Don't get caught in the trap of counting calories. This usually fails because after a month it gets tedious. Don't get into diets where you don't eat carbohydrates. That gets old after about three weeks. So, what DO you do? Very simple – you pretty much keep eating what you have been all along, just eat less. That way no one is asking you to give up pie or ice cream or pizza or burgers. Just don't eat as much as you usually do. However, if all you eat is pop tarts, pizza, ice cream, burgers, fries, tacos and pizza, you need to alter your diet. Don't give up any of the aforementioned items; just throw in some things like salad, fruits, vegetables, and milk to give you a more balanced diet.

If you find you lack the willpower to cut back on the amount of your servings (95 percent of people), have your father or mother dish out the proper amount for you and don't ask for second helpings. If you eat a snack, don't eat something like pretzels straight out of the bag. Place a few on a dish and limit yourself to that.

When I was a youth (1940s), my family never ate out at a restaurant. Mom home cooked all our meals. Modern families often eat out at a restaurant as many as two or three times a week. The problem with this is that when you order from the menu and the waiter/waitress brings out your food, it is usually twice the amount that you should be eating. The simple solution is to ask for a doggie bag or take home box and place half of your meal in it **immediately**. Take it home, put it in the refrigerator, and you can eat the other half at a later date.

If, in the beginning, you find you are slightly gaining weight instead of losing, you should remember that exercising builds muscle tissue and muscle weighs more than fat. This, however, should only be a temporary thing and you should start seeing results in your clothing sizes and in weight loss on the scales. Oh, about those scales. Don't check your weight every day or you will be disappointed. Weight loss is generally slow and methodical – not dramatic. It probably took years for you to add on all those extra pounds. Check your weight about once a week and record it in a notebook. This technique will help motivate you.

Most people, as they grow into maturity, begin making different food and drink choices. They start drinking tea and coffee. To keep their cholesterol levels low they start using skim milk instead of whole milk. They switch from white bread to whole grain wheat bread. Instead of pre-sweetened cereal they switch to cereal with fiber such as Cheerios, Grape Nuts, Shredded Wheat or Wheaties. And, if you pay attention, you'll notice that most adults even eat the crust on their bread – so they can whistle.

EATING A HEALTHY DIET

Do you know the definition of cholesterol? It's the stuff God put in red meat to make it taste so good. Do you know the three basic food groups? They are pizza, hamburgers and French fries. This may be hard for you to believe, but the word cholesterol didn't exist when I was a teen. If it did, I never heard a teacher, adult, or doctor ever mention the word. When I was born in 1939 (no, dinosaurs had all died off by then), the life expectancy for a male was about 61 years. Currently, that figure is somewhere around 77. Better nutrition has played an important part in increasing life expectancy.

As a teen you're too young to think about dying so terms and phrases like regularity, cholesterol, clogged arteries, diabetes, bypass surgery, high blood pressure, and stroke don't have much meaning. However, at some time in your life (the sooner the better), you need to start eating a healthy, balanced diet. The good news is that there aren't any certain foods you have to give up. When your youth group goes out for pizza, it's okay to enjoy the yummy cheese and delicious toppings. Your body actually needs some cholesterol to keep functioning properly.

Try to stick to cereal, milk and fruit for breakfast. Those grains are healthy for you and are a good source of fiber. As you become older, it's time to start thinking about giving up sugar coated kid's cereals such as Fruit Loops and switching to Wheaties or Grape Nuts Flakes. Top your cereal off with blueberries or blackberries. It's also time to ditch those Pop Tarts. If you just absolutely love bacon and eggs, that's okay, but try limiting this to just once a week.

For your noon meal at school, skip the burgers and fries and get the plate lunch. And instead of a soda or chocolate milk, try fruit juice. If you take your lunch, try eating a tuna sandwich once in a while instead of bologna or meat loaf. And have mom toss in an apple or a tomato. Scientists aren't really sure why, but they have determined that apples and tomatoes are really good for you. It has long been said that an apple a day keeps the doctor away.

By the way, here's another tip. Try masticating (chewing) your food well before you swallow. This will aid in the digestive process and help your body more readily absorb nutrients and enzymes.

Your mother will probably be the person who most determines what supper (that's what we call it in the Midwest) will be. Sweets, such as pie and cake, are normal for teens; just try not to go overboard. Limit yourself to one piece. If it's ice cream, limit yourself to one scoop or one bowl.

Here is perhaps my best recommendation. DO NOT BECOME A PICKY EATER! Now, I may not be able to eat head cheese (Google this term) or pickled pigs feet, but I can eat spinach, broccoli, peas, carrots, zucchini, beets, chicken, beef, cabbage and corned beef, pork, fish – you name it, I can eat it. (Yes, I can also eat rhubarb pie and mince meat pie.) I know a couple of teenage boys who mostly eat burgers and pizza and tacos. When the rest of the family sits down to a traditional Thanksgiving meal of turkey, dressing, sweet potatoes, cranberry sauce and pumpkin pie, mom or dad has to go out and buy the boys fast food.

In summary, try to eat a variety of foods, eat in moderation, and try cutting down a bit on sweets and foods high in cholesterol. A vegetarian diet has drawbacks because your body needs protein for muscle development that mainly comes from meat, beans and nuts. Another problem: Hitler was a vegetarian and this produced embarrassing bouts of flatulence (gas).

USING YOUR HANDS TO TOOT LIKE A TRAIN WHISTLE

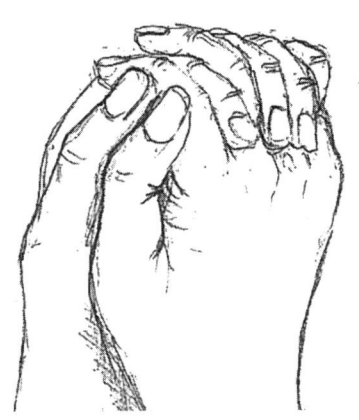

I learned how to do this so long ago I don't even remember who taught it to me. You'll amaze your friends because very few young people know how to do this.

Start your hands in a praying position and then slide them to where the fingers interlace with one another. Now adjust your hands slightly to form a small hollow cave area inside your hands. Next, make sure your thumbs are side by side and bend the knuckle joint outward toward your body. Make sure you maintain the hollow section but at the same time you must make a firm airtight chamber by pressing your hands together and keeping your fingers laced together firmly. There should be a small slit or opening between the lower half of the two thumbs. Place your mouth over the knuckles of your thumbs and blow slightly downward. If you don't get a whistle or a hooting sound, slightly adjust the opening between the knuckles and pretty soon you should be making a good hooting or tooting sound.

If nothing seems to work, keep blowing, and keep making adjustments. Don't blow too hard. Your chances of getting a good hooting sound are better if you blow with medium effort. In a way it's like learning how to whistle. You have to keep trying until suddenly you get the hang of it.

SHOULD CHRISTIANS CELEBRATE HALLOWEEN?

Halloween is an annual holiday celebrated on October 31. Its roots go back to pagan Celtic festivals and the Catholic holy day of All Saints, but in modern times has evolved into a secular celebration. The Celtics believed that at the end of summer, during the festival of Samhain, the dividing line between their world and the Otherworld became thin, allowing both harmless and bad spirits to cross over. On that night, families honored their ancestors and warded off evil spirits that were wandering around. To fool the evil spirits, people began wearing masks and later adopted costumes. This was also a time when livestock were slaughtered and meat was stored for the long winter ahead. Bonfires were lit for the purpose of roasting the meat. The bonfires also served the purpose of scaring away the bad spirits and lighting the way for the good spirits. The Celts were very superstitious and believed in elves, leprechauns, and bad spirits called bogeys. This is where the term **bogey man** is derived.

Townsfolk who attended these ceremonies would often take a burning ember from the bonfire and place it in a hollowed out gourd to help light their way home – thus the origin of the **jack-o-lantern**. These ghosts and spirits wandering around liked to play practical jokes on people. To appease these mystical beings, people left food and treats for them. As you can guess, this evolved into the "trick or treat" saying of current Halloweeners.

When St. Patrick brought Christianity to Ireland, the festival of Samhain was changed to All Saints Day, a day to honor all the Catholic saints. The day before was referred to as **All Hallows Eve**, and that evolved into the word Halloween. When the Irish migrated to America, they brought with them their old world language and customs. Soon young boys started the practice of playing practical jokes on Halloween. To keep them from getting into trouble, the adults encouraged the youngsters to dress up, wear false faces, and go door to door looking for treats.

Should Christian children be allowed to go trick or treating in celebration of a pagan ritual? I grew up in a conservative Christian church but my sister and I were allowed to participate in dressing up and ringing doorbells looking for free goodies. It was loads of fun. Yes, Halloween has an emphasis on monsters, witches, ghosts, skeletons and devils. But children brought up in the Christian tradition are not likely to take an interest in devil worship or witchcraft. These things usually appeal to those who lack self esteem and are without Christian values.

Spooky Halloween memories

A word of caution. Don't ever get caught up in the notion that it is all right to deface or damage property on Halloween. Even soaping windows is a no, no. That is a perversion of the whole idea of making it a fun night for youngsters. Always respect the property of others and honor those adults who go out and buy candy to give away to children on this night. My town has a traditional Halloween parade that is attended every year by about 10,000 people. Most trick or treating takes place the night before. For older teens, encourage your youth group to have a Halloween party where everyone dresses up as a character from the Old Testament. Bob for apples, play games, sing songs, perhaps watch an old classic such as *The Wolfman, Frankenstein, or The Mummy*. Stay away from the modern horror films that exploit teens with sex and excessive blood and gore.

A SPOOKY HALLOWEEN STORY

Halloween was always a fun, but scary, proposition back in the 1940s. This author's head is still filled with spooktacular memories of ghouls and ghosts, witches and goblins. Carving the Jack-O'-Lantern was unfailingly a highlight of the season. I would help my mother select a medium sized pumpkin. Mother wanted one that was symmetrical and blemish free, but I usually talked her into buying one that was misshapen and had character. Once we got home, mother cut the obligatory round hole in the top and scooped out the innards for making scrumptious homemade pies. Then she gave me a butcher knife to carve the face on front. "Don't cut your finger off and get blood all over my clean floor," she always warned. "Okay, Mom," I nonchalantly answered in my best Henry Aldrich voice. I had the choice of making it a "happy face" or a "spooky face." I usually opted for the sinister design with a menacing look.

It wasn't easy for kids in my neighborhood to go trick or treating. My older cousins warned me that witches were on the prowl and they liked to swoop down on their broomsticks and snatch kids off the streets. They would then whisk them off to some horrible cave, plop them in a cauldron of boiling water (bubbling with lizard tails, newt eyes, and salamander toes), and make stew of their flesh.

"If you ever encounter an evil witch that begins chasing you on her broom, be sure to take off your left shoe and spit in it. That will break the evil one's magic powers and she will be forced to search for a different victim," they explained.

Being caught in the clutches of evil monsters wasn't the worst thing that could happen to a kid back then. We also had to contend with **the ghost of Henry Lee**. According to the legend, Henry was a religious man who attended the Assembly of God Church. He worked the night shift in Washington Park at the St. Louis Bridge Company, next to the B & O railroad tracks.

It was Halloween Eve in 1930. Henry Lee lived in a desolate area called Jackass Flats. He loved going to the shallow Spring Lake next to the tracks to go frog gigging. A long pole with two prongs on the end proved useful for plucking the green amphibians from their murky habitats.

One fog-laden night he was walking home from work, carrying a kerosene lantern to light his way through a heavy mist that was as thick as pea soup. He accidentally stumbled upon a group of moonshiners who thought he was a "revenuer" (government agent). One of them quickly picked up a shotgun and fired. **The powerful blast knocked Henry clean out of his shoes**. The unlucky fellow never made it home.

After the incident, on every subsequent Halloween, people reported seeing a ghostly apparition, wandering around the area, carrying a lamp. The headless spirit of Henry Lee was just trying to find his way home.

Kids in my neighborhood were afraid to trick or treat. We usually made our rounds in the opposite direction where we were less likely to run into Henry Lee.   But one year, when I was eleven years old, I foolishly mustered up the courage to go looking for Henry Lee. I took along a Brownie box camera so that I would have proof of the encounter. It was a dark Halloween night barely lit by a gothic crescent moon. The cold night mist settled on my hands and face and sent a chill down my quivering spine. Undaunted, I made my way along an old gravel road hoping for success – yet praying that the grisly story had been a mere figment of someone's imagination. Suddenly, out of the ink-black

56

darkness of Hades, there it was. My hands trembling, I hurriedly snapped a picture and ran as fast as I could back to the safety of my home. When the roll was developed, I quickly shuffled through the snap shots looking for my prize. I gasped in shocked disbelief when I came upon the picture. All that you could see in the photograph was a lantern about three feet off the ground, slightly to the left of an empty pair of brogan shoes!

WHEN SOMEONE ASKS YOU FOR THE CORRECT TIME

Every once in a while a complete stranger will come up to you and ask what time it is. Most people simply look at their watch and tell the inquisitor the time, but if you want to give them a correct answer and leave them shaking their heads in wonderment, try memorizing this.

Stranger or friend: "Excuse me, can you please tell me what time it is?"
Your response after glancing at your watch: "I am deeply embarrassed and greatly humiliated that due to unforeseen circumstances over which I have no control, the inner workings and hidden mechanisms of my chronometer are in such unaccord by which time is ordinarily reckoned, that I cannot give you the exact time. However, without fear of being too far wrong I can tell you that it is approximately 3:05 post meridian" (or whatever the correct time happens to be).
If it is in the morning, instead of saying a.m. respond with ante meridian. In an earlier era when towns reckoned time by the position of the sun overhead, ante meridian referred to the time before the sun reached it's highest point in the sky (noon). After the sun crossed this imaginary meridian, time was referred to as p.m. or post meridian.

HOW TO MAKE A SUNDIAL

Take a sturdy piece of cardboard, 12 inches in diameter, and place a mark in the exact center. You can also go to a craft store and buy a 12 inch wooden disc with a hole pre-drilled in the center. If you think your cardboard is too thin, glue another piece on the bottom. Cut a pie shaped piece of wood, six inches long, to use for the hand (gnomon) of your sundial. The widest part of the block should be about three inches. Glue the block edgewise on your disc with the widest point at the edge and the narrowest part on the middle dot or hole.
Place your disc in an area where the sun will hit it most of the day. Once you position it, don't move it again. At the top of every hour go outside and write a number on your circle's edge where the shadow is made by the sundial's hand. Use a permanent fine point Sharpie pen for this. You can also affix pre-made plastic coated numbers instead of using the pen. It may take you two or more days to make all your time marks, but when you have finished you have a fairly actuate clock that you made yourself. Spray with clear acrylic sealer, allow to dry, and then apply a second coat for durability.
Another way to do this is to place a six or seven inch dowel in the hole in the

center of the wood disc and glue it upright with Elmer's glue. This will replace your block of wood. Then continue the project by placing the disc in the sun and marking the hours.

If you find your sundial gets out of whack by the end or the beginning of daylight saving time, simply go out rotate the face of the dial until the shadow falls on the correct hour.

If you check with friends or neighbors you'll probably find someone who has a decorative sundial out in their garden area. It will probably be made of brass and the numbers might be written with Roman numerals.

HOW TO MAKE A BUZZ BOMB

For this you will need a piece of wood 8 1/2 inches long, two inches wide and ¼ inch thick. A piece of ¼ inch plywood will do the trick. Use a saw or

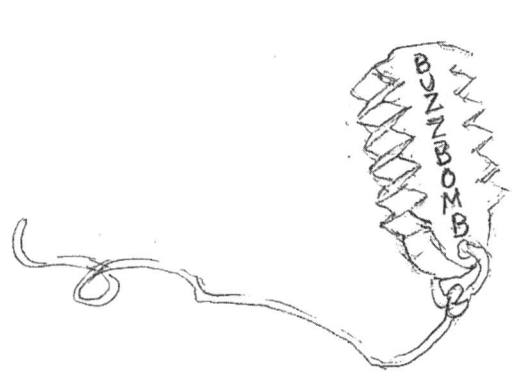

your pocketknife to carefully cut notches the entire length of the long sides of the block of wood. Taper one end of the block to a point by whittling or by cutting it with a saw. Drill a small hole in the pointed end. Attach some fairly strong string to the end with the hole and leave about three feet of length as your control mechanism. Take your buzz bomb outside and swing it around over your head and it will make a loud continuous noise.

HOW TO CARE FOR A DOG

American culture is full of famous dogs. If you watch any of the old Our Gang or Little Rascals comedies, the pet dog Petey was white and he had a big black circle around his eye. Rin Tin Tin was a dog found in a foxhole during World War I. He starred in numerous Hollywood movies in the 1920s. Roy Rogers had a German shepherd named Bullet who helped get him out of many a tight situation. The Phantom's faithful sidekick was Ace the Wonder Dog. For years the RCA logo showed the dog Nippur listening to "His Master's Voice" on a Victrola. President Obama's Portuguese Water Dog is named Bo. Abe Lincoln had a dog named Fido.

One way to convince your parents you are becoming a mature person is to have them get you a dog that you will be responsible for taking care of. This means you will need to feed him, let him out to do his business, bathe him, and see to it that his water bowl is changed daily. He will also need annual rabies shots. Whoever feeds a dog becomes its master. Even Adolph Hitler understood this and lovingly took care of his Alsatian dog named Blondi.

Dogs will love the person who takes care of them unconditionally. If you can't commit to responding back with loving care and daily exercise, you probably shouldn't get a dog. If you are going to tie the dog up outside most of the time, you shouldn't get a dog. Dogs live, on average, about 14 years. Small dogs have a longer life span than large ones.

Instead of getting a puppy that will need to be potty trained, go instead to an animal shelter. Not only will you save a dog's life, you can probably get one that is already trained. Another advantage is that you will be able to see the dog's personality.

HOW TO LEARN SPEED READING

Whether you're hitting the school books in history class, reading long articles in encyclopedias, or just reading the sports page of a newspaper, chances are at one time or another you've wanted to read a little faster. Teaching this skill has become big business: as numerous companies now offer training sessions and computer programs to increase reading speed. You may think that teaching your brain to scan lines is very difficult but scientists have discovered that your brain will adapt rather quickly to this technique and the more you use it the easier it becomes. In fact, many people get so good at speed reading that they can read a newspaper column just by running their eyes down the center. These lessons can be expensive but why spend your money for a speed reading class when you can start reading faster by following these simple steps?

First, time your current reading speed. It's important to find out how fast you read now so that you can track your improvement through subsequent timings. Not only will timing help you to tell if you're improving, but it will also serve as a motivational tool. You can get a novel and a stopwatch and time how long it takes you to read a certain number of words on a page.

Another way to time yourself is to take an online reading speed test. There are a variety of these available - just Google "reading speed test." Many of these have reading comprehension tests, as well, so you can see how well you're understanding what you're reading.

Be sure to read at your normal speed during the timing, and time yourself on a few different pages - the average of your times should approximate your average reading speed.

You should also eliminate distractions. Even if you think you read better when you have music playing, you can probably increase your speed if you reduce distractions to a minimum. Try to find an isolated place to read, and turn off the TV, radio and your cell phone. Even being in a room of people talking is distracting. If no solitary place is available, use earplugs to block out any distractions. In order to maximize comprehension while learning to speed read, you will need to focus on the material at hand as closely as possible.

You should also adjust your reading speed depending on the material. There are times when you should trade off comprehension for speed, so an important part of increasing reading speed is deciding how thoroughly you need to comprehend a particular piece of writing. Before you start reading, decide how fast you intend to go. If you're reading a newspaper article, chances are you just want to get the main ideas, and you can skim through the passages fairly quick. If, however, you're reading a mathematics textbook or a demanding piece on science - and you need to fully understand the material - you do not want to rush as much.

Learn to separate the wheat from the chaff with pre-reading. No matter what you are reading, there is frequently a lot of "filler" that you can read quickly through or even skim over. In the movie **Gross Anatomy**, Matthew Modine plays a first year med student taking an anatomy class. He seems lackadasical about his studies yet manages to come up with decent scores on the tests. "Concentrate on the material that is underlined or in bold print" he tells others in his study group. With practice, you will be able to determine the most important parts of a book as you skim it. When you get to such a passage, slow down. Before you begin a chapter or book, look over the entire piece very quickly. Try to find patterns of repeated words, key ideas, bold print and other indicators of important concepts. Then, when you actually do your reading you may be able to skim over large portions of the text, slowing only when you come to something you know is important.

Train yourself not to reread. Most people frequently stop and skip back to words or sentences they just read to try to make sure they understood the meaning. This is often unnecessary and you don't want it to become a habit. One exercise to help you avoid rereading is to take a sheet of paper or index card and drag it down the page as you read, covering each line once you've read it. Drag the card in a steady motion; start slowly, and increase your speed as you feel more comfortable.

Don't read to yourself. As you read you probably pronounce the words to yourself. Almost everybody does it, although to different degrees: some people actually move their lips or say the words under their breath, while others simply say each word in their heads. Regardless of how you subvocalize, it slows you down. To break the habit, try to be conscious of your behavior. When you notice yourself pronouncing words to yourself, try to stop doing it. Practice visualizing a word at the moment you see it, rather than confirming the word in your mind and then visualizing it. It may help to focus on key words and skip over others, or you may want to try humming to yourself or counting "1,2,3,4" repeatedly in order to prevent subvocalising. One exercise to stop your lips from moving is to put a finger on your mouth and keep it there while you read.

Practice reading with your hand. Smooth eye motion is essential to speed reading. You can maximize your eyes' efficiency by using your hand to guide them. One such method is to simply draw your hand down each page as you read. You can also brush your hand under each line you read, as if you are brushing dust off the lines. Your eyes instinctively follow motion, and the movement of your hand serves to keep your eyes moving constantly forward.

Practice reading blocks of words. Nearly everyone learned to read word-by-word or even letter-by-letter, but once you know the language, that's not the most efficient method of reading. Not every word is important, and in order to read quickly you'll need to read groups of words - or even whole sentences or short paragraphs - instantaneously. The good news is you probably already do this to some extent: most people read three or four words at a time. Once you make an effort to be aware of your reading style, you'll discover how many words you read at a time. Now you just need to increase that number. Using your hand as a guide may help, as may holding the book a little farther from your eyes than you usually do.

Practice and push yourself. While you may see some gains in speed the moment you start using these tips, speed reading is a skill that requires a lot of practice. Always push yourself to your comfort level and beyond - if you end up having to reread a section, it's not a big deal. Keep practicing regularly.

Time yourself regularly. After a week or so of practice, time yourself as in step two. Do this regularly thereafter, and keep track of your improvement.

As more and more people in the world begin to attend college, the greater the competition for jobs. You'll also see more competition in the classroom and anything you can do to give yourself an edge will be helpful. Speed reading will allow you to complete your reading assignments more quickly and give you extra time for lab work, research papers, or for socialization.

THINGS TO DO AND WHERE TO GO ON A DATE

It is up to your parents to decide when you are old enough to start dating and where you can go on a date, but sometimes you just run out of ideas. This list is based on the assumption that you live in an urban area and some of these are regionally specific to the metro-St. Louis area. If you live in or near a different city then you can support the specific sports team in that area. Many will apply and some will not.

Planetarium	Art Museum	Zoo
Cardinals' baseball	4 H Club activity	Tractor pull
Blues hockey	College basketball	Picnic
High school play	St. Louis Symphony	Roller skating

Ice skating	Ice cream social	Hiking
Bike riding	Eagle watching	Fishing
Camping with parents	Rams' football	Muny opera
Horseback riding	Music concert	Nascar races
High school basketball	High school football	School dance
Star gazing	Family game night	9 holes of golf
A chaperoned party	Miniature golf	Bowling
Batting cage	State Fair	Swimming
Tennis	Scavenger hunt	Ping pong
County Fair	Car Show	Boat Show
Amusement park	Church singspiration	Movie
Water Park		

HOW TO COLLECT STAMPS

Collecting things can be expensive and quite often you cannot get your money back if you decide to sell your collection at a later date. I know people who collected Avon after shave lotion bottles that came in the shape of classic cars. You can hardly give these things away now. The same thing can be said for beanie babies of the 1990s.

People collect things like guns, knives, swords, salt and pepper shakers, commemorative spoons, thimbles, beer cans, wine labels, plates, matchbook covers, figurines and coins (**numismatists**).

In the 1970s I started collecting plate blocks. These consisted of a block of four taken from a sheet of stamps that had a bottom tab with the sheet number when the stamps were printed. This distinguished it and made it more valuable than any other block of four from a sheet. These stamps can be purchased at the post office for face value.

After fourteen years I went to a stamp dealer to sell them. Incredibly, he offered me an amount below their face value. I said *no thanks* and started placing the stamps on letters that I mailed. That way I didn't lose any money. And if you buy a large album and put together a worldwide collection, when you take it to a dealer he will charge you a fee just to appraise its worth.

Despite these handicaps, millions of people globally collect stamps as a hobby. Former President Franklin Delano Roosevelt was a big **philatelist** (stamp collector). There is just something about these "miniature paintings" that fascinate people. Collecting stamps is a good way to learn about world geography and other cultures.

For young people on a very limited budget, here is what I recommend. Find an old three-ring binder and then purchase some paper from a place such as Staples or Office Depot. The paper should be marked off into little squares so that when you affix the stamps you can get them straight and evenly spaced. You can purchase stamp hinges from any stamp and coin dealer or from an auction on eBay. You can buy thousands of hinges for just a few dollars.

Check out sales on eBay and find a large quantity of USED stamps for sale in a packet rather than an album. Try to get a packet of large worldwide pictorials rather than the small "definitives" that are not nearly so interesting. Long Beach Philatelic and Lichtman Stamp Company sell these types of packets that will provide hours and hours of interesting activity. You might also need a small booklet called a stamp identifier. Since countries print stamps in their native tongue, it is difficult to determine the country of origin of many stamps. A stamp identifier will show you what to look for to help determine the country of origin. You can find these in used condition on eBay for about $3.

When I was a teen, stamps were 3 cents. Now U.S. first class stamps cost 44 cents. If you buy these at face value from the post office you'll be running up a pretty good tab. Collect U.S. stamps by buying cheap packets of used stamps. Then you can spread the word to families and friends that you'd like them to save envelopes for you with cancelled or used commemorative stamps on them. You can also ask mom and dad to save the ones that come in the mail to your house. The large stamps are called pictorials or commemoratives because they either depict a large scene or they have been issued to commemorate some notable event such as Lindbergh's 1927 flight or a World War II event.

HOW A POSTAGE STAMP CHANGED HISTORY:

The idea of building a canal somewhere across Central America gained currency in the U.S. during the 1849 Gold Rush in California. Some east coast Americans made their way to the gold fields by ship, traveling all the way from New York, around Cape Horn, and up the Pacific coast of South and Central America. This was a long, tedious route and it was expensive. The time and distance could be cut in half if a canal across Central America could be built.

Look at a map and you can immediately see two possibilities – the Isthmus of Panama and another across Nicaragua, at the site of Lake Nicaragua. The U.S. Congress was getting ready to vote on which place to secure a treaty and build a canal when something extraordinary occurred. The Nicaraguan government issued a postage stamp in 1902 that depicted a fuming, active volcano. Proponents of the Panama route sent letters to the legislators that had this stamp pasted to it. They warned that it would be foolhardy to build a canal in an area where volcanic and earthquake activity could wreck the entire project. The vote went in favor of building the canal at Panama – not Nicaragua.

At the time of the vote, the land we now call Panama was actually part of Columbia. Columbia didn't like the terms of the original lease treaty and demanded a new treaty that included more money. The American government knew there was secessionist sentiment in the isthmus area and let it be known that if the people there successfully revolted and formed a new country, America would sign a lease treaty with them. That is exactly what happened.

As of this printing, efforts are being made to construct a new canal through the old proposed Nicaraguan route. The Panama Canal was finished in 1914 and it has become somewhat dated as ships have become longer and bigger. The Panama Canal can handle ships of up to 65,000 tons. A new Nicaraguan route would handle ships of up to 200,000 tons.

President Jimmy Carter signed an unpopular treaty with Panama, which gave away the canal that the U.S. had built (at a cost of $352 million), along with thousands of auxiliary buildings that went with it. It was later learned that had the U.S. not ratified the treaty, there were plans by the Panamanian government to sabotage the canal.

Nicaraguan volcano stamp

It didn't take long to regret the treaty. Manuel Noriega, a military strong man, became dictator of Panama and quickly got involved in the drug trade. After an unarmed member of the U.S. military was shot and killed, President George H. W. Bush sent troops to invade Panama in 1989. The military incursion was called Operation Just Cause. Noriega was apprehended and is now in a federal U.S. prison.

LEARNING HOW TO SWIM

Swimming is another athletic skill that every boy and girl should learn how to do. You want to be careful because hundreds of teens drown annually. The top fourteen causes of older teen (15-19) deaths are: (1) auto accidents (2) homicide (3) suicide (4) cancer (5) heart problem (6) drug overdose (7) motorcycle, land rover accidents (8) diabetes (9) flu, influenza (10) drowning (11) farm accident (12) birth defect (13) respiratory disease (14) HIV infection from a contaminated needle or from having unprotected sex.

You can see that swimming by yourself, except perhaps in your home pool, might not be such a good idea. Also, don't dive headfirst into a pool or body of water without first making sure there is no submerged obstacle that you could hit with your head.

Swimming is also a good way to get your heart rate up and burn calories. Further, swimming is an excellent way to rehabilitate an injury. Johnny Weissmuller, the man who played Tarzan in the movies, may have been the greatest swimmer ever. He was never beaten in any swim competition. Not even Mark Spitz or Michael Phelps can make that claim. As a youth Weissmuller contracted polio and after he recovered his legs had atrophied and lost much of their muscle tissue. This Chicago youth rehabilitated himself by swimming in Lake Michigan. Your local YMCA is one of the best sources for swimming instruction and safety rules.

The most common and athletic looking swim stroke is the Australian crawl also known as freestyle. It is a simple hand-over-hand, kick your legs technique that gets you where you want to go in a hurry. To swim freestyle your body should be in the elongated position with the face in the water. Turn your head to the side and come up for air as needed. Keep your body near the surface of the water. Kicking your legs helps you maintain your buoyancy and propel you forward. Use your whole leg when you kick and move each leg alternately. Your main source of propulsion comes from your arms and cupped hands. Stretch your arms out on the water's surface and bring your arm downward, pulling your hand through the water toward your feet. When you bring your arm out of the water for the next stroke, try to lift your elbow out of the water first. Your other arm should begin its down stroke just as the other one is about to come up. Try to develop a rhythm of alternating strokes.

For some there is a fear of water that causes them to panic when their face goes in the water. Try standing under a showerhead and letting the water run completely over your head. If you feel like the water is taking your breath away as it runs down your face, you probably have some of this fear. The local YMCA starts you off with techniques for overcoming this fear when you take lessons.

When you take a breath while swimming, your head should be on its side, resting on top of the water. Practice until you can go three or four strokes in the water before you need to take a breath. Try not to splash too much when you swim this way, it makes you look like an amateur.

HOW TO TEAR A PHONE BOOK IN HALF

My grandson recently attended a service at his church where a group of strong men demonstrated incredible feats of strength and raw power. Afterwards they gave their testimony and advice on how to lead a Christian life.

These men used their hands and arms to break long, concrete blocks and other seemingly impossible items. They even impressed the audience by tearing thick phone books in half. Yet this feat isn't really all that difficult if you are moderately strong and know the proper technique. Here's how it's done.

Take the telephone book in your hands by the corners with the cover of the book facing you. Rest the bottom of the book against your outer hip with your thumbs pressing against the center of the book. Your hands should be forming an imaginary letter W. Form a U shape by pressing with your thumbs. Apply pressure and bend the middle of the book into a V shape. Keep a tight hold on the books edges and form a crease in the middle. Begin tearing the pages from the top to the bottom with the same motion you would use to break a twig in two. Keep applying force and try to make the ripping motion steady and smooth. Continue pulling the book apart with your hands and the book should completely rip in half.

HOW TO MAKE A MÖBIUS BAND

The Möbius strip has the unusual mathematical property of being non-orientable. It is something unusual you can easily make that will fascinate your teacher and your friends. It was discovered in 1868 by the German scientist August Möbius. In simple terms it is a loop with only one edge and one surface to it. A model can easily be made by taking a paper strip and then giving it a twist. Cut a strip of paper an inch wide and ten inches long. Mark the top left hand corner B and the top right A. Mark the bottom left corner D and the bottom right C. Give the strip a twist and in the process you turn the side marked C and D upside down. Using Scotch tape (or a staple), tape the ends together, A to D and B to C. Google "Möbius strip" if you can't quite figure out what this strip should look like when you are finished..

To prove that the band has only one side you can take a pen or pencil, starting at any point in the middle of the band, and draw a continuous line until you reach the point of origin. Notice that you did not have to lift your pen or pencil from the paper, proving the band has only one edge.

Now you can do some-thing astonishing. Take a pair of scissors and cut along the line that you have drawn. Instead of now having created two different loops you will merely have one much bigger loop.

HOW TO TREAT A POISONOUS SNAKE BITE

These instructions for treating poisonous snakebites assume that you have no special equipment such as a snakebite kit and do not have quick access to medical services.

Snake bites can be deadly so it is important to take action as quickly as possible. First, get the victim away from the snake. You want to make sure that neither you nor the victim receive any additional snakebites.

Remove clothing or constricting items since bites from venomous snakes can cause rapid and severe swelling.

Minimize activity by the victim. Moving around will increase blood flow and quicken the spread of poison through the body.

Do not cut an X into the bite site or use your mouth to suck out the poison. These are likely to be ineffective and can increase the likelihood of infection. Yes, I know; you've seen John Wayne do it this way in the movies. The movies do it that way to make it seem more heroic.

Clean the bite area with soap and water if it is available. Cover the wound with a dressing. Wrap the bite site with a tight elastic bandage. You can use something like an Ace bandage for this, or you can fashion one from an under-shirt or other article of clothing. The idea is to slow capillary and venous (veins) blood flow (back to the heart), but allow arterial blood flow (away from the heart).   Check for a pulse below the overwrap.   It should be

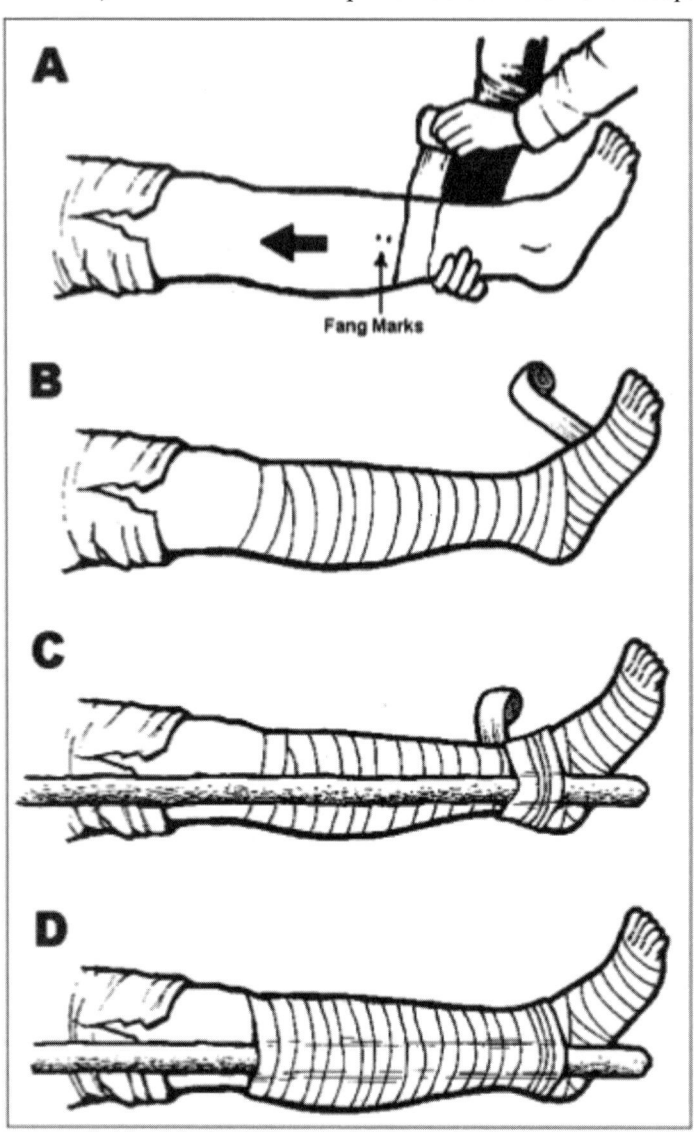

A

Fang Marks

B

C

D

present.
    Use a stick or branch to splint the bitten limb to prevent motion. Keep the
splinted extremity below the level of the heart. Allow the victim to rest until
you can get him/her medical attention. If the victim is conscious, try to make
him/her drink fluids.

If you or a victim are stung by a scorpion, clean the sting area with soap and water and apply a bandage. Get to a hospital as quickly as possible and make sure your victim gets a tetanus shot if the last shot hasn't been recent.

HOW TO SURVIVE A TORNADO

Tornadoes generally move in a slight south to north tangent, going from west to east. If your house has a basement, go to the southwest corner and try to get under a heavy table (perhaps a pool table) and place blankets or a mattress on top of you. If your house has no basement, go to a small closet in the southwest part of your house. Another alternative is to get in your bathtub and cover yourself with blankets or a small mattress.

If you are in the southwest corner and a tornado hits, chances are the tornado will strike near your location and then rip off the roof and timbers will be thrown away from you in a northeast direction.

Tornadoes are one of nature's most destructive forces. It so happens that where I live, in southern Illinois near St. Louis, is referred to as **Tornado Alley**. About six other states, such as Oklahoma and Texas, have tornadoes more frequently, but the ones to strike Illinois are **the deadliest**, having killed the most people over the years.

If you live in an urban area your town most likely has emergency warning systems over loudspeakers that give notice of approaching storms that have cyclonic wind potential. When the weather outside looks bad tune your radio to the National Weather Service or turn on your television to a local channel that will have meteorologists giving warnings and instructions.

This tornado killed 118 people in Illinois

1896 tornado damage on Eads Bridge

If you are in a building several stories high, go immediately to the lowest floor and take shelter in the southwest corner. Most tornadoes travel from west to east in a slightly north tangent. are in a If you are in a car and see a tornado moving towards you from your left or right, keep going forward and try to get out of its path. If you see a tornado coming toward you, get out of the car and find a culvert, low spot or ditch to lie in. Cover your head with your arms. Do not try to outrun the tornado for some of them attain ground speeds of over 60 miles per hour.

SHOULD YOU OWN A CAT?

Should you own a *felis domestica* instead of a loving, slobbering, rug peeing dog? It all depends. Cats are easier to take care of. They know how to use a litter box almost as soon as they are born. It's in their DNA. All a cat needs is food, water, annual rabies shots, and a clean litter box. The family can go on vacation for a week and there's no need to send the animal to an expensive kennel. On the other hand, man's best friend has long been the dog – not the independent and often indifferent cat. If you whistle and yell for Fido to come for an ear scratching session, he'll practically knock you down getting there as fast as he can. Cats can be affectionate but oftentimes it seems like they're in their own little world. No wonder man domesticated the dog thousands of years before the cat.

Dogs also can be taught more tricks and are useful as burglar alarms. If a burglar breaks into a home where there is a cat, the animal is likely to either run and hide or walk up to the intruder and rub up against his leg.

Another disadvantage is that cats produce more dander. Dander is not dandruff. It is microscopic bits of skin that cannot be seen with the eye and it plays havoc with some people who have allergies. A good air filter on your furnace can take care of most of this problem. They also sell room air filters that can help. Cats clean themselves frequently while dogs have to be bathed to remove the stink. However, cats regularly throw up disgusting hair balls.

Cats have the advantage when it comes to some behavior. Cats don't yap at strange sounds the way dogs sometimes do. And cats don't engage in stupid behavior such as chasing a car down the street. Cats also generally outlive dogs. They quite often will live to nineteen or twenty years.

There are exceptions to every rule, but women generally prefer cats while boys and men prefer dogs. In fact, cats have the same unpredictable behavior that sometimes makes the opposite sex so difficult to understand at times. (Naturally, girls say the same thing about boys.)

Here's an interesting oddity. Did you know that **dogs are mentioned in the Bible but there are no cats in the scriptures**? Here's another. Some historians think that the great plague of London (1665-1666), which killed over 100,000 people, was related to cats. People back then were very superstitious and cats, especially black ones, were associated with witches and witchcraft practices. Some people didn't like cats because they thought their elliptical eye irises made them look satanic. Cats were thusly killed off in large numbers. This allowed the rat population to increase substantially and the filth and disease they spread caused the plague. Londoners turned to smoking unhealthy tobacco in large amounts because it was thought the strong smoke somehow helped to ward off the disease.

HOW TO GET YOUR TONGUE UNSTUCK FROM A FLAGPOLE

Remember that famous scene in the classic film, *A Christmas Story*? Ralphie, the story's hero, is with two of his friends and they begin discussing whether or not one's tongue will get stuck if you stick it out and touch it to the frozen surface of a flag pole. After some back and forth discussion, Schwartz challenges Flick with a **"triple dog dare"** to try it. Flick unwisely doesn't want to back down from such a dare so, much to his subsequent dismay, sticks out his tongue. In the movie, the filmmakers hid a suction device inside the flagpole to grab Flick's tongue. In real life firefighters emergency response teams have been called out to deal with re-enactments. The solution to this dilemma is actually quite simple. Simply pour warm water where the tongue is stuck to the pole and it will easily come free.

There is a good lesson in all of this. Never be tempted to do something stupid or dangerous on a dare. Be resolute of character and mature enough emotionally to say, "No thanks, that's not for me!" (Even if it's a Triple Dog Dare!)

AMAZING ANIMAL FACTS

President Dwight D. Eisenhower hated cats and ordered the groundskeepers at the White House to shoot and kill any stray cat they saw.

During World War II movie stars helped raise money for the conflict by going around to large cities and urging people to buy bonds. A pig named Neptune, from Anna, Illinois, was taken around to numerous towns in Illinois and various parts of him were auctioned off to raise money for the war. Winning bidders would be given certificates instead of, let's say, a ham. Neptune raised more money for the war effort than many Hollywood celebrities.

During mating season, the deerfly can attain speeds of up to 60 miles per hour chasing the female of the species.

A horse named Comanche was the lone survivor of the Custer massacre of June, 1876.

In South Africa, **termites are cooked and eaten as delicacies**.

Olney, Illinois is famous for its **white albino squirrel population**. The city has passed ordinances protecting them and anyone maliciously harming one or removing one from the city is subject to large fines.

Giant stag beetles are popular pets in Tokyo due to lack of people living space. These creatures often sell in stores for thousands of dollars.

The DNA of chimpanzees and humans has a likeness of about 95 percent.

It is possible for lions and tigers to mate. When this happens the offspring are called ligers.

When it is first born, the human baby is one of the most helpless mammals in existence.

Elephants are the only mammals that can't jump.

DEALING WITH A CLOGGED TOILET EMERGENCY

Dealing with clogged toilets is one of those boy/guy/man things. Speaking of toilets, this reminds me of a joke. After a young man went to the bathroom and flushed, he forgot to put the seat lid down. The family dog went in and began slurping the clear water in the bowl. "Johnny," his grandmother yelled. "Please shut the lid to keep Fido from drinking out of the toilet." Johnny went back into the bathroom and closed the lid. "Grandma," Johnny asked, "why do dogs prefer toilet water to the water in their bowls?" "Because the water in the toilet is colder," Grandma replied. Johnny went upstairs where he found his mother making Christmas cards on the computer. "Mom, he quizzed, "how

70

does Grandma know the water in the toilet is colder than the water in Fido's bowl?"

Toilets become clogged when something, usually a lot of toilet paper, gets stuck in the drain section. The first rule is never to flush more than once. If you flush and it doesn't go down, get ready to use the plunger. If a friend comes over and this happens and he flushes twice, the excess water will spill over the edges of the bowl onto the bathroom floor. If this happens, there is an easy solution. Look behind the toilet and you will see a shut off valve. Shut off the water by turning the handle to the right. **Don't forget: lefty-loosey and righty-tighty.**

Make sure the clogging wasn't caused by little Mary dropping her rubber toy duck in the toilet. If you see something like this, get a pair of rubber gloves and pull the toy out. If you don't see anything blocking the flow, get the plunger out of the bathroom closet. If your dad hasn't showed you how to use the plunger, skip this step. The next time the two of you have some spare time try and persuade him to show you how to use it. The basic principle involved with a plunger is to force enough water down the drain to clear the drain and solve the problem. Make sure the plunger covers the drain hole completely before you push down. Try the plunger two or three times and if that doesn't work, put newspaper, paper towels or old bath towels on the floor to soak up most of the water. Shut the door and place an OUT OF ORDER sign on the door. Call Mom and Dad to tell them about the problem and let them deal with it.

Using a plunger

WHAT CAUSES FOG?

Fog is simply a cloud that has fallen out of the sky and is sitting on the earth. Well, something like that. Fog tends to settle in low places so sometimes you can be on a hill and look down and see a valley covered with fog. Another way of looking at it is fog is dew that should be on the grass but somehow is floating around in the air. As you might guess, fog occurs when the humidity (moisture in the air) is at or near 100 percent. Fog occurs when the difference in the temperature and the dew point is less than 4 degrees Fahrenheit. Fog begins to form when water vapor in the air begins to turn into tiny water droplets. Fog is quite common in the morning. As the sun comes up and warms the temperature of the air, the heat "burns off" the fog.

One of the foggiest places in America is Menomonie, Wisconsin which has, on average, 200 foggy days a year. London, England is also noted for being foggy. Much of this is due to the warm waters of the Gulf Stream meeting the cold water of the North Sea.

Just before the outbreak of World War II, London experienced a Killer Fog. Back then, we didn't know as much about pollution, and cars and factories spewed forth contaminants into the air. And back then most people heated their homes with coal and the dust in the smoke also went up into the atmosphere. Normally the wind disperses these contaminants and blows them away, spreading them out over large non-industrial rural areas.

However, for several days, the wind was almost non-existent and the contaminated air was not replaced by fresh air from the west. (Their prevailing winds blow from west to east, just as they do in the U.S.) Over 1,000 people died from breathing polluted air. It happened again in 1952, but this time it was worse. It lasted a week and nearly 16,000 people died. Nowadays we call this "thick as pea soup" pollution smog.

CHAIR TRICK AT A PARTY

For teens fifteen or older, this is what you do. Find a guy participant to stand close to a wall, leaving enough space between his toes and the wall to set a light chair between him and the wall. While facing the wall, tell him to bend over so the top of their head touches the wall. Tell him to pick up the chair and lift it to his chest. Guys cannot do this, because their center of gravity is in their chest. Now have a girl try it and everyone's mouths will fall open when she does it with ease. Women can do it because their center of gravity is in their hips.

Be sure you try this with your sister and yourself to make sure it works. If it doesn't, you might need a lighter chair or have the person move back from the wall an inch or so. If it still doesn't work, try this method reserved for slightly younger people.

Do the same experiment but this time have the volunteers get on the floor on their hands and knees. The legs and feet must be together. Next have the subject bend forward and place their elbows against their knees with their hands still flat on the floor. While they are in this position place a tube of Chap Stick at the end of their fingers. Now have them straighten up and clasp their hands behind their backs, above their waists. Tell them to keep that position and bend over and knock the Chap Stick over with their nose. Chances are the girls can do it and the guys can't. Once again it's because the girls' center of gravity is down in their hips, lower than the boys.

PUSHING A STRAW THROUGH A POTATO

This trick has been around a long time. You will need a room temperature uncooked potato and a regular plastic straw. Have someone wrap their fingers around a straw and tell them to try and push it through the potato. The straw will probably bend or possibly make a slight cut in the potato. Take the straw from the person and say, "Here, let me give it a try. Grip the straw with your fingers wrapped around it but this time place your thumb on top, trapping the air inside. Stab the potato with a quick thrust and you'll be amazed to see how deeply the straw goes into the potato. The air trapped inside the straw makes it much stronger, enabling it to easily penetrate the potato.

MONEY LAUNDERING DONE LEGALLY

In the movie *To Live and Die in L.A.*, a group of counterfeiters print fake bills on crisp paper. To make the bills look as if they've been in circulation, they are put in a home dryer with the heat turned low. Then they toss in some plastic poker chips and let everything tumble around.

Money laundering is a bit different. It's the process where you take illegally obtained dirty money and clean it by getting it back in circulation without getting caught by the authorities. In this exercise we're going to launder money but it will be perfectly legal. We're going to take dirty copper pennies and make them bright and shiny.

Pour ¼ cup of white vinegar into a china cereal bowl and mix in a teaspoon of salt. Mix thoroughly. Grab a handful of dirty copper pennies from the change jar and place them in the bowl. Watch carefully and you'll see the dirty pennies slowly become bright and shiny. Once they're clean rinse them and let them dry on an old towel. Be sure you also wash the bowl thoroughly.

The pennies you use are, most likely, 97.5 zinc and 2.5 percent copper. All pennies before 1982 were made of pure copper but the price of this metal increased to the point where the value of the copper in the penny was worth more than 1 cent so the government changed the penny's metallurgical properties.

The solution you created is actually a mild form of hydrochloric acid. Oddly, another cleaning agent that works well is Taco Bell hot sauce in place of the white vinegar. The next time you go to Taco Bell you can warn your friends that the sauce is so hot it will burn their innards. To prove it you can place a dirty penny on a napkin and pour on the sauce. Your friends' eyes will bug out as they see the chemical reaction!

When I was a youngster there were machines in stores that dispensed a stick of chewing gum for a penny. A pack of Wrigley's Spearmint gum cost a nickel. Today, the value of a penny is so small that many think it should be done away with and the nickel should be our smallest coin.

Abe Lincoln was the first president to have his image on a mass circulated coin. This occurred around 1909 and the Lincoln penny was 95 % copper. Southern states objected vehemently to the coin because there were still many Confederate war veterans alive.

IRON MAN SUPERHERO

Did you know that humans and other animals must have trace elements of various metals in their body in order to stay healthy? Included in this list are iron (for strong blood to distribute oxygen), cobalt (in vitamin B-12),

73

manganese (bone formation and reproductive health), magnesium (for bone structure), copper (copper deficiency results in anemia), and zinc (required for DNA binding).

Many cereals are fortified with vitamins, minerals and metals. Here's an easy way to prove it. Pour a half cup of cereal containing iron in a blender. Add a cup of water. Mix thoroughly. Pour this mixture in a bowl and add a silver colored magnet. Push the magnet around in the bowl with a plastic spoon. You should see tiny dark spots begin to form on the magnet. Those spots are the iron that was in the cereal.

WARNING: Too much of any of these metals in the human body, especially lead, can cause serious illness and possible death.

When a person dies, the value of the minerals and metals in their body is worth about $4.55.

HOW A FLINTLOCK WORKS

First you need gunpowder. This explosive material was discovered in China about 1,000 years ago, probably by accident. Gunpowder consists of potassium nitrate (saltpeter), charcoal, and sulfur. At first the Chinese merely used gunpowder to make fireworks. The Italian

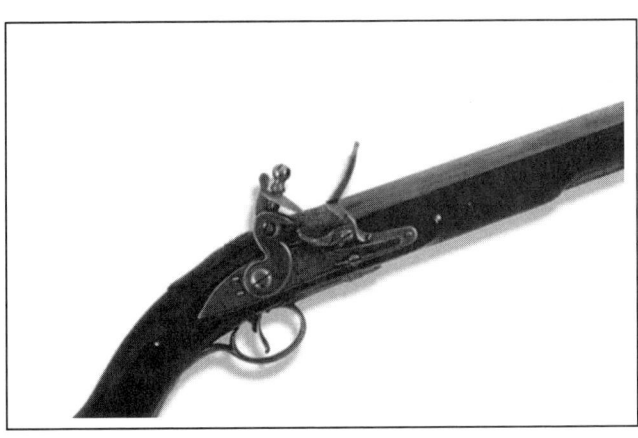

merchant **Marco Polo** visited China, around 1275 A.D., and brought back the gunpowder recipe with him. He also brought back an interesting food called pasta. That's right. **The Chinese invented pasta – not Italians**. The Chinese also invented kites and yo yos. It didn't take long for Europeans to figure out a way to use gunpowder to shoot cannon balls. A cannon is a simple weapon. It is a strong metal tube with a plug at one end. First you place gunpowder in the cannon and shove it to the back. Then you insert a cannon ball. There is an access hole in the top rear of the cannon. You can either insert a fuse in the hole or simply pour some gunpowder in it. When you light the fuse, or set fire to the gunpowder in the touch hole, a terrific explosion occurs, sending the ball out of the mouth of the cannon with tremendous force.

A similar principle was involved in early pistols, called flintlocks. The flintlock gun had a trigger mechanism. You would pull back the lock (hammer) and cock it in place. The hammer mechanism had a piece of hard rock on it called flint. When the trigger was pulled that hammer with the flint came down rapidly and struck a piece of steel. This created a spark that set off a bit of gunpowder that was in a small pan, which in turn ignited the gunpowder in the barrel. This sent the ball (round bullet) zooming out of the barrel. During the Revolutionary War, both the British and the Americans used flintlock weapons.

Sometimes the flint would set off the gunpowder in the pan but the gunpowder inside the barrel failed to explode. This was called a "flash in the pan." In my days of youth old timers sometimes used this expression. It meant that a young man might start out to accomplish something with a lot of fanfare but he never completed the project. Thus he was just a "flash in the pan."

MAKING PAPER HELICOPTERS

The autogiro, invented around 1923 by the Spaniard Juan de la Cierva, had

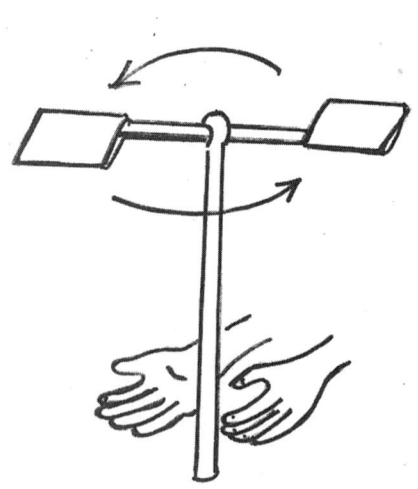

the body and propeller of an airplane and the rotors of a helicopter. The autogiro flew like an airplane but the helicopter blades gave it vertical lift, eliminating the need for a long runway to land or take off. With the development of the steerable rotor in the 1930s, the autogiro lost its wings, as these were no longer needed to fly the aircraft. Thus the autogiro, as it was first designed, fell into disuse. The first helicopter was invented and designed by the Russian-American Igor Sikorsky in the late 1930s. He got the idea from a 500 year-old drawing by Leonardo da Vinci depicting a crude aircraft with a spinning wing.

Make sure you ask your parents if it's OK to drop your helicopter from a rear deck that is one story high. If you have a friend or two with you, make a helicopter for each person and place something on the ground to indicate a landing zone. Then see which of you can make your helicopter land on or closest to the target area.

You can make a helicopter with some paper, two plastic straws, Scotch tape and a dab of Play Doh (see above illustration). Draw two rectangles on a piece of paper. They should be two and 5/8 inches wide and four and ¼ inches long. Form the letter T with the two straws and tape them together where they meet. Take one strip of paper and tape it over one end (the top of the T) of the horizontal straw. To hold your "wing" in place, use one piece of tape to fasten the edges of the paper together. Use another piece to attach the blade to the straw. Do the same thing with the other piece of paper, fastening it to the other end of the T. When finished, make sure both blades are in a flat horizontal position. Now take a piece of clay and shove it up into and around the bottom of the T.

To create a different paper helicopter Google *paper helicopter* and make your own replica by following the simple steps that are given.

You can now drop this helicopter from a deck and watch it maneuver, just like the other model. Compare the paper helicopter you made from instructions found through Google and compare it with the one shown in this book. Determine which one performs the best.

MAKE YOUR OWN MODELING DOUGH

When I was a youth, in the 1940s, nearly everyone had wallpaper in one or more rooms of the house. Houses back then were mostly heated with forced air coal burning furnaces. The warm air that came through the register of each room had tiny particles of coal dust that settled on the wallpaper, making it look dingy. A St. Louis company made a pink clay-like substance (**Absorene**) that came in a can. When it was time to clean the wallpaper my sister and I pitched in and helped Mom. You would take a chunk from the can and form it into a ball. Then you would rub the dough against the wallpaper and it was like an eraser removing a number that was written with a pencil. When the outside of the pink dough turned dark gray, you kneaded it until it was pink again. After there was very little pink left you got a fresh piece. When the task was finished we used the dough like modeling clay and made animal figures.

Forerunner of play dough

In 1951 most cities started using cleaner coal to generate electricity and many homeowners switched from coal to gas heat. The Absorene formula was slightly modified and the new product called Play Doh was created.

Play dough is a classic childhood toy everyone can have fun with, and it's so easy to make. Here are the basic ingredient ratios: 2 cups of flour; 2 cups warm water; 1 cup salt; 2 tablespoons of vegetable oil; 1 tablespoon of cream of tartar (optional for improved elasticity)....

Have Mom or Dad help you with this part. Mix all of the ingredients together, and stir over low heat. The dough will begin to thicken until it resembles mashed potatoes. When the dough pulls away from the sides of the pan and clumps in the center remove the pan from the burner and allow the dough to cool enough to handle.

Now place the dough on a clean counter or on wax paper and knead vigorously until it becomes quite smooth. Divide the dough into balls for coloring. Make a dimple in the center of the ball and drop in some food coloring. Fold the dough over and knead it, working the food color through the body of the dough

This stuff is completely edible but it's a bit salty. When you're done store it in an air-tight container. If it begins to dry out, you can knead a bit of water in again to soften the dough back to a useable form.

There are several projects in this book where the dough will come in handy.

BLASTOFF YOUR OWN HOMEMADE ROCKET

It was the Germans during World War II who used V-1 and V-2 rockets to terrorize the British. The rockets were launched from France and mostly aimed at London. The letter V stood for **V**engeance weapon. Hitler wanted to retaliate against the British for sending their bombers over Germany and dropping explosives on his cities. The V-l rocket was sub-sonic and did not fly faster than the speed of sound. The British were able to shoot down some of these rockets. Then along came the V-2 rocket which was supersonic – faster than the speed of sound. Although these weapons terrorized the British population, they came too late in the war to alter the outcome.

It is possible to purchase ready to fly rockets at hobby shops, but this ends up being a bit expensive. Here is an inexpensive way to build one of your own.

To do this fun project you will need the following... - One Estes Model Rocket Engine - one note card - 3 cardboard fins (these can be made out of the cover to an old notebook) - 1 two-inch long piece of balsa - Various tape (just about any kind will work) - You will also need a pair of scissors.

Make the body of the rocket with a 4 x 6 note card. Wrap it around the rocket engine - make sure it fits nice and snug; then tape the note card so that it will stay in a tube shape. Now tape the round note card to the engine.

To strengthen the rocket body, take some painter's tape and wrap it around the body of the rocket several times.

Use either a two-inch long piece of dowel or a piece of balsa wood to make the rocket's nose. The diameter should match the rocket body and the tip should be carved until it's pointed. If you use a knife, get adult supervision and remember: **always cut away from your body**. Slip the nose into the top of the cardboard rocket body and secure with more painter's tape. Wrap tape around the top of the body and the bottom of the nose piece.

Shape three heavy cardboard fins for the bottom of the rocket. Have your Dad do the next step. Use clear packaging tape which is a bit heavier than Scotch tape. Take a pen and mark three places on the bottom sides of the rocket body with each fin ending up 1/3 of the way around the body. Place tape on each side of the fin to hold it in place. YOU ARE NOW READY TO FLY.

With parental supervision, take your rocket to a large open area away from houses, cars, and trees. Carefully follow the detailed instructions that come with the rocket engine and get ready for blast off.

THE HOVERING COMPACT DISC

Someone sent this one to me by E-mail when they heard I was doing a book about boy things. To make this project you need glue, an old CD or a new blank one, a large empty wooden thread spool, glue, a button, and a round balloon.

Glue the button on top of the wooden spool with the button holes aligned with the spool hole. Set the wooden spool on top of the CD and make sure the spool hole is in the middle of the CD hole. The button is on top, then comes the spool, and on the bottom is the CD. Blow up the balloon and stretch it over the top of the spool. You might need Dad to stretch the balloon while you pinch the neck shut so very little air escapes. Set your hover-disc on the floor and watch it glide along and hover at the same time.

TEENAGE PIMPLES AND ACNE

With the onset of puberty the skin of most teens begins to produce more oils, sometimes clogging the pores. If bacteria and dirt are present this produces an inflamed area called a pimple. Nearly every teen gets zits but some conditions are worse than others. Back in the 1950s I had a friend with a bad case of acne. He worried endlessly about it and used a product called Clearasil. Despite his condition he somehow knew how to talk to girls and dated all the time in high school. As a senior he was voted the boy with the most pleasing personality. So you see, pimples aren't the end of the world.

Pimples are small inflammations of the skin. They are commonly caused by clogged or infected pores. This excess oil in a pore turns dark when exposed to air and dirt. A blackhead is the first stage in the development of a pimple. **A blackhead can be removed** if you do this before it becomes a pimple. Hold your face over a steaming bowl of water to open your pores. Then carefully remove the blackhead with an extractor which you can buy at most pharmacies. When finished, splash on some cool water to close the pores to their natural state.

Pimples usually develop after blackheads have become infected due to dirt and bacteria. When breakouts of pimples occur often, it is called acne. There are other causes of acne and the condition should be treated immediately. Often, if not treated, these conditions can lead to severe acne which can leave visible scars on your skin.

With Blue Ray DVDs and high definition TV, you frequently see actors and actresses on the screen who have scarring on their skin because of untreated acne.

Many teenagers experience pimple outbreaks. The best thing to do to maintain a good complexion is to address the problem of acne before it begins to exist. You can begin by following a regular skin cleansing regimen to rid your pores of unwanted particles and dirt. The easier it is for your skin to breathe, the fewer problems will occur. It requires some discipline and patience to maintain a skin regimen, but you will be glad you did it in the long run.

However, if you have an already existing skin condition, there are many things that can be done to help this ongoing problem. It is advised not to squeeze your pimples or a whitehead or blackhead. This could lead to further infection and scarring. Try to avoid touching your face often, especially if you already have pimples. Increased friction on the pimple will cause it to close up further, making extraction a lot more difficult.

You can purchase over-the-counter antibacterial cleansers made especially to combat pimple outbreaks. Be careful not to over scrub, however. Your skin needs a certain amount of oil to remain healthy. Some teens find that what works best for them is simply water and baby soap.

And what do you do if you have an acne outbreak several days before your big date with that cute girl in biology class? You can **go to a dermatologist** and get a shot that will help clear it up in time.

If over-the-counter medications and cleansing creams don't seem to be working for you, see a dermatologist and they can help.

There is an old saying: "Beauty is only skin deep." What it means is that nearly every teen thinks there is something wrong with their appearance. Those with curly hair wish they had straight hair and vice versa. Some think their nose is too long or perhaps they believe their neck is too long. If you can develop a pleasing personality, pay attention to good grooming, become a good listener, and avoid being a braggart or a showoff, you'll find that you will have lots of friends and will seem attractive by members of the opposite sex.

HOW TO FIX A DOOR THAT WON'T STAY OPEN

You can really impress your dad with this one because few men know this little trick. Let's say you have an interior door in your house that, after you open it, swings half way shut and stays there. No matter what you do, it always does this. Now there is a little rubber wedge-shaped device called a door stop you can use, but those are unsightly and unnecessary.

Here's the simple solution. Doors are held in place by metal hinges. One half of the hinge is affixed to the jamb (frame) and the other half to the door. The two are fastened together with something that looks like a long bolt called a pin. Tell your dad to remove the top pin with a hammer and small chisel. Then he should take the pin and place it on a hard surface such as the sidewalk or concrete driveway. Now tell him to lay the pin flat but then slip a 2 x 4 block of wood under the head of the pin. While holding the pin in place with one hand, your dad should strike the pin roughly in the middle just hard enough to put a very slight bend in it.

Have him place a light coating of thin oil on the pin and use it to refasten the two hinge halves. You can help hold the door in the correct position while your dad taps the pin back in place with the hammer. Problem solved! The slight bend will not affect the opening and closing of the door but once it is opened and pushed against the wall, it will stay there.

GOING HIKING AT SUMMER CAMP

If you do any significant amount of camping or hiking you should always have a good first aid kit in your pack. You should also have water, a red handkerchief, a whistle, a compass, a small flashlight, a couple of energy bars, a Swiss Army Knife and a cell phone (if it is in an area where there is a signal.) Every once in a while you see stories on TV about young people getting lost in the woods and it takes days to find them. Adhere to the Boy Scout motto: **Be**

Prepared!   Use your compass to determine your directions before you begin. (Luckily you only have to remember four – north, south, east and west.) Unless you have a defective compass, your needle should be pointing north.   South will be the opposite direction and west will be to your left and east to the right.

Hiking is good exercise and a lot of fun because you get to see squirrels, deer and other animals. When you go hiking at summer camp, do not go alone and always let others know when you are going. Before you leave, look out in the distance to get your bearings and note the location of your camp in relation to the rest of the landscape.   Take specific note of any landmarks such as an observation tower or an odd-shaped rocky cliff.   There are almost always marked trails to follow. While you are out in the woods try your very best to avoid snakes, skunks, bears and poison oak.   Skunk spray will, most likely, cause temporary blindness if it gets in your eyes.   You will also smell terrible for a long time unless you take a bath in baking soda and wash off with a vinegar rinse. Steer clear of these critters.

Use a certain amount of care.   You don't want to sprain or break an ankle. Don't be tempted to wander off very far from the marked trail.   That is a sure way to get lost. If you have a trail map keep it handy and refer to it frequently. If there is a rain shower and you spot a rainbow, don't go chasing after the pot of gold because you have no way of knowing on which end it will be.   Besides, it will be closely guarded by some nasty looking leprechauns.

When you go to sleep at night use netting, or a spray, to keep mosquitoes off of you.   You could get attacked by a million of them and they could drain your body of every single drop of blood. You just never know!

ABOUT THAT DUCT TAPE

There are numerous DIY projects in this book where duct tape will come in handy. Whatever you do, don't ever use up the last bit of tape on a roll without getting permission from a parent. You could get grounded for a month. Duct tape is one of the most indispensable household items in existence.   It can be used to tape a box together, bind two things together, repair book bindings, fix a leaking radiator hose, or mask something that needs to be spray painted.   It has a kazillion uses and you never know when duct tape will come in handy. For additional uses, read *2001 Uses For Duct Tape (Minus Seven or Eight Hundred)*.

Top Ten Back to School Uses for Duct Tape by the Duck Tape Guys
10. Backpack reinforcement - help that old backpack make it through one more year of school - reinforce the bottom and seams with duct tape.
9. Construct your own backpack! Cover a grocery bag entirely in Duct Tape, then duct tape the bag onto your kid's back (over clothing to avoid back skin and neck hair loss).
8. Book covers: Cover your books in paper, then cover the paper with duct tape. Don't tape right onto the book (school administrators are not real duct tape friendly, and will probably fine you for duct tape stickem all over your returned books).

7. Lunch money clip: Duct tape your lunch money to the back of your leg so you don't loose it or have it stolen by the school bully.

6. Note from home security: Tell mom to tape the notes from home onto your kid brother's forehead so he doesn't forget to give it to the teacher.

5. Reusable lunch bag: Tell your mom not to waste your money purchasing a nylon reusable lunch bag... simply duct tape over a paper lunch bag - you will be the envy of the classroom, and this bag will last you right through to college!

4. Sandwich safety belt. Avoid the stain and embarrassment of sandwich spills. Duct tape around the sandwich holds the fillings in place. You just eat down to the duct tape - then squeeze the contents out.

3. Book straps: Some schools are forbidding backpacks because of security issues. The Duct Tape Guys suggest making a book strap out of duct tape (like grandpa and grandma used as kids). To avoid books from spilling out of the strap, duct tape the spines of the books to the strap.

2. Duct tape fashion: Save HUGE bucks... instead of purchasing expensive brand name clothing, cover your last year's outfits entirely in duct tape. Go with silver for the space age look, black for a mysterious/artsy look, or try one of Duck® brand duct tape's NEW Xtreme Tape® - it's duct tape in dayglo colors: hot pink, lime green, citron yellow, and blaze orange. The same colors that are so trendy with the Xtreme Sports participants.

1. Make a knowledge magnet. Duct tape around your head sticky-side-out, and every word that your teachers say will stick to the tape and soak into your brain. (This has not been fully tested; it's just a theory at this point).

This savvy Internet list courtesy of www.ducttapeguys.com

Alternate tree fort

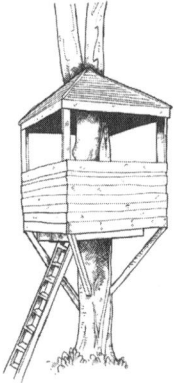

When I was born there was no such thing as duct tape. After America became involved in World War II, the tape was developed by the Army to protect ammunition from the weather. The color wasn't silver or gray, like most brands today. It was olive drab. Because the tape was also waterproof the GIs began calling it duck tape.

After the war the furnace people discovered the tape to be useful to seal the joints in sheet metal duct work. The name duct tape soon replaced the original duck tape.

BUILD A TREE FORT

This will be another one of those projects where you might want to have your dad's help. First, you and your friends must find an old tree in either your yard or theirs. Now find a friend or a neighbor who is tearing out an old wall or replacing their old decking. This will give you a supply of lumber and save you money. If there are any old nails in the boards you can pull them out with either a pry bar or a claw hammer. If you step on an old nail or get a puncture wound in your hand or leg from a nail, you must tell your parents so you can get a **tetanus shot** from your family doctor. THIS IS VERY IMPORTANT.

Ideally, the tree should have three forks to support the frame support for the floor. Try to use 2 x 6 boards for the frame with 12 inches on center between each support board (floor joist). Use rust proof screws to fasten the boards together.

Set the frame in the fork of the tree and determine where your fort needs firm extra support. A 4 x 4 post will give you the needed support. Drop a plum bob from your fort down to the ground to determine where you need to dig a post hole. If your dad doesn't have a plumb bob, a big nail on the end of a string will suffice. Use a post hole digger to make a hole. Make it two feet deep if you live below Cairo, Illinois and three feet deep if you live above Cairo. If you live in Alaska you'll need to dig to China. Place about 3 inches of small gravel in the bottom of the hole and then set the post in the center of the hole and, after you plumb check it with a level (to check vertical straightness) screw it to your base. Before you fix the post position with concrete, check your base and make sure it is totally level. Now fill the hole with ready mix concrete. Now check for stability and if you need another post on the other end, repeat this procedure.

Now you can add the floor to the tree fort. Use ¾ inch boards and place them perpendicular (crossways) to the joists. Trim the boards on all the edges so they are flush with the box frame. Determine if you want 4 ft. or 5 ft. high walls. Then use 2 x 4s to build the wall frame. This time you can space the vertical boards (studs) on 16 inch centers. Be sure you leave a 26 inch wide opening somewhere for your entrance ladder. After you make all four walls screw them in place. The walls of your fortress can be made of 6 inch wide dog-eared fence boards. These are about the cheapest construction boards you can buy from places such as Home Depot or Loews.

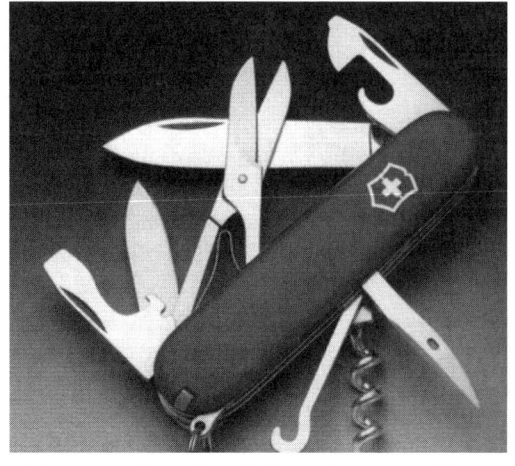

THE HANDY SWISS ARMY KNIFE

This ingenious little all-purpose tool was invented in 1891 by Karl Elsener, a Swiss knife maker. At first glance you might think it is a Red Cross knife because of the red body and white cross but that is just the coat of arms symbol for Switzerland. The knife first became popular in America due to its use by GIs (government issue) during World War II. At the time it was known as an Offiziermesser (Officer's knife) which the GIS promptly shortened to Swiss army knife.

Swiss Army knives can be bought for a reasonable price on eBay and among the tools are: ball point pen, scissors, corkscrew, awl, screwdriver, pliers, can opener, bottle opener, etc. Newer models have a laser light pointer.

This knife will come in handy for many of the projects in this book. Be very careful when you close the knife. Many accidental cuts occur at this point. Make sure you know that **you will be suspended from school if you take this knife with you**. Make sure you don't absentmindedly place the knife in a pair of jeans or trousers you normally wear to school.

ASTOUNDING FACTS ABOUT ADOLPH HITLER

Hitler believed in the stars and in destiny and employed an astrologer to tell him things such as the best date to launch an invasion. The British knew that Hitler held such beliefs and Churchill relied on his own astrologer to try and predict what Hitler's advisor was telling him.

Hitler was fascinated by toy trains but had no time to build his own layout. Instead he visited Herman Goering's impressive layout and the two of them took turns running the trains. Hitler's personal passenger train, which took him from place to place, was named *Amerika*.

Hitler had the ability to make bold and daring decisions, but once the troops were committed to battle he was plagued by nervousness and self-doubt.

Hitler was responsible for restoring German pride and gaining back territory lost by the 1919 Treaty of Versailles. He brought inflation under control and reduced unemployment. He annexed Austria and Czechoslovakia. Had he negotiated a settlement with Poland instead of invading that country, he could have avoided war. Hitler was chosen as Time Magazine's "Man of the Year" in 1938. Had he not overreached he might have been remembered as Germany's greatest leader.

Hitler invaded Russia mainly for two reasons. He wanted to destroy Bolshevism/Marxism and he wanted the Ukraine's grain and Russia's vast mineral wealth - iron ore, tin, zinc and manganese. He underestimated Soviet military capability mainly due to their poor performance in the Russian-Finnish war of the winter of 1939-40. He didn't realize that the Soviets had not yet recovered from Stalin's decimation of the Soviet military leadership through his cruel purges and Moscow trials. Hitler later remarked to Kesselring, "Had I known the Red Army was so determined and tenacious, I would have never invaded Russia."

Hitler originally wanted to be an artist but was turned down by the Art Academy in Vienna. While yet a teen he suffered this rejection and then went through the trauma of his mother's death in 1908. Many psychiatrists believe these events, combined with a domineering father, left Hitler emotionally damaged permanently. Until Hitler joined the German military in 1914, he was essentially a bum in Vienna, earning meager amounts by painting houses, drawing post card pictures, and wallpapering interiors. Though he lived the life of a tramp, he somehow managed to maintain his self-esteem.

Hitler had a remarkable memory for facts and figures. He constantly amazed his generals with the dimensions of buildings, industrial statistics, and the specifications of armaments which he used to confound his critics.

Through reading books and pamphlets he came to hate religion, Slavs, Orientals, Negroes and Jews. He detested abstract art and degenerate jazz music. He believed in Social Darwinism – all life was a struggle and only the fittest survived. Hitler was raised a middle-class Catholic and especially detested Protestantism. He saw Jews in prominent positions of leadership, and that they were successful in banking, manufacturing and commerce and blamed all of Germany's economic ills on them. To him the Aryans (Germans and northwestern Europeans) were the master race.

Hitler was arrested (1914) for evading military service in Austria. He pled poverty and ignorance of the law and claimed he was ready to serve. When doctors examined him he was declared unfit for combat and auxiliary duties on grounds of physical weakness – unable to carry a heavy rifle and bayonet.

However, he volunteered for the German army and after a couple months of training, his Bavarian regiment was sent to the western front. He was a courier and volunteered for many dangerous assignments. He was very cool under fire, was wounded a couple of times and his exemplary soldiering won him the Iron Cross first class. Seldom did a common corporal in the old Imperial Army receive such a prestigious award. He loved fighting and once said "War for a man is equivalent is what childbirth is for a woman."

Adolph Hitler

Hitler was accepted by his military comrades but they found him to be rather odd because he didn't drink, smoke, or show much interest in women. His superiors considered him for promotion but passed him over because they didn't think he demonstrated any qualities of leadership. At the end of the war, Hitler was in a hospital bed recovering from a poisonous gas attack on the battlefield. He turned his face to the wall and wept when he learned of Germany's surrender.

When Hitler came back to Germany, after the war, he saw hunger, inflation, street riots, political instability, and a people shamed by defeat in the recent war. He saw Germany on the verge of economic collapse and a Communist revolution. It was then and there that he decided his mission in life was to reverse the outcome of World War I. He remained in the army and they sent him on several assignments to investigate right-wing radical groups. Hitler quit the army and joined the small German Workers Party, deciding that he could transform it into a meaningful political force. He soon discovered that he had amazing powers of oratory. He learned to appeal to audiences - not through argument but by the powers of emotion. He honed his skills by standing in front of a mirror and practicing phrases, use of hands, and facial expressions.

Hitler's niece Geli Raubal, who was twenty years younger, was the one great love of his life. From 1929 to 1931, she was his constant companion in Munich. He was very possessive and she had very little social life except when she was with her uncle. Hitler forbade her from seeing other men and he refused to allow her to go to Vienna for singing lessons. **After she killed herself (in 1931)** Hitler was inconsolable for months and became a vegetarian.

Hitler's other significant female companion was Eva Braun. Eva was Hitler's wife for one day. Hitler's associate, Albert Speer, wrote of her: "She was a pretty, empty headed blonde with blue eyes." Hitler met her while she was working as a receptionist in a photographer's shop. She fell madly in love with him and told friends they would soon marry. But Hitler had little time for affairs of the heart and seemed to be consumed by politics and war. His lack of attention led her to attempt suicide in 1932. Hitler began paying her more attention after that, but he soon reverted to his old ways and she attempted suicide again in 1935. Her diary is full of complaints about Hitler's neglect of her. She was forbidden to smoke or dance or enjoy the company of other men. Nevertheless, the two remained a pair and she stayed with him to the end. Eva committed suicide with Hitler in the bunker as the Russians closed in on Berlin in the spring of 1945. Eva had no interest in politics and was of little consequence to Hitler in these matters.

Because Hitler created such controversy in the 1920s, he installed a searchlight in the back window of his car to blind the driver of any hostile car that followed him.

Hitler never went swimming because he thought it was unbecoming for a politician to be photographed in a bathing suit.

After the meals at Berchtesgaden, Hitler loved to sit and listen to guests gossip about the latest scandals of others.

If Hitler had died in December of 1938, he would have been hailed as Germany'sgreatest leader because he was more successful than Franklin D. Roosevelt.

Hitler could only speak German, didn't know how to dance, disliked snow, and didn't know how to swim.

Hitler was responsible for the murder of 6 million Jews. This is known historically as the Holocaust.

AMAZING WORLD WAR II STATISTICS

Roughly 50 million were killed in the global war – a terrible tragedy.

It cost $2 billion to build the atomic bomb.

The AAF gave about 360 hours of flying time to air crews before sending them into combat. The Germans, on average, gave their men 110 hours. Japanese and Italians had even less.

Between 1942 and 1945 Hollywood made 500 entertainment films that dealt with the war, one way or another.

The Army Air Corps lost 439 lives in primary training accidents.

The Italian navy performed reasonably well in the war, transporting men and material from one place to another, mostly in the Mediterranean. They lost 393 vessels, including 86 submarines.

The destroyer escort *USS England* was our champion sub destroyer with 6 kills.

An astounding 6.5 million American men failed their physicals and were classified 4-F

The Japanese lost 2,259 merchants ships to all causes. American submarines sunk 60 percent of Japan's merchant fleet. The submarine *Tang* alone sunk 24 vessels.

When the war began most of the Soviet Union's surface fleet was obsolete, but she had more submarines than any other country. The Soviets greatly inflated their successes and lied to cover up their losses. The Germans kept the Soviet fleet in the Baltic bottled up in port until progress in the land war freed them in 1944.

Nearly 240,000 women served in the American military. One old shovel could be recycled to make four hand grenades.

Children's war outfits available in catalogs

During the war America out produced the rest of the world, Axis and Allied powers combined.

6 million – Number of Jews killed by Hitler

1,078,674 – American soldiers killed in the war

During the war the U.S. government sold $135 billion dollars worth of war bonds.

At the time of Pearl Harbor the U.S. had only 55 submarines in the Pacific, half of which were obsolete. American subs sank so many Japanese tankers that her oil imports plummeted by 80 percent.

U.S. subs sunk 200 warships and over 1,000 merchant ships. Twenty-seven U.S. battleships saw action in World War II.

There were 136,216 prisoners of war in World War II and about 111,000 made it back home.

The Battle of the Atlantic cost the Allies more than 20 million tons of merchant shipping and cost the Germans 781 submarines.

About three million men participated in the D-Day invasion at Normandy

Before the P-51 Mustang came along in 1943, only 35 percent of bomber crews survived 25 missions. After the plane arrived the number rose to 66 percent.

At Pearl Harbor the Japanese lost 55 pilots, 29 planes, 9 midget submariners and a number of others on an "I" class submarine.

The fighting in eastern New Guinea cost the Allies 8,500 men; Guadalcanal losses amounted to about 5,800

American losses at Pearl Harbor were 18 vessels sunk or severely damaged, 347 airplanes lost, 2,403 Americans dead.

In 1942 the U.S. had 3 heavy aircraft carriers and the Japanese had 6. By 1945 the Japanese had 2 carriers and the USA had 14.

At Hong Kong the Japanese lost about 3,000 men while the entire British garrison of 12,000 men were either killed or captured.

15 million American men and women served in the armed forces between 1941 and 1945.

One out of every seven American submarines was sunk during the war.

5,640 British "Churchill" tanks were built during the war.

Japan produced 65,000 aircraft during the war. By the end there were only 9,000 left.

Hitler's stubborn determination to take Stalingrad was one of the war's great blunders. It cost the Germans 150,000 dead and of 91,000 taken prisoner, only 6,000 ever returned to Germany. Apparently the Russians were even more barbaric than the Japanese.

The Germans produced 36,000 ME – 109 fighters.

The Germans lost 80,000 men at Leningrad.

The V-1 and V-2 rocket attacks on England caused about 31,000 casualties.

Japan lost 20 aircraft carriers during the war.

The German Messerschmitt ME 109 was faster and could climb better than the British Spitfire, but it only had a 90 minute fuel supply.

England lost 60,000 seamen in the Battle of the Atlantic and lost 4,786 merchant ships during the war – the most of any nation.

Germany lost 630 U-boats and 27,491 submariners during the war.

Allied losses in the recapturing of the Philippines were about 3,000 – the Japanese lost 56,000 troops.

Doctors and nurses at Bataan in 1942 had a 2,900 bed open air hospital unit for wounded men. As doctors probed for shell fragments they discovered metal parts made in the U.S. and sold to Japan as scrap metal. Parts of Ford automobiles and a screwdriver from a Singer sewing machine were items retrieved from the bodies of American soldiers.

About 75,000 men were on the Bataan Death March. About 12,000 were American, the rest Filipino. About 9,000 died.

In the battle for Okinawa, the U.S. lost 36 ships and the Japanese lost 200 ships, including the huge *Yamato*.

The Germans lost around 500,000 men in fighting around Normandy and the Allies lost about half that amount.

At Guadalcanal the Japanese lost 25,000 soldiers, 1,000 airmen, and 3,500 sailors, 680 planes and 24 warships. The Americans lost 1,700 soldiers and Marines, 400 airmen and 5,000 sailors as well as 600 planes and 24 warships.

German losses in the Battle of the Bulge, an offensive conceived by Hitler, amounted to 100,000 men and 1,600 airplanes.

The Japanese lost 100,000 men in Burma, nearly a third of their force in that country.

135,000 civilians were killed in the Allied raids on Dresden February 13-14, 1945.

Had General Omar Bradley given gasoline to Patton instead of Bernard Montgomery, the Germans could not have launched the Bulge offensive.

M & M candy was invented during World War II as a way for soldiers not to get their hands messy.

UPSIDEDOWN CARD TRICK

Take a deck of cards and before you begin this trick, turn the bottom card over and keep it in the bottom position. Ask for a volunteer in your audience to come forward to pick a card. Tell the audience that after your volunteer places the card back in the deck, you will correctly identify it. Spread out the cards to let the volunteer make his selection, but keep that bottom card covered up so the volunteer doesn't see that it's turned over.

Turn your back on the audience and tell them that you don't want to see that card. You plan to pick it out solely from exercising your mental powers, much like Patrick Jayne of *The Mentalist* television program. While your back is turned you can flip the deck over. The cards in the deck will all be face up except for the top card.

Hold the deck loosely and let him put the card back in the pile, but don't let the volunteer take the deck from you or spread the cards. Your volunteer has just placed his card back in the deck upside down.

Hold the deck behind your back and say "Abra cadabra, palooka shazam!" While the deck is behind your back, turn the top card of the deck over so it will match the rest. Now spread the cards on a table and the volunteer's card will be face up. Pick it up and say, "This must be the card you picked, am I correct?"

KICK THE CAN OUTDOOR GAME

This game is for 3-7 players. It should be played in a location where there are plenty of good places to hide. Agree in advance on what the farthest perimeters should be. A little experimenting should be done and it won't take too long to find out how far away is *too far*. Place a tin can in an open area. Designate another area close by to be the "prison." Determine who will be IT by rolling the dice. Low score is IT.

The strongest kicker in the group gets to kick the can away from its designated spot. The farther the better. While the designated IT person walks, not runs, after the can to replace it, the others run to a hiding place. The IT person then tries to find the players in hiding while at the same time guard the can. When he/she discovers a hiding place he calls out that person's name and their location. That person is now "captured" and must go sit in the prison area.

The goal is for the IT person to discover the hiding places until he/she captures everyone and then the game is over.

However, captured players can be set free from prison. When IT wanders away from the can, a player in hiding can rush forward and try to kick the can before IT can get back to the can. If the player kicks the can first, then the player that has been in prison the longest can escape and find a new hiding place. While IT walks after the can to restore it to its place, the player kicking the can runs and hides in another location. If IT gets to the can first he calls out that person's name and he has captured another prisoner.

CAPTURE THE FLAG: CLASSIC OUTDOOR TEAM GAME

For this game you divide up into teams with three or more on each side. Next, divide the playing area into two territories. Trails, creeks, roads, and fence lines all make good boundary markers. Each team should have different colored flags, roughly a foot square in size. There are three options for players who get captured. They can be "out" for the rest of the game. They can be forced to switch over and play for the team that captured them. Or they can go to a prison area and hope to be rescued.

Each team decides where to hide their flag. It must be hung at least head high and be visible for about 20 yards away on at least one side. Each team should then split in half for "defenders" and "attackers." The job of the attackers is to sneak into enemy territory, capture the opponent's flag, and safely make it back to their own territory. The job of defenders is to protect their flag and capture enemy attackers. To capture an enemy attacker you must chase them down and tag them.

The team that wins is the one that is successful in capturing the enemy flag and carrying it back to their territory.

If you decide to have a prison for captured enemy combatants, it should be located ten yards away from the flag location. Prisoners can be "rescued" if one of their teammates is able to find and rescue them by a tag. Both can then run back to their side of the border. If the would be rescuer gets tagged by the enemy, then he/she also must go to the prison area. The rescued player can be recaptured again if he/she gets tagged again before reaching their border.

You can modify this game and use **paintball guns** to replace the tagging process. Be sure to **wear safety goggles**.

THE OUTDOOR GAME OF STATUE

This game is probably more age appropriate for the 8-12 age category. It can easily be played on a front lawn or rear yard. Designate one player to be the store owner and another to be a statue buyer. The buyer comes to the store owner and says he/she would like to buy a statue. The store owner explains that he has a good selection from which the buyer can choose. The owner then takes both hands of a potential statue and spins them around two times and then lets go. The potential statue person then tries to regain his balance and then turn into a statue by "freezing" into the first position they can achieve. All the other players in the game, one-by-one, are also spun into statues.

The buyer then goes around to each statue and asks him/her what kind of statue they are. The ones who end up on hands and knees might be an elephant or a tiger. The ones who manage to freeze into position while on their feet might say they are a model, a Hollywood actor, a soldier, an Indian, or an

Olympic athlete. Each person gets to use his own imagination.

Then the buyer makes a selection and the person chosen gets to be the buyer in the next round of play. The former buyer now gets the opportunity to be a potential statue.

HOW TO SURVIVE A BAD SITUATION AT HOME

Most teens grow up in homes where the parents are doing the best they can to raise their children. There may be occasional marital spats or sometimes there might be a significant shortage of money but, as a whole, there is nothing highly traumatic in the children's lives. However, some teens must cope with an alcoholic parent or one that is on drugs. It is all too common today for teens to grow up without a father figure because of a divorce or abandonment. And lots of teens grow up in homes that largely subsist on welfare.

Another problem can be parents who are too lenient. This might sound like hog heaven to some, but most likely it will lead to trouble down the road. Teens need rules and boundaries. They also need to learn discipline. Undisciplined teens often get into trouble and by the time they turn eighteen they are a complete mess. There have been numerous cases where boys in this situation find themselves facing a stern judge who gives them the choice of jail or joining the military. I have heard many adults tell me they joined the military because they lacked focus, direction and discipline, and they matured into responsible adults after joining the military.

If you find yourself in a home where parents don't want any conflict (so they give their children almost complete freedom), there are some things you can do to prevent yourself from becoming a loser. Find someone you admire and try to live by a similar set of rules that they abide by. Another thing you can do is start going to church regularly and become an active member of a vibrant youth group. Youths who have spent their teen years in a church with a dynamic youth group have only a 5 % statistical chance of running afoul of the law or becoming dependent on drugs or alcohol.

If you find yourself in a home without much guidance, stay loyal to your family no matter what. They are the only parents you have. You'll just have to work that much harder at reaching maturity on your own.

There is a story about two brothers who grew up with an irresponsible and mean father who was a drunk. One grew up and found himself doing a twenty-five year stretch in a federal prison. The other brother ended up becoming a minister. A newspaper found out about this oddity and decided to interview the two men. "Why do you think your life has been such as mess so far?" the reporter asked the distraught man. "If you knew my father, you wouldn't have to ask that question," the man replied. Then the reporter went to talk to the other brother. "How is it that you ended up leading such an exemplary life?" the reporter asked. "If you knew my father, you wouldn't have to ask that question," the man replied.

As you can see, **what you make of your life is really all about choices**.

HOW DO YOU COPE WITH PARENTS WHO ARE VERY STRICT?

Parents worry about their kids. They worry about their sons getting into trouble with the law and they worry about their daughters becoming a victim of some predator. I was fortunate in that I was able to earn the trust of my parents at a fairly early age. I went to church with my mother and sister ever since the 5th grade and never went through any period of rebellion. I didn't run around a lot and was usually home by 9 p.m. on school nights. Quite often I was with a couple of my best friends who lived right across the street from us. I was smart enough not to violate my parents' trust. I made decent grades in school and never got into any trouble.

My sister had pretty much the same situation except once she started dating she had a bit of a conflict with my parents because she wanted to stay out late on dates. However, this never became really a huge issue that led to a big blowout argument. As a result, my sister and I can look back and be thankful that we never had any regrets about our relationship with our parents. We didn't cause them sleepless nights or cause the hair on their heads to turn gray with worry.

There will be times when your parents say *no* to a new bicycle or *no* to going out on a date at age 13. Maybe they won't let you go to a party because they don't think it will be properly chaperoned. You might think your parents are living in a different century. Instead of sulking or throwing a fit, learn to accept the word *no*. The great American humorist Mark Twain once wrote: "When I was a boy of fourteen my father was so ignorant I could hardly stand to have the old man around. But when I got to be twenty-one, I was astounded at how much the man had learned in seven years."

Parents are sometimes too strict because the behavior their child has exhibited leads them to believe they need a short leash. Perhaps they made mistakes during their coming-of-age years that they are afraid you might make and being strict is the only way they know how to deal with it. You might have to work extra hard to convince them of your trustworthiness. And if they never quite come around, learn to live with it and give in a little. It won't be that long before you turn eighteen and in the eyes of the law you will be considered an adult. Don't make the crucial mistake of running away from home. So many young lives are ruined because they can't get along with one or both parents. Follow the Ten Commandments and honor your mother and father. This is something you will never regret.

FAMOUS PIECES OF CLASSICAL MUSIC

Beethoven's 5th Symphony, Ode to Joy
Rimsky Korsakov's Scheherazade, Flight of the Bumblebee
William Tell Overture by Rossini
Symphonic Poems by Franz List (Lone Ranger music)
Schubert's Unfinished 8th Symphony
1812 Overture by Peter Tchaikovsky

The Planets by Gustav Holst
Clair De Lune (Moonlight) by Claude Debussy
Franz Haydn – Father of the Symphony (composed 106)
Frederick Handel's The Messiah
Wolfgang Mozart - The Magic Flute, Eine Kleine Nacht
Giuseppi Verdi's Rigoletto (hunchbacked court jester)
Ottorino Respighi – The Fountains of Rome
Jean Sibelius – Finlandia
Edvard Grieg – Peer Gynt Suite
George Gershwin – Rhapsody in Blue
Johann S. Bach – Brandenburg Concertos
Giacomo Puccini – Madam Butterfly, La Bohéme

Franz List of Hungary

Johann Strauss – Blue Danube
Aram Khachakurian – Saber Dance
Edward Elgar – Pomp and Circumstance
Felix Mendelssohn – Wedding March
Frederic Chopin – Funeral March
John Phillip Sousa – Stars and Stripes Forever
Johannes Brahms – Lullaby
Sergei Prokofiev – Peter and the Wolf
Saint Saëns – Carnival of the Animals
Ferde Grofe – Grand Canyon Suite
Aaron Copeland – Appalachian Spring
Igor Stravinski – Firebird Suite
Mussorgsky – Pictures of an Exhibition
Antonin Dvorák - New World Symphony
Niccolo Paganini – Carnival of Venice
Sergei Rachmaninov – Symphony #2
Richard Strauss – Zarathustra

USA GEOGRAPHY

49TH Parallel of Latitude – Boundary between USA and Canada
Rio Grande River – Boundary between USA and Mexico
Panhandle – narrow strip of land in a state; Florida, Texas and Oklahoma have panhandles
Grand Canyon – In Arizona – one of the 7 Wonders of the Modern World, the Colorado River flows through it
Florida – Our flattest state topographically; topography means the shape of the land, flat, hilly or mountainous
Mountain – Must be at least 1,000 feet high; Colorado has the most
Ozark Mountains – In southern Missouri and Southern Illinois
Appalachian Mountains – In eastern USA running north-south from Pennsylvania to Georgia
Rocky Mountains – In Western USA running north-south from Montana to

Mexico

Continental Divide – Rainfall on west side of the Rockies flows into Pacific; rainfall on east side flows into Mississippi

Sierra Nevada Mountains – In California on the Nevada border; sometimes called the "snowy mountains"

Cascade Mountains – Located in Washington, Oregon and Northern California; like the Rockies, they extend into Canada

Catskill Mountains – In New York, Northwest of New York City and southwest of Albany which is on the **Hudson River**

Pocono Mountains – In Northeastern Pennsylvania

Wasatch Mountains – In Utah near Salt Lake City; Great Salt Lake is also in Utah

Green Mountains - Vermont

White Mountains – New Hampshire

Black Hills – South Dakota – Mount Rushmore with the faces of Washington, Jefferson, Lincoln, Teddy Roosevelt

Mississippi River – Begins in Minnesota at Lake Itaska and flows into Gulf of Mexico at New Orleans, Louisiana

Missouri River – Begins in the Rocky Mountains & flows into Mississippi River just north of St. Louis; longest river in USA

Ohio River – Begins at the juncture of the Allegheny and Monongahela rivers (Pittsburgh's Golden Triangle) and empties into the Mississippi at Cairo, Illinois

Illinois River – Begins near Chicago and empties into the Mississippi just north of Alton near the town of Grafton

Chicago River – **Only river in world that flows backward**; empties into Illinois River instead of Lake Michigan

Tennessee River – Empties into the Ohio River near Paducah, Kentucky

Snake River – A major tributary of Columbia River; flows through Wyoming, Idaho, Oregon, Washington

Columbia River – Starts in British Columbia, Canada; forms border between Oregon & Washington and flows into Pacific

San Andreas Fault – In central and southern California, where two sets of tectonic plates in the earth's crust come together; when they move you get an earthquake like the big one in **San Francisco** in 1906

New Madrid Fault – At New Madrid, in Southern Missouri, where two sets of plates come together; these plates moved in 1811 causing the Mississippi River to flow backward; Reelfoot Lake in Tennessee was formed by this massive earthquake

Niagara Falls

Great Lakes – Lake Superior, Lake Huron, Lake Michigan, Lake Erie, Lake Ontario

Niagara Falls – On Niagara River on USA-Canadian border near **Buffalo, N.Y**. and Toronto, province of Ontario

Everglades – Huge swamp area in Florida

Okefenokee Swamp – Largest swamp in USA, located in southeastern Georgia – full of alligators; crocodiles are in Africa

Old Faithful – Geyser in Yellowstone National Park, Wyoming, erupts every 90 minutes & shoots water up 150 feet high

Stone Mountain – Atlanta, Georgia – carvings of Confederate heroes Robert E. Lee, Stonewall Jackson, Jefferson Davis

Four Corners –Where four western states meet; you can stand in 4 states at once – Utah, Arizona, New Mexico, Colorado

Minnesota – Land of 10,000 Lakes (made by Paul Bunyan and Babe, his huge blue ox, according to folklore)

Indiana – the Hoosier State, Illinois – The Prairie State; the Land of Lincoln, Texas – The Lone Star State; Missouri – the Show Me State; the Cave State, Tennessee – the Volunteer State – sent the most volunteers to fight in the Civil War, North Carolina – Tarheel State –Tar is made by slowly burning longleaf pine tree. North Carolina soldiers in Revolution wouldn't flee or retreat; it was as if they were stuck to the ground with tar on their heels

Space Needle – In Seattle, Washington; has revolving restaurant on top; built for Seattle Worlds Fair in 1962

Golden Gate Bridge – Located in San Francisco, stretching over harbor area near old Alcatraz Prison and the Presidio military base

Norfolk, Virginia – Home base for USA Atlantic Ocean fleet of ships

San Diego, California – Home base for USA Pacific Ocean fleet of ships for the Navy; ships are also at Pearl Harbor, Hawaii

Brooklyn Bridge

Liberty Island, NYC – where Statue of Liberty located, NYC is located on Manhattan Island, Hamptons on Long Island is where rich people live; Brooklyn Bridge goes across East River and connects NYC to Brooklyn, which is on Long Island

Basin – depressed area shaped like a bowl – much of the state of Nevada is a basin

Plateau – large raised section of land that is relatively flat on top

Mountain = 1,000 feet high or higher – Illinois has three mountain peaks in southern Ozarks.

Bitterroot Mountains – a sub-range of the Rocky Mountains; found in Montana and Idaho

94

Blue Ridge Mountains – a subsection of the Appalachian Mountains running from Georgia to Pennsylvania; also called the Smoky Mountains

Berkshires – mountains in western Connecticut and Massachusetts

Petrified Forest – In central Arizona, it has numerous examples of fossilized or petrified wood from the late Triassic Period

Painted Desert is in Arizona near the Grand Canyon and not far from the Petrified Forest.

Monument Valley is in Utah and is noted for its beautiful buttes and mesas. A **butte** is an isolated hill with steep sides and a flat top. A **mesa** is similar to a butte but it is larger.

Mount McKinley is in Alaska and it is the highest peak (20,000 feet high) in North America

Mount Hood is in the Cascade Mountains near Portland, Oregon.

Mount Rainier is in Cascade Mountains (14,000 feet high) near Seattle, Washington

Grand Coulee Dam is on the Columbia River in Pacific Northwest

Carlsbad Caverns are in New Mexico; Mammoth Cave is in Kentucky

The Brooks Mountain range is in Alaska

The Hudson River - named for explorer Henry Hudson - is in New York

An easy way to remember the Great Lakes in order of biggest to smallest is the mnemonic: Super Man Hates Eating Oreos (Superior, Michigan, Huron, Erie, Ontario)

IT'S ALWAYS THE FOURTH CARD TRICK

Shuffle a deck and deal them one at a time, from left to right, forming three columns of seven cards each. While your back is turned, have a volunteer pick a card from one of the piles without telling you what that card is. Tell him to remember that card. Now push the three columns into three piles. Ask the volunteer which pile the card is in. Take that pile and set it on any of the other two piles. The remaining pile now goes on top of the other two. Take your shortened deck and form three columns once again, dealing from left to right. While your back is turned have the volunteer find his card and remember which column it is in. Turn around and have the volunteer tell you which column the card is in. Reform the columns into three piles. Pick up the pile the card is in and set it on top of another pile. Now take the remaining pile and place it on top of the other two.

Deal the cards again into three columns, forming them from left to right. Ask once more what column the card is in. Once he tells you which column you can identify his card. It is always the fourth card down from the top. It comes up this way every time.

CHOOSING A STEADY GIRL FRIEND

For older teens going steady simply means that a particular boy and girl decide to see each other exclusively and not date anyone else. Sometimes this involves exchanging class rings. Perhaps the biggest advantage is that you always have someone to talk to and go with. Also, you don't have to worry about who your date will be to the fall dance or the prom. Your teen years should be a time of discovery and exploration. If you go steady too soon, you'll lose the opportunity to compare and contrast personalities and temperaments. How do you know Rocky Road is your favorite ice cream if that is the only flavor you have tried? Also, you probably should not go steady with someone unless they have many of the traits you would be looking for in a life partner – your wife. Here are some qualities to look for.

Is she sincere or does she sometimes put on a front?

Is she honest?

Does God and religion play a significant role in her life?

Is she loyal? Does she harp on your faults and overlook your virtues?

Is she trustworthy? Can you tell her something in confidence?

Is she good company? Does she have good manners, put others at ease. Is she courteous, easy to talk with, or is she argumentative?

Is she thoughtful and dependable?

Do you have many of the same interests?

Is she an extreme extrovert – a showoff?

Does she easily lose her temper?

Is she a good friend?

There is a tendency for guys to be dazzled by a woman's good looks and overlook her bad qualities. Sometimes you think you can change them but, more often than not, what you see is what you get.

And while you're at it, you might want to use this list to **see how you measure up** as someone a nice girl would want to go steady with or possibly marry.

HOW TO FIX A LEAKY FAUCET

This is a task appropriate for older teens. Certified plumbers charge about $80 an hour so the more things you learn about plumbing the better off you'll be. Ask your dad to show you how to repair a leaky faucet. If you don't have a leaky faucet, simply take one apart in your bathroom and put it back together again. It's a relatively easy task and once you do it you'll have the confidence to do it again should the need arise. Have dad work with you the first time.

The first thing you do is shut off the water supply, located near the floor below the basin. Turn the shutoff valve to the right (righty tighty). Plug the sink drain either by pulling up on the control lever by the faucet handle or stuff a rag in it. You don't want to lose a nut or washer. Now remove the screws that hold the faucet handles in place. Either a flathead or Phillips will be required. Sometimes the screws are hidden by a cover and you either have to unscrew them off or pry them with an awl or a very thin flathead screwdriver. Once the screws are removed, pry the handle off with a flathead screwdriver. Mask the area you will be prying on with duct tape so you don't scratch it.

Most faucets are made of brass and coated with chrome or nickel.

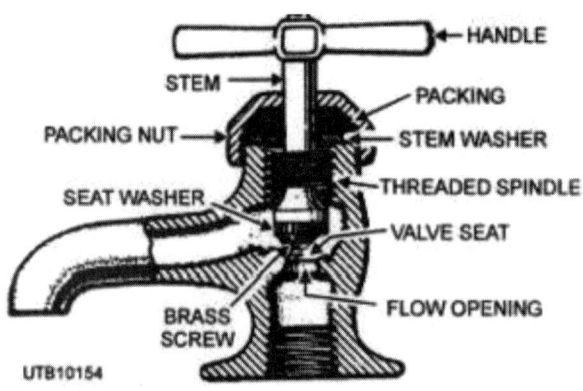

HANDLE
STEM
PACKING
PACKING NUT
STEM WASHER
SEAT WASHER
THREADED SPINDLE
VALVE SEAT
BRASS SCREW
FLOW OPENING
UTB10154

If the faucet has been leaking out the top, you probably need a new stem washer or packing nut. If the faucet has been dripping, you probably need a new seat washer. There are many kinds of seat washers so make sure the one you purchase from a hardware store matches the original.

You are now ready to replace the handle. Carefully screw it back on straight. If it doesn't go back on easily, back it off and start over. You don't want to cross-thread (strip) it and ruin the mechanism. Tighten it snug but not too tight. Now replace the screw and then replace the cap that goes over the screw. Turn your water supply back on and check for leaks. If it still leaks, try tightening the screws a bit. If it still leaks you might have to call a plumber.

HOW TO FIX A TOILET LEAKING ON THE FLOOR

This is a project for older teens. The procedure is fairly easy but it can be messy so don't expect your dad to take the toilet apart if it isn't leaking. First make sure the water on the floor wasn't merely spilled by someone. You can test this by wiping up the liquid, letting the floor dry, and then flushing the toilet. If water seeps out, then you have a problem. Turn off the water supply pipe behind the toilet and near the floor. Turn the handle clockwise to shut it off. The toilet is fastened down with two bolts. Two bolts fasten the toilet to a metal flange at the top of the toilet drain. The tops of the two bolts are covered with plastic caps near the bottom of the toilet. Pry or unscrew these caps off and examine the bolt. If it is broken, there is your problem. Simply replace it. If the bolts are okay, then you must pull the toilet off the flange.

Flush the toilet to drain the water from the tank. Use a small cup to drain most of the water from the bottom of the toilet bowl. Disconnect the water supply pipe from the toilet bowl with a small Crescent wrench. Lift the toilet up off the flange and set it down nearby. Examine the flange to see if anything is broken. If it is, replace the flange. Remember to take the old one with you to the hardware store to get a proper match. While you're there, buy a new wax gasket ring. The ring is in the bottom of the toilet so you have to tilt it to pull the old one out and replace it with a new one. When this is done, carefully put the toilet back in its place and fasten the bolts to the flange. Reconnect the water supply pipe and turn it on. After the tank fills, flush the toilet and check for leaks. If it still leaks, call a plumber. If it doesn't leak, put the caps back in place to cover the bolts.

HOW TO UNCLOG A VANITY SINK DRAIN

This project is for older teens and, hopefully, you can get your dad to stand by and assist in this learning process, even if the drain isn't clogged. Let's assume it is clogged. Push the drain stop lever down to lift the stopper a bit. Oftentimes, hair gets clogged up around this plunger and pulling the hair out with your fingers, tweezers, or needle nose pliers will do the trick. Now let's assume the clog is in the gooseneck (P trap) and Draino or Mr. Plummer doesn't do the trick.

You will either need a monkey wrench or a pair of large adjustable pliers to loosen the large nut on both ends of the 180 degree curve gooseneck. Remember to turn the nut counterclockwise. Place some kind of container underneath the gooseneck to catch any overflow water. After the nuts have been loosened, slide the gooseneck out from under the sink. Then take a "snake" or a long flexible brush and clean out the accumulated gunk. Take outside and use a hose stream to clean the inside thoroughly. Reconnect the gooseneck and then run water down the drain to make sure there are no leaks.

Doing minor household repair is quite satisfying and saves money. If you really get into the home handyman thing there are books you can buy that give step by step instructions and are illustrated. Cleaning up your room, taking out the trash, and doing minor repairs also builds self-esteem and makes you feel like a contributing member of the family.

By the way, it's called a monkey wrench because it was invented by Charles Moncky of New York. An adjustable crescent wrench is so named because it was first manufactured by the Crescent Company. The wrench is sometimes called a "knuckle buster" by those who often use it improperly. The strong crescent-shaped part of the wrench should always be on top of a nut or bolt when pulling down on it.

HOW TO PLAY CORKBALL

The game of corkball was invented at St. Louis taverns as a diversion from hard work - six days a week at the factory. The game was played in an alley behind the tavern. A sawed off broomstick served as the bat and the ball was the cork from the bung hole of a keg of beer.

In my youth the bat was a Louisville Slugger – an exact replica of a major league bat, only smaller in diameter. It was the same length, made of ash wood, and it was a bit thicker on the meat end than a broomstick. The ball was a miniature baseball, slightly bigger than a golf ball. It had a horsehide cover with red stitching, and it was made by the Rawlings Company of St. Louis.

The game apparently was played only in the metro St. Louis area. There were organized adult leagues, but as a youth we played the game in a vacant lot. The big advantage to this game is that you only need three players – a pitcher, batter and catcher. There were no balls and strikes. The pitcher threw the ball hard – fast balls and curves. If the batter swung and hit the ball fair it was a single. If the ball went past a designated distance on the fly, we called it a home run. There was no running the bases and there were no doubles or triples. If the pitcher or catcher caught a pop fly, it was an out.

They say the single most difficult thing to do in sports is to hit a ball safely for a base hit. If you can do this just one out of three times, you will be in the Hall of Fame. One out of three successful surgeries is unacceptable. A 33 percent shooting average in the NBA doesn't cut it. In corkball, if you swing and miss, and the catcher catches it, you're out. If you hit a foul tip or a foul ball, you're out. You get three outs to an inning. It would seem that the hardest thing in sports is hitting a corkball – not a baseball.

Each player keeps track of his own score and you play nine innings. After a batter makes his third out, you rotate positions. The catcher becomes the batter, the batter becomes the pitcher, and the pitcher takes the spot behind the plate.

And if you want to play on the high school baseball team, there is no better game than corkball to develop your batting eye. If you can't find a corkball or a corkball bat on the Internet, use a rubber ball and a broomstick.

HOW TO PLAY INDIANBALL

Indianball is another one of those games that was largely confined to the metro St. Louis area. You need four players for this game plus something like part of an old roofing shingle to serve as first and third bases. As in corkball, you do not run the bases in this game.

There are two players on each team. The team at the plate has one player pitch and the other one bats. The pitcher tosses the ball (baseball or softball) underhanded. If the hitter likes the pitch he swings. If he doesn't like it, he bunts it back to the pitcher. The two players take turns being the batter.

One opposing player is the infielder and plays even with first and third bases which only serve to designate fair or foul. His teammate is the outfielder. Any ball hit foul that goes past first or third is an out. Any grounder or line drive fielded cleanly is an out. Any ball caught on the fly by the outfielder is an out. There are only singles and home runs – no doubles or triples. A ball hit over the outfielder's head is a home run. There are three outs to an inning.

As a youth, my buddies and I played this game in the street. Now to hit safely, you usually swing as hard as you can, especially if you are trying to hit a home run. Not once did we ever hit a neighbor's house or porch. Neither did we ever break a window. I'd say that was some pretty good hitting.

TO TATTOO OR NOT TO TATTOO, THAT IS THE QUESTION

Primitive tribes have long used decorative body art to represent inner qualities like tribal status, personal achievements, and personality traits. Red might represent success in love or combat, while a jaguar image could suggest traits such as speed, strength, and quickness.

During my youth the only people who had tattoos were low ranking military personnel who, at the urging of their buddies after a night of drinking and carousing, decided to give in to peer pressure and get one. In today's world, tattoos are worn by the rich and famous as well as the poor and obscure. Conversely, in the eyes of many, tattoos are still disdained as a means of defacing the body and are seen as low class. Perhaps the trait shared by those who get them is the desire to enhance self-image through the use of colorful skin designs. It's another way of expressing themselves the same way they do when they choose what to wear.

Take a good look at most tattoo artists. Is their setup in a nice clean facility? Probably not. Are they dressed like a professional or are they wearing wife-beater undershirts and dirty jeans? Probably the latter. Tattoo artists use a hollow needle to inject colored dye below the skin's surface. Tiny dots of color are inserted along a pre-selected design. Tattoos can be placed on just about any part of the body, some for public display and others for private screening. Sizes range from a tiny heart about the size of a nickel to designs that surge the length of a torso or limb. Many people who get one tattoo return for more later. Many also come to regret the decision and have to learn to live with it.

The primary concern with getting a tattoo is the possible health risk. If the needle has been used by others infected with blood-borne diseases, you may become exposed to the same bacteria and **develop conditions like hepatitis or HIV**. Another possible concern is blood poisoning or a skin infection if the needle happens to become contaminated by airborne or localized germs. Take a look at the tattoo artist's equipment and hands. Considering what he is about to do to you; the environment should resemble your dentist's examining room – pristine and germ free.

A skin tattoo is designed to last. However, it may need a later touch-up to brighten the colors, which will fade over time. If you are not sure whether to get a permanent tattoo, you can try a temporary one that will wash off in a few days. If, after getting a permanent tattoo you wish to have it removed, good luck. You will need to visit a skin specialist and have the dye removed from your skin. This can be a difficult and painful process, as well as expensive.

There are still large segments of the population who think that a tattoo is a mark of immaturity. Getting a tattoo may impact your personal or professional life. Some employers do not want their workers to exhibit tattoos when clients are around. Tattoos are widely used by gang members. You may have to cover up your tattoo or stay away from clients at the workplace.

Weigh the risks and benefits to having this procedure done before making a decision that is likely to be permanent.

All in all, I'd say that getting a tattoo is not a good idea. Resist the peer pressure. And for goodness sake, don't make that idiotic mistake of getting your girlfriend's name tattooed on your body. If you know that 46 percent of marriages end in divorce, guess what percent of steady couples break up and move on to someone else. If you're dating Mary Jane, it's a bit embarrassing to have Lois Lane tattooed on your arm.

IMPRESSIVE CARD TRICK

Card tricks need to be practiced until you have every detail down pat. There is nothing more embarrassing than a botched card trick. Get an ordinary deck of cards and shuffle the deck in front of the audience. Now have a volunteer pick a card from the deck. Tell the audience that you have just learned the trick of seeing a person's recent fingerprints on an object and that you will use these powers to identify the card the volunteer picks. As the person selects the card pick up the deck and tell the audience that you don't want to look at the card. While your back is turned, sneak a peek at the card on the bottom of the deck. Let's say it's the queen of hearts.

Now turn around and have the person place their card on top of the deck. Tell them to cut the deck by randomly dividing the deck in two halves, placing the two stacks next to each other. (Be sure you remember which half has the queen of hearts on the bottom. Now take the stack with the queen and place it on top of the other stack. As you do this, tell the audience you are burying the card somewhere in the pile.

Here is what has occurred. The queen of hearts, once on the bottom, is now on top of the card your volunteer selected. Start sifting through the deck and act like you are looking for fingerprints. As you sift through the deck come close to picking the wrong card and then back off, saying the fingerprints don't seem as fresh as they should be. Now find your queen of hearts and hold up the next card, ask the volunteer, "Is this your card?" Your audience will think your trick is impressive.

HOW TO GET GOOD GRADES IN SCHOOL

When I went to school in the 1950s, America was an industrial giant. We were a nation that manufactured everything from Aluminum to Zinc. Jobs were so plentiful that a saying developed in my home town: "If you can't find a job in East St. Louis, you won't find work anywhere." Teachers complained that their biggest problems were kids chewing gum in class and dropping out of school at age 16 to go to work at a local factory. How different things are today. We are now a service oriented economy and school shootings are a common occurrence.

I never saw much need for schooling because I figured that after graduating I would get a job in a factory, just like my father. I looked around in my classes and decided that God had essentially made three kinds of people. The intelligent kids took math and chemistry and science classes. They would become the doctors, lawyers and engineers of tomorrow. The average kids made mostly Cs in school. They would get factory jobs, marry, have two or three kids, and pretty much live the life of my parents and just about everyone else in my neighborhood. The dumb kids skipped school, stared out the windows in class, and got into mischief. I figured these students would get in trouble with the law, become heavy drinkers, and end up with low-paying jobs or on welfare.

Despite my lack of enthusiasm for school, I knew that flunking out was a bad idea. I almost never missed school, paid attention in class, and earned Cs because much of what was on Friday's test the teacher had talked about previously during the week. I didn't study a lick.

After I graduated I asked my dad to get me a job at his plant where he was a foreman. He said he didn't want me working around all that dust at the paint mill. I ended up getting a low-paying, entry level office job at Midwest Pipe in St. Louis. I soon realized that I didn't have any real skills to offer an employer. I saved my money and decided to go to college. My first year of college was mostly general studies but I took a chemistry class, figuring that would be my major. My only D in college came from the first semester of the chem class. **I didn't have the math skills needed to succeed**. My second year was more general studies but now I decided to major in electronics. I quickly dropped out of those classes because, once again, I didn't have enough math background.

My first year grades were mostly Cs because I tried the same formula that had worked for me in high school. Unfortunately, the results were pretty much the same. I pondered my future and decided that few employers would want to hire a graduate with a C average. Fortunately, the second semester, I got involved with a study group for a history class. It was there that I learned that studying was the best path to good grades. I decided to spend more time going over the material until I mastered it. I knew it so well that, from that point on, I didn't worry about what kind of test the teacher gave – multiple choice, true-false, fill-in-the-blank, or essay. I had the confidence to ace the test, no matter what.

What a great feeling it was. Bill Nunes, Mr. Nobody, Mr. Average, King of the C Grade, was now getting the same high scores as all those "brains" he had looked up to in high school.

Unfortunately, most youth in school have about the same motivation I had a half a century ago. Unfortunately for today's youth, competition for jobs is keener than ever. Many American companies have either gone out of business or they have "outsourced" their jobs overseas to places such as Bangladesh, China, Korea, India, Pakistan or Hong Kong. They, too, will soon discover that, like me, they have graduated from high school without any real skills.

The solution, of course, is to buckle down and start putting in more time on your studies. You should spend at least two hours a night going over your homework and studies. Don't fall into the trap of thinking that you have no homework because the teacher didn't assign anything. There will be a test on Friday. Sometime during the week, go over your material two or three times. Make sure you have mastered it.

Many of you will say that no matter how much you study, nothing seems to stick. That's just a poor excuse. I taught school for thirty years and discovered that even the worst student in school managed to learn all the rules of the road and qualify for a driver's license. Why? It's simple. The goal in front of them was important and they buckled down and mastered the material.

If you follow my advice and find you're still having trouble, consider registering for special tuition classes at places such as Sylvan Learning Centers. There are costs involved but it will be worth it if they can get you on the right track to success.

SHOULD YOU PLAN TO GO TO COLLEGE?

From grades 1-12 I had no plans whatsoever to go to college. Then, after securing a low paying office job after graduation, I packed my bags and went off to college the next year. My first year was at a private church-affiliated school and the first year expenses wiped out everything I had saved up after working for a year. After that, I transferred to Southern Illinois University at Edwardsville, Illinois. Instead of paying $800 tuition, the cost was now (Are you sitting down?) **$180 a year**. Currently, a single textbook can sometimes cost nearly that much. I not only graduated debt free, I continued my studies and went on to earn a Masters degree and a Specialist degree. Imagine that, going from no plans whatsoever to go to college to obtaining three degrees. I also had no encouragement from anyone to go to college – not my parents, not my teachers, not my counselor (I don't ever remember meeting with a school counselor.), not my friends. It was entirely all my idea.

Now, I suppose college isn't for everyone. On top of that, high schools have about an 85 percent graduation rate. The dropout rate in college is about 50 percent. Why so high? The reasons are varied – expenses, a minimum four year commitment, inability to get decent grades, sickness, accidents, etc. I saw peers I had gone to high school with who had earned mostly As and Bs. But they really didn't have to study that hard because they had high IQs. However, now that they were in college, students were more motivated and competition was tougher. For the first time they had to do some real studying and they didn't like the regimen.

Some students drop out of college because it's pretty much like high school for the first two years. They make you take courses in art appreciation, geography, speech, literature, English, math, science, history and foreign language. I've also seen many a youth go off to college with the intent of becoming an accountant. They are forced to take a psychology class and end up loving it and decide to major in that instead.

History is the second most disliked subject in high school, right behind English and poetry. Yet there never seems to be a shortage of history teachers. After I couldn't cut it in chemistry and electronics, my wife-to-be asked me what subjects I had taken that I liked. "History and geography," I said, after giving it some thought. And that is what I taught in high school for 30 years. Young people in high school are mostly not quite mature enough to appreciate what history is all about. Studying "dead white males" and memorizing dates and events seems useless and boring to them. But the older you get the wiser and more mature you become (hopefully).

The first two years of college are intended to be mostly exploratory. Institutions of higher learning don't want to graduate accountants who are ignorant of their country's history, have little knowledge of biology or zoology, have no idea what is going on in the world, couldn't find Vietnam on a map if their life depended on it, and have little or no appreciation for music or art.

They also know that students often change their majors, based largely on classes they were forced to take.

College also brings with it a lot of freedom. Mom and Dad aren't there anymore to hound you about hitting the books. Many students get distracted and spend too much time at drinking parties, doing drugs, messing around in the gym. They get poor grades, get discouraged, and drop out.

Talk it over with your parents. If you decide college isn't for you, at least acquire some kind of skill in carpentry, plumbing, electrical, computers, automotive, real estate, insurance, etc. Another possibility is a two-year junior college to obtain a certificate to be something like an X-ray technician or a dental assistant. Perhaps this is the best motivation. Typical people with high school degrees earn, let's say, $35,000 a year. People with a degree will earn, on average, $55,000 a year. Think of how that translates over a lifetime. Money doesn't buy happiness, but a lack of it causes numerous problems.

TIPS FOR DOING WELL ON TESTS

Like many other things in life, test taking is a skill that needs to be worked on and developed. There are certain strategies to follow that nearly all educators agree on. Let me give you an example of how mastering the material worked well for me.

In 1977, while teaching high school, I decided to study real estate and sell property after school, on weekends, and during the summer vacation. I took the required class, studied hard, mastered the material and looked forward to the date of the test. Unfortunately, it was going to be given from 9-12 noon on a school day. I applied for a ½ day leave of absence to take the test at Southern Illinois University. My school district said they would allow me to take the test, but they would deduct a half day salary from my paycheck because it wasn't an illness or family emergency. That seemed fair to me.

I arrived at SIU ten minutes early, but when 9 a.m. arrived the proctor said that everyone scheduled to take the test hadn't arrived and we should wait another fifteen minutes before beginning. That wasn't fair to me because I had to be back at the high school by 12:05 p.m. However, I didn't complain. The test was in three parts and the last part, dealing with real estate math, left me with less time to finish than I would have had if we had started on time.

I knew that passing the test required 70 percent correct or higher. With most questions I knew the answers, but the ones I was unsure of I placed a little mark by them on my answer sheet. When the time approached 11:45 a.m., I knew I had to hand my paper in to get back to school on time. I quickly counted up the little marks and knew that even if I missed all of the last 15 questions I would still pass the test. For all the remaining multiple choice questions I quickly marked the letter C for every answer. A month later the state of Illinois sent me my score and I passed with a mark of 87. My mastery of learning skills paid handsome dividends.

These are some techniques to better understand your material:
Take good notes in your class lectures and from your textbooks

Review your notes soon after class/lecture, while what was said is fresh in your mind

Review your notes briefly before the next class

Schedule some time before the test for a longer review

Take good notes as your teacher tells you what will be on the test

Organize your notes, texts, and assignments according to what will be on the test

Estimate the hours you'll need to review materials

Draw up a schedule that blocks units of time and material

Test yourself on the material

Finish your studying the day before the exam

Get plenty of rest the day before the test.

TAKING A TRUE-FALSE TEST

Every part of a true sentence must be "true." If any one part of the sentence is false, the whole sentence is false despite many other true statements.

Pay close attention to negatives, qualifiers, absolutes, and long strings of statements.

Negatives can be confusing. If the question contains negatives, as "no, not, or cannot," drop the negative and read what remains. Decide whether that sentence is true or false. If it is true, its opposite, or negative, is usually false.

Qualifiers are words that restrict or open up general statements. Words like sometimes, often, frequently, ordinarily, and generally open up the possibilities of making accurate statements. They make more modest claims, are more likely to reflect reality, and usually indicate "true" answers.

Absolute words restrict possibilities. No, never, none, always, every, entirely, or only, imply the statement must be true 100% of the time and usually indicate "false" answers.

Long sentences often include groups of words set off by punctuation. Pay attention to the "truth" of each of these phrases. If one is false, it usually indicates a "false" answer.

Often true/false tests contain more true answers than false answers. You have more than a 50% chance of being right with "true". However, your teacher may be the opposite. Review past tests for patterns...

Your first instinct on a particular question is probably the right one. Don't try to read too much into the question.

ANSWERING MULTIPLE CHOICE QUESTIONS

Improve your odds by thinking critically: Read the stem carefully and answer by selecting the option or choice that **most closely matches** your answer.

Treat each option as a true-false question and choose the "most true."

Eliminate options you know to be incorrect.

If allowed, mark words or alternatives in questions that eliminate the option or choice.

Give each option of a question the "true-false test." This may reduce your selection to the best answer.

Question options that grammatically don't fit with the stem.

Question options that are totally unfamiliar to you.

Question options that contain negative or absolute words.

Try substituting a qualified term for the absolute one, like *frequently* for *always;* or *typical* for *every* to see if you can eliminate it.

How do you deal with "All of the above" as a choice? If you know three options seem correct, "all of the above" is a strong possibility.

If the question calls for a number answer, try tossing out the high and low and consider the middle range numbers.

How do you handle two options that "look very similar?" Probably one is correct; choose the best but eliminate choices that mean basically the same thing, and thus cancel each other out.

If two options are opposite each other, chances are one of them is correct.

Favor options or choices that contain qualifiers. The result is longer, more inclusive items that better fill the role of the answer.

If two alternatives seem correct, compare them for differences, and then refer to the stem to find your best answer.

Always guess when there is no penalty. Don't guess if you are penalized for guessing and if you have no basis for your choice.

Use hints from questions you know to answer questions you do not know.

Sample question: Which of the following was **not** a British victory in the American Revolutionary War? (That was the stem.) (A) Brandywine Creek (B) Germantown (C) Yorktown (D) Brooklyn Heights

Now for some reason you don't recall much about Brandywine Creek, Germantown, or Brooklyn Heights. However, you do remember that the entire British army surrendered to Washington at Yorktown and that led to the Treaty of Paris that ended the war. Thus you know the answer is C.

ESSAY TESTS

Before writing out the exam answers, set up a time schedule to answer each question and to review/edit all questions.

If six questions are to be answered in sixty minutes, allow yourself only eight minutes for each.

If questions are "weighted" (some are worth more than others), prioritize that into your time allocation for each question.

When the time is up for one question, stop writing, leave space, and begin the next question. The incomplete answers can be completed during the review time.

Six incomplete answers will usually receive more credit than three, complete ones.

Read through the questions once and note if you have any choice in answering questions.

Pay attention to how the question is phrased, or to the "directives," or words such as "compare," "contrast," "criticize," etc.

Answers will come to mind immediately for some questions. Do these first to get your brain engaged and reduce anxiety.

Write down their key words, listings, etc, as they are fresh in mind. Otherwise these ideas may be blocked (or be unavailable) when the time comes to write the later questions. This will reduce panic (anxiety - actually fear which disrupts thoughts).

Before attempting to answer a question, put it in your own words. Now compare your version with the original. Do they mean the same thing? If they don't, you've misread the question. You'll be surprised how often they don't agree.

Think before you write: Make a brief outline for each question.

Number the items in the order you will discuss them; get right to the point.

State your main point in the first sentence.

Use your first paragraph to provide an overview of your essay.

Use the rest of your essay to discuss these points in more detail.

Back up your points with specific information, examples, or quotations from your readings and notes.

Teachers are influenced by compactness, completeness and clarity of an organized answer.

Writing in the hope that the right answer will somehow turn up is time-consuming and usually futile.

To know a little and to present that little well is, by and large, superior to knowing much and presenting it poorly--when judged by the grade received.

Avoid very definite statements when possible; a qualified statement connotes a philosophic attitude, the mark of an educated person. Example: "Vietnam was a stupid war!" With this statement you have reduced a very complex war to oversimplified terms.

Qualify answers when in doubt. It is better to say "toward the end of the 18th century" than to say "in 1790" when you can't remember, whether it's 1780 or 1790. In many cases, the approximate time is all that is wanted; unfortunately 1790, though approximate, may be incorrect, and will usually be marked accordingly.

Summarize in your last paragraph.

Restate your central idea and indicate why it is important.

If you think you had pretty good answers but didn't receive the grade you thought you deserved, try this. After the teacher has passed out all the graded essays, raise your hand. Ask the teacher to state what he was looking for in a particular answer in order to receive an A. Or, you might ask the teacher to have another student, who earned an A, to read their essay. You can justify this by telling the teacher that this, or a similar question might come up on the final exam and you want to do the very best you can. What teacher could refuse such a sincere request?

I would wish you luck on future tests but someone once said, "Luck is the residue of design."

HOW TO TALK TO A GIRL

Getting butterflies in your stomach when mustering up the courage to talk to a girl, or ask her for a date, is quite common. The best thing to remember is that girls have the same fears and insecurities that boys do. Girls want to be liked and have friends, just like the boys. They also worry about how they look, even more than boys do. For some boys, going up and talking to a girl is a bit scary. What if she doesn't like you? What if she says *no* to a proposed date? What if she says she's not interested in you? I know. It seems as if you'll die of embarrassment if you get turned down, but you'll get over it. It's like anything else. "If at first you don't succeed, try, try again." People who work in sales learn to live with rejection. They are taught that when they are trying to sell a product, they might get as many as seven negative responses before they get a "yes" for a sale.

If you watch a romantic comedy movie, almost all of them have the same formula. When the guy and the girl meet for the first time they are almost repulsed by each other. As the plot goes on, circumstances cause them to keep in contact with each other. Their original hostility begins to dwindle and they slowly warm up to each other. By the end of the film they are madly in love. IT DOESN'T WORK THAT WAY IN REAL LIFE! If a girl tells you she's not interested, continued pursuit is harassment and instead of mildly not liking you, she'll end up hating you. Move on to a different girl. There's an old saying: "There are plenty of other fish in the ocean."

In school, unfortunately, there is a pecking order. Nerds generally date other nerds. Heavy set people tend to date other heavy set people. The prettiest girl in the class doesn't date the ugliest boy in the class. Girls from rich families don't date guys from poor families. The pretty cheerleader dates the high school quarterback. That's life. Fortunately, that usually leaves a large number of girls available who roughly match up with your IQ, looks, and social status.

I came from a lower middle-class family and ended up marrying a girl from a higher middle class family. However, I had several things going in my favor. We both went to the same church and Christian values were important in her life. She also wouldn't date boys who smoked, drank or cussed. Once we started dating, I knew that her parents would not approve of someone who didn't have a good education or good earning potential. No parent wants their children to marry a loser and end up poor. Her mother and grandmother had Masters degrees so I knew that a college education was important in her family.

If there is a girl in your class that you like, try giving her a friendly "hello, Carlie" as you pass her in the hall. If she smiles or says hello back to you, the next time you see her tell her hello and pay her a compliment on her outfit. Never, never say: "Wow! You look hot!" It will make her feel as if she is an object instead of a person. You might catch up to her some time on the way to class and say: "That was a big assignment Mr. Roberts gave us yesterday, wasn't it?" If she responds in a friendly or enthusiastic manner, you can be pretty sure she likes you.

If you are too shy to talk to a girl directly, here's another possibility. See who her girl friends are and call or go up to one of them and tell her you are interested in dating her friend. Ask her what she thinks your chances are. If she doesn't know, she'll soon find out and let you know. That's the way girls are. It's part of their DNA.

If you are part of a youth group at church, this makes it a bit easier because boys and girls are thrown together in informal social activities where interaction is a bit easier. In some cases there might even be activities (such as a potato sack race) where a boy and girl are paired together. You can use the same technique. Start with a friendly *hello*. The next time say hello and pay her a compliment. Then begin a conversation by making a comment about a recent event or an upcoming activity.

How do you keep a conversation going? **Try to be yourself.** Say something funny occasionally that will make her laugh and put her at ease. Show interest in things that seem important to her by asking follow up questions. Don't start talking about sports or cars. That's a definite turn-off unless she lets you know she's into those things in a big way.

Here's another good rule to follow. **Be a good listener**. Try to listen twice as much as you talk. If the ratio is the other way around, the girl will think you are self-centered and more interested in yourself than her. Have you ever noticed this? Many popular girls in school will end up marrying one of most handsome and popular boys. Five years later they get divorced. The next time this beauty marries, her second husband is quite often average in looks. Here's what happens. When she marries that handsome hunk, it's mostly about looks. After they've been married a while she discovers he's more interested in himself than her. Also, those handsome devils with the chiseled good looks are more prone to have affairs. Before she marries a second time, she makes sure the guy is in love with her instead of himself. The second time around, looks aren't quite as important to her as having a companion who treats her like a queen.

A final suggestion. **Pay attention to your personal hygiene**. Make sure you're not a turn-off because of bad breath, dirty fingernails, body odor, shabby clothes, or unkempt, dirty hair.

I knew my wife going back to the 5th grade. That's when my family started going to her church. During all those years I never said a word to her. I was too shy and didn't know how to talk to a girl. I didn't date until after I graduated from high school. When I did finally ask her out, I telephoned her and asked her to come watch me play in our church league basketball game and then go for a burger and fries afterward. She said yes, and that was a beginning. We celebrated our 50th Wedding Anniversary in September of 2010. Life has been good! God has blessed my family. You never know where your life is going to take you. Because I became a teacher, sold real estate, and have written 16 books, I have gone from being a shy introvert to an outgoing extrovert.

HOW TO BUILD A COOL SNOWMAN

You generally need at least two inches of snow to build a decent snowman. Dress warm and wear gloves or mittens. Since heat rises, much of your body heat will exit from the top of your head unless you **wear a cap or knit hat**. This is a good project for two so have your dad, best friend, or that special girl come over and help. If you want her mom and dad to get to know you better, suggest building the snowman at her house. During the building process, take time out to be playful. Girls like that in a guy. Accidentally on purpose, softly toss some snow on her head in a way that she gets some on her face. She'll probably get you for that and do the same to you. A playful snow fight should ensue. This isn't a snowball fight with some other guy. Be gentle. Let her win. Then you can gently tackle her and the two of you will end up on the ground. Lean over and give her a playful kiss on her forehead. From there you can go to making snow angels. After that – time to get busy finishing the snowman.

Test to see if you have *packing snow*, which clumps together easily and isn't too wet or too dry and powdery. The snow must pack to make a snowman. Grab a handful of snow and shape into a ball. Continue adding more snow and packing the ball until it's too large to hold. Place the ball on the snow in front of you and slowly roll it forward. As more snow accumulates on the outside of your ball, pack the snow tighter by pressing on it with your gloved hands. Roll and pack the ball over and over until it is the size you want for the bottom of the snowman's body. Repeat for the thoracic midsection and noggin'. The bottom should be the biggest ball, and the top should be the smallest (obviously). Pack some extra snow between the layers to make them stick together. Place sticks or a metal rod down the center where the sections meet if your snowman is having trouble standing erect. Give the snowman a happy face. Use coal, rocks, buttons, or anything dark and round for the eyes. A

horizontal stick or twig will make a good mouth, and a carrot will do fine for the pointed nose. If you don't have a carrot, a banana or a candy cane will suffice. Cover the top of his head with an old plant for hair, or give him a knit hat to wear. Top hats will blow away unless secured. An old silk top hat would be perfect but he might then come alive and run away and you'd have to start all over again. Add arms, legs and other accessories. Push sticks into the sides of the middle section and hang old mittens on the ends, then place boots at the bottom for legs. Also consider adding a scarf or sun glasses.

Oops, you forgot to give your snowman rosy cheeks. The simple solution is to add some food coloring to a spray bottle and spray them on.

BUILDING A SNOW FORT

When there is a big snow, you have an opportunity to do many things - snowball fights, snowmen building, ice carving, sledding, and more! One big favorite is building a snow fort. Here is how to build one effectively. **Be sure there is an adult helping you in case there is a cave in**. First find a good snow drift. If you don't have one, make it! Use shoveled or blown snow from the driveway and snow from anywhere else. Make a huge pile, or find your own.

Make sure the snow is strong and not loose. You will need to dig a tunnel through, and if the snow is loose, it will cave in too easily. If you can't get strong snow, either pat it all down well with a shovel, or pat it and then pour cold water over it, to make a layer of ice. Make sure to leave a space with no water poured over it so you can easily start your tunnel. Start your tunnel by using a shovel or your hands. Try making a circle shaped tunnel, since square ones can cause people to get stuck, and then you may need to destroy the fort to free them. Make sure your tunnel doesn't go too far as to leave no space for your room area. Also, make sure your tunnel is tall and wide enough so visitors can fit in. Once your tunnel is finished, crawl in and start clearing out your room area. To do this, dig in a little farther, and then dig on the sides. Sometimes, you may have trouble fitting a shovel in when doing this, so you may have to use your hands. Continue to dig for a little while, then check how close you are to your walls. To check if you are too close to the outer walls of your fort, do the following. Find a wooden stick or use the end of your shovel. From inside or out, make a horizontal hole with the stick, just simply jab it through. Do this until you get into your fort. If you are close to the inside or outside of the fort, you may need to stop with where you are. If you have different amounts of snow in different places, you may have to do this a few times. You can also use these as ventilation holes, which you will need to help circulate air. There you have it! A snow fort. But wait...isn't something missing? Well, there may be! You can add extra rooms, snow or ice sculptures and decorations, and even a chimney if you have good snow! Beware though, you may cave in your tunnel with really complex structures added onto it!

A DIFFERENT KIND OF SNOW FORT

Here are instructions for building a more complex type of fort. **Be sure there is an adult around to help in case there is a cave in.** Again, try taking advantage of an existing large drift. A side of a house or shed can provide good support for at least one wall you don't have to build, but make sure you don't rely too heavily on it. The walls of your finished fort should optimally be all snow, because that's niftier.

Another thing. Determine where you can assemble the biggest pile of snow with the least amount of effort. Getting your snow is going to take a lot of work, but that's what kids are for, right? After you've selected your location, begin moving snow from the rest of your yard into a pile.

As you pile the snow, compress it. This is very important. The weight of the snow will gain you some free compression, but you'll need to pound it with your shovel, roll around in it, or take little jaunts down the mound with a flat-bottomed sled. This is a good job for younger kids who are too small to give real help.

Build your compressed mound up about five feet high. Then build it up a little more. Now build up the sides of the mound so it looks less like a mountain and more like a rectangle.

Here's where it starts getting fun because now it's time to excavate. You can do some room planning, but really the shape of your room (or rooms) will be dictated by the shape of your mound. It would be best to enter from the south side, presuming the coldest winds generally blow from the north. Begin by carving a slot into the side of the mound just wide enough for your sled, which will now serve as a snow cart, removing the carved snow from inside the fort and form a second, adjacent mound which can be carved into a second room.

Try to get your entrance as close to the ground as possible without hitting the grass or dirt, then move inward. (Don't worry if you cut a little deep; you'll naturally build up the floor as you excavate.) Push the front of the sled into your slot until it butts against the bottom of the mound, then use your hands to cut snow out of the mound into the sled. Once the sled is full, slide it out of the slot and dump it. (Again, this is great work for kids, especially with two sleds that can be set up in rotation.)

(Don't hog the fun part all to yourself, but make sure you are keeping a vigilant eye on younger kids during the initial excavations, when it's possible several pounds of snow could fall in on them if you didn't do a good job packing your mound.) That's why you need an adult present.

Carve out your rooms, leaving about a foot of snow for walls. If you can see sunlight shining through the snow, you've gone too far. Your goal is to always carve *through*, if possible, after you've made your initial punch into the side for your door. Once you have enough room inside your fort to fit inside, start carving from the bottom of the mound up, the better to prevent a cave-in. (Don't get under a big snow pack if you can help it.)

The trick is to be conservative as possible with your dimensions while not leaving too much snow above to weigh down your ceilings and walls. It's very easy to cause a structural failure but very difficult to repair one. The shape of your rooms should be domed rather than squared off. Fortunately, that's the natural shape your excavations will make. A decently-packed mound will allow you to build rooms that are just big enough for an adult male to sit upright within, but probably not able to totally stretch out. You can try to buttress the ceilings with load-bearing walls, but it's a challenge. Instead, consider carving out a second room if you have the mound real estate for it.

You've got your fort basically built, with as small of an entrance as possible and strong, opaque walls. It's probably going to be pretty dark inside, which is a good sign that it won't immediately come crashing down—especially when you roll up a big ball of snow or stuff an old blanket in the hole for the door.

You can light up a candle, but make sure you leave a couple of air holes for fresh air to come in and mix. A candle won't give off much light, but it can provide a surprising amount of heat—snow is a great insulator. (Just the body heat of its occupants will keep most forts plenty toasty.) This is why Eskimos (Inuits) build igloos out of blocks of ice. If your best girl is helping you with the fort, you can tell her about the Inuit tradition of rubbing noses together after they finish a joint project.

THE SEVEN WONDERS OF THE ANCIENT WORLD

The **Great Pyramid of Cheops** was built as his tomb nearly 3,000 years before the birth of Christ. The pyramid originally stood 481 ft. high, although somewhere along the line, somebody stole the capstone. The base at the bottom is perfectly square. It took about two million blocks of stone to complete the structure. Each stone weighed about two tons. Most of the stones fit together so well that the blade of a knife cannot be inserted between them.

The **Hanging Gardens of Babylon** were built on the Euphrates River in modern day Iraq. King Nebuchadnezzar made it for his queen who was not accustomed to living in a dry desert climate. The gardens were built sometime between the 6th and 7th centuries B.C. Thousands of gallons of water had to be drawn daily from the river to keep everything green and blooming. Historians believe a water lifting device based on the principle of the screw, invented by the Greek Archimedes, was the method employed to lift the water.

The **Temple of Diana at Ephesus** was built in what is now the country of Turkey. Alexander the Great, during his journeys of conquest, was awed by its magnificence and beauty. The temple was burned the night Alexander was born by a man named Herostratus just so history would record his name. The temple was rebuilt by the time Alexander became a young man. The temple fell into ruin by the Third Century A.D.

The **Mausoleum at Halicarnassus** was built for King Mausolus of Persia who died in 353 B.C. Halicarnassus is now in the country of Turkey. The building had a pyramid-shaped top that was sup-ported by 36 columns. On top was a statue of Masoulus his wife and his sister in a chariot. The 140 ft. tall building was destroyed in 1522 when Christian knights on a crusade dismanteled it and used the stones to build a fort. From the name Mausolus comes the word mausoleum, which means a fancy and ornate tomb.

The **Statue of Zeus** at Olympia depicted the chief Greek god in a seated position. In one hand he held a statue of Nike, the winged goddess of victory. The other hand held a gold scepter topped by an eagle. The statue was made of gold and ivory. The statue was later moved to Contantinople and was destroyed by fire in the fifth century. Olympia was the site of the original Olympic games.

The **Colossus of Rhodes** was a 100 ft. tall statue of Helios that towered over the harbor. The frame was made of iron and the outer layers were bronze. A

113

strong earthquake brought it crashing down around 230 B.C. It lay there in ruins for about 800 years before conquering Arabs sold it for scrap.

The **Lighthouse at Alexandria**, Egypt was built for Ptolemy, the Greco-Egyptian king who ruled from 285 B.C. to 247. Ptolemy's ancestor was a former general of Alexander the Great. Ptolemy's most famous descendant was Cleopatra, who was queen of Egypt during the time of Julius Caesar. The lighthouse was on Pharos Island, in the harbor. Its light could be seen from a distance of 35 miles and the structure was estimated to have been about 500 feet high.

HOW TO MAKE A COIN BATTERY

Colossus of Rhodes

A battery needs three things – a positive end (cathode) a negative end (anode) and a solution or electrolyte. Electricity is simply the flow of electrons, which are negatively charged particles. The anode is frequently made of some material, such as zinc, which gives up electrons easily. Copper makes a good cathode. When **Alessandro Volta** made the first battery, he used zinc and copper. His electrolyte solution was seawater soaked in blotter paper.

For this project you will need **ten copper pennies**, some **tin foil**, and a **paper towel** instead of blotter paper. We honor Volta by using his name for a unit of energy (volt), as in a 1 & ½ volt flashlight battery. A good way to understand a volt is to think of it like the speed of water flowing through a water pipe. Amps are the power units behind the volts. Think of them in terms of the diameter of the pipe. A one inch pipe produces a small flow but a 5 inch pipe gives you a greater volume (power).

Using the penny as a pattern, cut ten circles from the tin foil, slightly larger than the penny. Now cut ten circles from the paper towel, just a bit larger to prevent the two metals from touching. Use a small bowl in which to mix some **salt** in **white vinegar**. Acids are used to make electrolytes and vinegar is acetic acid. The electrolyte in your car battery is sulfuric acid. The purpose of the salt (sodium chloride) is to increase the strength of the electrolyte. Soak your paper towel circles in the electrolyte solution.

You need a **LED (light emitting diode) light** from Radio Shack and **two small lengths of copper wire**. Attach the two wires to the wires coming from the led bulb. **Duct tape** the other end of one of the wires to the bottom of a piece of foil. Stack everything in this sequence on top of the foil with the wire on it. Foil, paper, coin, foil, paper, coin until you have used up all the

114

materials. A coin should be on top of your stack. Tape the other wire from the LED bulb to the top coin. The top coin is your cathode and your bottom foil is the anode. On a flashlight battery, the flat bottom is the anode and the other end, with the raised button in the middle, is the cathode.

Your home-made coin battery should be able to light the bulb. Here's something else you can try. Remove the bulb and let the ends of both wires touch your tongue. You should feel a slight tingle.

When you shake a flashlight battery, you don't hear any electrolyte sloshing around inside. That's because the electrolyte is a gel paste. Sometimes an old battery will leak. When it does, the material that oozes out is the electrolyte.

LEARNING MORSE CODE

America's most famous spy was Benedict Arnold, an American officer in the Revolutionary War. Arnold, a courageous and able general, was upset that he had been passed over for promotion. His life was further complicated because his wife, Peggy Shippen, was a Tory - sympathetic to the British cause.

Arnold plotted with British Major John Andre to give information that would enable the English to capture West Point, a fortified position overlooking the Hudson River. Andre was caught out of uniform with a message in his boot **and was hanged**. Arnold made his way to the British lines and lived out his

MORSE CODE

Letter	Code	Letter	Code	Number	Code
A	•−	N	−•	1	•−−−−
B	−•••	O	−−−	2	••−−−
C	−•−•	P	•−−•	3	•••−−
D	−••	Q	−−•−	4	••••−
E	•	R	•−•	5	•••••
F	••−•	S	•••	6	−••••
G	−−•	T	−	7	−−•••
H	••••	U	••−	8	−−−••
I	••	V	•••−	9	−−−−•
J	•−−−	W	•−−	0	−−−−−
K	−•−	X	−••−		
L	•−••	Y	−•−−		
M	−−	Z	−−••		

life in London. Had their message been written in cipher (code), the Americans might have been unable to translate it. The telegraph, invented by Samuel Morse, sent electrical impulses from one place to another by wires attached to poles. With his electromagnetic device, an operator could send a pulse to another machine at some distant point. His device could send long and short pulses. Translated on paper, the shorts were called dots and the longs were called dashes. The first message Morse sent said: "**What hath God wrought**?" He established a chart that operators learned to memorize, with a certain number of dots or dashes representing every letter in the alphabet and numbers 0 through 9. The telegraph, a simple machine, was considered a revolution in communications (See chart on page 115).

The best known Morse code signal is a distress call sent out by ships in trouble – SOS (save our ship). The correct sequence for SOS is dit, dit, dit – dah, dah, dah – dit, dit, dit. When Senator John McCain was captured during the Vietnam War, the enemy posed him for a televised press conference to show he was being treated according to the Geneva Conventions. To let U.S. intelligence know it was all a lie, he acted as if the bright lights were hard on his eyes. They finally figured out that he was blinking **T-O-R-T-U-R-E** in Morse Code.

Check again the universal chart for Morse Code. Who knows, perhaps some day it could save your life if a building collapses, trapping you inside. You can tap out SOS on a water pipe.

WEATHER SCIENCE

4 types of clouds: A – Cirrus = high level wisps and tufts of ice crystals; when sky is full of them referred to a cirrostratus sky   B – Cumulus = look like mashed potatoes; C – Stratus = horizontal low cloud, looks like a buttermilk sky; D – Nimbus = storm cloud; E =Cum-u-lo-nimbus is tall storm cloud

Meteorology – the scientific study of weather

Barometer – Instrument that measures air pressure – high pressure = clear weather, low pressure, = approaching storm

Fahrenheit thermometer – 32 degrees = freezing and 212 degrees = water boiling – USA uses this type

Celsius thermometer – zero degrees equals freezing and 100 degrees = boiling point of water – scientists use this type

Tornado – Dark cumulonimbus cloud has destructive rotating funnel that comes down and touches the ground; in some parts of US tornadoes are called cyclones. In weather map terms, a **cyclone** is a large mass of low pressure with wind rotating in a counter-clockwise direction in the **Northern Hemisphere** (everything from equator to North Pole)

Rain – Warm air, which holds more moisture than cold air, releases droplets when it meets a cold front. If the temperature is above freezing, it occurs as rain; if it is below freezing, it falls as ice crystals known as snow

Anemometer – device to measure wind speed

Climate – weather conditions over a long period of time; dry or arid over long period results in a desert

Windward and **lee** side of mountain – air approaching windward side rises and produces rain. The far or other side of the mountain is the **lee side** and it is often dry or desert-like because all the moisture fell on windward side.

Longitude – long lines running north-south on a map grid. Everything starts at zero degrees at **Greenwich**, England and goes 180 degrees West and 180 degrees East. The earth is a circle and there are **360 degrees in a circle;** a **marine chronometer** calculates longitude

International Date Line – 180 degrees longitude; there are 24 time zones in the world

U.S. Time Zones – Eastern, Central, Rocky Mountain, Pacific – Illinois is in the Central zone, Virginia is in the Eastern, Oregon the Pacific

Sextant (Wikipedia)

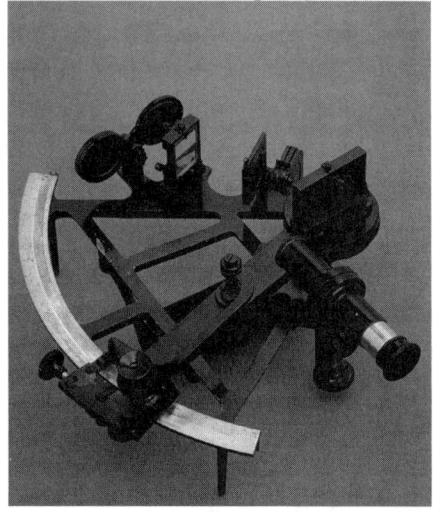

Latitude – lines running east-west on a map grid. The **Equator** is zero degrees. From the Equator to the **North Pole** is 90 degrees; a device known as a **sextant** measures latitude

Compass – floating magnetized needle which points to the earth's magnetic north; it helps you find direction; if you are in the woods without a compass, **moss always grows on the north side of a tree**.

4 Seasons – Earth is tilted on its axis as it travels around the sun. When the sun's rays hit earth directly, temperature is warm. When the rays hit the earth at an angle, the temperature is cooler. Near the equator, sun's rays are always direct and hot.

Jet Stream – Current of rapidly moving air in the upper atmosphere between a large mass of warm air and a large mass of cold air; first discovered by the Japanese in World War II

Gulf Stream – First noticed by Ben Franklin, it is a river of warm water that comes up from the Caribbean and flows along our eastern coast as far north as Newfoundland and then heads toward England, giving it a milder winter climate

Isobar – Lines indicating areas of equal air pressure on a weather map

Isotherm – Lines indicating areas of equal temperature on a weather map

Dew point – As night temperatures cool, the point at which moisture is released from the atmosphere and condenses on grass; in a similar manner moisture forms on the outside of a glass when you put ice in a cold drink.

THE FIFTY STATES

STATE	CAPITAL	NICKNAME
Alabama	Montgomery	Heart of Dixie

Alaska	Juneau	Last Frontier
Arizona	Phoenix	Grand Canyon State
Arkansas	Little Rock	Natural State
California	Sacramento	Golden State
Colorado	Denver	Centennial State
Connecticut	Hartford	Constitution State
Delaware	Dover	First State
Florida	Tallahassee	Sunshine State
Georgia	Atlanta	Peach State
Hawaii	Honolulu	Aloha State
Idaho	Boise	Gem State
Illinois	Springfield	Prairie State
Indiana	Indianapolis	Hoosier State
Iowa	Des Moines	Hawkeye State
Kansas	Topeka	Sunflower State
Kentucky	Frankfort	Bluegrass State
Louisiana	Baton Rouge	Pelican State
Maine	Augusta	Pine Tree State
Maryland	Annapolis	Old Line State
Massachusetts	Boston	Bay State
Michigan	Lansing	Great Lakes State
Minnesota	St. Paul	North Star State
Mississippi	Jackson	Magnolia State
Missouri	Jefferson City	Show Me State
Montana	Helena	Treasure State
Nebraska	Lincoln	Cornhusker State
Nevada	Carson City	Silver State
New Hampshire	Concord	Granite State
New Jersey	Trenton	Garden State
New Mexico	Santa Fe	Land of Enchantment
New York	Albany	Empire State
North Carolina	Raleigh	Tar Heel State
North Dakota	Bismarck	Peace Garden State
Ohio	Columbus	Buckeye State
Oklahoma	Oklahoma City	Sooner State
Oregon	Salem	Beaver State
Pennsylvania	Harrisburg	Keystone State
Rhode Island	Providence	Ocean State
South Carolina	Columbia	Palmetto State
South Dakota	Pierre	Mount Rushmore State
Tennessee	Nashville	Volunteer State
Texas	Austin	Lone Star State
Utah	Salt Lake City	Beehive State
Vermont	Montpelier	Green Mountain State
Virginia	Richmond	Old Dominion State
Washington	Olympia	Evergreen State

West Virginia	Charleston	Mountain State
Wisconsin	Madison	Badger State
Wyoming	Cheyenne	Equality State

FAMOUS PEOPLE OF THE NEW TESTAMENT

John the Baptist – Forerunner of Jesus; baptized Jesus in the River Jordan

Matthew – Former tax collector, disciple of Jesus; wrote first Gospel

Mary – Mother of Christ, virgin birth

Mary Magdalene – Devoted follower of Jesus who cleansed her of seven demons

Mark – Disciple of Christ; wrote 2nd Gospel, founded Christianity in North Africa

Saint Stephen

Luke the physician – Disciple of Christ, wrote Gospel of Luke and the book of Acts

John - Disciple of Christ; author of 4th Gospel and book of Revelation; brother to James

Peter the fisherman– Disciple of Christ, brother of Andrew; called the Rock

Pontius Pilate – Procurator of Judea; washed his hands absolving himself of responsibility for the crucifixion of Jesus

Nicodemus – Pharisee & member of Jewish senate; showed favor toward Jesus

Joseph of Arimathea – He and Nicodemus removed the body of Christ from the cross

Stephen – First Christian martyr - stoned to death for his beliefs

Saul of Tarsus – Christian persecutor; became Apostle Paul after his conversion

Joseph – Husband of the Virgin Mary; he was a carpenter by trade

Silas – Right hand man of Paul; helped to recruit Timothy

Timothy – Paul wrote two books of the Bible instructing his young colleague

Salome (Sal-ohm) – Danced for King Herod and asked for the head of John the Baptist as reward

King Herod – King of the Jews; reconstructed the second temple in Jerusalem

Dismas – Thief crucified (the good thief) alongside Christ who repented and was saved

Cornelius – Roman Centurian who was first gentile (non Jew) to be converted to Christianity

Judas – One of the original 12 who betrayed Jesus for 30 pieces of silver; hanged himself

Thomas – Disciple who doubted resurrection of Christ and wanted to feel his wounds

Simon the Cyrenian – Man who carried the cross for Jesus when he faltered due to its weight

James and John – Disciples of Jesus who were also his cousins

119

Salome (Sal-oh-may) – Sister to Mary and aunt to Jesus
Woman at the well – Sinning Samaritan who gave Jesus a drink and believed he was the Messiah
The Good Samaritan – Cared for an injured man (he didn't know) that others had passed by

GROW YOUR OWN CRYSTALS

Anyone can grow their own crystals. Growing a crystal on your windowsill is fun, easy, and educational. You don't need to buy a special kit or any unusual chemicals to grow great crystals. All you need are ones you probably already have at home. A crystal is a substance that has a highly ordered internal structure. Crystals can be composed of atoms, molecules, or ions.

Examples of common crystals include sugar, alum and salt. Most gemstones are crystals, such as diamonds, emeralds, and rubies. Some materials that are called crystal, but really aren't, include all types of glass and faceted plastic. Crystals can be shaped or cut, but their internal repeating structure often gives them a characteristic shape without any treatment.

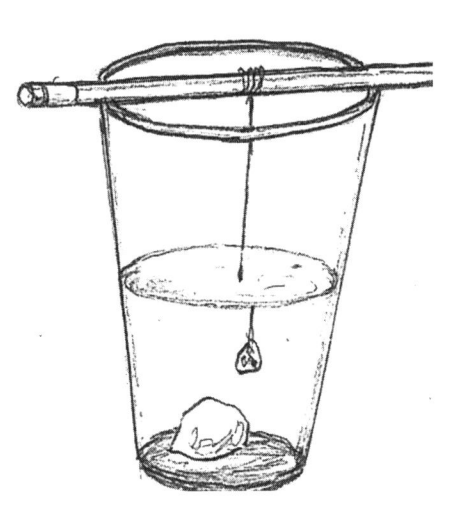

Crystals that you can grow at home are developed from solutions in water. To grow a crystal, you dissolve a chemical in water, then either evaporate the water or cool the solution so that the substance starts to crystallize. Usually you hang a string or a seed crystal in the growing solution to provide a surface for the crystals to form. You want water to be able to evaporate from the solution, so you don't want to seal the container. However, you can place a coffee filter or paper towel over your solution to keep it clean. Crystals grow best if they are undisturbed. You can watch them grow, but don't pick up the container or shake it.

To make an alum crystal you must find some alum power at home or at a pharmacy. Alum can be used as a tanning agent and as an astringent (shrinking agent) on small cuts or sores. Find some small, flat stones. Pour enough warm water in a glass to fill about 1/3 of it. Add about 10 grams of alum and stir vigorously. Leave one stone on the bottom of the glass and suspend the other by tying a piece of string around it. Tie the other end of the string around a pencil and place the pencil horizontally over the mouth of the glass so the rock is suspended in the water. Adjust the string length if it is too long. Set the glass somewhere in the sun where the water will evaporate. It will take a few days for the first crystals to appear.

To make a salt crystal add salt to boiling hot water until no more will dissolve. For a fast crystal, soak a piece of cardboard in the salt solution, then set it in a sunny spot to dry. Numerous tiny salt crystals will form on the surface of the cardboard.

For larger crystals, you need a seed crystal. Get a seed crystal by pouring a small amount of this solution onto a saucer. Let the liquid evaporate. Carefully scrape the best crystal from the saucer and attach it to a nylon line or a string. Tie the other end of the line to a pencil or butter knife and hang the crystal in the growing solution. The best salt crystals take several days or weeks to grow. Allow the solution to sit undisturbed in a cool, dry location. Remove the crystal when you are happy with it or when it stops growing.

To make sugar crystals (rock candy) Stir 3 cups of sugar into 1 cup of boiling water. Keep stirring until as much sugar has dissolved as possible. You can add food coloring to the solution if you like to get a prettier crystal. Pour the solution into the glass you have selected for growing the crystal. Avoid getting any undissolved sugar in this container, since the sugar will provide a growing surface for the crystals, causing them to grow on your container. Suspend a rough string into the solution. Remember: allow the solution to sit undisturbed. Check it out once a day and observe the changes and the crystal that is slowly forming.

HOW TO THROW A BOOMERANG

The boomerang was invented by the Australian aborigines and originally the "kylie" was used as a war club. It later developed into a tool for killing rabbits and other small game. A hunting boomerang is more delicately balanced and harder to make than a returning one. Over the years, as the natives tried to improve their throwing stick, the returning boomerang was accidentally discovered.

You can buy a decent boomerang on e-Bay or at any sporting goods store.

Most children who receive one as a birthday or Christmas gift usually give up on them after a few tries because they don't realize that successfully throwing a boomerang is a skill, like hitting a baseball or throwing a Frisbee. It will probably take numerous throws before you are able to have your boomerang regularly return to you.

Select a large grassy area, clear of trees and bushes for your throwing area. A soccer field or baseball field usually works well. Avoid areas with high weeds or bodies of water because these make perfect hiding places for wayward boomerangs. Do not throw in the vicinity of people, animals, cars or buildings.

A warm day with little or no breeze is usually ideal for boomeranging. Some boomerangs will not return in a dead calm. Gusting winds could cause you to lose control of your boomerang and should be avoided until you have gained some experience.

Do not throw in the rain because moisture may have an adverse affect on the boomerang itself, depending on its finish. Your boomerang could swell with moisture, possibly cracking the finish or warping it.

A boomerang is always thrown overhand like a baseball. Never throw your boomerang side-arm. There are two basic ways to grip your boomerang, the pinch grip and the cradle grip. The pinch consists of simply pinching the boomerang between your thumb and forefinger, allowing friction to keep the boomerang in your hand during the throw. Snap your wrist at the end of the throw to create spin, and momentum will help pull the boomerang from your hand. The cradle grip is similar to the pinch grip, the difference being that you wrap your forefinger around the front of the boomerang. At the end of your throw, snap your wrist and "pull the trigger" to create spin.

Creating spin is essential for a successful throw. So whichever grip is most comfortable and allows you to create maximum spin is the one to use. The first time you throw it the weapon will, in all probability, not go anywhere near its mark but, soaring aloft, perform some of the most extraordinary maneuvers you have ever seen. It will then, with renewed velocity, either return near the spot from which it was thrown or take off for parts unknown into the wild blue yonder.

The boomerang has two arms: the lift or leading arm and the trailing or dingle arm. The boomerang can be thrown from either of these arms.

The most curved side of the boomerang must be toward your face with the flat side facing away. Otherwise the boomerang will rotate backwards and the airfoils will not generate lift.

The direction of the throw, relative to the wind, is critical. The boomerang must be thrown across the direction from which the wind is blowing at about a 45 degree to 90 degree angle. To determine the proper direction of the throw, pick up some leaves or grass clippings and drop them. Watch which way the wind blows the clippings. Face directly into the wind so it's blowing directly into your face. Turn about 60 degrees to your right. The wind should now be blowing from your left to your right. Throw your boomerang in the direc'' you are facing. If the boomerang returns and lands somewhere in fron turn slightly to your left and throw more into the wind. If your boomerang lands behind you, turn to your right and face more away from the wind. If it returns to where you are standing but is too high to catch, throw with less arm strength. If the boomerang heads back in your direction but hits the ground before it gets to you, throw a bit harder. If the boomerang flies straight out and hits the ground, you either need more spin or you've thrown it upside down.

Experimenting with different throws and in differing wind conditions will improve your skill in having the boomerang fly exactly how you want it to. Another tip is to mark the spot you throw from, so if you have to move to catch or retrieve your boomerang, you can see how close it returned to the spot from which you threw it. Always return to this spot to throw again.

The sport of boomeranging is a developed skill, like throwing a disc or hitting a golf ball. It will take some practice. To take a carved piece of wood and throw it 150 feet away, only to have it turn and fly back to you to be caught, is like having a hole-in-one shot in golf. Except you have to go and get your disc or ball. Your boomerang, on the other hand, is back with you and waiting to be thrown again.

The best way to catch a returning boomerang is to trap it between the palms of your hands. Wait until your boomerang is below shoulder level, then place one hand above and one below your boomerang, "clap" your hands together, trapping the boomerang between. If you want to try one handed catches, stick your hand into the open hole in the center of the spinning boomerang and grab. Try this technique only if your boomerang is well above your head or below your shoulders, because the boomerang can spin off your hand changing directions abruptly, and could strike your head or face.

The flight path of a boomerang changes constantly during a flight. Do not look away from a returning boomerang and expect to find it in the air again

easily. If you do need to look away (you trip over your marker) glance quickly in the area you expect the boomerang to be. If you don't see it right away, don't stand there and stare! A boomerang returning at close to eye level is almost impossible to spot and will hurt if it hits you in the face. If you don't spot it immediately, turn your back, cover your head with your arms, and crouch down. If the boomerang lands on your back, you know it was a good throw.

MAKING A WHIP BOW

This interesting weapon is similar to the English long bow that won the Battle of Agincourt in 1415. The big difference is that the bow string is fastened to just one end, similar to that of a whip-lash. The end of the bow string should be tied into a hard knot. The bow itself should be a flexible sapling (branch) from a tree about two feet long. Using a pocket knife, strip off all the branches from your main stick. Remember to always cut away from your body. Purchase an arrow with a pointed metal tip from a sporting goods store. In one side of the arrow, approximately at the mid-point, cut a notch that the bow string will slip into where the knot is located. The knot at the end prevents the arrow from slipping off until thrown by the archer.

Take your whip bow to a large, empty ball diamond or soccer field. Make sure there isn't anyone in sight of the direction from which you plan to launch the arrow. Do not do this on any playground. **Safety should always be paramount in these activities.** To launch your arrow stand sideways with the end of your bow gripped firmly in your right hand. Hold your arrow with the notch string in place with your left hand. Sway your body back and forth and then fling the arrow in whip-like fashion, extending your right arm outward to give the arrow velocity. This double action of a bow and a whip should send the arrow a very long distance.

MAKING A THROW STICK

The same aboriginal race that invented the boomerang also invented the throwing stick. A throwing stick can be fashioned from a small tree branch about a foot long. Make sure one end has a harpoon-like knob on one end (see illustration). Next you need a lance or throwing spear about three feet long. The lance can be made from a piece of bamboo or a horseweed that has turned brown in the fall and stripped of its branches.

As a young boy I engaged in spear fights with neighborhood buddies. This was a bit dangerous and something I wouldn't recommend. Every young boy thinks he is agile enough to dodge these spears. However, a man I came to befriend in later life was playing this game and a spear he didn't see coming caused him to lose an eye at the age of 8. For the rest of his life he had to wear a porcelain eye in his eye socket. He was probably a good enough baseball pitcher to play in the majors. However, that artificial left eye made it difficult for him to hold runners on first base and that cost him his shot in the major leagues. His uncle, Hank Bauer, holds the New York Yankees' record for the most games played in right field. He also holds the World Series hitting streak record of 17 games in a row.

To throw your lance (see illustration), place the end of the spear in the knob end of your throw stick. Grasp the throw stick by wrapping your last three

124

fingers around it. Hold the spear in place with your thumb and forefinger (pointer finger). Throw the device pretty much as you would a spear. It will take you a while to get the hang of it but the throwing stick gives you additional leverage and you'll be able to throw the spear farther because the stick acts as a sling.

HOW TO TEACH YOUR DOG TO RUB HIS NOSE

This is usually not a difficult trick to teach a dog. Blow in the dog's face and at the same time say, "rub your nose." Your breath, coming into contact with his sensitive snout, will probably cause your dog to rub his nose with his paws. Each time you do this reward the dog with a small treat. Say the exact same words every time you give a command. Pretty soon, your dog should rub his nose with his paws without you blowing in his face, just to earn a reward.

You can also turn your dog's peculiar habits into tricks. If he is one of those dogs that likes to carry a stick around in his mouth, you can teach the animal to carry a basket instead and show him off to your friends. The Russian scientist Pavlov rang a bell just before he fed a dog. He did this repeatedly and pretty soon all he had to do was ring the bell and it would cause the dog to salivate. This became known as a conditioned response. By rewarding the dog with a treat every time he does a trick, you are conditioning the animal to repeat the trick when you give a certain command.

PAPER, SCISSORS, ROCK

This little game is played to determine who goes first in a game or for various other decisions. The two people face each other and count to three. As they say "one," they throw their right hand out from their body toward the other person so it is plainly in sight. They do the same thing with the count of "two." As they finish the word "three," they must use their hand to describe one of the three items. A closed fist indicates rock. A flat extended hand means paper, and two crossed fingers signals scissors. The winner is determined thusly: rock breaks scissors, paper covers rock, and scissors cut and triumph over paper. There you have it – a quick and easy way to decide something.

SNOWBALL WARFARE

It is that time of the year. Jack Frost, the lively sprite, comes along and blows his breath to decorate the window in your bedroom. Cold, gray clouds have chased away the fleecy white cumulus cotton balls of summer. Like migratory birds, they have flown away to warmer climates, destined to return in springtime when the red, red robin comes bob, bob bobbing along.

Swim season is long over; the boys of summer have put away their Rawlings gloves and Louisville Slugger bats. Indoor basketball is now the chief spectator sport. Many elderly, known as snowbirds, have left for their condos in Florida and Arizona. Shoppers walking along sidewalks are puffing two streams of steam from their nostrils. They clap their hands together in a vain effort to warm their benumbed fingers. Most seem unhappy with this unwelcome visit from Old Man Winter – everyone, that is, except the schoolboy who sees winter as a great opportunity to ice skate, build snowmen, and engage is rowdy snowball fights.

This robust breed of youngster has rosy cheeks and eyes that twinkle. In his chest lives that spark of inward merriment for he knows that these dull, leaden skies are full of promise. These skies herald the advent of a big winter storm that will blanket the ground with layers and layers of pristine snow – perfect for building a snow fort and providing opportunity for exciting snowball warfare.

The rules are as follows: (**Be sure to wear safety goggles**.)

Each side elects a team captain. The captains decide, by drawing the high card from a deck, (or paper, scissors, rock) their choice of position. The attack army moves away to a pre-determined position, while the defenders retreat to the snow fort. The attackers' camp is marked by driving stakes into the ground or by marking with large snowballs at the four corners. Each group designs its own battle flag. This can be done with felt cloth for the base flag and words or emblems can be cut out and glued from other colored pieces of felt and glued or sewn on. Battle flags must be placed in the middle of the fort/camp and attached to a three-foot long stick.

War is waged completely with snowballs. There is no hitting with fists or kicking. Pushing, pulling and shoving are allowed. Also, no ice balls are allowed. Fort defenders use the walls of the fort for protection while attackers may use small shields to ward off blows. A Frisbee can be turned into a small shield by wrapping one strip of duct tape completely around the Frisbee. Do not press the duct tape to the underside of the Frisbee. Leave it loose and take another 5 inch long piece of duct tape and press both sticky sides together. This will give you a handle for your shield. The attackers can throw snowballs with one hand and ward off incoming missiles with their plastic shield.

If any member of the attacking force gets pulled into the fort, he becomes a prisoner of war and must remain there until his forces capture the fort and win the battle. Any member of the defending team who gets pulled *from* the fort is thusly captured and must go to the camp of the attackers and wait for the outcome of the battle. Prisoners of war can be put to work making snowballs or repairing any damages to the fort. They cannot be forced to fight against their comrades.

If, by any means, the defenders can somehow capture the flag of the attackers and bring back their flag inside their fort, the battle is over and the game is won.

HOW TO MAKE A WHIRLIGIG BUZZER

A whirligig buzzer, also known as a sawmill, is an ancient mechanical device used as a toy. It is constructed by centering an object at the midpoint of a cord and winding the cord while holding the ends stationary. The object is then whirled by alternately pulling and releasing the tension on the cord. The whirling object makes a buzzing or humming sound, giving the device its common name.

Such a buzzer can also be constructed by running string through two of the holes on a large button and is a common and easily made toy.

Native American Indians used the buzzer as a toy and also to call up the wind. It was also used ceremonially. Early Indian buzzers were constructed of wood, bone, or stone.

Use a protractor to draw a circle on a stiff piece of cardboard about 3 ½ inches in diameter. Or you can use any round object you find, such as the mouth of a glass, as a pattern. Make a mark to designate the exact center of the cardboard. Now drill two holes, one 3/8 of an inch above the center and the other 3/8 inch below the center. Get two pieces of string about a foot long. Insert one string through the top hole and another through the bottom. Push your cardboard circle to the middle of the two strings. Use both hands to hold the ends of each string, pressed between your thumb and forefinger. Allow the wheel to droop and swing the wheel around and around to wind up your buzzer. When the string becomes tightly twisted, the device is fully wound. Now alternately pull and then slacken the ends of the strings. Your mechanism will spin around and make a buzzing sound.

A similar device can be made by using an old, large coat button, using two of the four pre-drilled holes.

UNDERSTANDING PERSISTENCE OF VISION

Movie films have long operated on the principle of persistence of vision. If you examine film from an old 8 mm movie camera, you will see that it consists of a string of frames, each with a slightly different image to give the appearance of motion. As a kid I once bought a flipbook for 10 cents that consisted of pages with Popeye imprinted on each page. If you held the bottom of the book with your thumb and forefinger, and then slid your thumb upwards, the pages came down rapidly and gave Popeye the appearance of motion. Movie theaters had projectors where the celluloid sat in a reel and the projector pulled the film past the opening of the projection lens at a rate of 16 frames a second, and this gave viewers the impression of smooth, realistic motion. The sound track was etched on the edge of the film and the projector had a sound drum that pulled the music and words from the film and sent them to amplified speakers. Modern theatric film runs at 24 frames a second. The new film system MaxiVision films at 48 frames per second.

Instead of the eye seeing each image distinctively and separately, enough of each image lingers on the retina just long enough to give the appearance of motion.

HOW TO MAKE A PRESSMAN'S HAT

Google the words "make a pressman's hat." You will find two or three sites that give directions for making such a hat. These hats, made from a single double page of a standard newspaper, are made by the men and women who work in the print room where the newspapers are printed on machines. The hats are designed to keep ink and grease out of one's hair. Follow these directions and you'll end up with a really cool hat that will impress your friends. The directions are a bit complicated so you might have to make several attempts before you are successful.

THE PAPER GAME OF SQUARES

This is a paper game for two players that can be very interesting. Take a half sheet of blank paper. About a half an inch from the top make a horizontal row of dots and space them about 3/8 of an inch apart. Make a second row of dots about 3/8 of an inch below the first row. Keep doing this until the entire page is filled with dots.

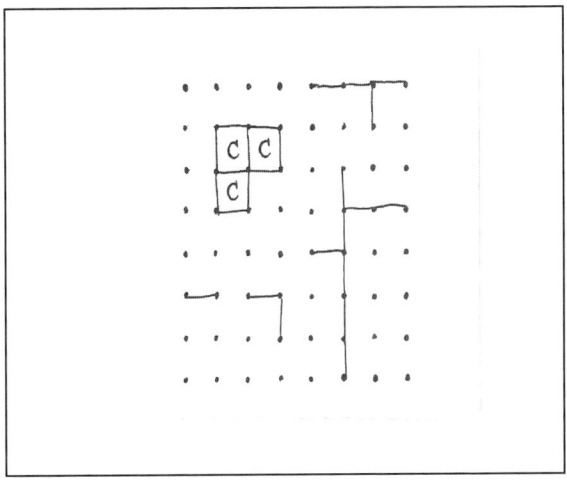

The first player draws a line connecting any two dots. The line can be horizontal or vertical but it cannot be diagonal. At first the line drawing will be pretty mundane but soon the game gets very interesting. The player who draws a line that makes a square box gets to place his initial in that square. He also gets another turn. The object of the game is to be the player with the most boxes that have your initial in it. What makes the game fun is that there is some strategy involved and no two games are ever alike.

HANGMAN

Here is another paper game for two players. The first player thinks of a word and draws a series of dashes to represent the exact number of letters in the word. The other player tries to guess the word by saying a letter of the alphabet he thinks is in the word. For each wrong guess the other player writes the wrong letter at the bottom of the sheet and then begins to draw a hangman's platform. As

128

you can see by the illustration, after six wrong guesses, the scaffold is complete. With the next wrong guess he begins to draw the man. It takes six wrong guesses for him to complete the man. Every wrong guess of the word also results in one more step towards the drawing being completed. After the twelfth mark and the completion of the drawing, the person trying to guess the word is hanged and loses the game. If twelve guesses proves to be too many, reduce it to ten with five steps to complete the platform and five to complete the man.

THE IMPOSSIBLE GAME

Here is a paper game that is perfect for you to give to that person (perhaps an older brother) who thinks he is good at solving these kinds of puzzles. Take a half sheet of paper and about 1/3 of the way down draw three 1 inch long rectangles across the page horizontally. About three inches below

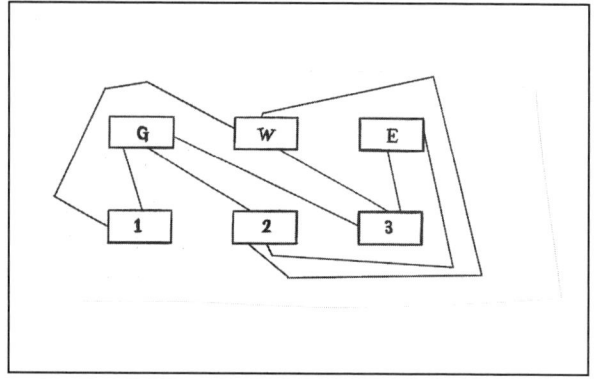

these rectangles draw three more rectangles, with each one directly below the one on top. Mark the first box on the top left with a G; mark the box directly on its right with a W; mark the final box in the top row with an E. Now number the boxes below 1, 2, and 3.

Explain to the challenger that the numbered boxes on the bottom represent three houses. The boxes on top represent utilities – gas, water, and electricity that must be delivered to each of the three houses. The object of the game is to deliver all three vital services to each house by drawing 3 lines from each utility box to each of the three houses. The only catch is that none of the 9 lines that they draw can cross or intersect another line.

Most players will spend quite some time trying to do this but then give up in frustration. You will finally have to tell them that there is no solution to this little gem. It is possible to draw 8 lines to the three houses but there isn't any way to draw that 9th line without it crossing another one. It's one of those puzzles that looks solvable, but isn't.

HOW TO MAKE A CATAMARAN

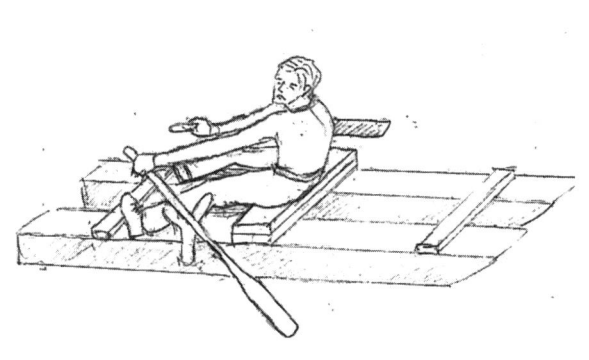

Here is how to make the simplest and safest of all boats – a catamaran.

The catamaran is a two hulled boat that has been around since time immemorial among the Polynesians.

For your double hulls you will need two eight foot long 6 x 6 pieces of wood. Start building this boat on the shore near your pond, lake or stream. Sharpen one end of each piece and fashion it to resemble the forward prow of a ship. Cut two pieces of 2 x 12 lumber into three foot long lengths. Place your two 6 x 6 pieces next to each other horizontally about three feet apart. Span your 6 x 6s with one of the 2 x 12s and fasten in place with rustproof screws. This piece should be slightly forward of the exact middle of the 6 x 6s. Now screw the other 2 x 12 directly on top of the first one to create your boat seat. Cut a 2 x 4 three feet long to act as a stabilizer cross piece. Screw this in place across the span of the two 6 x 6s about eight inches from the front end of your boat. Cut two more three foot long 2 x 4 pieces for your foot rest. Screw the first one in place across the span of 2 x 6s. It should be about two feet below the seat toward the rear of the boat. Screw the next 2 x 4 directly on top of the first one.

Find two small branches, about an inch and a quarter in diameter, with forks in them. This will serve as your rowlocks. Drill two holes in each 6 x 6, midway between your seat and footrest. Make the holes slightly larger than the diameter of your branches and drill them about 2 ½ inches deep. Make sure the Y of the fork is parallel with the length of each 6 x 6 before you fix them in place with waterproof glue.

Add a skull and crossbones ensign (flag) to the front crosspiece and you and a pal are ready to go off on a great adventure. **Be sure to wear a life jacket**. You could act as if you are a distant cousin to Daniel Boone and make an oar out of pine, but just go to a boat store and buy two paddles made of plastic. Be sure they are guaranteed to float. Notice that as you row the boat your back is to the direction you are headed.

HOW TO MAKE AN ELECTROMAGNET

Electromagnets are magnets that only become magnetic when there is a coil of wire with electricity running through it. This is also known as a solenoid. The strength of the magnet is proportional to the current flowing in the circuit. Electromagnets are used for a variety of purposes. In a simple example, an electromagnet can pick up pieces of metal, iron, steel, nickel, and cobalt. The most obvious everyday example of a magnet is the crane at an auto junkyard with a magnet on the end of a cable instead of a hook. The huge magnet picks up the car and the crane lifts it and drops it in the crusher.

The electricity running through the wire is called a current. The current is a flow of electrons which is a flow of negatively charged particles.

Electromagnets can be made stronger by adding more coils to the copper wire, or adding an iron core through the coils (for example a nail). You can also increase the current to make the magnetism stronger.

A British electrician, William Sturgeon, invented the electromagnet in 1825.

An electromagnet is very useful because it can be deactivated (turned off) easily, whereas a permanent magnet cannot be deactivated and will continue to affect its immediate environment. Iron stops being an electromagnet very quickly, but steel takes more time to wear off.

To make your electromagnet, wind copper wire around an iron nail. Then connect one end of the wire to the + (positive) and the other end to the - (negative) side of a D battery. (The negative side is the flat bottom.) To turn on your electromagnet simply touch the two screws together. Your electromagnet should be strong enough to pick up a paper clip. (If the coil wires get too hot, you can wrap duct tape around them.

Electromagnets are also used in everyday items such as burglar alarms, electric relays and fire bells. Their ability to change from the state of non-magnetic to magnetic just by passing an electric current through it allows it to be used in many different items.

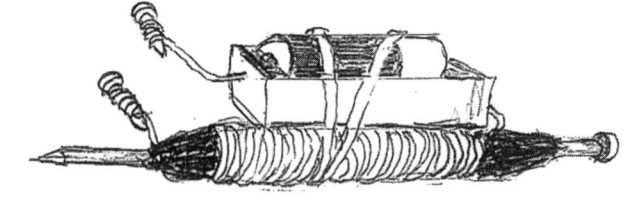

131

HOW TO PLANT A VEGETABLE GARDEN

As a youth I can remember the time when my mother would buy four quarts of strawberries for a dollar. Bread was 20 cents a loaf. Food prices have risen dramatically in recent years. A single onion nowadays can cost over a dollar. Gardening has several benefits. First, it will save your family money. Also, your family usually ends up eating a wider variety of fruits and vegetables (the tomato is actually a fruit). And this is another one of the self-esteem builders for a young man because it adds another arrow of confidence to your quiver (arrow holder) of abilities.

Get permission from your parents to set aside a plot of ground for a garden. See if your dad will rent a tiller to chop up the soil. If the soil is mostly clay, which packs hard, you might want to mix in bags of peat moss or top soil. These can be bought for a rather cheap price at stores like K-Mart. Draw a plan (to a scale) of the ground at your disposal. (Try to select a spot that gets plenty of sunlight.) Make allowances for paths, borders, etc. It's fun and interesting after you get started.

Next, take inventory of your family's likes and dislikes in vegetables. Put down on paper every vegetable you wish to grow. Then go back to your plan and mark out a definite space or number of rows for the different vegetables. Select early, midseason and late sorts of these vegetables, which you like best. This will give you a constant supply of them. When garden operations start, be sure to follow your plan. A disregard of your carefully planned program may easily spoil results. I cannot place too much emphasis upon this point, since many gardens fail to yield satisfactory crops for lack of adherence to the original plan.

Study the peculiar characteristics of certain vegetables and utilize them to best advantage. Some vegetables thrive, even in partially shaded positions, while others require lots of sunshine for best results. Some of the finest lettuce I ever saw was grown between rows of early peas. The two-foot tall pea vines, rows running east and west would shelter Wayahead, Black Seeded Simpson, etc., which form perfect heads of lettuce.

Though the pea rows were standing only 2 1/2 feet apart, the lettuce did splendidly since peas root deeply while lettuce is a shallow, rooting plant. Keeping the lettuce row free from weeds gives additional cultivation to the pea vines, which will, under such conditions, stand considerable dry weather and still yield heavy crops.

A good many vegetables are of exceedingly slow growth during the seedling stage of development. Take advantage of this by utilizing space between such rows for quick-growing crops. For example, sow beet seed by middle of April and set young lettuce plants between the rows. By the time the beet tops develop, the lettuce will be used.

A distance of **20 inches between the rows** is ample for most vegetables in a carefully managed home garden. Tall peas, tomatoes and corn should be allowed at least 2 to 2 1/2 feet and should be staked for best results. The proper thinning out of all kinds of vegetables is advisable. Do not permit root crops to

132

crowd each other in the row. Thin out radishes, beets, onions, turnips, etc., to stand about from 2 to 4 inches apart in the row, according to variety. Beans will yield more and better pods if plants stand 4 to 6 inches apart in the row.

Where space is rather limited; the French method of intensive cultivation may be employed. Here is how it is practiced:

Combine a packet of spinach seed and carrot seed, mixing seeds thoroughly. Make your row uniformly half an inch deep and sow this mixture in the row. Cover, and soon the quick-growing spinach seed will break the crust, making it easier for the weak carrot seedlings to see the light of day. In four weeks, the spinach may be "thinned" to make room for the slowly developing carrots. In six weeks the spinach will be all used up, and the carrots will find room to develop. If an early carrot, such as Early Scarlet Horn, is selected, this will be ready for the table use by July 15th, when the last may be pulled to make room for endive, celery, late cabbage or any other fall crop.

This method may be employed with quite a number of vegetables. Care should be taken in experimenting along these lines, that kinds are combined having seed of about the same coarseness, but possessing different characteristics as to growth. Lettuce and radishes go well together, so do radishes and parsley; the last named being an exceedingly slow grower. The French gardeners plant extra early radishes, midseason lettuce and turnips' in, the same row, at one operation. This gives about as ideal a succession as can be worked out.

As to the actual location of the different rows and crops, here is a good rule to follow: If the land runs east and west the taller plantings should be on the north, so that the light will not be shut off from the lower growing vegetables. Corn grows so much taller than anything else cultivated that it should, if possible, be placed in the rear. In front of it the few hills of early potatoes which it is possible to grow on a city lot may be planted, as they are the least ornamental of vegetables.

Beans, beets, carrots, chard, corn, lettuce, melons, peas, pumpkins, squash and turnips are planted as seeds directly into the ground. Starting with seeds is, of course, much less expensive than planting seedlings sold in flats, packs and pots. Follow the directions on the back of the seed packets. Start with nursery seedlings of certain other crops unless you are an experienced vegetable grower. These plants tend to do better when set out in the garden as seedlings: eggplant, peppers, tomatoes, broccoli, cabbage and cauliflower. Squash and cucumbers are among a few you can plant just as effectively as either seeds or seedlings.

Cabbage and cauliflowers grow of corresponding height, and may be planted side by side and given the same treatment. Tomatoes, which need two feet of space between each plant, may follow the potatoes, and so on in the order of height until the front of the garden is reached, and such ornamental vegetables as remain may be placed.

During the dry season of mid-summer, be sure to water your garden at least twice a week.

During the month of either October or November, spread natural fertilizer

133

over your garden plot to get good yields the next growing season. If you want to do a minimum of re-tilling the next spring, cover everything with several layers of newspapers. Pile leaves, hay, grass clippings on top of the newspapers and wait until spring. The ground won't be compacted because you have created a happy home for earthworms that will do much of the work for you.

Here's another idea. Find someone in your neighborhood who has been growing a vegetable garden on a regular basis. People like this are usually more than willing to give you tips.

HOW TO MAKE A COMPOST PILE

No garden is complete without a compost pile! Compost is a soil conditioner, mulch and fertilizer all wrapped into one. It feeds the soil microorganisms that help plants stay healthy, adds nutrients to the soil, and helps clay soil drain better and sandy soil retain water. Plus, composting reduces your contribution to the waste stream by recycling yard and kitchen waste into the world's best soil amendment. Here's how to build a pile that breaks down fast and never smells bad.

Choose a site that is handy to your garden and kitchen, yet out of plain sight. You don't need a bin to make compost-a pile of leaves, grass clippings and other yard wastes will do, but a bin keeps the compost contained and looks neater. You can corral compost in a simple wire column made from a 4-foot wide by 8-foot long piece of stiff wire mesh.

You can also buy a more permanent bin or build a three-bin compost system made from slatted wood or recycled pallets. Leave the bins open on one side so you can add compost materials and turn the pile easily. Cover the top of the bins with a sheet of plywood if you live in a very rainy climate. A three-bin system allows you to turn the compost from one bin to another and store finished compost until you are ready to use it.

The two basic elements that make up compost are green garden debris (grass clippings or old annuals) and brown garden debris (dry leaves). Green ingredients are high in nitrogen and brown materials are high in carbon. Adding too many greens can make the pile smell bad. Do not add animal waste, meats, oils, dairy, diseased plants, weeds that have gone to seed, or plants treated with pesticides or herbicides to your compost.

Compost piles with a balance of one part green to two part brown materials break down fastest. The easiest way to achieve this balance is to add one garden forkful of green material to the pile, top it with two forkfuls of brown material, and mix them together. Continue adding greens and browns until the pile is at least 3 cubic feet (3 ft. x 3 ft. x 3 ft.). Piles of this size heat up quickly and break down faster.

Add in a shovelful of finished compost or garden soil to help kick start the microbial activity in your pile. Compost also needs the correct amount of moisture to breakdown. Compost with the right moisture level should feel like a damp, wrung-out sponge. Too much moisture can cause temperatures to fall within the pile (and make it smell). Too little moisture slows down the decomposition rate and keeps the pile from heating up. Check your compost pile's moisture level once a week and adjust it if necessary by adding water to increase moisture or more browns to help dry the pile out.

Turn the pile once a week to move material from the outside of the pile in. Turning also keeps the pile from compacting, which reduces airflow and slows down decomposition.

You should have finished compost in about two months. You'll know your compost is finished when it no longer heats up and you can't identify any of the original materials. The compost should be dark brown, moist and earthy smelling. Dig finished compost into your garden's soil. You can use partially composted material as mulch.

You can also build a very basic, passive compost system by simply piling up leaves, grass clippings and other yard waste into a pile in a secluded corner of your yard. The compost will be ready when the original ingredients are unrecognizable, usually in about 6 to 12 months. Compost at the bottom and middle of the pile typically "finishes" first.

HOW TO SHARPEN A MOWER BLADE

A dull mower blade doesn't cut grass - it tears the blades leaving the grass vulnerable to disease or damage from the sun. How often the mower blade needs sharpening depends on the size of your lawn and how often you mow, but plan on doing the job at least every six weeks.

Drain the gas and disconnect the spark plug wire in your power mower so the motor doesn't turn over while you're working. Tilt the mower on its side, and wedge a block of wood between the blade and the mower deck to keep the blade from turning. You can also buy a device called a Blade Buster that locks the blade in place while you work on the mower. Use a scraper or putty knife to clean any built-up debris from the underside of the mower deck.

Using a socket or crescent wrench, remove the bolt from the center of the blade. Pull off the blade and clamp it in a bench vise. Check the blade edges for small nicks, and remove them using a flat medium file. Sharpen the blade by moving the file toward the cutting edge with smooth, even strokes. Follow the original bevel of the blade as closely as you can. Make the same number of strokes on each edge. If you take more metal off one side than the other, the blade will be out of balance. An out-of-balance blade cuts unevenly; it also makes the mower vibrate which can cause serious damage to the engine. Test the balance by resting the blade on a dowel or the handle of a screwdriver. If one side points up, sharpen the other until the blade lies flat. (Or use a blade balancer, available at garden centers.)

Another way to sharpen a blade is with a nifty little device called a Dremel tool. It is a rotary tool with a large variety of grinder attachments. A third way to sharpen the blade is with a power grinder wheel. If your dad is a good handyman he might already have one of these. Try to get him to show you how it is done, and then see if he will let you try it. Just remember to grind at the original bevel angle of the blade. If you use a grinder or a Dremel tool you should **wear safety goggles**.

HOW DO YOU PRUNE A BUSH?

First you need a good pair of gloves and some pruning scissors. These can be bought at any nursery or store such as Wal-Mart. Bushes should be pruned and maintained each year for a well shaped and healthy plant. The plants should be full looking, yet not overly bushy. If the plant is too bushy, the inner leaves do not get sun and air circulation, an invitation to plant disease.

Trim larger stems from the center of the bush to increase ventilation. It will also afford more room for newer shoots on the outside of the plant to develop.

Pruning should be done immediately after the flowers have died off. Cut small suckers and shoots at, or near, ground level, or where it comes out of the main trunk. Leave a few strong and healthy new stalks each year, especially if you are planning to trim back old wood.

Trim back any branches that stick out from the main bush, and are not appealing to look at.

Topping the bush is not recommended. A flat top is not an appealing shape to most lilac lovers. A slightly rounded top looks best. It is okay to clip off old, dead flowers at the base.

In trimming and pruning bushes, remember, beauty is in the eyes of the beholder. If you like a tall bush, let it grow tall; if you prefer a wide bush, encourage shoots that have spread out from the main bush. Be sure you have one of your parents with you the first time you trim any of their bushes.

If a bush has become overgrown, or is too large or tall for the area allotted it, there are a couple of ways to prune it.

Try the three year plan. A lilac shoot takes about three years before it produces a flower. Plan to eliminate 1/3 of the shrub each year, selecting the oldest stalks first. Cut them down to just above the level of the soil. As you do, allow new shoots to grow to replace the old ones. By the end of three years, the entire shrub will have been replaced, and you will not go without lilacs for that period of time. Then, continue the cycle each year.

If you become completely unhappy with an overgrown shrub, remove all old stock and leave just new shoots. This is pretty drastic and you probably will go a couple of years with out flowers. But most bushes are hardy. As long as there are a few healthy new shoots they will grow back.

One of the most popular shrubs is the burning bush due to its spectacular red color in the fall. These bushes grow fast and they can get quite tall. If you want to keep them from getting out of hand you can trim them annually with a pair of hedge trimmers. This should be done in the early spring.

CUTTING EVERGREEN BUSHES WITH A HEDGE TRIMMER

Your dad probably owns a pair of hedge trimmers. You might want to watch him a few times to see how he does it. The trimmers should have comfortable grips and be long enough to reach into the center of your bush. For detailed work, you want to be able to reach in to even tight spots to make certain the bush adheres to symmetry (pleasing appearance).

Do not trim the bushes when they are wet or while it is raining. There is danger of electrical shock. Always be aware of where the extension cord is. Most beginners, at one time or another, end up cutting their own electrical cord.

Place a drop cloth around the bottom of the bush you are trimming. This will make it much easier to collect the trimmings when you are finished. **Do not trim bushes in the late fall when there is danger of frost**. This will cause the edges where you have cut to turn brown and instead of a beautiful winter evergreen, your bush will have ugly brown spots. Fortunately, the bushes will recover from this by late spring. Don't take too much off the top or you'll end up with brown instead of green. If you make this mistake, the bush will grow enough in one month for the greenery to return.

Trim along the top of your bush at first, making sure it is level all the way across. You occasionally need to take a few steps back to make sure you've maintained a good line.

Work around the edges, taking off no more than 3 to 4 inches per pass. If more bush than that must be trimmed you can come around a second time, making sure you keep from cutting unevenly. When cutting the sides of a bush, I always like to start at the bottom and go straight up to the top of the bush. Finally, I go all the way around the top edge of the bush to give it a rounded look.

Collect your bush trimmings and place them in a proper garbage bag for disposal. Leaving clippings on your lawn destroys the manicured effect you have just achieved.

Make a note of when you have trimmed your bush so that you can set up a regular grooming schedule. Every two months during the summer should be sufficient, depending on the amount of sunlight and rain.

PHONE FISHING

This might be difficult to beliefe but your grandparents, if they lived on a farm, probably did this. They took an old wall crank kitchen telephone that goes back to about 1945 or earlier. When you turned the crank on these phones they rotated a coil inside a group of U-shaped magnets, creating an electrical current. Such a device was called a magneto. This electrical current rang up a telephone operator who asked the caller what number he/she wanted. The switchboard operator would then plug you into the right connection so you could complete your call.

To go fishing, they took the entire unit down to the pond. They took the two wires coming out of the back of the unit and placed them in the water. Then they turned the crank. This sent an electrical charge into the pond that either stunned or killed fish that were close to it.

It simply isn't considered a very sporting way to fish. If you want to see what this feels like, get a group of about 10 people and have them form a line and hold hands. Secure an old crank phone and have the first person in line hold onto the two wires with one hand. Now have a responsible adult in the group **slowly** turn the crank and the electricity should pass through everyone's body and travel all the way to the last person. People with weak hearts, pacemakers, or women who are pregnant, should not participate. UNDER NO CIRCUMSTANCES SHOULD THE PERSON TURNING THE CRANK DO SO VIGOROUSLY BECAUSE THE VOLTAGE WILL BE TOO HIGH AND IT WILL BE QUITE UNCOMFORTABLE. THIS IS NOT THE TIME FOR A PRACTICAL JOKE!

ELECTRONIC AND SCIENCE KITS

The world of today is run by computers and electronics. The more you know about these things the better equipped you will be to face life's challenges. This book is mostly about things you can make and fun things you can build with household items. At some point you might want to consider kits that can be purchased at Radio Shack, through e-Bay, or through places such as KITS USA at www.kitsusa.net or 1-800-379-6664. These kits are sometimes challenging and are more suitable for boys age ten and older. Kits available include chemistry sets, electronic projects, and biology kits that include a microscope. With some kits soldering is a requirement but this is a useful skill to possess. Soldering kits are inexpensive to buy and they come with complete instructions.

As a young boy my parents bought me a Gilbert Chemistry Set that I found fascinating. Because of this set, I went on to take chemistry in high school and in college. While I ended up becoming a high school social studies teacher, I have still retained much of what I learned in those courses.

Instead of asking Mom and Dad for some flashy robot that merely moves and blinks lights and talks (you'll quickly tire of it) ask them to get you one of these kits that is not only fun, but educational as well. Even radio controlled cars quickly lose their appeal.

HOW TO ELECTROPLATE SOMETHING

Take an empty half-gallon milk container and carefully use a boxcutter knife to take off the lower ¼ of the container. Fill the plastic container with enough vinegar to submerge the host metal completely! Add salt by tablespoons, until the salt will not dissolve into the vinegar anymore. That's when there will be extra salt on the bottom of the container with the vinegar in it.

You need a foot long piece of non-copper wire, a penny made before 1983, and a nickel. (Bell wire usually fits the non-copper requirement.) Cut the wire in half, and then cut off enough of the rubber coating to attach one end of the wires to both the nickel and the copper penny by twisting the wire around them.

Attach the other ends of the wire to either ends of the battery with duct tape (one to the negative end and the other to the positive end). Do not place the battery in the solution.

You will notice that as soon as you put the nickel in the vinegar, it will begin to fizz. Eventually, bubbles will form on the nickel; these will need to be wiped off periodically. Notice that after about two days, the nickel will be completely coated in copper.

If you can't find a penny that is old enough, buy a small strip of copper from a craft store about four inches long and an inch wide.

The process used in electroplating is called **electrodeposition**. It is roughly equal to a galvanic cell acting in reverse. The part (nickel) to be plated is the cathode of the circuit. In this activity, the anode is the metal to be plated on the part (penny). Both components are immersed in a salt and vinegar solution, called an electrolyte, which contains ions that permit the flow of electricity. The battery supplied a direct current to the anode, oxidizing the metal atoms that comprise it and allowed them to dissolve in the solution. At the cathode, the dissolved metal ions in the electrolyte solution were reduced at the interface between the solution and the cathode, so that they "plated out" onto the cathode. The rate at which the anode is dissolved is equal to the rate at which the cathode is plated, related to the current flowing through the circuit. In this manner, the ions in the electrolyte bath are continuously replenished by the anode.

In the 1950s, automobiles had lots of chrome parts on the outside, especially the bumpers. To keep the metal bumpers shiny and rust free, they were electroplated with chrome.

HOW TO GRAFT PLANTS AND TREES

Grafting is a method of asexual plant propagation widely used in agriculture and horticulture where the tissues of one plant are fused with those of another. It is most commonly used for the propagation of trees and shrubs grown commercially.

One plant is selected for its roots, and this is called the **stock** or rootstock. The other plant is selected for its stems, leaves, flowers, or fruits and is called the **scion**. The scion contains the desired genes to be duplicated in future production by the stock/scion plant.

In stem grafting, a common grafting method, a shoot of a selected, desired plant is grafted onto the stock of another type. In another common form called budding, a dormant side bud is grafted on the stem of another stock plant, and when it has fused successfully, it is encouraged to grow by cutting out the stem above the new bud.

For successful grafting to take place, the vascular cambium tissues of the stock and scion plants must be placed in contact with each other. Both tissues must be kept alive until the graft has taken, usually a period of a few weeks. Successful grafting only requires that a vascular connection takes place between the two tissues. A physical weak point often occurs at the graft, because the structural tissue of the two distinct plants, such as wood, may not fuse.

Grafts are often made with apple trees to induce dwarfing. Most apple trees in modern orchards are grafted on to dwarf or semi-dwarf trees planted at high density. They provide more fruit per unit of land, higher quality fruit, and reduce the danger of accidents by harvest crews working on high ladders.

Apples are notorious for their genetic variability, even differing in multiple characteristics, such as, size, color, and flavor, of fruits located on the same tree. In the commercial farming industry, consistency is maintained by grafting a scion with desired fruit traits onto a hardy stock.

A practice sometimes carried out by gardeners is to graft related potatoes and tomatoes so that both are produced on the same plant, one above ground and one underground.

Here is how to make a plant graft. Cut a small growth off the plant you wish to transplant. You should cut the plant near the central trunk. The piece you cut off should be roughly equivalent in size to the plant or tree you wish to graft it to.

Store the cutting in your fridge. Remove the cutting in winter, as this is when plants are dormant. This means they are storing up their growing energy for spring. Keeping the cutting in the fridge tricks it into thinking it is still in an extended winter.

Decide where on the host plant you wish to apply the graft in the spring. You will then need to cut into the plant at that spot. Cut deep enough to get through the outer layers of bark to the nutrient rich inner area of the tree that is actually responsible for the growth of the plant.

Notch the host plant in your garden in such a way so that the grafting piece interlocks with the host plant or tree. If you can't match it exactly, try to get at least one side well aligned.

Bind the two plants together by either string or grafting tape. This will hold the cut sides of the pieces together encouraging them to fuse.

Apply a light coat of sealant before taping; this can be found at your plant store and is designed especially for grafting. You can use stakes if the weight of your small plant is pulling it away from the larger one. Then wait a couple of years and the graft will be complete.

Here are some instructions for grafting fruit trees. Cut a twig from a compatible fruit tree species. The twig should be cut at a 45 degree angle to form a close bond with the host tree. Cut a wedge-shaped slit in the tree and angle it downward to match the final position of the graft twig. Insert the twig in the slit allowing the small band of cells called the cambium (just under the bark layer) to match up as closely as possible. Secure the two twigs together using a commercially available grafting tape. Duct tape may also be used. Place a rubber band around the grafting site firmly but not too tightly. Let the twigs fuse over two to three months for successful buds. Once the graft seems sturdy, you should remove the tape and string.

HOW TO MAKE ROPE

Rope is one of the oldest tools used by mankind, with uses ranging from decoration to supporting loads, among an infinite number of applications. Rope is strong because of a few basic physical principles, and because of the simplicity, it is easy to make rope yourself out of twine.

Cut 3 (or more) pieces of twine the same length. As a general guideline to follow, it is a good idea to cut the strands 6 feet for every 5 feet of rope you wish to make, just to have a little extra. Tie the strands along a fixed rod, about 1 inch in diameter. They should be tied separately, but close together.

Holding the twine taut, twist each strand individually, rotating the fibers about a central axis. You should twist each strand in the same direction (usually clockwise, although for lefties, I suggest going counter-clockwise).

The strands do not have to be twisted the same number of times, but the rope tends to have fewer kinks when they are more twisted and when the number of twists in each strand is about the same.

Still holding taut, twist the strands around one another in the opposite direction (if you went clockwise before, now go counterclockwise), bringing them together in one rope.

Let go of the ends of the twine, letting the tension from the winding cause the rope to try to unravel itself. If you have done the twisting correctly, the rope should catch itself, finding a stable equilibrium.

Untie the end of the rope. Then pull the rope out taut again, but do not make it too tense. Fuse the ends of the rope to keep it from unraveling at the ends. There are two methods for fusing a rope. You can burn the ends or tie them together using string. If you plan on cutting the rope into smaller ropes later, I suggest just burning the ends, but you can decide which method to use.

FUN BOOKS TO READ

The Raft by Robert Trumbull
The Book of Cowboys by Holling C. Holling
Hot Rod by Henry Gregor Felsen
The Kid Who Batted .1000 by Bob Allison
The Bobbsey Twins
Nancy Drew Mysteries
Hardy Boys Mysteries
Black Beauty by Anna Sewell

Life on the Mississippi by Mark Twain
The Time Machine by H.G. Welles
Harry Potter series by J.K. Rowling
Treasure Island by Robert Louis Stevenson
20,000 Leagues Under the Sea by Jules Verne
Chasing Lincoln's Killer by James Swanson
The Chocolate War by Robert Cormier
The Distance From Normandy by Jonathan Hull
Fahrenheit 451 by Ray Bradbury
The Heart is a Lonely Hunter by Carson McCullers
The Hitchhiker's Guide to the Galaxy by Douglas Adams
The Hobbitt by J.R.R. Tolkein
Hound of the Baskervilles by Arthur Conan Doyle
Lord of the Flies by William Golding
A Night to Remember by Walter Lord
Call of the Wild by Jack London
Dracula by Bram Stoker
Frankenstein by Mary Shelly
The Prince and the Pauper by Mark Twain
The Spirit of St. Louis by Charles Lindbergh
Watership Down by Richard Adams
Tarzan of the Apes by Edgar Rice Burroughs
Raise the Titanic by Clive Cussler
Old Yeller by Fred Gipson

RECOMMENDED MOVIES

Silver Bullet – Gary Busey
The Great Santini – Robert Duvall
Ben Hur – Charlton Heston
King Kong (1933)
Don't Cry, it's Only Thunder – Dennis Christopher
Breaking Away – Dennis Christopher, Dennis Quaid
October Sky – Laura Dern
Batman I– Michael Keaton
Superman I– Christopher Reeve
Spiderman I– Tobey McGuire
Captain Blood – Erroll Flynn
Shane – Alan Ladd
The McConnell Story – Alan Ladd
A Walk to Remember – Mandy Moore
Rocky – Sylvester Stallone
Last of the Dogmen – Tom Berenger
Big – Tom Hanks
To Kill a Mockingbird – Gregory Peck
The Magnificent Seven – Yul Brynner

Pearl Harbor – Josh Hartnett
Believe in Me – Jeffrey Donovan
Dragonheart – Sean Connery, Dennis Quaid
Electric Dreams – Virginia Madsen
Wind – Matt Modine
F.E.D.S - Rebecca DeMornay
Rebel Without a Cause – James Dean
A Christmas Story – Peter Billingsley
Searching for Bobby Fisher – Joe Mantegna
Sergeant York – Gary Cooper
Remember the Titans – Denzel Washington
Lucas – Charlie Sheen
Pistol: The Birth of a Legend – Adam Guier
The Iron Mistress – Alan Ladd
Kings of the Sun – Yul Brynner
Starman – Jeff Bridges
Spartacus – Kirk Douglas
Remo Williams – Fred Ward
Our Man Flint – James Coburn
On Her Majesty's Secret Service – Roger Lazenby
Live and Let Die – Roger Moore
Amelia – Hillary Swank
The Curse of the Pink Panther – Peter Sellers
Hondo – John Wayne
The Blind Side – Sandra Bullock
The Ultimate Gift – James Garner
White Feather – Robert Wagner

HOW TO TELL IF AN EGG HAS BEEN BOILED

Let's say you have a half dozen eggs in the refrigerator and you can't remember which ones are fresh and which ones have been hard boiled. To determine whether the egg is fresh, set it lengthwise on the table and spin it, much as you would a top. If it keeps spinning, it has been hard boiled. If it is fresh, it will fall over on its side after a spin or two. With the fresh egg, the yolk slushes around in the egg white and throws everything out of kilter.

INVISIBLE INK

Suppose there is a girl in your English class that you think is cute and you want to send her a note. Now if you write a message that says, "Hi! I'm Tom. I sit two seats behind you and I think you're cute." Things could get embarrassing. What if the person in front of you decides to read the message first before sending it along? What if the note gets intercepted by the teacher and he/she reads it out loud in front of the entire class? You can eliminate this possibility by writing two messages. Your first note, written in ballpoint, can say something such as: "Hello! I hope you have a nice day. Save this message." Your second message, written in invisible ink, can be written below the first message. You can call the girl that evening and tell her how to read the secret message. Or, you can tell her best friend at school how she can do it.

Apply the invisible ink to the writing surface with a fountain pen or toothpick or the bottom of a matchstick. Once dry, the written surface should appear blank, and of a similar texture as the surrounding paper. With letters, a cover message is usually written over the invisible message, as a blank sheet of paper might arouse suspicion that an invisible message is present. This is best done with a ballpoint pen, since fountain pen ink may 'run' when it crosses a line of invisible ink, thus betraying the presence of invisible ink. Invisible ink should not be used on ruled paper as it might also alter or streak the color of the lines.

The ink is later made visible by different methods according to the type of invisible ink used. Most invisible ink can be developed by heat or by application of an appropriate chemical, or it may be made visible by viewing under ultraviolet light.

For your secret ink you can use something carbon based - either egg white, lemon juice, or milk. When it comes time to read the secret message all one needs to do is apply a warm iron to the paper and the words should appear like magic. If the words don't appear, turn up the heat on the iron.

Good luck with your message to that cute young girl!

THE TEN COMMANDMENTS

The 10 Commandments are found in the Bible's Old Testament at Exodus, Chapter 20. They were given directly by God to Moses and the people of Israel at Mount Sinai after He had delivered them from slavery in Egypt.

ONE: '*You shall have no other gods before Me.*' (There is only one true God. People all over the world are worshiping false gods.)

TWO: '*You shall not make for yourself a carved image--any likeness of anything that is in heaven above, or that is in the earth beneath, or that is in the water under the earth.*' (Do not worship idols.)

THREE: '*You shall not take the name of the LORD your God in vain.*' (Do not use the name of God or Jesus in curse words. Unfortunately, this is almost totally ignored in many Hollywood movies.)

FOUR: '*Remember the Sabbath day, to keep it holy.*' (Sunday should be reserved as a day of worship.)

FIVE: '*Honor your father and your mother.*' (Obey your parents, do not back talk, do not rebel against them.)

144

SIX: '*You shall not murder.*' (Killing in just warfare is not considered murder.)

SEVEN: '*You shall not commit adultery.*' (Be faithful to your wife.)

EIGHT: '*You shall not steal.*' (Respect the property of others.)

NINE: '*You shall not bear false witness against your neighbor.*' (Do not tell lies.)

TEN: '*You shall not covet your neighbor's house; you shall not covet your neighbor's wife, nor his male servant, nor his female servant, nor his ox, nor his donkey, nor anything that is your neighbor's.*' (Be content with what you have; work hard to obtain your own personal comforts.)

PERFORMING THE HEIMLICH MANEUVER

When I was about three years old I put a marble in my mouth and it got stuck in my breathing passage. My mother saw me choking and ran over and held me upside down. She then slapped me on the back and the marble became dislodged. A flap of tissue called the **epiglottis**, attached to the base of the tongue, usually prevents food or objects from getting into the trachea when swallowing.

If a person chokes on something and is able to cough, they will probably be able to dislodge the offending object by themselves. **If they are unable to cough, they are probably in trouble**. You shouldn't try to do the Heimlich maneuver if you are too young or too small. If that is the case, get another nearby adult to do it and you can help with instructions if they don't know the technique.

Ask the choking person to stand if he or she is sitting. Place yourself slightly behind the standing victim. Reassure the victim that you know the Heimlich maneuver and are going to help. Place your arms around the victim's waist. Make a fist with one hand and place your thumb toward the victim, just above his or her belly button. Grab your fist with your other hand. Deliver five upward squeeze-thrusts into the abdomen. Make each squeeze-thrust strong enough to dislodge a foreign body. Understand that your thrusts make the diaphragm muscle move air out of the victim's lungs, creating a kind of artificial cough. Keep a firm grip on the victim, since he or she can lose consciousness and fall to the ground if the Heimlich maneuver is not effective. Repeat the Heimlich maneuver until the foreign body is expelled.

THE ART OF SKIPPING STONES

What red-blooded American boy doesn't love the opportunity to skip stones across the surface of a lake or pond? And if you have a friend along, you can see which of you can make the stone skip the most times before it sinks to the bottom.

During World War II the British tried to bomb German dams in the industrial Ruhr Valley. Conventional bombing didn't work because the Germans had the dams heavily defended with anti-aircraft guns. This forced bombers to fly too high for the bombardier to be accurate enough to destroy the dams. A suicide mission would have worked, but Judeo-Christian ethic holds life too dear to do something similar to the Japanese kamikaze suicide missions.

British scientists finally figured out how to destroy the dams. They developed "skip bombs" that were dropped at low levels in the lake behind the dam. The bombs skipped along the water and did not explode until they hit the dam. The story is told in the film, *The Dam Busters*, starring Richard Todd.

Before you throw, **make sure there are no people boating, fishing or swimming near you.** The trick to being a good stone skipper is in finding a fairly flat rock that is not too large or too small. Grip it with your thumb and curl your forefinger around it, with your middle finger resting behind it. When you throw the stone, do so with a sidearm motion and bend your knees so the stone hits the water at a shallow angle of about 20 degrees. If the angle is too steep, the stone will sink. The more you practice, the more skips you'll get across the water.

In case you're wondering, the world record is 40, set by Kurt Steiner in 2002. I know, this seems impossible, but you can Google it if you don't believe me.

HOW TO STUDY AN ECLIPSE

A solar eclipse occurs when the moon passes between the Sun and the Earth. The last solar eclipse occurred on January 15, 2010. The next solar eclipse that can be seen in North America will be on December 21, 2010. Although the Sun is 93 million miles away, its rays can cause

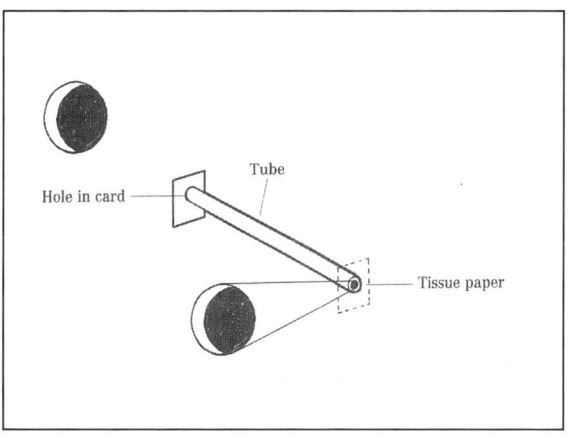

permanent retinal damage so you should **never look at it directly for any extended length of time**. And during an eclipse, it should never be looked at directly, even briefly. Regular sunglasses do not work either. You can purchase specially made sunglasses from science stores. Another alternative is to obtain a piece of #14 welder's glass from a welding supply store. Fortunately, you can also make a device that will allow you to see an eclipse safely. Even with the special glasses, do not look at the eclipse for any extended period of time. Also, don't use the glasses if they are scratched.

Get one of those rolls of Christmas wrapping paper and remove the cardboard tube (with mother's permission). Cut the tube in half. Glue a square 3 ½ inch piece of thin cardboard over one end of the tube. Oak tag or cardboard from an old file folder should suffice. Make a small pinhole in the center of the cardboard. Now glue a 3 ½ inch square piece of tissue paper over the other end. Lift the device toward the direction of the sun and an image of the eclipse will appear on the tissue paper. **Remember to look at the image on the tissue paper and not the sun.**

If you have no special glasses, don't despair. The next best approach (and a very simple one) is to project the Sun with a mirror. Use a small mirror, like a makeup mirror. With masking tape, cover all but about a 1/2" square in the center of the mirror. Then hold the mirror at an angle and project the sun onto a shaded wall or onto a white garage.

HOW TO GET A CAT TO "SIT PRETTY"

Dogs are smarter than cats when it comes to getting them to perform tricks or obey commands. However, my wife taught our female calico cat to "sit pretty." The bed in our bedroom has a footboard attached to it. She walked over to the dresser and took out a cat treat. Dianchi, our calico, came to the edge of the bed, placing her paws on the footboard and looked at my wife in anticipation. My wife, who has the patience of Job, gently pushed down on Dianchi's hindquarters and said, "sit pretty." Then she rewarded our Calico with the treat. After about three repetitions, Dianchi learned to obey the command and sit on her haunches all by herself.

My wife started with Dianchi because both of us, after observing her behavior for years, thought she was the smartest of our cats. What totally stunned us was our big, clumsy (but lovable) black tomcat – Dominy. He was also on the bed and had been carefully observing what was going on and how his sister was getting freebie treats. The next time my wife gave the "sit pretty" command to Dianchi, he jumped up on the other end, placed his paws on the footboard, and lowered his haunches. He, too, was given a treat! He learned the procedure by the simple process of observation.

Our cats are very smart. Their brains are stimulated at one end of the house by 1950s rock 'n' roll music and classical music at the other end. Be patient. Yours might require ten or twenty repetitions before they get it.

By the way, if you have a dog and want to teach him/her this trick, follow the same procedure on the living room floor. A firm low voice command generally works better than a shrill high one.

HOW TO CHANGE A WIPER BLADE

Examine the wiper blades on the family car. Are there pieces of rubber missing? Is the rubber hard and brittle? Have you noticed the blade streaking badly when it rains? If so, it's a good idea to replace the blades. It's one of the easier things you can do.

Purchase the correct replacement windshield-wiper blades for your car at an auto parts store. You need to know the year, make and model (example: 1955 Porsche Spyder). Buy the entire wiper blade assembly, not just the rubber blade insert.

Open the package and find the attachment that matches the one on the wiper blade on your car. Read through the directions to see how to connect the attachment to the blade. Pull the wiper arm up so it is no longer resting on the windshield. Remove the old wiper blade from the wiper arm. This typically involves pushing on a tab and pulling the wiper blade off or lifting a tab with a small screwdriver. Insert the attachment onto the new blade or onto the wiper arm. On some cars, it may be easier to put the attachment on the wiper blade first; on other models it is easier to first put the attachment onto the wiper arm. Listen for a click. Tug on the wiper blade to make sure it is securely attached and won't fly off later. Gently lower the wiper arm onto the windshield.

By the way, that Porsche Spyder sports car was the car iconic actor James Dean was driving when he was killed in a September 30, 1955 car accident.

TEDDY ROOSEVELT'S INSPIRATIONAL SPEECH

The Man in the Arena is the title of a speech given by Teddy Roosevelt at the Sorbonne in Paris, France on April 23, 1910. It was subsequently reprinted in his book *Citizenship in a Republic*.

Teddy Roosevelt

The speech is notable for the extended passage:

"It is not the critic who counts; not the man who points out how the strong man stumbles, or where the doer of deeds could have done them better. The credit belongs to the man who is actually in the arena, whose face is marred by dust and sweat and blood; who strives valiantly; who errs, who comes short again and again, because there is no effort without error and shortcoming; but who does actually strive to do the deeds; who knows great enthusiasms, the great devotions; who spends himself in a worthy cause; who at the best knows in the end the triumph of high achievement, and who at the worst, if he fails, at least fails while daring greatly, so that his place shall never be with those cold and timid souls who neither know victory nor defeat."

RUDYARD KIPLING'S "IF"

"**If**" is a poem written in 1896 by the then-31-year-old Rudyard Kipling. It was first published in the "Brother Square Toes" chapter of *Rewards and Fairies*, Kipling's 1910 collection of short stories and poems. Like William Ernest Henley's "Invictus", it is a memorable evocation of Victorian stoicism and the "stiff upper lip" that popular culture has made into a traditional British virtue. Its status is confirmed by the widespread popularity it still draws amongst the British (it was voted Britain's favourite poem in a 1995 BBC opinion poll). The poem's line, "If you can meet with Triumph and Disaster and treat those two impostors just the same" is written on the wall of the centre court players' entrance at the British tennis tournament, Wimbledon. The entire poem was read in a promotional video for the Wimbledon 2008 gentleman's final by Roger Federer and Rafael Nadal.

The beauty and elegance of 'If' contrasts starkly with Rudyard Kipling's largely tragic and unhappy life. He was starved of love and attention and sent away by his parents; beaten and abused by his foster mother; and a failure at a public school which sought to develop qualities that were completely alien to Kipling. In later life the deaths of two of his children also affected Kipling deeply. His only son John was killed in World War I.

IF

If you can keep your head when all about you others
Are losing theirs and blaming it on you,
If you can trust yourself when all men doubt you,
But make allowance for their doubting too;
If you can wait and not be tired by waiting,
Or being lied about, don't deal in lies,
Or being hated, don't give way to hating,
And yet don't look too good, nor talk too wise:

Rudyard Kipling

If you can dream - and not make dreams your master,
If you can think - and not make thoughts your aim;
If you can meet with Triumph and Disaster
And treat those two impostors just the same;
If you can bear to hear the truth you've spoken
Twisted by knaves to make a trap for fools,
Or watch the things you gave your life to, broken,
And stoop and build 'em up with worn-out tools:

If you can make one heap of all your winnings
And risk it all on one turn of pitch-and-toss,
And lose, and start again at your beginnings

And never breathe a word about your loss;
If you can force your heart and nerve and sinew
To serve your turn long after they are gone,
And so hold on when there is nothing in you
Except the Will which says to them: "**Hold on!**"

If you can talk with crowds and keep your virtue,
Or walk with kings - nor lose the common touch,
If neither foes nor loving friends can hurt you,
If all men count with you, but none too much;
If you can fill the unforgiving minute
With sixty seconds' worth of distance run,
Yours is the Earth and everything that's in it,
And - which is more - you'll be a Man, my son!
    Rudyard Kipling (1865-1936)

INVICTUS

Invictus" is a short poem by the English poet William Ernest Henley (1849–1903). This is a poem about taking charge of one's destiny. There will be forks in the road of life that will largely determine your fate. Decisions that you make will determine what kind of friends you will have, your success in school, whether or not you go to college, whether you will have a successful marriage and what kind of financial success you will have. Some people spend everything they make, but never abuse credit or go into debt. Some people start saving money at age 21 and are able to retire at age 58. Some people regularly spend more than they earn and have money problems throughout their life. Life is full of challenges and victories and defeats. How you handle these situations will largely determine whether you have an unhappy and stressful life or a successful one.

This poem was written in 1875 and first published in 1888 in Henley's *Book of Verses*, where it was the fourth in a series of poems entitled *Life and Death (Echoes)*. It originally bore no title; early printings contained only the dedication *To R. T. H. B.*—a reference to Robert Thomas Hamilton Bruce (1846–1899), a successful Scottish flour merchant and baker who was also a literary patron. The familiar title "Invictus" (Latin for "unconquered") was added by Arthur Quiller-Couch when he included the poem in The Oxford Book of English Verse (1900).

Henley became a victim of tuberculosis of the bone. A few years later the disease progressed to his foot, and physicians announced that the only way to save his life was to amputate directly below the knee. It was amputated at the age of 25. In 1867 he successfully passed the Oxford local examination as a senior student. In 1875 he wrote the "Invictus" poem from a hospital bed. Despite his disability, he survived with one foot intact and led an active life until his death at the age of 53.

Invictus is a 2009 film directed by Clint Eastwood, starring Morgan Freeman and Matt Damon. The film is a look at the life of Nelson Mandela after the fall of apartheid (racial segregation) in South Africa, during his term as president, when he campaigned to host the 1995 Rugby World Cup event as an opportunity to unite his countrymen. The title comes from the fact that Mandela had the poem written on a scrap of paper on his prison cell while he was incarcerated. In the movie, Mandela gives the "Invictus" poem to his national rugby team's captain Francois Pienaar before the start of the Rugby World Cup. In reality, Mandela provided Pienaar with an extract from Theodore Roosevelt's "The Man in the Arena" speech from 1910.

INVICTUS

Out of the night that covers me,
Black as the pit from pole to pole,
I thank whatever gods may be
For my unconquerable soul.
In the fell clutch of circumstance
I have not winced nor cried aloud.
Under the bludgeonings of chance
My head is bloody, but unbowed.
Beyond this place of wrath and tears
Looms but the Horror of the shade,
And yet the menace of the years
Finds and shall find me unafraid.
It matters not how strait the gate,
How charged with punishments the scroll,
I am the master of my fate:
I am the captain of my soul.

WHAT CAUSES A RAINBOW?

The dispersion of colors in a prism occurs because of something called the **refractive index** of the glass. Every material has a different refractive index. Take a look at a prism in your science class. When light traveling through the air enters the glass of a prism, the difference in the refractive index of air and glass causes the light to bend. The **angle of bending** is different for different wavelengths of light. As the white light moves through the two faces of the prism, the different colors bend different amounts and in doing so spread out into a rainbow.

In a sky rainbow, raindrops in the air act as tiny prisms. Light enters the **raindrop**, reflects off of the side of the drop and exits. In the process, it is broken into a spectrum just like it is in a triangular glass prism. Rainbows occur most frequently after a summer shower when the bright rays of the sun breaks through the clouds and strikes lingering droplets of rain in the sky. The angle between the ray of light coming in and the ray coming out of the drops is 42 degrees for red and 40 degrees for violet. You can see that the angles cause different colors from different drops to reach your eye, forming a circular rim of color in the sky -- a rainbow! The next time you spot a rainbow, you will see it in a whole new light – literally.

HOW TO PLAY A GAME OF MARBLES

The ancient Romans were among the first to play this game and the stones they used were usually made of marble. Marbles is mostly a game for grade schoolers. It is generally thought of as an old fashioned game but it requires a certain amount of skill and it can be fun. I was an average player and yet I enjoyed the competition and the skill of those who were really good at the game. The only spanking I got in grade school was due to a lingering game of marbles after the bell rang ending recess. Our game was nearly finished so we hurried to complete it. When we finished, we ran to the school doors to go inside. We were the last ones to re-enter the building but we were right behind other children. Our principal, Mr. Buzzell, had been watching us and he met us at the top of the steps. We were taken to his office and given swats. After that, when the bell rang to end recess, we yelled "hobbles squabbles." All the remaining marbles still in the ring went to those who grabbed them first.

Select a level spot of ground with no grass. Don't try to play on concrete or asphalt. Draw a circle with a stick about four feet in diameter. This game is best played with three to six participants. Decide in advance if the game will be funsies or keepsies. In funsies, all marbles are returned to their original owners at the end of the game. Marbles are so cheap we usually played keepsies.

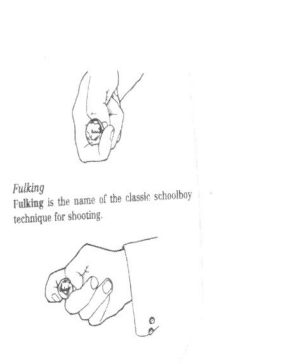

Fulking
Fulking is the name of the classic schoolboy technique for shooting.

Select your shooter (a taw) and place six marbles you wish to play with as targets inside the circle; the other players do the same. The marbles should be scattered rather than bunched up. Shooters are designated marbles used to knock targets out of the ring. Your shooter should be slightly larger than the other marbles so it's powerful enough to do its job. It should also look different from other marbles so you can distinguish it from them.

There are two different ways to shoot a marble. The easiest is known as "fulking." The marble is cradled in the crook of the index finger with the thumb behind it. The bottom of the index finger sits flat on the ground. The thumb is then flicked forward which gives propulsion to the marble. This is a rather wimpy way to shoot. A better way is to cradle the marble on two sides with the bent thumb on one side and the tip of the pointer finger on the other side. The back of the marble rests against the middle finger. Actually, the middle finger is wrapped around the part of the thumb containing the thumbnail. This produces far greater power. I knew boys who could use this shot to knock a marble out of the ring and after the shooter did its work it would sit where it had landed against the target marble and spin furiously.

Large marbles, called boulders, are not allowed in the game. Neither are "peewees" or "steelies." Take your turn when the time comes by shooting your marble from outside the ring at any marble or marbles inside the ring. Shoot by kneeling on the ground and flicking your marble out of your fist with your thumb. The object is to hit one of the marbles in the ring. If you hit one, you can place your shooter close to that marble and try to knock it out of the ring. Gather any marbles you've knocked out of the ring. Shoot again if you knocked any marbles out of the ring. Let the next player shoot if you haven't knocked any marbles out and/or your shooter remains in the ring. If someone knocks your shooter out of the ring, you lose a turn. Continue shooting in turn until the ring is empty.

Fudging is against the rules and any player who fudges loses a turn. Fudging is when a player gives additional power to his shot by pushing his hand forward just as he lets go with a shot.

Count your marbles at the end of the game. The winner is the player with the most marbles.

The world championship of marbles is played every year in West Sussex, England.

HOW DO SAILBOATS GO
AGAINST THE WIND?

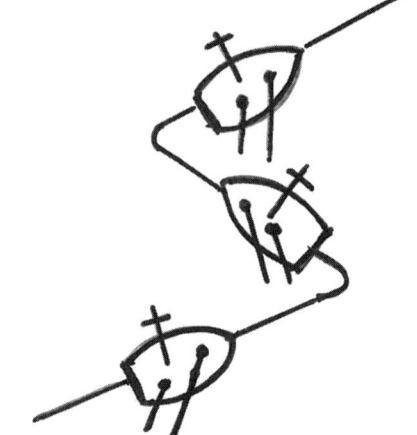

In the time of Christopher Columbus, many people thought the world was flat and that if you sailed too far your ship would fall off the edge. It was also thought that the Earth was the center of our universe and the Sun and planets revolved around it. There were also tales of sea monsters that could swallow ships whole.

In those earlier times boats were either powered by oars or sails or both. It was the early Phoenicians who learned the technique of sailing against a strong headwind. Sailors called this process "beating against the wind." The entire thing is accomplished by turning the angle of the sail and having the rudder in the right position.

Sailing against the wind must be done in a zig zag pattern. The rudder and sails are turned at corresponding angles to the direction of the wind. The boat makes some forward progress but only by going off on a tangent, first to the right (starboard), then to the left (port). To get back on course the rudder and sail are then turned at corresponding angles in a different direction. To continue making progress in a direction with a headwind, this zig zag pattern is simply repeated over and over.

The term port side comes from the fact that the ships pull into port and dock on their left side. To determine latitudinal position on the Earth, sailors would use sextants to "shoot the stars" from the right which became known as the starboard side.

SELECT WORLD CAPITALS

China – Beijing	Japan – Tokyo	South Korea - Seoul
U K - London	Germany –Berlin	Poland - Warsaw
Spain -Madrid	Portugal – Lisbon	Russia - Moscow
Finland - Helsinki	Norway – Oslo	Denmark - Copenhagen
Sweden – Stockholm	Romania – Bucharest	Hungary – Budapest
Bulgaria – Sophia	France – Paris	Belgium – Brussels
Italy – Rome	Switzerland – Bern	Egypt – Cairo
Libya – Tripoli	Brazil – Brasilia	Argentina – Buenos Aires
Venezuela – Caracas	Chile – Santiago	Iran – Teheran
Turkey – Ankara	Iraq – Baghdad	Ecuador - Quito
Syria – Damascus	Israel – Jerusalem	Mexico – Mexico City
Jordan – Amman	Lebanon – Beirut	India – New Delhi
Nicaragua – Managua	Kenya – Nairobi	Ghana – Accra
Senegal – Dakar	Liberia – Monrovia	Colombia – Bogota
Australia – Canberra		New Zealand – Wellington
Philippines – Manila		Singapore – Singapore City
Slovakia – Bratislava		Czech Republic – Prague

RHETORICAL QUESTIONS THAT DON'T NEED AN ANSWER

If you throw a cat out a car window, does it become kitty litter?
If corn oil comes from corn, where does baby oil come from?
If there is no God, who pops up the next Kleenex in the box?
Why do they put Braille on the number pads of drive-through bank machines?
How did a fool and his money GET together in the first place?
How do they get a deer to cross at that yellow road sign?
If it's tourist season, why can't we shoot them?
What's another word for thesaurus?
Why do they sterilize the needles for lethal injections?
What do they use to ship Styrofoam?
Why is there an expiration date on my sour cream container?
How do you know when it's time to tune your bagpipes?

When you choke a smurf, what color does it turn?

Does fuzzy logic tickle?

Do blind Eskimos have seeing-eye sled dogs?

Do they have reserved parking for non-handicapped people at the Special Olympics?

Why do they call it a TV set when you only get one?

Do radioactive cats have 18 half-lives?

If you shoot a mime, should you use a silencer?

What was the best thing before sliced bread?

Is it true that cannibals don't eat clowns because they taste funny?

Do fish ever get thirsty?

Why does a 10 gallon cowboy hat hold only ¾ of a gallon?

Why do we call some people *airheads* when their brain is 80 percent water?

If you melt dry ice, can you swim in it without getting wet?

Does Hawaii have any interstate highways?

If you jog backwards, will you gain weight?

If one synchronized swimmer drowns, do the rest have to drown too?

What does cheese say if someone takes its picture?

If you spin an Oriental person around, does he become disoriented?

Why are flotation devices used on planes instead of parachutes?

If people from Poland are called Poles, why aren't people from Holland called Holes?

Why do we say something is out of whack? What's a whack?

If a pig loses its voice, is it disgruntled?

Some of the people in Europe are Flemish. Does this mean there is a country called Phlegm?

When someone asks you, "A penny for your thoughts," and you put your two cents in, what happens to the other penny?

Why is the man who invests all of your money called a broker?

Why do croutons come in airtight packages? It's just stale bread.

Why is a person who plays the piano called a pianist, but a person who drives a race car is not called a racist?

Why are a wise man and a wise guy, opposites?

Why do overlook and oversee mean opposite things?

Why isn't the number 11 pronounced onety one?

"I am" is reportedly the shortest sentence in the English language. Could it be that "I do" is the longest sentence?

If lawyers are disbarred and clergymen defrocked, doesn't it follow that electricians can be delighted, musicians denoted, cowboys deranged, models deposed, tree surgeons debarked, and dry cleaners depressed?

If Fed Ex and UPS were to merge, would they call the resulting company Fed UP?

Do Lipton Tea employees take coffee breaks?

What hair color do they put on the driver's licenses of bald men?

I was thinking about how people seem to read the Bible a whole lot more as they get older. Then it dawned on me.....they're cramming for their final exam.

If it's true that we are here to help others, then what exactly are the others here for?

How come no one ever says, "It's only a game" when their team is winning?

Ever wonder what the speed of lightning would be if it didn't zigzag?

Whatever happened to Preparations A through G?

Why do people sing "Take me Out to the Ballgame" when they're already at a ballgame?

If you try to fail and succeed, which have you done?

If 7-11 is open 24-7 for 365 days a year, why do they have locks on their doors?

If a cow laughs really hard, does milk come out of her nose?

If you were in a car going the speed of light and then turned on the lights, what would happen?

Why is it called "after dark" when it's really "after light?"

Why do we park on driveways and drive on parkways?

Why do they always report power outages on TV?

If a mime swears, does his mother wash his hands with soap?

When it rains, why don't sheep shrink?

Is it permissible for vegetarians to eat animal crackers?

If a cop arrests a mime, does he need to tell him he has the right to remain silent?

Why are boxing rings square?

Can fat people go skinny dipping?

How do you know when you run out of invisible ink?

Why do you need a driver's license to buy liquor if it's illegal to drink and drive?

Why isn't phonetic spelled the way it sounds?

Have you ever imagined a world with no hypothetical situations?

How does the guy who drives the snowplow get to work early in the morning?

If nothing sticks to Teflon, how do they get it to stick to the pan?

If you tied buttered toast to the back of a cat and dropped it from table height, what would happen?

Why is it that when we transport something by car it's called a shipment, but if we transport by ship its called cargo?

You know that little black box they put on planes that's indestructible, why can't they make the whole plane out of that substance.

Why is it that when you're driving and looking for an address, you turn down the volume on the radio?

Why are cigarettes sold at gas stations when smoking is prohibited there?

Who decided what was going to be the order of the alphabet?

Why is it so hard to remember how to spell the word Mnemonic?

Why do hot dogs come 10 to a package, yet there are only 8 buns in a package?

156

If you keep trying to prove Murphy's Law, will something keep going wrong?

Shouldn't there be a shorter word for monosyllabic?

If 75 % of all accidents happen within 5 miles of home, why not move 10 miles away?

Why doesn't onomatopoeia sound like what it is?

Why is it that when two planes almost collide it's called a "near miss?" Shouldn't it be called a near hit?

Why isn't palindrome spelled the same way backwards?

If you see a heat wave, should you wave back?

Why is it called a toothbrush instead of a teethbrush?

Why is brassiere singular and panties plural?

If someone invented instant water, what would they mix it with?

Why do *fat chance* and *slim chance* mean the same thing?

If love is blind, why is lingerie so popular?

Why does your alarm clock go *off* by going *on*?

Why do we wash bath towels? Aren't they clean after we use them?

Why do we always press harder on a remote control when we know the battery is dead?

Why are they called apartments when they're all stuck together?

If a vegetarian eats vegetables, what does a humanitarian eat?

Why do our noses run and our feet smell?

Is it true that Eskimos use refrigerators to keep their food from freezing?

Why does quicksand work so slowly?

Why are there no eggs in an eggplant? Why is there no ham in hamburger? Why are there no apples in pineapples?

How is it that a burning building burns up as it burns down?

If the # 2 pencil is so popular, why is it still number 2?

Why is it when the stars are out they're visible, but when the lights are out, they are invisible?

Can anyone name the technical medical term to describe boogers?

Do amphibians need to wait an hour after eating before going into the water?

DAYS OF YORE REMEMBERED – 1902

The average life expectancy in the US was forty-seven (47).

Only 14 percent of the homes in the US had a bathtub.

Only 8 percent of the homes had a telephone. A three-minute call from Denver to New York City cost eleven dollars.

There were only 8,000 cars in the US and only 144 miles of paved roads.

The maximum speed limit in most cities was 10 mph.

Alabama, Mississippi, Iowa, and Tennessee were each more heavily populated than California. With a mere 1.4 million residents, California was only the 21st most populous state in the Union.

The tallest structure in the world was the Eiffel Tower.

The average wage in the US was 22 cents an hour.

The average US worker made between $200 and $400 per year.

A competent accountant could expect to earn $2,000 per year, a dentist $2,500 per year, a veterinarian between $1,500 and $4,000 per year, and a mechanical engineer about $5,000 per year.

More than 95 percent of all births in the US took place at home.

Ninety percent of all US physicians had no college education. Instead, they attended medical schools, many of which were condemned in the press and by the government as "substandard."

Sugar cost four cents a pound. Eggs were fourteen cents a dozen. Coffee cost fifteen cents a pound.

Most women only washed their hair once a month and used borax or egg yolks for shampoo.

Canada passed a law prohibiting poor people from entering the country for any reason.

The five leading causes of death in the US were:
1. Pneumonia and influenza
2. Tuberculosis
3. Diarrhea
4. Heart disease
5. Stroke

The American flag had 45 stars. Arizona, Oklahoma, New Mexico, Hawaii and Alaska hadn't been admitted to the Union yet.

The population of Las Vegas, Nevada was 30.

Crossword puzzles, airplanes, canned beer, and iced tea hadn't been invented.

There was no Mother's Day or Father's Day.

One in ten US adults couldn't read or write. Only 6 percent of all Americans had graduated from high school.

Marijuana, heroin, and morphine were all available over the counter at corner drugstores. According to one pharmacist, "Heroin clears the complexion, gives buoyancy to the mind, regulates the

Eiffel Tower

stomach and the bowels, and is, in fact, a perfect guardian of health."

Eighteen percent of households in the US had at least one full-time servant or domestic.

There were only about 230 reported murders in the entire US.

STRANGE & UNUSUAL CIVIL WAR FACTS

About 300 women disguised themselves as older boys and participated in the war. Illinoisan Jennie Hodgers (she enlisted as Albert Cashier) holds the record for maintaining her disguise the longest. Her true identity was not discovered until 1910 when she was injured in an accident and taken to a hospital.

Northerners, largely from cities, were impressed with natural objects and named battles after hills or streams. Southerners lived in rural areas and named battles after artificial objects on the field of action. Thus the first battle of the war was called the Battle of Bull Run Creek by the North and the Battle at Manassas Rail Junction by the South.

The Civil War was the first conflict to be photographed (Matthew Brady)

The Civil War had the first ironclad ships (Monitor & Merrimack)

Trench warfare was used extensively for the first time.

For the first time in U.S. history men were drafted into a war.

The decoration known as the Medal of Honor was introduced in this war.

The bugle call "Taps" was introduced in the war.

Many of the opposing generals were good friends having been schooled together at West Point and having served together in the war against Mexico 1846-1848.

Lincoln's Emancipation Proclamation of 1863 did not immediately free any slaves because it did not apply to any of the Border States and the South was still in control of the states it affected.

Missouri was never a Confederate state but it was represented on the Confederate flag as the 12th star because Missouri had so many southern sympathizers.

Writer Mark Twain participated in a few battles and then quit the war and went out west to attend to his writing.

Northerners had the advantage of more railroad tracks, more states (22-11), better finances and more population.

Jenny Hodgers/Albert Cashier

The South had the advantage of better generals and better knowledge of the terrain; also, it is always easier to fight a defensive war. The South had higher motivation for it was their homeland that was being invaded.

When the North invaded the South they tore up railroad tracks. To prevent the rails from being used again they were heated and bent around a tree. They were called Sherman's Bowties.

Historians speculate that Lee might have won at Gettysburg if Stonewall Jackson had been there. Unfortunately, Jackson was previously killed by his own men who fired on him in darkness after the Battle of Chancellorsville. They mistakenly thought Jackson was part of a Union patrol.

During the war Abe Lincoln issued a proclamation that the last Thursday of November should be set aside as a special day of thanksgiving – hence the origin of Thanksgiving.

More than half of all deaths of soldiers came from disease and not bullet wounds.

The Battle of Antietam was the bloodiest single day of the war with 23,000 being killed or wounded. This is nine times the number of casualties suffered by Americans at D-Day in World War II.

There were more American casualties in the Civil War (650,000) than in the Revolution, War of 1812, Mexican War, Spanish-American War and World War I combined.

Stonewall Jackson had the unusual habit of only eating food that tasted bad. He assumed anything that tasted good was probably unhealthy.

Wives whose husbands were killed in battles mourned them for two years. This meant not going to parties or social functions (only church) during that period. Men usually mourned their wives for four months.

There were no funeral parlors then. People were laid out in a wooden coffin in the parlor of their home for one day and then quickly buried to prevent disease since there was also no embalming. It became the practice of using flowers at a funeral to mask the odor of the deteriorating body of the deceased.

President Lincoln's favorite tune was "Dixie."

General Nathan Bedford Forrest had 29 horses shot from beneath him during the war. He later became one of the founders of the KKK.

During the war colored glasses were used to treat people with mental illnesses. Rose colored lenses were used to treat people with depression. This is where we get the expression "seeing the world through rose-colored glasses."

The largest mass lynching in history occurred at Gainesville when a Confederate mob lynched 12 union sympathizers and shot 28 others.

Both Abraham Lincoln and Jefferson Davis had sons who died while they were in office.

Confederate General Joseph Johnston was a pallbearer for the funeral of Union General William T. Sherman. While out in the cold and the rain at the funeral, Johnston contracted pneumonia and died.

It only took Abraham Lincoln two minutes to deliver the Gettysburg Address, arguably the most famous speech in American History.

The Civil War started and ended on property belonging to Wilmer McLean. The first battle, fought in 1861 at Bull Run Creek, was practically fought in his front yard. After the battle he moved to southern Virginia to escape the conflict. When Lee surrendered to Grant in 1865, it was at McLean's second house near Appomattox Courthouse.

General Arthur MacArthur was awarded the Congressional Medal of Honor for his heroism during the Battle of Chattanooga. His son, Doug, won the award for his actions in the Pacific during World War II. They are the only father and son team to be given that prestigious award.

Abe Lincoln has no living descendants. Three of his sons died before reaching maturity. Son Robert had a son and two daughters. The son died at age 17. The daughters married and had children but the last Lincoln descendant died in 1985.

COIN FLIP

Remember This: The next time you flip a coin to decide something, choose tails. The side with the head usually weighs more than whatever is on the other side. Because the heads side of the coin is a tad heavier, it has a tendency to land face down a bit more. This means that out of 1,000 flips, it doesn't come out 500 times heads and 500 times tails. Heads only comes up about 450 times and tails comes up 550 times. To increase your chances of winning the flip, TAILS NEVER FAILS.

THE STRANGEST OLYMPICS EVER

With much of regular television programming sidetracked for two weeks, many of us in the metro area watch the Olympic Games when they are held. We sit glued to our sets to watch competing athletes experience the thrill of victory and the agony of defeat. But, let's rewind and go back to a time when the Olympics were very different. In fact, the 1904 Olympics at St. Louis weren't even the main attraction, and they were very poorly attended because they were a mere sideshow.

The city of Chicago back then was a fierce competitor of St. Louis for the title, "Queen City of the Midwest." Missourians derisively called Illinoisans "Suckers," and denizens of the Prairie State returned the favor deriding Missourians as "Pukes." Chicago had won the original bid to host the 1904 Summer Olympics, but the organizers of the Louisiana Purchase Exposition in

St. Louis pressured the Olympic Committee to hold the games in St. Louis in conjunction with the World's Fair.

Pierre de Coubertin, the founder of the modern Olympic movement, at the urging of President Roosevelt, gave in and awarded the games to St. Louis. This is the only time in history where the games have been taken away from a city that was previously awarded them.

St. Louis organizers repeated the mistakes made at the 1900 Olympics in Paris. Competitions were reduced to a side-show of the World's Fair and were lost in the chaos of other, more popular cultural exhibits. Many of the competitive events were held on the property of Washington University, at what is now called Francis Field. It was located at the far west end of the fairgrounds, which consisted of more than 1,000 acres. David Francis, the President of the Exposition, declined to invite anybody else to open the Games and, on July 1, did so himself in a rather humdrum ceremony.

The participants, from twelve countries, totaled 651 athletes - 645 men and six women. However, only 42 events (less than half) actually included athletes who were *not* from the United States. The actual athletic events that formed the bulk of the recognized Olympic sports were held from Monday, August 29 to Saturday, September 3, a period of just five days.

European tension, caused by the Russo-Japanese War and the difficulty of getting to St. Louis, kept many of the world's top athletes away. The expense of trans-oceanic travel was also a hindrance since participants had to pay their own way.

Boxing, dumbbells, freestyle wrestling and the decathlon made their debuts as Olympic events. One of the most remarkable athletes was the American gymnast George Eyser, who won six medals even though his left leg was made of wood, due to a train accident.

The exhausting marathon was the most bizarre event of the Games. It was run by 39 participants in brutally hot weather, over dusty roads, with horses and automobiles leading the way. The runners were literally forced to eat dust along a tortuous route that was marked with red flags. Back in 1904, paved roads were almost nonexistent, and there was only one water station - located at the mid-point of the race. One of the bedraggled runners was chased by vicious dogs and ran a mile out of his way to escape them.

The first to arrive at the finish line was Frederick Lorz, who actually was just trotting back to the finish line to retrieve his clothes. Lorz ran for about nine miles and then hopped in a car and rode in it for twelve miles. When the officials thought he had won the race, Lorz played along with his practical joke until he was found out shortly after the medal ceremony. Lorz was banned for a year by the AAU for this stunt but later won the 1905 Boston Marathon.

Thomas Hicks (a Brit running for the United States team) was the first to cross the finish-line legally. He tired a few miles from the finish line and his trainers had him stop for a pick-me-up which consisted of brandy, raw egg white, and strychnine sulfate. Drunk, poisoned, and exhausted, Hicks staggered toward victory. He was so weak and ill he had to be supported by his trainers when he crossed the finish line. Alice Roosevelt, the President's daughter was there, waiting to crown him with a laurel wreath, but she couldn't. Hicks had to be carried off the track, and possibly would have died in the stadium had he not been treated by several doctors.

Perhaps the most interesting marathon story was that of a Cuban postman named Felix Carbajal. Felix quit his job and made it to New Orleans by boat. He then lost all of his money to a street gambler and had to hitchhike and walk the next 700 miles to St. Louis. He had no running outfit so he cut around the legs of his street clothes to make them look like shorts. Felix enjoyed himself, sometimes running the race backwards. He also paused to chat with bystanders along the way. He detoured through an orchard to have a snack on some apples, which turned out to be rotten. The spoiled apples caused him to have to lie down and take a brief nap. Despite falling ill to apples, he managed a fourth place finish.

The marathon included the first two black Africans to compete in the Olympics. However, they weren't there to compete in the Olympics, they were actually the sideshow. They had been brought over by the Exposition as part of the Boer War exhibit (both were really students from the Orange Free State in South Africa). One African finished ninth and the other came in twelfth. Many observers were sure the one who finished ninth could have done better if he had not been chased nearly a mile off course by those aggressive dogs.

Incredibly, the organizers of the games held "Anthropology Days" on August 12 and 13. Various natives from around the world, who were at the World's Fair as part of national exhibits, competed in various events for anthropologists to see how they compared to the white man. Unfortunately, their events were largely confined to rock throwing, pole climbing, spear tossing, and mud fighting.

The Fair was held long before the advent of political correctness and racial sensitivity, so it should not be too surprising to learn that organizers also set aside a Watermelon Day to attract local "Negroes" to the gala event.

HOW TO BIND A BOOK WITH GORILLA GLUE

This process, using Gorilla Glue, involves just a few basic steps with no sewing. The most time consuming part of this procedure is just waiting for glue to dry. How many times do you print up an E book or a school report only to lose some of the pages, or have them fall out of your hands and jumble the pages? It's easy for accidents to happen. You can't read them if there is any wind blowing. You can't pull them out five minutes before a class and turn to your bookmark. Even turning the pages becomes annoying after awhile. That's why you should consider this easy DIY project.

Aside from printing and glue drying, the whole process takes only about five minutes. Like a deck of cards, grab all your book pages and tap them so all the sheets are flat and in line. You can make a simple book binder jig out of scrap wood to hold the sheets in place. If you don't feel like building one, you can use a heavy phone book to hold everything flat and in line. Building a binder jig has its advantages. First the two blocks of wood keep the pages in line on two sides. Also, it's very easy to clamp them using the clamp bar and wing nuts. Clamp the pages tight so nothing moves.

Now wet the spine and use Gorilla Glue to bind the book. It's great for several reasons. One, it expands and fills in any unintentional gaps. Two, it holds firm and tight.

Use a cotton ball slightly wet with water to wet the spine. Make sure you make a pass or two over the spine so it's damp. Now squeeze all the water out of the cotton ball and use it to apply the glue. While the glue is drying, measure out the cover. Typically, you can use some heavy card stock in legal size. It's smart to go ahead and fold the edges of the cover **before binding** so it will fold over the pages without you having to strain. If you are going with pages 5 1/2 inches wide, then measure 5 1/2 inches and make a light mark on the cover. Then measure the thickness of the newly bound pages and mark there. (In this case the pages measure 1/2 inch.) Use a ruler to make the folds.

After the glue has dried, loosen the wing nuts and insert the cover (back side) underneath the newly bound pages.

After applying a touch more water and spreading glue to the spine, fold over the cover and make everything tight. Then clamp it in the book binder.

You probably can see an overlap in the cover. It's best to cut too large so you can always cut back. It's better to have too much than too little. Now just leave everything to dry – overnight is preferable.

FUNNY THINGS TO DO ON AN ELEVATOR
Courtesy of Dave Winer

What's the fun of being a kid if once in a blue moon you can't do something a bit goofy that is essentially harmless and won't get you thrown into juvenile detention? Just one thing. Never get on an elevator and push all the buttons. We live in a time oriented world and making people late isn't funny so you shouldn't ever do it. If you're brave enough, here are some really stupid things to do on an elevator.

Make race car noises when anyone gets on or off.
Grimace painfully while smacking your forehead and muttering: "Shut up . . . all of you just shut UP!"
Whistle the first seven notes of "It's a Small World" incessantly.
Sell Girl Scout cookies.
On a long ride, sway side to side at the natural frequency of the elevator.
Offer name tags to everyone getting on the elevator. Wear yours upside-down.
Stand silent and motionless in the corner, facing the wall, without getting off.
When arriving at your floor, grunt and strain to yank the doors open, then act embarrassed when they open by themselves.
Lean over to another passenger and whisper: "Noogie patrol coming!"
Greet everyone getting on the elevator with a warm handshake and ask them to call you Admiral.
Stare, grinning, at another passenger for a while, and then announce: "I've got new socks on!"

When at least eight people have boarded, moan from the back: "Oh, not now, darn motion sickness!"

Meow occasionally.

Bet the other passengers you can fit a quarter in your nose.

Frown and mutter "Gotta go, gotta go," then sigh and say "Oops!"

Show other passengers a wound and ask if it looks infected.

Holler "Chutes away!" whenever the elevator descends.

Walk on with a cooler that says "human head" on the side.

Stare at another passenger for a while, then announce "You're one of THEM!" and move to the far corner of the elevator

Ask each passenger getting on if you can push the button for them.

Wear a puppet on your hand and talk to other passengers "through" it.

Start a sing-along.

When the elevator is silent, look around and ask: "Is that your beeper?"

Play the harmonica.

Shadow box.

Say "Ding!" at each floor.

Listen to the elevator walls with a stethoscope.

Draw a little square on the floor with chalk and announce to the other passengers that this is your "personal space."

Carry a blanket and clutch it protectively.

Make explosion noises when anyone presses a button.

Stare at your thumb and say "I think it's getting larger."

None of these goofy stunts should get you sent to reform school; however, you should be prepared to get grounded for a month when your parents find out about it.

HOW TO USE A MULTI-METER

WARNING!!!!!   Volt-ohm meters are great for testing toys and small appliances. Testing anything larger such as a washer, for example, would be best left up to an electrician.   Also, stay completely away from microwave ovens which emit dangerous waves.

When you are using the probes, be sure you do not touch the metal tips because you will then become part of the circuit which could result in an electrical shock. Have your dad or mom to guide you if you attempt to use an ohm meter on anything else besides household batteries and light bulbs.

Ohm's law breaks down into the basic equation: Voltage = Current x Resistance. Current is generally measured in amps and resistance in ohms. **Select an ohmmeter suitable for your project.**   Another term for an ohmmeter is a **multi-meter** because they usually measure voltage as well as resistance. Analog ohmmeters are very basic and inexpensive, and usually range from 0-10 to 0-10,000 ohms; digital devices may have similar ranges or "auto-range", reading the resistance of your device or circuit and selecting the correct range automatically. Some people prefer the analog because they prefer seeing the old fashioned dial move across the face of the meter. **Check the ohmmeter to see if it has a battery.** If you just bought an ohmmeter, the battery may have come pre-installed in your unit, or packaged separately with instructions for installing it.

Plug your test leads into the sockets on your meter. For multi-functional meters, you will see a "common," or negative plug, and a "positive" plug. These may also be colored red (+) and black (-). **Zero your meter if it is equipped with a zeroing dial.** Notice that the scale reads in the reverse direction of most conventional measuring scales, that is, less resistance is to the right, and more resistance is to the left. Zero resistance should be observed when your probes are connected directly to each other, and you can adjust this by holding them together and turning the "adjust" dial until the needle on the scales is at zero ohms.

Choose the circuit or electrical device you want to test. For practice, you can use almost anything which conducts electricity, from a piece of aluminum foil to a pencil mark on a sheet of paper. To get an idea of the accuracy of your readings, buy a few different resistors from an electronics supplier, or some other device with a known resistance value. Touch one probe to one end of a circuit, the other to the other end, and note the reading on the instrument. If you bought a 1000 ohm resistor, you can place a probe on each conductor on the resistor, and select the 1000 or 10,000 ohm range, then read the meter to see if indeed it reads 1,000 ohms. Isolate components in a hard wired electrical circuit to test them individually. If you are reading the ohms on a resistor in a printed circuit board, you will have to unsolder or unpin the resistor to assure you are not getting a false reading through another path in the circuit. Read the resistance of a run of wire or a branch of a circuit to see if there is a short or open break in the circuit. If you read "infinite ohms", there is no path for the electrical current to follow, and in simple terms, this suggests a burned out component somewhere in the circuit, or a broken conductor. Because many circuits contain "gate" devices (transistors or semiconductors), diodes, and capacitors, however, you may not read continuity even when the complete circuit is intact, which makes it difficult to test complete circuits with only an ohmmeter.

Test the life of batteries safely by using a volt-ohm meter. The meter will show if there is still life in the batteries. Use the meter to test battery operated toys also. Be sure you match the polarity of the probes with the batteries. Touch the red positive probe to the nub on the top of a C or D battery, the black negative probe to the bottom of the battery. Some batteries, such as a 9 volt battery, have both the positive and negative on top and are marked with a plus or a minus (negative). To check batteries, you must set the dial on the Ohmmeter to DC voltage. To check whether a light bulb is still good you must switch the dial over to resistance, which is symbolized on the dial by a horseshoe. Touch the black probe to the metal bottom of the bulb with screw markings. Touch the red positive probe to the bottom of the bulb that connects to the bulb's filament.

Turn the ohmmeter off when not in use. Occasionally the test leads will become shorted while the device is stored, draining the battery.

LINCOLN AND KENNEDY SIMILARITIES

Not long after Kennedy was assassinated, someone started doing some research and discovered a startling number of similarities in their deaths. Now these just happen to be coincidences, but the sheer number of them is a bit spooky.

Abe Lincoln was elected to Congress in 1846 and John Kennedy was elected to Congress in 1946. Lincoln was elected president in 1860; Kennedy was elected in 1960, exactly 100 years apart. Lincoln championed the cause of civil rights for blacks and Kennedy did the same. Both men were shot on a Friday and in the presence of their wives. Each of their wives lost a child while living in the White House. Both men had vice –presidents with the name Johnson – Lyndon Johnson and Andrew Johnson. Both were southerners. Each of their names contains 13 letters. Andrew Johnson was born in 1808 and Lyndon Johnson was born in 1908. Lincoln was shot in Ford's Theater. Kennedy was shot while riding in a Lincoln, manufactured by the Ford Company. John Wilkes Booth, Lincoln's assassin, has 15 letters in his name. Lee Harvey Oswald, Kennedy's assassin, also has 15 letters in his name. Lincoln was shot in a theater and his assassin was captured in a warehouse. Kennedy was shot from a warehouse and his assassin was captured in a theater. Both Booth and Oswald were killed before being brought to trial.

THE CURSE OF TENSKWATAWA

When the British colonized America there was a major problem. The land already belonged to the Native-Americans living here. Much of the land desired by whites was obtained by treaty, but a good deal of it was simply taken by force. What happened to the Indians is a sad fact of life, but here's another fact. Mark Twain once commented that there probably isn't a square foot of earth that, at one time or another during the centuries, hasn't been fought over with the strong taking it away from the weak. The Greeks took land from the Persians, then lost it to the Romans. The Roman Empire was later overrun by Goths, Visigoths, Huns and Vandals.

Mark Twain (Wikipedia)

The Portuguese, Dutch, Spanish, French and English had hundreds of colonies they took by force. The Australians took land away from the aborigines.

It should also be remembered that the varying Indian tribes engaged in vicious warfare with each other.

William Henry Harrison won the presidency in 1840 with the slogan, "Tippecanoe and Tyler Too." This refers to his participation in the Battle of Tippecanoe in 1811, in what is now the state of Indiana. He was hailed as a hero when Tecumseh's forces were defeated at this battle. Harrison delivered a very long inaugural address on a cold, windy day. Then he was caught in a rainstorm. He fell ill which turned into pneumonia and led to his death. He 'served' as president from March 4 - April 4, 1841. His death would be seen as the first in a long series of what became known as **Tecumseh's Curse**: Presidents elected in a year ending in a zero would die in office.

The curse is attributed to Tenskwatawa, a Shawnee mystic who was known as "the Prophet." He was a half-brother to the great chief Tecumseh, who led the uprising against the encroaching whites. When Tenskwatawa learned that his half-brother had been killed in battle by Harrison's forces, he invoked a curse. "Harrison will die, I tell you," the Prophet reportedly said. "And after him a number of other Great White Chiefs will die on a regular basis by the curse I place on them."

Now, nobody really believes in curses, but this one is pretty eerie. You see, every president elected in a year ending in zero died in office over a span of more than a hundred years. Harrison (1840) of pneumonia, Lincoln (1860) from an assassin's bullet; Garfield (1880) from the hands of an assassin; McKinley (1900) from an assassin's bullet to the stomach; Harding (1920) from a stroke (some think his wife poisoned him); Roosevelt (1940) cerebral hemorrhage, and Kennedy (1960) from a rifle shot. Ronald Reagan, of Dixon, Illinois was elected in 1980. The next spring he was shot in the side by John Hinckley and very nearly died, but managed to survive. The curse was finally broken. George W. Bush was elected in 2000 and also survived.

Tecumseh (Library of Congress)

IMPORTANT FACTS ABOUT COLONIAL AMERICA

Christopher Columbus lands in the Bahamas in 1492.

America gets its name from **Amerigo Vespucci**, an Italian who sailed for Spain and made numerous voyages to the New World.

Ponce de Leon, looking for the Fountain of Youth, discovers Florida in 1513.

Hernando DeSoto of Spain discovers the Mississippi River in 1541.

Walter Raleigh establishes the colony of Roanoke, Virginia in 1585, but after a few years it becomes known as the Lost Colony.

The first permanent English colony is established at Jamestown, Virginia in

1607.

In 1612, **John Rolfe** (the man who married Pocahontas) grows tobacco at Jamestown and exports it to England, placing the colony on a good financial footing.

The first slaves are brought to Jamestown in 1619.

The *Mayflower* lands the English Pilgrims at Plymouth, Massachusetts in 1620.

The Dutch settle New York in 1626 when Peter Minuit buys Manhattan Island from the natives for about $24.

King Charles II establishes a colony in Carolina in1663.

In 1674 the Duke of York occupies New Amsterdam by threat of force and renames it New York. It is now a British colony.

William Penn and the Quakers establish the Pennsylvania colony in 1681.

Twenty people are executed in Salem, Massachusetts in 1692, being accused of practicing witchcraft.

Georgia, the thirteenth colony, is founded in 1732 by **James Oglethorpe**.

Parliament passes the hated **Stamp Act** in 1765, taxing the colonists on newspapers, legal documents and playing cards.

British troops fire on a protest mob and kill five in the **Boston Massacre** of 1770.

Sam Adams and fifteen colonists, disguised as Indians, dump British tea into the harbor in 1773 during the **Boston Tea Party**.

Skirmishes at **Lexington and Concord** in 1775 mark the beginning of the American Revolution. This is when **Paul Revere** made his famous ride warning the Americans, "The British are coming!"

Nathan Hale (National Archives)

In June of 1775, the colonists show they can stand up to British regulars by their brave actions at the Battle of **Bunker Hill** in Boston.

France and Spain send millions of dollars to help the Americans who declare their independence on July 4, 1776.

Nathan Hale, executed in 1776 by the British for spying, proudly declares: "I regret that I have but one life to give for my country."

Washington boldly crosses the Delaware River on December 25, 1776, and defeats the Hessians at Trenton, New Jersey.

General **Benedict Arnold** defeats the British in a key battle in 1777 at Saratoga, N.Y.

Washington barely keeps his rag tag army together at Valley Forge, Pennsylvania during the winter of 1777-1778.

John Paul Jones refuses to surrender his sinking ship (*Bonhomme Richard*) to the British in 1779 exclaiming, "I have not yet begun to fight!" He manages to capture the British ship *Serapis* before his sinks.

Benedict Arnold commits treason in 1780 by trying to turn over the fortifications at West Point to the British in exchange for a large sum of money.

Washington and **Lafayette** trap the British into surrendering at **Yorktown**, Virginia in 1781, losing an entire army and unofficially ending the war.

The British sign the Treaty of Paris 1783, granting the Americans their independence. They gain control of everything from the Atlantic Ocean to the Mississippi River, except for Spanish Florida.

They obtain the land west of the Appalachians, thanks to the exploits of **George Rogers Clark**.

THE BALANCING FORKS

This little gem has been around forever. As a youth, I remember making one of these do dads out of Tinkertoys. Take a large coin – either a quarter or 50 cent piece - and slip it through the tines of two forks. The handles of the two forks should be at opposite ends with one fork cradled on top of the other so it is possible to connect them with the coin. You may need to do a little experimenting to find the right size forks and the right size coin. The coin should be placed in the center of the tines (prongs).

Have enough coin protruding from the tines (prongs) that you can set the entire assembly on the lip of a tall glass. You may have to do a little adjusting to get the forks to balance on the outer lip of the glass.

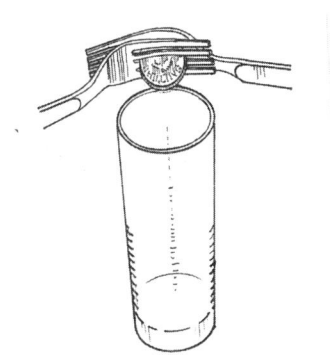

If you can't get that to work, try inserting a wooden kitchen match in the tines of the fork and set the match on the outer lip of the glass.

And if that doesn't work buy a set of Tinker Toys that has this little device in its set of instructions.

HOW TO FLOAT AN EGG IN WATER

Set two glasses of water in front of a friend. Tell him you bet he can't get an egg to float in the water, but you can. Place your egg in the glass of water and it will readily float. Then hand him the egg and tell him to try it with his glass of water. His won't float. The difference is that you placed a lot of salt in your glass of water, making it more dense, thus supporting the egg. Make all the preparations with your glass beforehand so you are sure there is enough salt in your glass to make the egg float.

HOW TO MAKE A CODED SPARTAN MESSAGE

In ancient Greece there was often constant warfare with surrounding enemies and there was a need to be able to send messages in code that the enemy couldn't decipher. The Spartans found that the easiest way to do this was to wrap a strip of paper around a stick and then print their message along the length of the stick. Then they would go all the way around the stick and write random letters of the alphabet in a long row, matching up with the message line. If the enemy intercepted the message it would look like gobbledygook. Once delivered to its intended receiver, the message would be taken and re-wrapped around a stick that was the same diameter, making sure that the letters lined up perfectly. Then all they had to do was look for the line that made sense.

To make your own Spartan Code Stick you need the inside cardboard tube from some Christmas wrapping paper. Now take some Christmas wrapping paper and cut a one inch wide strip from it. You will write your message from the reverse blank side. Tape one end of your strip to one end of the tube and begin coiling around it, making sure the edges don't overlap. Cut off any excess strip and tape this end to the tube also. Print your message in a straight line along the tube using all capital letters. If you need to separate words you can use the letter X or Z to do this.

After you have written your message, rotate the tube and start a new row of nonsense letters.
After you have gone completely around the tube, mail the message to a friend. You can call them in advance (or see

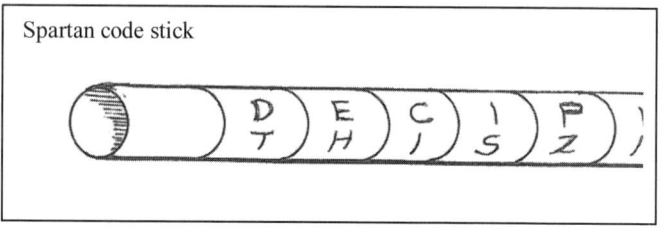

Spartan code stick

them at school) and tell them how to decode the message.

HOW TO MAKE A SHADOW PORTRAIT

When I was in grade school one of the art projects we did in February was to make a folder with two portraits inside. One was of Abe Lincoln and the other was George Washington. Back then there was no such thing as Presidents' Day. We celebrated Lincoln's birthday on February 12 and Washington's on February 22. What makes this interesting is that when Washington was born in 1731, his birth certificate said it was on February 11. That's because at the time the western world was using the Julian calendar. In 1752 Great Britain and all her colonies switched to the modern Gregorian calendar which placed his birthday on the 22nd. In 1968 a law was passed making the third Monday in February Presidents' Day, celebrating the birthdays of both men while giving

171

people a three day holiday weekend.

Our teacher gave us two pieces of black construction paper. She passed around heavy cardboard silhouette profiles of Washington and Lincoln. We traced their profiles on our construction paper, cut them out, and then glued them in our folder. Naturally we were proud as peacocks when we took them home to show our parents.

Here's how to do your own:

Wait until it gets dark and then attach an 8.5 x 11 sheet of black paper to the wall, portrait style. Place a chair sideways in front of the wall and place a table in front of the chair. Place a desk lamp on the table, the kind with a flexible stem and a metal shell that covers all of the bulb except the front portion.

Find someone in your family willing to sit still long enough for you to draw their silhouette. You may have to do a little adjusting of the chair and lamp (closer or farther) to get a sharp image on your paper. Once you get a crisp image take a well sharpened #2 pencil and draw the person's profile on the paper. Thank the person who sat for you and tell them their job is finished. Take a pair of scissors and carefully cut out the likeness with care. Glue your black silhouette to a sheet of white or beige paper. If you did a really good job, you might want to frame it.

If you still have pencil marks on the silhouette after you cut it out, simply turn it over and then glue it down.

MAKE A PAPER MILITARY-STYLE HAT

If the pressman's hat was too complicated, here is an easy one that, with practice, you can learn to make in about 25 seconds.

Take a large single sheet of newspaper and trim it to 15 x 23 inches. Newspapers come in double sheets so you might have to cut the other half off with scissors. Place this single sheet on the table with the centerfold in a horizontal position. Take the top of the newspaper and fold it in half as you pull it toward you. Make the crease sharp. Fold the paper over from left to right, just as if you were closing a book. Make a light crease not a sharp one.

Now fold the paper back to the original position. All you were doing was marking the center.

Take hold of the top left corner and pull it over and down until what was the top edge now sits vertically along that crease you just

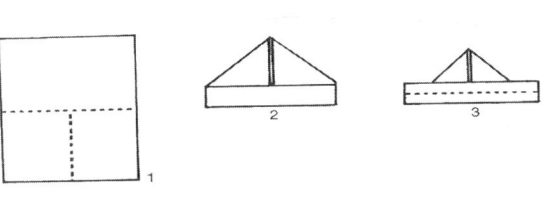

made. Now take the top right corner and pull it over and down until its top edge sits vertically next to the other side. The top of your sheet should now be

172

pointed. Press the creases to make them sharp.

Now take the bottom horizontal flap and fold it up horizontally over the bottom of the pointed section. Turn the project over and do the exact same thing to the other bottom flap. In order to make the whole thing shaped like a pyramid, grab the protruding right-angle corner on one side and bend/tuck it around the base of your pyramid. Flip it over and take the other protrusion and bend it around to the other side. Fasten it in place with a small piece of Scotch tape. Now do the same thing with your protrusions at the other end. Those two little pieces of tape will keep your hat from coming undone.

If your hat has the complete shape of a pyramid, you are finished. If not, go back over the steps and try to figure out what you did wrong. You can now open up your hat and place it on your head at a cocky angle. **Ten Hut!**

HOW TO MAKE A HUGE PAPER TREE

Making a tree from newspapers that reaches to the ceiling can be impressive. Here's how you do it. Take about six sheets of newspaper and spread them lengthwise on the kitchen or garage floor. Overlap each sheet just enough to glue one strip to the next until you have one long strip. Allow time for the glue to dry.

Roll the strip into a fairly tight cylinder with enough room to poke your forefinger (pointer finger) into it. If you have trouble, try rolling the newspaper around a pencil or pen. Take the leftover loose end flap and glue it down to the roll. Take a pair of sharp scissors and make two cuts down opposite sides of your newspaper roll. The length of your cuts should be about halfway down the tube. The next time you make a paper tree you can experiment with the depth of your cut to see how it affects the outcome. Now take another newspaper sheet and wrap it around the floppy cut lengths of the newspaper. Trim and glue in place to make everything neat and tidy.

When you are ready to demonstrate what you have made to others, tear your outer sheet along the line of the previous cuts. Hold the tree trunk in your left hand and stick your right forefinger into the middle of the hole, and pull up on the paper with a twisting and tightening motion as you go. (It will quickly become obvious which way to twist it to make it tighter. You'll be amazed to see how much your tree will grow.

MAKE YOUR OWN HALLOWEEN BLOOD

When Halloween rolls around, you might want to dress up as some ghoul or fiend. Wouldn't it be cool if you had some blood on your cheek or some dripping down the corner of your mouth? Making your own blood isn't that difficult but for years Hollywood used a product that looked more like red paint than red blood. The first movie to use a recipe with corn syrup and food coloring, similar to this one, was *Midnight Cowboy* in the 1970s. Now it's just about the standard.

Here's how you make it. Combine 1 tablespoon of water with 1 measuring cup of clear Karo corn syrup. Add red food coloring and mix by stirring. Continue adding drops until the shade resembles that of real blood. Add a small amount of blue food coloring to achieve a more realistic shade.

If you need to add a thickener, add sifted flour or corn starch to your mixture and gently stir it all again. Small lumps may form at the top of the mixture. Wait a bit and they will float to the top where you can remove them. If you need a wet thickener, stir in chocolate syrup until the desired consistency is reached. It will also add a realistic brown tone to the blood.

Let the mixture sit for ten minutes at room temperature. This will give it some time to thicken. And then you can freak people out with it; this is lots of fun. You might want to mix up an extra batch for the local vampires in your area. Note: this recipe yields blood that is very sticky initially, especially in hair.

Be careful with your food coloring and don't spill it on anything because it causes a stain that is difficult to remove.

HOW TO USE HALLOWEEN MAKEUP

Make your own makeup. Determine what color makeup you want. Mix together 2 tsp. solid shortening, 5 tsp. cornstarch, 1 tsp. flour and 4 drops of glycerin (laxative suppositories at a pharmacy) in a bowl. Mix and blend well. Add food coloring a little at a time until you get the color you want. Apply the makeup, using only enough to cover. Wash makeup off with warm water and soap when your Halloween fun is over.

Make sure you plan ahead. Don't start making your costume and makeup plans the night before Halloween. Do some advance planning and get all the materials, props, costume, and makeup items you'll need for your creative Halloween costume ideas ahead of time. If you wait too long, what you need or want may not be available.

When Halloween finally arrives, start your preparations early in the day. Set all your materials and makeup out to make sure you have everything you'll need. Give yourself time for a last minute trip to the store.

Now you must decide if you should put your makeup on before or after getting in costume. If your costume is one that can easily be put on without touching your face and messing up your makeup, go ahead and do your makeup first. It's easier to put makeup on when you are not in costume because you don't have to worry about messing up your costume. However, if your costume is going to be difficult to put on, go ahead and get into it before putting on your makeup. Simply drape a towel around your neck to protect your costume from makeup splatters and drips. This way you can do a great job on your makeup and not accidentally mess it up while putting on your costume.

Now that you are ready to begin with the makeup, secure a scarf around your

174

head so that all your hair is covered. This will keep your face makeup out of your hair, prevent your hair from messing up your makeup and will give you a clear view of your whole face.

Use a couple of mirrors (one on either side) to study your face. Take a moment to imagine the makeup on your face before applying it. Taking a little time to mentally plan how you're going to put on your makeup can help prevent frustrating mistakes and may give you some new ideas.

Nothing is too strange for Halloween, so be creative! If you decide at the last minute that you want to try something wild, go for it! If it doesn't work out, you've (hopefully) started early and will have time to clean up and go back to the original plan.

When trying to look like an old hag, don't just draw dark lines on your skin to look like wrinkles. First cover the skin in a lighter than normal color using baby powder or white blemish cover stick. Then draw the dark lines and slightly blend them to the surrounding area with your finger. Now add baby powder to give the skin that old, dry look. You can also use the baby powder in your hair to get that gray look.

If you want to be a vampire, first cover your face in white powder makeup or white blemish cover stick. Outline sharp eyebrows, and then fill in with black makeup. Draw lines on the face with reddish-brown makeup, and blur the edges a bit. Outline the eyes and draw a line up about an inch from the outside edge of the eye. Drip fake blood from the edges of the mouth (see above for details on making fake blood). Comb hair into a point in the middle of the forehead. Use fake teeth to complete the transformation.

To look like a witch, follow these techniques. Cover the face in green or white powder makeup or white blemish cover stick. With a black makeup stick, draw lines in a "V" in the middle of the forehead and create some lines around the mouth. Draw lines on the hands with an eyeliner pen; almost follow the veins to make the hands look old. Tease and spray hair with a super stick hairspray. Add a few plastic bugs. Don't forget you will need a realistic looking old-fashioned broom.

Do you have a pair of boxing gloves? To get that recently punched look you will need to defiantly plan in advance and you will need some not entirely easy to find tools. Modeling Wax and Spirit Gum are required to undertake this look. Place a thin layer of the Spirit Gum on the area of your face to appear bruised. Then take the Modeling Wax and shape it into the desired size and apply to the Spirit Gum. Blend the edges into your skin until they are flat and the wax appears to be part of your skin. Once the edges are blended, clear your face of excess wax and gum using your finger tips and a tiny bit of cleansing cream. Next, use a base or makeup foundation to blend your new bruise into your skin color or with a purplish color to make it more realistic. If you'd like to kick it up a notch, carve a small circle into your bruise and apply fake blood or a gooey green substance so it can fester.

If you really get into this make-up thing, you can check your local yellow pages to find places that sell professional makeup for actors and actresses. Max Factor is a well known brand.

HOW TO MAKE A FROGMAN THAT DIVES

You will need to use a bit of imagination on this one. You must pretend that an eyedropper is your frogman. The actual name for this little trick is the Cartesian Diver. It's named for Rene Descartes, the Frenchman who said, "I think, therefore I am."

Find an empty 2 liter plastic soda bottle and fill it with cold water, stopping about two inches below the neck of the bottle. Now find an eyedropper and empty it of all oils and fluids. Check the buoyancy of the eyedropper by placing it in a glass of water. It will probably fall over sideways. Use the dropper to draw in a small amount of water and try again. Keep adding more water until your frogman floats upright. Once you have the right amount of water take your diver and place him upright in your soda bottle and screw the cap on tight.

To make your diver go up and down, just squeeze the shoulder of the bottle with both hands. There is a simple principle of physics involved here. Air can be compressed but liquids cannot. That's why fluids are used in hydraulics (such as your car's brakes). When you squeeze the bottle the air in top will be squished up a bit but, since the water can't be compressed, some of it will go up into the dropper. This will make it too heavy to float and it will begin to sink. You'll find that you can control the rate of your diver's descent and ascent by varying the amount of pressure you apply as you squeeze the bottle.

THE GAME OF SPROUTS

Sprouts is a pencil-and-paper game with interesting mathematical properties. It was first played by mathematicians John Horton Conway and Michael S. Paterson at Cambridge University in 1967.

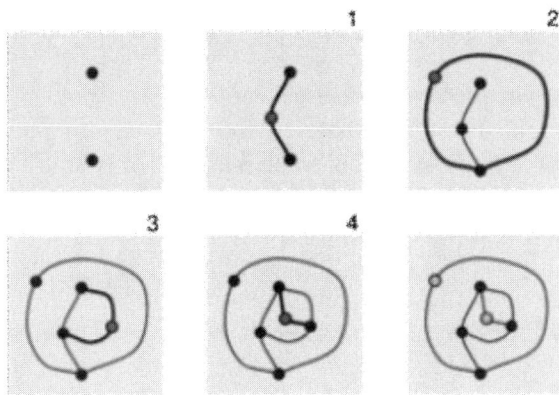

The game is played by two players, starting with a few spots drawn on a sheet of paper. Players take turns, where each turn consists of drawing a line between two spots (or from a spot to itself) and adding a new spot somewhere along the line. The players are constrained by the following rules.

176

The line may be straight or curved, but must not touch or cross itself or any other line. The new spot cannot be placed on top of one of the endpoints of the new line. Thus the new spot splits the line into two shorter lines. No spot may have more than three lines attached to it. For the purposes of this rule, a line from the spot to itself counts as two attached lines and new spots are counted as having two lines already attached to them.

The player who makes the last move wins. The diagram above shows a 2-spot game of normal-play Sprouts. After the fourth move, most of the spots are *dead*–they have three lines attached to them, so they cannot be used as endpoints for a new line. There are two spots (the one in the center and the one of the top left) that are still *alive*, having fewer than three lines attached. However, it is impossible to make another move, because a line from a live spot to itself would make four attachments, and a line from one live spot to the other would cross lines. Therefore, no fifth move is possible, and the first player loses.

BALLOON MAGIC

Have another person help you with this. Blow up a regular egg-shaped or round balloon. As you inflate it, have someone press a small plastic bathroom cup on each side. As the balloon fills with air the balloon will expand into the cups. After you tie a knot in the end of the balloon you can use a magic marker to draw a funny face on the balloon, using the protruding parts as ears.

Here's another! Wait until you are the only one home at your house. Take a long sausage-shaped balloon and blow it up. Now rub the balloon against your hair to give it a charge of static electricity. Now stand on a chair and press it to the kitchen ceiling. When the rest of the family gets back home the balloon will still be there, clinging as if by magic. When someone asks how it got up there simply shrug your shoulders. Such balloons have a tendency to stay in place for a very long time.

At school you can trick your classmates with this one. Ask your science teacher permission to do this trick. Blow up a balloon and put it in a bag and take it to school with you. Have a small square of Scotch tape already stuck to the side. Show the balloon to the class, with the piece of tape facing away from them. Tell them you can insert a needle in it without popping the balloon. Hold the needle prominently in front of you so the class can see it is a sharp instrument. Rotate the balloon so that the Scotch tape is on the side of the balloon. Insert the needle and, amazingly, the balloon won't pop. Act as though you forgot the other half of the class couldn't see the needle so rotate it so the rest of the students can see the needle in the balloon but can't get a good look at the tape.

Now comes the shocker. Hand another needle to the person sitting in the front middle and ask them to stick it in the balloon, while pointing to the front/middle part of the balloon. Naturally, it will make a loud pop. Quickly place the balloon and both needles back into the bag.

HOW TO MAKE A LEPRECHAUN HAT

Get one of those large bowls that you can buy at K-Mart made out of paper. Like paper plates, many of these are basically sturdy like cardboard. Buy the sturdy type that looks like it will fit your head. (These will probably come in a pack.) Paint the bowl green. While it is drying, make a band of black construction paper. Glue the band around the hat. It should be sitting on the brim. Take an index file card and cut out a piece two inches square. This will be a buckle. In the middle of the square draw a letter C facing backward. Instead of rounding the corners of the letter make them square. Cut out your letter with scissors. Make the two prongs of the letter about 1/8 inch wide and make the inside curve cutout about ¼ inch wide. When finished your cutout letter should resemble a backward letter C. Paint the buckle gold. After it dries glue it to the front/middle part of the hatband so the black shows through the cutout area, making it resemble a buckle. Cut out a shamrock from a piece of foam and attach it to a pipe cleaner. Trim the pipe cleaner to the desired length and paint the shamrock and pipe stem green. After it dries, shove one end into the rear/side of the hat and you are ready to celebrate St. Patrick's Day in a big way.

St. Patrick was an English Christian missionary sent by Rome to convert the Irish. It is thought that he died in 493 A.D. He has come to be revered as the Patron Saint of the Irish. Although St. Patrick's Day is a non legal holiday in America, it is celebrated with festivities. In the Windy City that sits next to Lake Michigan, the Chicago River is dyed a festive green. Even Protestants quite often fix a meal for supper consisting of corned beef and cabbage and cornbread.

There are two legends concerning St. Patrick. One is that **he banished all snakes from the island country**. Ireland is currently free of snakes and it is illegal to take them into the country. The other tradition is that he used the three-leafed shamrock to teach the Irish about the concept of the trinity – God the Father, Jesus the Son, and the Holy Spirit.

New Zealand is another snake-less country. The fact is, both places are snake free because their land became isolated from the continents before the snake, as a creature, evolved. Snakes can swim across rivers but they can't swim across large bodies of water.

HOW TO MAKE YOUR OWN BAROMETER

A barometer is a scientific device used to measure air pressure. Everyone on Earth essentially lives at the bottom of a sea of air that is pressing down on us. This principle can be demonstrated by making a simple barometer.

Blow up one of those egg-shaped balloons and then let the air out of it again. This is done to stretch it. Cut the balloon in half and discard the part with the neck on it. Now take the balloon and stretch it over the mouth of an empty and clean jar of mustard (or some other similar jar). Make it airtight around the edges with a rubber band.

Keep it stretched firmly across and sealed down with the rubber (elastic) band, around the rim of the glass jar. To make an airtight seal, avoid gaps between the balloon and the glass. Now tape a straw horizontally across the top of the balloon.

Tape the straw onto the balloon lid; the straw should be sitting 3/4 of the way on the lid, with the tape nearly in the middle of the balloon lid. The straw will serve as your indicator "needle." You can trim the straw if it is too long, but leave more length off the jar compared to what is on it. Put the finished glass jar on a table next to a wall and tape a piece of paper or card to the wall behind it. Take a pencil and mark the current position of the straw on the paper. Arrange the paper so there is room above and below the straw for you to make more marks when the straw moves.

Check your straw regularly and keep marking its location on the paper for a

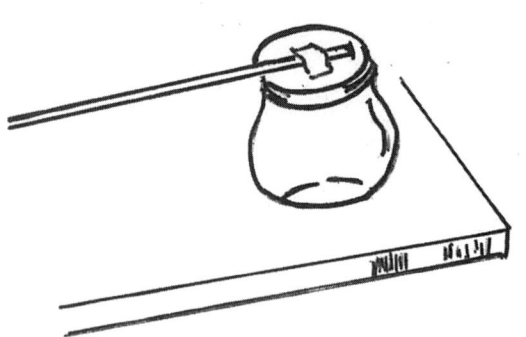

few days. Add notes that tell you what the weather is like (e.g. "rainy," "windy," or "sunny,") next to the mark. Try to do your readings when the room temperature has been about the same because warm air expands and cold air contracts.

Examine the paper after several days and take notice of your marks and comments. What conclusions can you draw?

When you fitted the balloon over the glass, you captured air under a certain pressure. The balloon now indicates changes in the atmospheric pressure, i.e. the pressure of the air around you. Higher air pressure pushes the balloon into the jar and makes the straw go up. Conversely, the air inside the jar expands against lower pressure and will bulge the balloon, moving the straw down. The straw makes it easier to see the motions of the balloon.

As the straw moves up with higher air pressure, the days should be sunnier. As the straw lowers, the skies may be looking gray and you should expect cloudy or rainy weather on the way.

Also notice that the straw moves up or down just before a weather change since a change in weather typically coincides with a change in the atmospheric pressure.

Try this over a longer period of time if you are having a week of rain or a week of sunshine. Try and choose the seasons likely to bring the most changes during a short period of time in your part of the world.

Check your results against the pressure from weather reports for your area. Do the direction and degree generally agree?

This is a delicate apparatus. Place it away from traffic and activity.

The first barometer was built by **Francis Bacon**. Later in 1644, **Evangelista Torricelli**, built the first instrument with mercury. When I was young it was common to see barometers that consisted of glass tubes filled with liquid mercury which was known as quicksilver. Because mercury is poisonous, it is no longer used to make barometers. As atmospheric pressure increased, it caused the mercury in the barometer to rise, signaling the arrival of sunny weather. As low pressure moved into the area, the barometer fell, signaling the advent of rain. Modern aneroid barometers have a piece of metal in them which expands and contracts as the atmospheric pressure changes.

MAKE A FISH THAT SWIMS

Do the best you can to draw a two inch long fish. Give him a mouth, eyes, and a two pronged tail fin at the end of his body. Look at the bottom of this article if you need an example. Now draw a black circle in the middle of his body and draw a straight black line from the circle to the tail of the fish and end it in the V of his tail fin.

Here is where the fun begins. Take a small bowl and fill it with water. Place the fish in the water with his tail close to one edge. Make sure the top of the 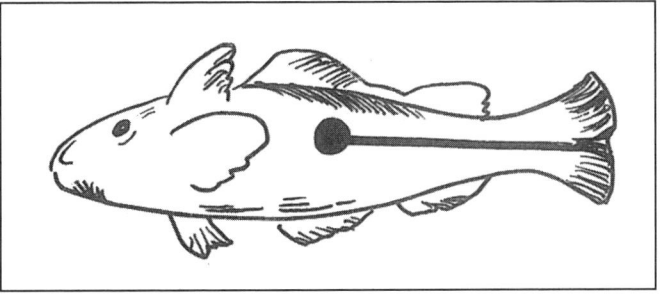 fish stays dry. Take a can of 3-in-1 Oil and place a drop on your black dot. Oil and water do not mix so the oil will run down the line to the tail of the fish and enter the water from the tail. As it does so this will cause the fish to zoom across the water in the opposite direction. When you show this to your friends they will be amazed.

A BUNCH OF USELESS, YET INTERESTING, FACTS

The word "queue" (pronounced Q) is the only word in the English language that is still pronounced the same way when the last four letters are removed.

Beetles taste like apples, wasps like pine nuts, and worms like fried bacon.

Of all the words in the English language, 'set' has the most definitions!

The phosphorous match was invented in France in 1831.

Boston Celtics star Danny Ainge is the only high schooler to become a first string All-American in football, baseball and basketball.

What is called a "French kiss" in the English speaking world is known as an "English kiss" in France.

"Almost" is the longest word in the English language with all the letters in alphabetical order.

"Rhythm" is the longest English word without a vowel.

In 1386, a French pig was publicly hanged for the murder of a child.

The wettest place on Earth is Lloro, Columbia, which receives an average of 40 feet of rain a year.

So many vessels have disappeared in the area known as the Bermuda Triangle that a number of researchers have suggested the existence of a time warp there that transports the crafts to an alternate universe.

For every ten people who climb Mt. Everest, one person dies in the attempt.

John Wayne and Doris Day are the top movie box office stars of all time.

The center of the Earth is estimated to have a temperature of 9,000 degrees Fahrenheit.

The Indianapolis Speedway is the largest sports facility in the world. It can hold 255,000 people during the race.

The largest college football stadium is at the University of Michigan and it holds 107,501 fans.

A cockroach can live several weeks with its head cut off!

Human thigh bones are stronger than concrete.

You can't kill yourself by holding your breath

There is a city called Rome on every continent.

Your heart beats over 100,000 times a day!

Horatio Nelson, one of England's most illustrious admirals, was throughout his life, never able to find a cure for his sea-sickness.

The skeleton of Jeremy Bentham is present at all important meetings of the University of London

Right handed people live, on average, nine years longer than left-handers.

Your ribs move every time you breathe, about 5 million times a year!

The elephant is the only mammal that can't jump!

One quarter of the bones in your body, are in your feet!

Like fingerprints, everyone's tongue print is different!

The first known transfusion of blood was performed as early as 1667, when Jean-Baptiste, transfused two pints of blood from a sheep to a young man

Fingernails grow nearly 4 times faster than toenails!

181

Most dust particles in your house are made from dead skin!

The present population of 5 billion plus people of the world is predicted to become 15 billion by 2080.

Women blink nearly twice as much as men.

The 12" action figure GI Joe was first created in 1964 by the Hasbro Toy Company in response to the immense popularity of the Barbie Doll among girls. The term GI stands for "government issue."

The first Batman story appeared in May of 1939 in issue #27 of Detective Comics. The Bat Man character proved to be so popular that in the spring of 1940 a self-titled Bat Man comic book series was started.

Statistically, the player going first in Monopoly has the best chance to win.

Superman first appeared as a hero in Action Comics #1 in 1938.

Peter Parker debuted as "The Amazing Spider-Man" in a March 1963 Issue #1. He was an unusual super hero because he was just a teenager.

Adolf Hitler had only ONE testicle.

Honey is the only food that does not spoil. Honey, found in the tombs of Egyptian pharaohs, has been tasted by archaeologists and found edible.

Months that begin on a Sunday will always have a "Friday the 13th."

Coca-Cola would be green if coloring weren't added to it.

On average, a hedgehog's heart beats 300 times a minute.

More people are killed each year from bees than from snakes.

The average lead (graphite) pencil will draw a line 35 miles long or write approximately 50,000 English words.

More people are allergic to cow's milk than any other food.

Camels have three eyelids to protect themselves from blowing sand.

The placement of a donkey's eyes in its' head enables it to see all four feet at all times!

Queen Elizabeth I (Wikipedia)

The six official languages of the United Nations are: English, French, Arabic, Chinese, Russian and Spanish.

Earth is the only planet not named after a heathen god.

It's against the law to burp, or sneeze in a church in Nebraska.

You're born with 300 bones, but by the time you become an adult, you only have 206. Some of the bones grow together.

Queen Elizabeth I regarded herself as a paragon of cleanliness. She declared that she bathed once every three months, whether she needed it or not.

Some worms will eat themselves if they can't find any food!

Dolphins sleep with one eye open!

It is impossible to sneeze with your eyes open.

182

The world's oldest piece of chewing gum is 9000 years old!

The longest recorded flight of a chicken is 13 seconds.

Slugs have 4 noses.

Owls are the only birds that can see the color blue.

A man named Charles Osborne had the hiccups for 69 years!

A giraffe can clean its ears with its 21-inch tongue!

The average person laughs 10 times a day!

An ostrich's eye is bigger than its brain

The Bible, the world's best-selling book, is also the most shoplifted book.

In Monopoly, Illinois Avenue is landed on more than any other property.

Your tongue is the only muscle in your body that is attached at only one end.

More than 1,000 different languages are spoken on the continent of Africa.

In the U.S.A. over twelve thousand people have seen a tortilla chip that appears to have the face of Jesus Christ burned into it.

The English ruler Richard II is credited with inventing the handkerchief.

Men's suit coats have buttons on the sleeve thanks to Frederick the Great. He did not want his officers messing up their uniforms by wiping their noses on their sleeve. He placed buttons on the sleeve to discourage the practice.

A kiss lasting one minute can burn more than 30 calories.

Buckingham Palace in England has over six hundred rooms.

There was once an undersea post office in the Bahamas.

Abraham Lincoln's mother died when she drank the milk of a cow that grazed on poisonous snakeroot.

The sandwich was invented around 1772 by the Earl of Sandwich who was First Lord of the Admiralty. He did not want to leave the gaming tables so he ordered a piece of meat with a slice of bread on each side.

St. Louis Municipal Opera

171—St. Louis Municipal Opera, St. Louis, Mo.

After the death of Albert Einstein, his brain was removed by a pathologist and put in a jar for future study.

Milk from a Yak is colored pink.

In 2002, the most popular boat name in the U.S. was Liberty

One out of 20 people have an extra rib

44% of kids watch television before they go to sleep

In 1865, the U.S. Secret Service was first established for the specific purpose to combat the counter-feiting of money

Istanbul, Turkey is the only city in the world located on two continents

In 1967, the IMAX film system was invented by Canadian Ivan Grame Ferguson to premier at Expo 67.

Approximately 40% of the U.S. paper currency in circulation was counterfeit by the end of the Civil War

Every three days a human stomach gets a new lining

In 1873, Colgate made a toothpaste that was available in a jar

The Kodiak, which is native to Alaska, is the largest bear and can measure up to eight feet and weigh as much as 1,700 pounds.

The three best-known western names in China: Jesus Christ, Richard Nixon, and Elvis Presley.

The largest outdoor stage in America is the Muny Opera in Forest Park in St. Louis.

Mars is the home of Olympus Mons, the largest known volcano in our solar system.

It was Charlie Chaplin who said, "a day without laughter is a day wasted."

It takes more muscles to frown than to smile.

Queen Elizabeth I is credited with inventing the gingerbread man.

The Gastric Flu can cause projectile vomiting.

The name Wendy was made up for the book "Peter Pan."

The fur of the binturong, also known as the "Asian Bear Cat," smells like popcorn. The scent is believed to come from a gland located near the tail.

In 1894 the first big Coke sign was placed on the side of a building located in Cartersville, Georgia and still exists today.

The longest distance a deepwater lobster has been recorded to travel is 225 miles

Orcas (killer whales), when traveling in groups, breathe in unison

The Great Pyramids used to be as white as snow because they were encased in a bright limestone that has worn off over the years

The percentage of American men who say they would marry the same woman if they had it to do all over again: 80%

Paul Hunn holds the record for the loudest burp of 118.1 decibels, which is as loud as a chainsaw

A monkey was once tried and convicted for smoking a cigarette in South Bend, Indiana

There are six million parts in the Boeing 747-400.

The first TONKA truck was made in 1947

In the U.S., over one million gallons of cosmetics, drinks, and lotions are sold per year that contain aloe in them

Sugar Bear (the mascot for Golden Crisps cereal) was born in 1963

The Tonle Sap River in Cambodia flows north for almost half the year and then south for the rest of the year

For more than 3,000 years, carpenter ants have been used to close wounds in India, Asia and South America

Baskin Robbins plain vanilla ice cream is the number one selling flavor and accounts for a quarter of their sales

Elizabeth Taylor has appeared on the cover of Life Magazine more than anyone else

Michael Jordan has appeared on the cover of Sports Illustrated more than anyone else (49)

The word "toy" comes from an old English word that means "tool."

Smokers are twice as likely to develop lower back pain than non-smokers.

The reason hair turns gray as we age is because the pigment cells in the hair follicle start to die, which is responsible for producing "melanin" which gives the hair color

The two factories of the Jelly Belly Candy Company produce approximately 100,000 pounds of jelly beans a day. This amounts to about 1,250,000 jelly beans an hour

Pucks hit by hockey sticks have reached speeds of up to 150 miles per hour.

The Planters Peanut Company mascot, Mr. Peanut, was created during a contest for schoolchildren in 1916.

Most lipstick contains fish scales.

The sentence "the quick brown fox jumps over the lazy dog" uses every letter in the English language.

No piece of paper can be folded in half more than 7 times.

More people are killed by donkeys annually than are killed in plane crashes

Asthma affects one in fifteen children under the age of eighteen

Barbie Roberts is the full name of a Barbie doll.

Throughout the South, peanuts were known as "Monkey Nuts," and "Goober Peas," before the Civil War.

Scallops have approximately 100 eyes around the edge of its shell.

In 1810, Peter Durand invented the tin can for preserving food.

The fear of peanut butter sticking to the roof of the mouth is called Arachibutyrophobia.

Men in their early twenties shave an average of four times a week.

Color is not an indicator for the taste or ripeness in cranberries.

Each year there are approximately 20 billion coconuts produced worldwide.

A chicken with red earlobes will produce brown eggs, and a chicken with white earlobes will produce white eggs.

Not all polar bears hibernate; only pregnant female polar bears do.

Superman: The Escape rollercoaster, located in California at Six Flags Magic Mountain, goes from 0 to 100 miles per hour in only 7 seconds.

Five thousandths of a millimeter is the tolerance of accuracy at the LEGO mould factories in Denmark.

2.5 cans of Spam are consumed every second in the United States.

In 1836, the Mexican General Santa Anna held an elaborate state funeral for his amputated leg.

A meteor has only destroyed one satellite, which was the European Space Agency's Olympus in 1993.

The Koala bear is not really a bear, but is really related to the kangaroo and the wombat.

The largest employer in the world is the Indian railway system in India, employing over 1.6 million people.

The word "comet" comes from the Greek word "kometes" meaning long hair and referring to the tail.

The hydra, which is related to the jellyfish, can grow its body back in a couple of days if it is cut in half.

Native Indians have been known to paint their doors blue, which they believe keeps the bad spirits out.

Before air conditioning was invented, white cotton slipcovers were put on furniture to keep the air cool.

It costs about 3 cents to make a $1 bill in the United States.

Colgate faced a big obstacle marketing its toothpaste in Spanish speaking countries. Colgate translates into the command "go hang yourself."

The cross bow was invented by the Chinese and records of its usage goes back to as far as the Three Kingdom Period (220 a.d.-280 A.D.).

It is estimated that by the end of 2000, there has been 142,600 tons of gold mined in the world.

One-third pound stalk of broccoli contains more vitamin C than 204 apples.

The Flintstones cartoon was the first thirty-minute cartoon to be aired during prime time.

The abbreviation Xmas for the word Christmas is of Greek origin. Since the word for Christ in the Greek language is Xristos, which starts with the letter "X," they started putting the X in place of Christ and came up with the short form for the word Christmas.

President Lyndon Johnson smoked three packs of cigarettes a day.

It takes 17 trees to make a ton of paper.

Statistically, if there are as few as 23 people in a room, there's a 50-50 chance that two of them will share a birthday.

Dipsomania refers to an insatiable craving for alcoholic beverages.

China has more English speakers than the United States.

Pitcher Darold Knowles once pitched all seven games in a World Series.

In a day, kids in the U.S. that are between the ages of 2 - 8 spend 28 minutes of their time coloring.

Herbert Hoover, who was the 31st president of the United Stated, turned over all the Federal salary checks he received to charity during the 47 years he was in government.

Macadamia nuts are not sold in their shells because it takes 300 pounds per square inch of pressure to break the shell.

Japan has approximately 200 volcanoes and is home to 10% of the active volcanoes in the world.

Before 1928, yo-yos used to be called bandalores in the United States.

The only South East Asian country that has never been colonized by a Western Power is Thailand.

The shortest war in history was between Zanzibar and England in 1896. Zanzibar surrendered after 38 minutes.

Irish Wolfhound dogs have a short lifespan and live about 7-8 years.

The climbing perch, a fish native to India, can walk on land.

When Queen Elizabeth I of England died she owned over 3,000 gowns.

Female alligators lay about 40 eggs that hatch in 60 - 70 days.

Emus cannot walk backwards.

The external tank on space shuttles is not painted. It is the only part of the shuttle that is lost after launch, so it is not necessary to worry about metal corrosion.

The most popular Twizzler candy flavor is strawberry.

The famous playboy Casanova (Giacomo Casanova) was a librarian for many years before he died.

The only species of turtle that lives in the open ocean is the sea turtle.

Toronto was the first city in the world with a computerized traffic signal system.

Seniors who drink a cup of coffee before a memory test score higher than those who drink a cup of decaffeinated coffee.

Venus is the only planet that rotates clockwise.

Some octopuses have been known to eat their arms off when they are exposed to stressful situations.   On average, 749 pounds of paper products is used by an American individual annually.

The skeleton of a spider is located on the outside of the body. The name for this is exoskeleton.

The letter J does not appear anywhere on the periodic table of the elements.

Over 200 varieties of watermelons are grown in the U.S.

The most dangerous job in the United States is that of a fisherman, followed by logging and then an airline pilot.

French soldiers during World War I had the nickname "poilu" which translates to "hairy one."

Spandex was invented in 1959 by Dupont. It can stretch 500 percent without breaking.

Former U.S. President William Taft converted the White House stable into a four car garage in 1909.

People living on the east coast prefer creamy peanut butter, while people living on the west coast prefer chunky peanut butter.

Some snails live on branches in trees.

The first two extra-inning All-Star games were won by Cardinal hitters Stan Musial and Red Schoendinst who slugged home runs.

Wilmer Mizell of the baseball Cardinals holds the record for walking the most batters in a game and pitching a shutout – 9.

Stan Musial also holds the record for hitting 5 home runs in a doubleheader.

The youngest pope was 11 years old.

Ducks on the outer edge of a group sleep with one eye open. The rest close both eyes.

There is a historical marker at St. Charles, Missouri that indicates it was where the nation's Interstate Highway System began. From St. Charles, it headed in two directions, east and west.

The cruise ship *S.S. Admiral*, on the St. Louis riverfront, was the world's largest boat traveling on inland waterways.

BALL OF STRING TRICK

Try to arrive at school early one day. Take a small ball of string with you. Find a student and ask him/her to hold one end of the string for a brief moment. Tell them you have to take the other end around the hall corner for a science experiment. Tell them it will only take a minute. After you go around the corner with the string, hand the ball of string to another student and ask them to hold it a moment. Tell them you are doing a science experiment but need to get your "stramulator." Tell them you'll be back in a minute. Disappear for a while and then come back, hidden behind a much larger classmate who is in on the joke. It won't take very long for one of the victims to start heading toward the other end of the string. You will want to be there (still hidden) to see the expression on their faces when they meet the person at the other end of the string.

This also might be a good way for you to "accidentally" meet a girl you see in school that you'd like to know better. Let your friend be the one who first hands the string to the girl and then takes it around the corner and gives the other end to you. The event will serve as an "ice breaker" and give you an excuse to introduce yourself and start talking to her.

HOW TO MAKE A GROTESQUE NOSE

You need a used rubber nipple from a baby bottle. Take a sharp knife and enlarge the hole in the end of the nipple. This is what you are going to breathe through. Get some of your mom's makeup and put it on the inside of the nipple to make it match the color of your skin as much as possible. Now shove the nipple up one nostril. You may find it a bit easier to breathe with your mouth while the nipple is up your nose. When you are through, you'll notice that your nose looks pretty grotesque. You can probably think of numerous ways to give your friends the willies when they look at your sorry condition. This might also be useful as part of a Halloween costume.

HOW TO OVERCOME MAN'S #1 FEAR

Man's #1 fear isn't snakes, heights, or spiders – it's getting up in front of a group and giving a speech. There comes a time when the need for a speech presents itself in almost everyone's life. It might be a eulogy at your grandpa's funeral; it could be a tribute to a wedding couple where you are the "best man;" it might be a public prayer.

I was quite the timid soul as a youth, and in a moment of temporary insanity

I chose to take a speech class in high school. Registering for this class also meant I would have a speaking part in the school play.

Needless to say I was petrified at the thought of getting in front of the class and giving a five minute talk to convince others to buy an imaginary product I was selling. And during my student teaching my mouth turned to cotton when my college evaluator showed up to watch me teach a class. But if you are going to survive as a teacher you lose those jitters pretty quick. Later on I obtained a real estate license and worked on weekends and summers selling real estate. After I retired from teaching I began writing books and giving talks for civic groups and library groups. Not long after that, my wife said that I missed my natural calling. "You should have been a salesman," she commented.

Now that is interesting because some of the better paying jobs around are in sales. Pharmaceutical sales people who call on doctors and hospitals make very good money. Yet there are few, if any, college courses designed to teach students salesmanship.

The secret of speaking in public is twofold – know your subject well and exude confidence. Let the audience know right off the bat that you are in charge and that what you are going to say will be worth their time. Dress well, keep your head up, maintain eye contact, and speak clearly and decisively. It's what all the experts have learned to do.

Be yourself, but in a slightly exaggerated form. Design a well formed speech with a beginning, middle and an end. Don't be apologetic, foul-mouthed, or crude. If your mouth gets a bit dry, bite the tip of your tongue and the saliva will flow. Try to throw in a funny story to illustrate a point. Most good speakers use their hands a bit to give the speech some animation. Adolph Hitler used to stand in front of a mirror for hours and practice his gestures. Say what you will about him, his speeches had a mesmerizing effect on his audiences. That is how he went from being a bum in Vienna to Time Magazine's Man of the Year in 1938.

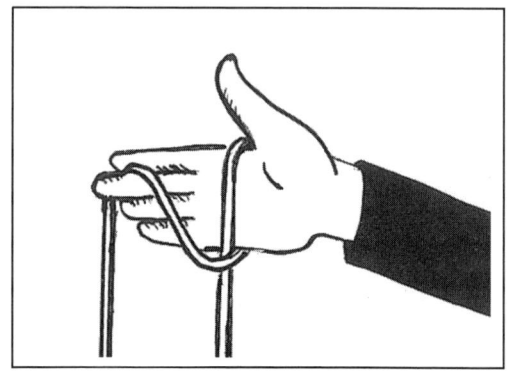

When you speak into a microphone, talk a bit over it; that way you should avoid that awful feedback noise. If you have a hand held mike, hold it near your chest and speak a bit over the top of it.

There is one last piece of advice. Before every speech remember the letters XYZ – Examine Your Zipper. There is nothing more embarrassing than to give a speech and later discover that your fly was open.

TYING A KNOT WITH ONE HAND

Like most rope tricks, this one becomes fairly easy with a little practice. Drape a thick string about 20 inches long over your dominant hand at the point where your fingers start jutting out from your hand. Now drape the tips of your string on your other arm and with your first and second fingers take hold of the string that is behind your hand. The part of the string behind your hand should come up to the front of your hand and be sitting in front of the string that drapes down from the palm of your hand. This is the only way a knot will form. You must pull the string from the back of your hand so it is in front of the other string. Now flick your wrist down so the loop on your hand will slide off from your fingers and the knot will automatically form as you maintain your hold to the end that is still grasped by your two forefingers.

WHOLE LOTTA SHAKIN' GOING ON

The San Francisco earthquake of 1906 was mere child's play. The Alaska quake of the 1960s hardly moved the state. The absolute worst earthquake in U.S. history, according to some experts, occurred in Southern Illinois and Missouri due to the New Madrid fault near the Missouri bootheel. The San Francisco earthquake affected some 60,000 square miles, but the New Madrid jolt affected an area sixteen times greater – over a million square miles.

The Big One struck on December 16, 1811, and a series of lesser aftershocks continued through February 7, 1812. The largest quake, estimated by scientists to have been an 8.2 on Richter's deadly scale, was strong enough to ring church bells in belfries as far away as Philadelphia. It even collapsed scaffolding erected around the Capitol Building in Washington, D.C.

The air was filled with the smell of sulfur, the screeching of birds, thunderous roaring sounds and dust that turned day into night. Most deaths occurred on the Mississippi where boats were swamped or struck by uprooted trees or collapsing banks. Some areas sank and formed new lakes. Mother Earth shrugged and earthen cliffs fell into the Mississippi; boats disintegrated and sank at their moorings. The tremors radiated all the way to Canada and as far south as Mexico. Part of Missouri broke away from its moorings and ended up in Kaintuck (Kentucky). Much of **New Madrid**, in the bootheel of Missouri, was destroyed. Five towns in three states were swallowed up. Nicholas Jarrot's two story mansion in **Cahokia**, the oldest brick structure in Illinois, sustained a large crack in a wall. Islands in the Mississippi disappeared, and new lakes were formed on previously solid ground. Ripley's Believe-It-Or-Not reported that the cataclysmic quake had caused the Mississippi River to *flow backwards* for a spell.

The steamboat *New Orleans* was traveling on the Mississippi at the time. That night the ship was moored to an island in the river. The next morning, the crew reported that the **quake caused the island to disappear**.

The earthquake, caused by slippage of tectonic plates, collapsed some bluffs along the Mississippi River and formed Reelfoot Lake on the Missouri-Kentucky-Tennessee borders. Because the area of southern Missouri was so sparsely settled, there were few deaths. The entire state of Missouri had a population of only about 4,000 at this time. This "prime event," the "great shakes" as old timers called it, was said to have shaken the ground in long waves that would rock and roll. Due to the basket-like construction of pioneer homes back then, where no iron or nails were used, there was minimal damage. Reports talked about horrible smells and dark sulfur vapors filling the air. One eyewitness said that the stock was very much disturbed and frightened; horses nickering, cattle lowing, hogs squealing, chickens squawking. The domestic animals all came running to the house for protection. One neighbor woman collapsed and died from fright.

The New Madrid quake turned solid ground into a swampy morass over-night. A region in Missouri near the area is named Pemiscot County and the name literally translates into "**liquid mud**." Sand boils – geysers of sand and water dredged up from the bowels of the earth – shot up more than 100 feet into the air. There are some places where evidence of these nearly 200 year-old boils still exist as infertile spots on Southern Missouri farms. They can readily be observed from the air.

Seismologists are on a continuing lookout for another big quake from the New Madrid fault. In 1990, a respected St. Louis climatologist named **Iben Browning** said there was a 50/50 chance that another quake would occur on or near December 3. He based the prediction on a series of circumstances including the gravitational pull of the moon. Everyone knows that earthquakes can't be predicted, but a media frenzy ensued and *millions of tax dollars were wasted* in useless drills and preparations for the impending disaster. School officials, terrified of criticism or lawsuits, caved in and ordered school buses with drivers to park beside the schools on standby in case evacuations were necessary.

The designated day came and went with nothing happening. T-shirt sellers were quick to capitalize on the non-event with clothing that shouted "**I Survived the 1990 Earthquake**."

W. Atkinson wrote a book in 1989 titled *The Next New Madrid Earthquake.* He predicts that a big new quake will

San Francisco 1906 quake

kill about 5,000 people and result in billions of dollars in property damage. The probability of a 6.5 magnitude quake hitting again by the year 2040 is rated at 90 percent. Such an event would destroy about 60 percent of Memphis, Tennessee. Southern Missouri is particularly vulnerable since few of its large buildings possess earthquake resistant construction.

In 1900, geologists concluded that the 1811 quake was due to slippage from great artesian pressure, which for centuries had undermined beds of clay by the steady removal of sand. Sinkholes were formed as far north as St. Louis.

Abraham Bird was a farmer near New Madrid who lost his land when it was swallowed up by the earthquake. The federal government issued him an "earthquake certificate" which entitled him to other unsettled land in Missouri.

New Madrid residents face the uncertain future with black humor. Stores sell T-shirts that read, "**It's Our Fault**." The historic and scientific aspects of the 1811 earthquake can best be studied by visiting the New Madrid Museum on 101 Main Street, New Madrid, Mo. (573-748-2378) By the way, the pronunciation is different from the capital of Spain. In Missouri it's pronounced Mad-rid instead of Muh-drid.

DO YOU NEED TO WORRY ABOUT KILLER BEES?

We wouldn't have to worry about this if some nincompoops in Brazil hadn't let some bees escape. Interestingly, there were no bees in our country until European settlers brought some with them when they came over on boats to colonize. The Native-Americans called them "**white man's flies**."

It all goes back to 1956 (this author's junior year in high school) when some bee keepers in Brazil imported 47 queen bees from Africa. They did this to see if these bees would give them an increase in honey output. Later on, some visitor removed the grid that kept the queen bees from escaping and 26 colonies fled the scene.

As the bees interbred with the local populations they slowly moved their way northward. The fierce name "killer bees" came to be applied to them because this new breed seemed more ferocious than the existing bees when it came to defending their hive. So far, over 1,000 deaths have been recorded due to attacks by these bees. As deaths from bee stings mounted, creative reporters started calling them "killer bees" to sell more newspapers. Keep in mind that more people die annually from bee stings than from snake bites.

These bees have arrived in the southern parts of Texas, Arizona, and New Mexico, but they probably won't go much farther north due to a colder climate. One way scientists think they can control killer bees is by drone flooding. With this technique European male drones are released in large quantities into areas where Queen bees like to go to mate. Scientists know these areas the same way we know that teenagers like to flock to malls for activities. This increases the chances that the new hives will not become Africanized.

HOW TO TIE THREE BASIC KNOTS

If you need to tie two ropes together that are approximately the same thickness, you should use what sailors call a **reef knot**. You can Google this knot for a diagram to make it easier. Lay one rope on the floor (or ground) and bend it at the end to form a narrow loop. Take your other piece of rope and start at the closed end of the other rope's loop. Start on the right side of the loop, going over the end and then under the right side. Now bring your rope across the two strands of the rope on the floor and then bring it under that rope.

When you get to the closed end of the loop bring it back on top. Now pull the two ends tight without letting any of the ends slip out of their position.

If you need to tie two ropes together of a different thick-ness you need what is called a **sheet bend**. Again, Google this knot for an illustration. Place the thicker rope on the floor and put a loop in the end but make sure that one end of the rope comes across the top of the other, forming a closed circle. Now take your smaller rope and start working at the end of the circle loop. Slip the rope under the loop and then take it over the rope where the other rope forms an X. Now slip it under the piece of straight rope on the right and then come back with it toward yourself and go over the two thick rope pieces and then tuck it under the circle loop end where you star-ted. When you finish, pull the knot tight without letting any loose ends slip through.

The last knot is called the **clove hitch** and it is used to attach a rope to a fixed item such as a pipe or a tree limb. Take your rope and drape one end of it over the horizontal pipe. Pull it toward you and then go over the pipe again, staying a bit to the left of your first loop. Take the rope over the pipe and come back with it by

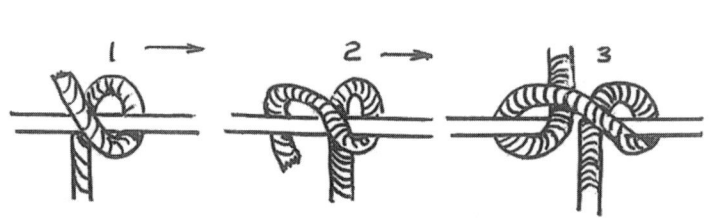

pulling back toward yourself. Now tuck your rope end under the top left loop and then pull everything snug.

MAKE YOUR OWN KAZOO

This is just about the simplest of all instruments to make. Take that cardboard tube at the end of a toilet paper roll and spray paint it to whatever color you wish. Now cut a piece of waxed paper 5 inches square. Place the waxed paper over one end of the tube and secure it in place with a rubber band. Hum into the open end and the waxed paper at the other end will vibrate, enhancing your tune. If this doesn't work, go to K-Mart and buy one for 97 cents.

HOW TO GET RID OF THE HICCUPS

There are many tried and true ways to get rid of the hiccups. If none of these seem to work, you can just wait it out and, most likely, they will go away on their own. Many of these recommendations were thought of by our pioneer ancestors who were a superstitious lot.

Try holding your breath for 60 seconds. Swallow a teaspoon of sugar. Jump up and down five times. Gulp down a glass of water. Breathe into a small brown paper bag for several minutes. (Or is that what you do if you hyperventilate? Oh, well, you might as well give it a try.) Eat a piece of bread

slowly. Have someone try to scare you by saying BOO! Try gargling water.
Take a drink of water from the far side of the rim of a glass. Careful . . . don't
spill. Count backward from 500. Have someone sneak up behind you and
scare you by popping a balloon. Have someone pinch you hard enough to
make you yell! If none of these work just go to bed and sleep for a half an
hour. When you wake up, you'll be just fine.

OPTICAL ILLUSION

Take one of those cardboard tubes from either a paper towel roll or a toilet
paper roll. Look through it with your right eye. Now take your left hand and
place it over the end of the tube with your palm facing you. Now, with both
eyes open stare at the point where the tube and the edge of your hand meet and
it will appear as if you have a hole in your hand.

HOW TO SPEAK PIG LATIN

This is a way to talk in code with your best friend. With a little practice
you'll be speaking it fluently and you can drive other people crazy with it
because they can't understand what you are saying. I did this with a close
friend when I was about 12 and it was a lot of fun. Don't keep doing this
forever because it wears on other people's nerves after a while.

Here is the formula. You simply move the first letter of the word to the end
and tack on the letters "ay" to it. Here's an example:

Arymay, ouldway ouyay ikelay aay isskay?

Mary, would you like a kiss?

HOW TO TREAT STINGS

It isn't hard to recognize if someone is allergic to a bee sting because it won't
take long for them to have difficulty breathing. If you see this happening, call
911 immediately. Ask the person affected if they have anything with them to
counteract the effects of the sting – a pill or an injection.

If they have no serious reaction simply follow a few easy steps to make them
feel more comfortable. Holding a cool cloth to the sting will be soothing.
Rubbing the affected area lightly with an ice cube is also helpful.

If it is a bee sting you should pull out the stinger with tweezers. Follow that
up with a solution of baking soda. Wasps don't leave their stingers behind so
all you need to do is to dab some vinegar on their sting.

If the sting is from a jellyfish, rinse the sting area and put calamine lotion on
it. Much worse than the jellyfish is the Portuguese Man of War. This is a
dangerous sea creature recognizable as it floats on the water due to its purplish-
blue bladder. Avoid this creature like the plague.

HOW TO MAKE A SQUEAL STICK

Take two strips of wood that are about 6 inches long, one inch wide and a half an inch thick.

Mark the center on each stick and then cut a notch all the way across the width of each piece. Each notch should be ¾ of an inch on each side of the center mark for a total length of 1 ½ inches long. Make the depth of the cut 1/16th of an inch. Have your dad or another adult help you with these cuts. They can either be made with a saw or a knife. Take a rubber band 3 ½ inches long and about 3/16 wide, unstretched. Stretch it lengthwise over both ends of one stick. Make sure it is flat and that it runs over the middle of the part you notched out. Place the other stick on top of the other, so the two notched areas are face to face. Use two smaller rubber bands wrapped 2 or 3 times around each end to hold the entire contraption together.

When you are ready to test your instrument hold it in front of your mouth

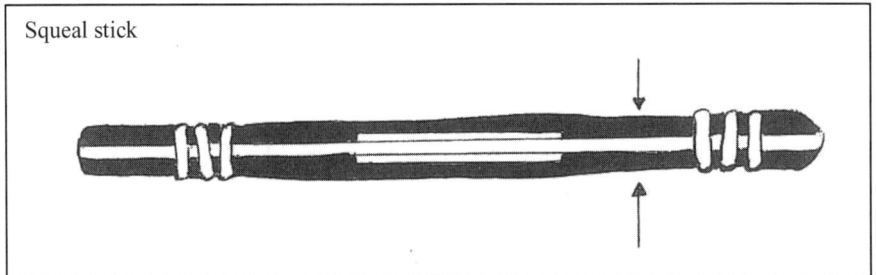

Squeal stick

with your lips over the dip in the center. Blow gently and you should get a high pitched scream that sounds like an animal being attacked at a watering hole by a pack of hyenas.

You might want to go outside and conceal yourself in some bushes and make your weird sounds. No telling what kind of strange animals might be attracted to your noises.

HOW TO REPAIR A BIKE FLAT

When I was a young boy we used to take old car inner tubes and cut them up to make rubber guns. Then we would play cops and robbers with our guns. This was back in the days when there was no such thing as tubeless tires. Our ammunition was a strip of inner tube tied in the middle. Then we would stretch the strip over one end of a wooden block and attach it to the other end that had a trigger mechanism. If you got hit with one of these rubber bands you were considered dead and out of the game. This was the forerunner of paintball.

A bicycle from 1950

THE NEW

monark

All of the bicycles I ever owned were hand-me-downs so it was important that I knew how to take a bike apart and be able to reassemble it if a part was broken. Knowing how to fix inner tubes that went flat was also a necessary skill.

If your bike tire goes flat, turn the bicycle upside down and pull off the wheel. Take a valve stem cover that has a stem remover on it and use that device to take out the valve stem and let all the air out of the tire. Now take a flathead screwdriver and insert it between the inner edge of the tire and the rim. Push up and out to pull part of the tire up and out so that it goes over the rim instead of inside it. Leave that screwdriver in place and take another one to go all the way around the rest of the rim until the entire tire rim is outside the spoked rim. You should now be able to reach in and pull the inner tube out.

If you don't have a patch kit, buy one at a sporting goods store or bicycle shop. The top of the can should be very rough. Use this to lightly roughen the area around the puncture. Roughen an area slightly larger than the patch. This allows the glue to hold better to the rubber. Squirt some of the glue solution over the area where the patch will go. Use your finger to smooth the glue over the entire area. Don't get it too thick and don't lick it off your finger. Wipe your finger off with a shop cloth (one of those square red things). Allow the glue to set for about four minutes and then set the patch in place and smooth it down to get rid of any air bubbles. There may be a backing on the patch that you will have to pull off. Press down firmly around all the edges of the patch for at least a minute.

Be sure to read the instructions on your repair kit and follow them if they are different from mine. In my day we set fire to the glue on the patch area and let it burn about four seconds and then blew out the fire. Then we applied what was called a *hot patch*. It was pretty cool!

Before you insert the tube back in the tire, apply a light coating of French chalk so it doesn't stick to something and get pinched inside the tire. After the tube is inside the tire, adjust it so the valve is sticking perfectly straight out the rim hole. Reinsert the valve stem and inflate. Pump up the tire to its recommended level and keep a watchful eye on it for a while.

HOW TO MAKE A RAFT

Find or cut four wooden poles 6 feet long and about 4 inches in diameter. You will also need three cross poles that are 4 inches in diameter but only 4 feet long. Additionally, you will need nine empty mineral water bottles with caps that secure firmly. You will also need lots of nylon cord or strong twine to lash the poles together. Form a rectangle with the two long poles and two of the shorter poles. Lash all four joints together as indicated in the diagram. Now take the extra short pole and lash it in the center of the raft - crossways. Take the last two long poles and lash them side-by-side parallel to the other long poles and in the center of the raft. The distance between them should be just enough to accommodate a water bottle. Now lash all 9 empty containers in place at various points around the raft.

Test your raft by taking it out in shallow water. If it doesn't seem buoyant enough, add some more empty water bottles.

Always wear a life jacket anytime you go out in the water.

HOW TO HYPNOTIZE A CHICKEN

I grew up in a city of 82,000 but we lived on the distant edge of town. In 1945 my parents bought a house that had a chicken coop and a fenced-in area of the back yard so for several years we raised chickens. We had one bantam rooster and about eight hens. Anyone who's been around chickens, or spent a lot of time on a farm, is probably familiar with this trick. Those who've never heard of this will be amazed to see a chicken lie perfectly still after these instructions are followed. No one quite knows how or why this works, but it's fun to watch, and it can even be of use if you need to keep a chicken in one spot for a minute while you go do something else.

Find a flat surface such as a sidewalk. You'll need a piece of chalk and a chicken. You can also do it on bare earth using a stick in a pinch. Catch your chicken but be gentle with it. Hold the chicken in one hand by

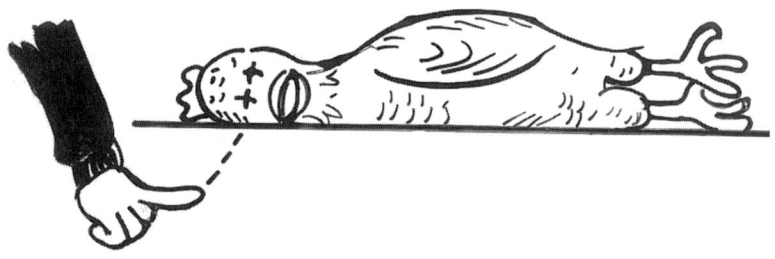

both feet and place it down on its side so that its breast is carrying most of its weight and rests on the sidewalk or dirt. The fowl's head/beak will therefore also be on the sidewalk/dirt as you continue to hold its feet.

Wave the chalk in front of the chicken to get its attention. Then draw a line 12" to 18" STRAIGHT OUTWARD from the end of the chicken's beak. If you use bare earth or ground, use a sharp stick to draw the line.

The chicken will go into a hypnotic trance and cease to struggle. If you release its legs, it'll just lie there, mesmerized by the straight line for a time. Eventually, the chicken will "come to" and take off running.

For those who have never seen this done it is an absolutely amazing thing.

AMAZING WAR HERO STORY

Illinoisans had an early hero in World War II. Edward "Butch" O'Hare grew up in south St. Louis. His father thought the young teen lacked focus and discipline and sent him to the **Western Military Academy in Alton**. Butch was there the same time as Paul Tebbets of Quincy, Illinois, the man who flew the atomic bomb-equipped *Enola Gay* over Hiroshima.

Butch was a fighter pilot assigned to the aircraft carrier *Lexington* in the South Pacific. One day his entire squadron was sent on a mission. After he was airborne, he looked at the fuel gauge on his F-4-F Wildcat and realized that someone had forgotten to top off his fuel tank after his last mission. He would not have enough fuel to complete his new mission and get back to his ship. His flight leader told him to return to the carrier. Reluctantly, he dropped out of formation and headed back to the fleet.

As he was returning to the mother ship, he spotted some-thing that turned his blood cold – a squadron of Japanese bombers was speeding its way toward the American fleet. The American fighters were gone on a sortie and the fleet was all but defenseless. He couldn't reach the squadron and bring them back in time to save the fleet. Nor was there time to warn the fleet of the impending danger. There was only one thing to do. He must somehow divert the enemy from the fleet. Laying aside all thoughts of personal safety, he dove into the formation of

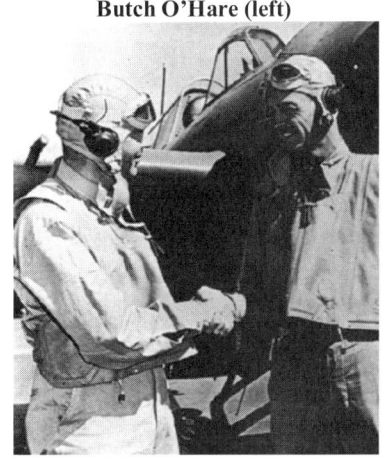

Butch O'Hare (left)

Japanese planes. Wing-mounted .50 calibers blazed as he charged in, attacking one surprised enemy plane and then another. Butch weaved in and out of the now broken formation and fired at as many planes as possible until finally all his ammunition was spent. Undaunted, he continued the assault. He dove at the planes trying to clip off a wing or a tail, in hopes of damaging as many planes possible and rendering them unfit to fly. He was desperate to do anything he could to keep them from reaching the American ships.

The men on the carriers saw what was happening and a few planes were sent airborne to assist O'Hare. Finally, the exasperated Japanese squadron took off in another direction. Deeply relieved, Butch O'Hare and his tattered fighter limped back to the carrier. Upon arrival he reported in and related the event surrounding his return. The film from the camera mounted on his plane told the tale. It showed the extent of Butch's daring attempt to protect the fleet. He had become an ace in a single day, destroying five enemy dive bombers. This made him **the first American pilot to shoot down five enemy aircraft in a single day**.

That was in February of 1942, and for that action he became the Navy's first Ace of the war and the first naval aviator to be awarded the Congressional Medal of Honor. He was given a huge welcome home parade in St. Louis. A year later the "Savior of the Lexington" was killed in aerial combat at age 29, shot down by "friendly" fire. Today, O'Hare Airport in Chicago is named in tribute to the courage of this great man. So the next time you're in O'Hare visit the memorial with his statue and Medal of Honor. It is located between terminals 1 and 2.

MAKE A TIN CAN TELEPHONE

Tin can telephones were those kind of simple toys when I was a youth that cost almost nothing, was simple to make, and gave us hours and hours of pleasure. It is believed that Alexander Graham Bell made a tin can telephone and this is what gave him the idea for the electronic telephone he later invented.

The tin can was patented in 1810 by the English inventor Peter Durand, based on experimental work by the Frenchman Nicolas Appert. Durand did not produce any food cans himself, but sold his patent to two other Englishmen, Bryan Donkin and John Hall, who set up a commercial canning factory, and by 1813 were producing their first canned goods for the British Army.

Early cans were sealed with lead soldering, which led to a few cases of lead poisoning. Famously, in the Arctic expedition of Sir John Franklin in 1845, **crew members suffered from severe lead poisoning after three years of eating canned food**.

Modern tin cans are actually made of steel and are merely coated with a thin layer of tin.

Here's how to make your listening device. Remove one end completely from each of two tin cans, and leave one end intact. The end that has been removed will be the phone's "receiver," and the intact end will hold the phone's "wire."

Turn one can upside-down, so that its intact end is facing up. Drive a small nail through the center of the intact end using a hammer. The nail should make a neat hole in the end of the can. Repeat with the other can.

Obtain a piece of string about 22 feet long. Thread one end of the string through one of the nail holes. Make a knot in the string on the inside of the can, so that the string remains attached to the can. Repeat with the other can and the other end of string. The tin cans should now be tied to either end of the string.

Hold one tin can and give the other tin can to someone else. Walk away from each other until the string between the cans is taut.

Speak into the open end of one tin can while your partner listens to the open end of his/her tin can. Switch roles, and listen to the open end of your tin can while your partner speaks into the open end. This neat toy also demonstrates the principle that sound travels through solid materials. You might also want to try using bell wire instead of string.

HOW TO MAKE A WATER XYLOPHONE

This project will show a principle of physics that the more matter that sound must travel through, the lower the pitch. Conversely, the less matter the higher the pitch. You can make a water xylophone to prove this principle. Find 8 identical glasses and fill them with different amounts of water. Arrange them in a row starting with the glass that has the least amount of water to the one that is nearly full. Tap each container with a spoon to see what pitch you get. Experiment with the water levels until you can play a tune that resembles "Mary Had a Little Lamb."

10 inch 1949 Zenith television

A BUZZ FROM THE GOOD OL' DAYS

Not long ago my wife and I were eating breakfast with a group of friends at a restaurant. A pesky fly was flitting about and every once in a while it would be necessary to shoo him away from our food. It made me think back to the days of my youth when restaurants had a quick solution for the problem – **fly paper**.

Fly paper hung from ceilings in barns, kitchens, restaurants, ice cream parlors, porches – just about anywhere flies gathered in squadrons for strafing missions against humans. They would land on the strip, become hopelessly stuck, and eventually die from starvation. Now fly paper looked pretty much like someone took a roll of Kodak film, let it uncoil, then hung it from the ceiling. One side of the roll was coated with a sweet smelling sticky substance that attracted flies and held them fast when they landed. Coated with dead flies and squirming lives ones, it wasn't pretty, but it was effective. You don't see them in restaurants anymore. I guess the health department considers them unsightly and unsanitary.

Before fly paper was invented our ingenious forefathers came up with a solution for dealing with flies at mealtime – **shoo fly pie**. This rich dessert was first concocted by the Amish, sometimes referred to as the Pennsylvania Dutch. It consists of a gooey mixture of molasses beneath a crumb topping. During mealtime, a small portion of this would be set in a corner of the room. The flies wouldn't bother the goings on at the meal because they were preoccupied with a different and more irresistible food.

In the 1920s, there was a product called Flit. "Quick, Henry - the Flit," was a well known advertising phrase at the time. Magazine ads featured a cartoon "Henry" character busily killing the critters wherever he went by shooting them with poisonous clouds from a small garden sprayer.

To my young adolescent brain the Nobel Prize should have been given to the man who invented window screens and screen doors. What a boon to mankind. Since almost no one had air conditioning in 1950, everyone left windows and doors open for summertime ventilation. Had it not been for screens, flies

200

would have been a huge problem. Mothers, of course, were far more vigilant about this than youngsters. Many a time our household would reverberate with a thunderous, "Sonny, close that front screen door; you weren't reared in a barn!"

My childhood friends and I devised an ingenious way of killing flies with rubber bands. Yes, rubber bands. Sometimes we sat near a porch railing and waited for a fly to land. Then we took a rubber band that had been cut and pulled one end back, much as you would a sling shot. After taking dead aim at the fly, we let one end go and quick as lightning its zooming tip would cut the fly in two. The rubber band was a bit messy, but about 95 percent effective. It was also considered more civilized than pulling wings off butterflies, which some young boys were known, on occasion, to do.

Around 1900, the fly problem in the metro St. Louis area was so bad that **public schools offered youngsters a penny for every 100 dead flies that they brought to class**. I suspect that these children probably used old-fashioned fly swatters to collect their bounty.

When we visited our farm relatives in Kentucky, I noticed that over in the dairy stall the milk cow was perpetually annoyed by flies. Bossie's only line of defense was her tail which she swished in near perpetual motion. This made milking often hazardous since you could be squeezing and tugging on a spigot and suddenly get smacked in the face by the cow's tail. Now this wasn't like getting hit with a feather duster. The texture of a bovine's tail in no way resembles a feather duster. Think more like one of those lashes administered to seaman Alan Ladd in *Two Years Before the Mast*.

My dad was quite adept at killing flies with a rolled up newspaper. However, even a good newspaper like the *St. Louis Star* was reduced to shreds after about 22-25 swats. Our local paper, the *East St. Louis Journal*, became tattered more quickly.

Flies were also an annoyance for picnickers, horses, cats and dogs. An outdoor meal attracted flies for miles around. Some of them even came from different ZIP codes.

It seems as if flies aren't as big a nuisance anymore. My wife and I have solved the problem by keeping several cats as pets. They're pretty good at trapping the flies against the window and then eating them. I try not to think about that when one of them occasionally saunters over to me and gives me a lick on my cheek.

CHARLES LINDBERGH'S 1927 FLIGHT

Every schoolboy should know the story of Charles Lindbergh because it is about courage and determination. Charles Lindbergh was an early aviation pilot who sometimes did barnstorming and worked for Robertson Aircraft of St. Louis as a mail pilot. He flew the mail route from St. Louis to Chicago, often following Chicago & Alton Railroad tracks to keep from getting lost.

A New York man offered a $25,000 prize for the first man to fly solo from New York to Paris across the Atlantic Ocean. In 1925, the twenty-five year-old Minnesotan sought financial backing for his endeavor. After failing to interest

New Yorkers in the venture, he sought help from a fellow St. Louis aviator, A. B. Lambert - the pioneer for whom Lambert Airport is named. **Lindbergh's dare-devil reputation** preceded him. He had barely survived four crashes already and was remembered notoriously for the dangerous stunt of flying under the Eads and Municipal bridges at an air show. The St. Louis Flying Club, the *Post-Dispatch*, and the *Globe-Democrat* all refused to have anything to do with an inexperienced long distance pilot flying an underpowered single engined plane. Finally, the fledgling Ryan Aircraft Company of San Diego agreed to build Lindbergh's plane for about $10,000. The plane had an oversized wingspan for added lift to counteract the weight of the extra fuel needed to cross the Atlantic. Since the huge fuel tank was directly in front of the pilot, **there was no windshield. To see where he was going, Lindbergh used a periscope**.

All of the other pilots who planned to compete for the prize were more experienced and had co-pilots with them. Richard Byrd was one such entrant, having already accomplished the feat of flying over the North Pole. Charles Nungesser and Francois Coli, two flying veterans from the Great War, took off from Paris on May 8, were spotted over Ireland, and **were never seen again**.

While flying his 5,250 pound plane from San Diego to New York, "Slim" Lindbergh broke the coast-to-coast record in his pewter-colored plane by 5 ½ hours. Lindbergh dubbed his 28 foot-long bird the *Spirit of St. Louis* to honor his adopted city. Meanwhile, another contestant (Noel Davis) was killed during a practice run.

While Richard Byrd and Clarence Chamberlin hesitated because of a slight drizzle, Lindbergh took off (May 20, 1927) in his monoplane at Roosevelt Field, his aircraft barely clearing obstacles at the end of the runway. For the

next 33 ½ hours, Lindbergh flew the Great Circle Route by dead reckoning, an incredible feat, ultimately landing at Le Bourget Airfield in Paris, France.

The entire world went crazy over "Lucky Lindy." In an age of ballyhoo and cynicism, the masses had a real hero who didn't drink anything stronger than coffee. President Coolidge sent a cruiser to bring him back home. Most thought it should have been a battleship. He was given a ticker-tape parade in NYC and a special banquet in St. Louis to honor his achievement. They even named a dance for him – **the Lindy Hop**. St. Louis was bursting with a pride that hadn't been seen since 1904. Foreign nations issued stamps in his honor. Lindy became a goodwill ambassador to Nicaragua and

Mexico. In Mexico, he met his future wife, Ann Morrow, the daughter of the U.S. Ambassador to that country.

Unfortunately, Lindbergh and his wife were to suffer through the personal heartbreaking tragedy of having their baby kidnapped and murdered. A German immigrant, Bruno Hauptmann, was executed for that crime. Subsequently, the Lindbergh Kidnap Law was enacted which allowed for the feds to intervene when state lines were crossed. Further, the death penalty was invoked if the kidnap victim was harmed in any way.

Lindbergh's reputation suffered when he became an isolationist in the 1930s and opposed war preparedness measures by President Roosevelt. Lindbergh saw limited participation in World War II and managed to shoot down one Japanese plane.

THE MURDER OF ELIJAH LOVEJOY

Alton mob attacking Lovejoy warehouse (ISHS)

In 1836, **St. Louis** enhanced its reputation for violence in the Francis McIntosh Affair. McIntosh, a mulatto steward on a steamboat, was arrested after a skirmish down on the river levee. He was charged with interfering with the duties of law enforcement officials. McIntosh broke free as he was being taken to jail. He killed George Hammond by cutting his throat and then seriously wounded the other officer, William Mull.

Historian James N. Primm says McIntosh was captured and sent to jail where an angry crowd of about 2,000 people gathered. They rushed the jail, overpowered the sheriff and took the prisoner out to hang him. When someone in the crowd suggested that hanging was too good for him, they took him to a tree at 10th and Market and bound him to it. A fire was lit, and **he was slowly roasted alive**. One eyewitness to the event said the flames caused his bowels to fall out of his body. Someone in the crowd asked if he "felt any pain," and he replied with an anguished *yes*. He expired after about eighteen minutes of torture. None of the newspaper accounts of the incident ever identified any specific persons as the ringleaders, and no one was prosecuted for the crime. The *Alton Telegraph* was highly critical of the lack of government initiative in stopping the mob. And Elijah Lovejoy, editor of a St. Louis religious weekly, incurred the wrath of locals by keeping the issue alive week after week. Judge Luke Lawless (actual name, no kidding) held a grand jury probe that, to no one's surprise, indicted no one.

Lovejoy stepped up his attacks and lambasted Judge Lawless and the jury. He inferred that Judge Lawless's faulty logic was attributable to his Irish birth and Catholic upbringing. After Lovejoy's editorial attacks, his office was twice broken into and damaged. He opted to move to a *safer* location in **Alton**, Illinois, 20 miles north of St. Louis and located in a "free" state.

Lovejoy was a Yankee New Englander who grew up in a religious home where the precocious youth learned to read from the Bible at age four. He graduated from college, taught school for a spell and then his restless bones compelled him to head west. He arrived in St. Louis at age 27. St. Louis was a rough and tumble city in a state where slavery had been extended by the Missouri Compromise of 1820.

At this point in time, Lovejoy was no abolitionist. He personally hated slavery but thought abolitionism was too extreme and divisive. More than anything else, he was interested in spreading the gospel to the "godless" frontier. In 1833, backed by a coalition of St. Louis businessmen, Lovejoy printed his first issue of the *St. Louis Observer*. Lovejoy was an ardent Presbyterian, and he frequently attacked Baptists with his scathing pen for their unorthodox views. Like so many other Protestants, he thought Catholics were destined for hell.

The McIntosh affair and memories of degrading slave auctions hardened his views toward slavery. He increasingly began to preach against and publish articles denouncing slavery. Missourians, who would later run the Mormons out of their state, did not take kindly to these acerbic criticisms. St. Louisans, in particular, did not take kindly to being called sinners because they supported slavery. After a particularly inflammatory article, a large mob gathered and wrecked his print shop in 1836. Dismayed, Lovejoy left for Alton where he thought his views would be more acceptable.

Part of Lovejoy's press at the *Alton Telegraph* office

These high expectations were quickly dashed, for as soon as his printing press arrived from St. Louis, another mob smashed it and threw it into the Mississippi. A new press was ordered and, for about a year, Lovejoy was able to continue his divine mission. He further enraged the locals and St. Louisans when he broached the subject of sex, a hitherto unprintable subject for the press. He castigated slave owners for immorality by having sex with their female slaves and producing mulatto children. The subject of miscegenation (mixing of races) was a touchy subject with southerners.

Alton, the largest city in the state, was on the northern fringe of downstate Illinois that was referred to as Egypt. Pro-slavery sentiment was so strong in southern Illinois that they came very close to amending the state constitution to allow slavery back in 1824. Lovejoy further angered people when he said the Depression of 1837 might be God's way of punishing the people of **Alton**.

One hot August night in 1837, another mob, filled with agitators from St. Louis, destroyed Lovejoy's press. When a new one arrived a month later, it too was pitched into the river and destroyed. A fourth press arrived on November 7 and this time a group of armed supporters moved the equipment to a stone warehouse near the riverfront. But tempers festered and flared when opponents gathered in local taverns and, aided by "Demon Rum," worked themselves into a frenzy. An armed mob of about 150 men gathered and, bearing torches, marched on the warehouse. At first the crowd was content to shout epithets and hurl paving stones. Soon nearly every window in the place was broken.

Lovejoy was inside with fifteen of his loyal and armed supporters. Lovejoy refused to surrender the press and soon shots rang out. Supporters at Alton's First Presbyterian Church rang the bell to alert law enforcement officials, but no help was forthcoming. Alton's mayor, John Krum, tried to stop the violence, but no one heeded him.

The mob then raised a ladder to the roof so they could set it on fire, but Lovejoy and a few others ran outside to push it aside. **A number of shots rang out and Lovejoy was mortally wounded.** He managed to struggle back inside where he died from his wounds. He had been shot five times. Lovejoy's supporters fled the warehouse and the mob finished the dastardly deed by destroying the press and throwing it into the river.

No one was ever convicted of Lovejoy's murder. His friends buried him the next day on, what would have been, his 35th birthday. Owen Lovejoy, his brother, took up the cause and became a leading abolitionist. Alton paid a heavy price for Lovejoy's murder. Once the largest city in the state, its growth now stagnated. A dark pall hung over the once bustling metropolis. Prominent townspeople, who had been supporters of Lovejoy, moved away and the economic and population boom which had marked previous decades was reversed.

In 1915, a piece of Lovejoy's press was salvaged from the river. It is now proudly on display in the office of the *Alton Telegraph.* Alton since has erected a beautiful monument in his honor. When the SIUE campus was built in Edwardsville, Illinois, the university library was named for him.

The Lovejoy incident illustrated just how much the country was becoming divided over slavery. His murderers intended to silence him, but their heinous crime had the opposite effect. His death played a significant role in pricking the conscience of a nation and awakened it to the evils of slavery. **History's most outstanding example of martyrdom, for the cause of freedom of the press, happened in St. Louis and southern Illinois.**

BUILDING THE FAMED EADS BRIDGE

The Mississippi River: discovered by Desoto, explored by Marquette and Jolliet, navigated by Mark Twain, spanned by James B. Eads. In 1795, Captain James Piggott built the first ferry service to operate between St. Louis and Illinoistown (East St. Louis). He died in 1799 and his widow eventually sold out to other interests. By 1820, Samuel Wiggins had gained control of the company and made a fortune after being granted a monopoly of the transport business by the Illinois legislature.

The first railroad from the East (B&O) made its way into Illinoistown in 1857. As more and more railroads arrived, they were all forced to terminate at Illinoistown for lack of a bridge. The Wiggins Company charged exorbitant rates to transfer goods from boxcars and ferry them across the Mississippi to St. Louis. In 1870, responding to the threat of a bridge being built, Wiggins installed inclines at Choteau Avenue to enable railroad cars to be run onto barges equipped with rails.

St. Louis merchants were so frustrated by the expenses incurred in the movement of goods across the river that they formed a corporation with the intent of building a bridge to circumvent the Wiggins ferry monopoly. Washington Avenue was chosen as the site for the foot of the bridge because it was wider than most other St. Louis east-west streets. Washington Avenue is the second oldest street in St. Louis.

Another source of growing pressure for a bridge came from the cotton trade. St. Louis was ranked third, behind New Orleans and Savanna, in the cotton business. The St. Louis Cotton Compress Company was founded by J.W. Paramore and had a plant on the St. Louis levee that was the **largest of its kind in the world.** (Paramore and several others were responsible for founding the Cotton Belt Railroad.) Cotton Compress occupied fifteen acres and had another large warehouse across the river in East St. Louis. It took southern cotton bales that weighed five hundred pounds and squeezed them with hydraulic presses down to a thickness of nine inches. The smaller cotton bales were then shipped by rail to New York and cotton mills in New England.

Another disadvantage to the ferry monopoly is that there were times, during the months of January and February, when the river froze over and the eight boats that belonged to Wiggins couldn't operate.

The St. Louis and Illinois Bridge Company was formed in 1867 by Edgar Ames, Charles Dickson, and others, with James B. Eads as its chief engineer. A rival group formed the Illinois and St. Louis Company, headed by the noted Chicago architect and bridge builder, Lucius Boomer. It was referred to in documents as the Boomer Company. The Boomer design called for a span farther north supported by five piers while the Eads plan called for only two with an unheard of distance of 515 feet between the piers.

The powerful Wiggins Ferry monopoly saw both bridges as a threat to its future growth and used its considerable influence to undermine efforts to build them.

A fierce rivalry existed between Chicago and St. Louis back then. There is evidence to suggest that Boomer had no immediate plans for building a bridge at St. Louis and the company's proposal was merely a smoke screen. Many in the Illinois state legislature wanted such a bridge to be built at Alton, not East St. Louis.

After months of legal wrangling, the two companies merged with Eads as the principal stockholder. The bridge was financed with three-fifths of the bonds being sold to Europeans and eastern U.S. investors, while the remainder

206

was sold to local investors. The finished cost of the bridge was around ten million dollars.

According to historian James Neal Primm, James Buchanan Eads built ironclads for the North during the Civil War and, before that, ran salvage operations on the Mississippi. **Eads was also a cousin to President Buchanan**. A self-taught engineer, he developed a diving bell for the salvage operations. His fifteen years in this business gave him thorough knowledge of the river and its tricky currents. Eads personally made about 500 trips below the water. **What a thrill it must have been, in 1859 to actually walk on the bottom of the Mississippi River**.

Salvage profits were good since ship owners offered 50 percent of the take on salvaged goods. Eads (1820-1887) was the perfect person to build the bridge because of his knowledge and talent.

By 1867, work had begun on the bridge and Eads reached bedrock, laying the first 3,000-pound Grafton lime-stone for the western pier. By 1869, excavation had begun on the east pier of the bridge. By 1870, both piers were protruding above the water line. The west pier was 70 feet deep and the east pier was 110 feet deep. In 1871, both piers were completed and work was started on the superstructure. A tornado that year caused some damage to the bridge work.

The piers caused new currents in the river, forcing the Wiggins Ferry Company to move its riverfront operations in St. Louis/East St. Louis farther south.

Eads and his assistant, Colonel Henry Flad, used carbon steel and a new chrome steel for some of the bridge-work and the arched-tube sections. Unfortunately, American steel companies were unable to meet Eads' requirement and he was forced to use wrought iron on much of the bridge.

Of the roughly 600 men who worked on the bridge, fourteen died as a result of the bends.

Partially completed Eads Bridge (Missouri Historical Society)

About 118 suffered severely from the mysterious disease caused by going below water level in caissons with compressed air, and then coming back to the surface too quickly. **Caisson disease**, as it was called, was caused by nitrogen forming in the bloodstream during decompression. Many of the workers began wearing copper bracelets to ward off the mysterious illness.

The bridge had three spans of 497, 515 and 497 feet respectively. The roadway was 34 feet wide and there were two footways each eight feet wide for pedestrians.

Andrew Carnegie, a substantial investor in the Bridge Company, provided much of the iron and steel with his own company.

In early 1874, St. Louisan U.S. Grant made a personal inspection of the bridge and fearlessly walked out with Eads on planks laid on the superstructure.

By April of 1874, struts, braces and the upper roadway were completed. A 4,480 ft. train tunnel was built on the west end to take traffic past the downtown area of St. Louis.

The bridge was completed by the end of June. There were many fears that the distance between the piers was too great and that it would not support rail traffic designed for the lower deck below the main roadway. One of **the first to test the bridge was John Robinson, an African-American, who walked across it leading an elephant. Strange as it may seem, there was a common belief back then that elephants had an uncanny sixth sense that made them balk at going across an unsafe structure**.

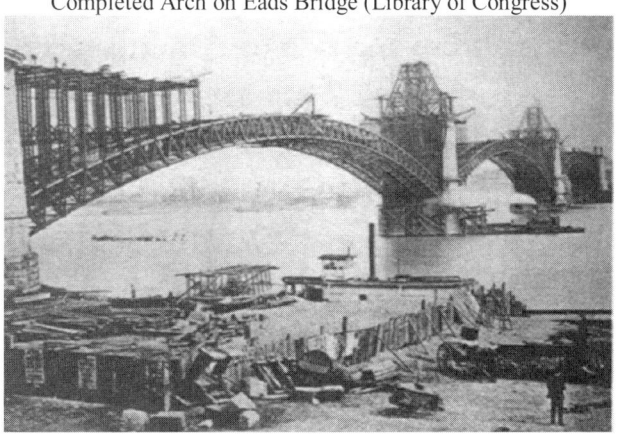

Completed Arch on Eads Bridge (Library of Congress)

Next, a fully loaded train went across. On July 2, fourteen locomotives with loaded tenders were parked in the middle of the bridge, convincing everyone that the bridge would hold.

A huge 4th of July opening ceremony was officiated by President Grant. Symbolic figures were painted on a canvas, signifying Illinois and Missouri shaking hands. It was a symbolic wedding of East and West. Missouri Governor Beveridge was a featured speaker at the dedication.

Ironically, the bridge did not put the Wiggins Ferry Company out of business. It survived until 1913 by reducing rates and by giving cases of whiskey to those who used their services.

Eads, who had never before built a bridge, was quickly hailed as one of the greatest engineers of modern times. Roebling, who later built the Brooklyn Bridge, admittedly used many of Eads's ideas for his project.

INCREDIBLE FACTS: In 1898, the Eads Bridge, **the first people/traffic bridge to span the Mississippi**, became the first bridge to be depicted on a U.S. stamp when it was featured as part of a Trans-Mississippi issue.

In its heyday, the Eads Bridge carried **more railroad freight than any other bridge in the world.**

ST. LOUIS WOMAN POPULARIZES THE OUIJA BOARD

The Ouija game, invented shortly before the turn of the century, was first met by the public with mild interest. The name was derived from the French and German words for *yes* –oui and ja. It became a sensation only after Mrs. John (Pearl) Curran of **Mound City, Illinois** began making fantastic claims in 1913. She told others that the board enabled her to get in touch with the spirit of **a woman killed a hundred years earlier by Indians** in the New England area. This deceased woman, by the name of Patience Worth, now proceeded to dictate to Mrs. Curran thousands of words of poetry and prose that also produced six novels on the eve of World War I. Mrs. Curran eventually left Mound City and moved to St. Louis.

In 1919, the American Society for Psychical Research invited Mrs. Curran to come to New York and give a public demonstration. She did, giving an impressive performance before a large audience, receiving words and messages from Confucius and Walt Whitman.

Skeptics, of course, called this housewife with the world's busiest Ouija board delusional. They claimed the long-departed Patience Worth was but a figment of Mrs. Curran's imagination. Harvard Psychologist William James explained the phenomenon by comparing her to rare persons with an "alternating personality" who could sit down at a piano and, with no previous training, play a concerto.

Debunkers claimed that Pearl had this poetry and prose writing ability all along, but hid it so that some day she could make a big splash on the literary scene. Yet Pearl was a woman of limited education, having quit school after completing the eighth grade.

Mrs. Curran went to New York once again in 1928, this time for an audience at St. Marks in the Bouwerie. By now her message of spiritualism was very popular, and she had quite a following. She performed magnificently, producing poems on split-second notice in response to requests from the audience. Mrs. Curran grew quite wealthy from her enigmatic abilities.

As historian Paul Sann explains in his 1967 *Fads and Follies* book, "Miss Patience Worth of New England never called to the bench for a pinch hitter, so the Niagara of words finally dried up when Mrs. Curran died in December of 1937 at age forty-six." The *St. Louis Globe-Democrat* used the following title to introduce her obituary: "Patience Worth is Dead." Was this a case of afterlife communication with the dead or just another hoax? Or is this just another one of those unexplained mysteries?

It is noteworthy that Mrs. Curran's emergence coincided with a rising interest in spirituality. There were those in the 1920s who held séances on each anniversary of the Halloween death of **Harry Houdini** and claimed to have communicated with him.

Arthur Conan Doyle, of Sherlock Holmes fame, was a firm believer in having once lived in a previous life through reincarnation. And then there was **Edgar Cayce**, the man who once a day would lie down on his couch, fold his hands and go into a self induced trance. An observer would then ask him questions about some individual from the past and he would relate answers, called readings, given to him as a result of having communicated with that person.

The improbable Ouija board gained even greater notoriety when it became the subject of a murder trial. A lonely Dorothea Turley, in the American Southwest, found an Ouija board and a handsome cowboy to keep her company. Just one problem - there was still a Mr. Turley. Dorothea asked the board to help her decide between her husband and her young lover. The board replied that her future was with the cowpoke, and that the problem could be solved by having daughter Mattie shoot her father –

The famous Ouija board

which she did. Despite the fact that the Ouija board had told them they wouldn't be prosecuted for the act, young Hattie was sent to reform school until she was 21, and mother was given three years behind bars.

In Chicago, the Ouija board was involved in another interesting case. In an odd decision the court held that a woman could not be prosecuted for slander against a neighbor because she had been directed to do so by a Ouija board.

The Fuld brothers, of Baltimore, invented the Ouija board in 1892, but they eventually sold out to Parker Brothers. Used by thousands in the hope that it could tell them whether their loved ones would survive the Great War, it remained a popular game throughout the 1920s. The lapboard had ten numbers on it plus all twenty-six letters of the alphabet. The user asked the board a question and relied on the three-legged planchette to "discover" the answer. All you had to do was place your fingers lightly on the planchette and a magical energy guided it to the letters or number that gave you an answer. Women often used the board to determine how many children they would bear or how many times they would be married. For answers to simplistic questions, the board had a *yes* and *no*.

The amazing Ouija board is still around and it has been updated and modernized. You can Google the term "Ouija board" and click on an internet hocus pocus site. There is a reproduced image of a board and you are told to type in a question on your computer. Then you are instructed to place your mouse arrow on the pointer (planchette) and follow it to your answer. Now, I never have believed in nonsensical tom-foolery, but curiosity got the better of me. I asked the talking board if I would ever marry again. Despite the fact that I am over the hill at age 71 and have been, uh, happily married 44 . . . 45, no . . . 50 years, some unseen force took my mouse up to the answer "yes." Hmm!

SPOOKY ST. LOUIS

McDowell Medical School (Mo. Historical Society)

Do you believe in ghosts? Do I believe in ghosts? – nah! Well . . . maybe some. Over the past several hundred years time has woven some incredible supernatural stories into the history of St. Louis. My friend from **Decatur**, Illinois, Troy Taylor, has written about many of them. He wasn't the first to do so and he probably won't be the last. Some of these stories will raise goose bumps and make the hair on the nape of your neck stand straight up.

If you're really into this kind of thing, Jason Offutt's *Haunted Missouri* (2007) will also fit the bill. Reviewer Amy Stapleton says the "book brings Missouri's haunted sites to life and beckons the reader: come visit."

The earliest reasons for hauntings date back to the Mound Builders who gave St. Louis its earliest nickname – Mound City. Explorer Stephen Long made reference to about 27 of these mounds. The biggest of them, La Grange de Terre (earthen barn) was used as a sighting landmark by riverboat pilots. It was located between Second and Broadway. There was another large mound at Kingshighway and Martin Luther King Drive. The French called it Cote Brilliante – Shinning Hill. It was razed in 1877 to make way for Christian Brothers College. Two more large mounds, located in Forest Park, were destroyed as preparations were made for the 1904 World's Fair.

Though long gone from the scene, these Mississippians are best remembered for burying their dead in earthen mounds. As the city of St. Louis grew and expanded, these sacred mounds were razed by insensitive developers. There are those who will tell you that the restless native spirits, whose graves were desecrated, haunt the city.

The Casino Queen, in East St. Louis, sits on land that was once in the Mississippi River. That famous **Bloody Island** was the scene of several bloody duels that resulted in death for St. Louisans. In 1817 Charles Lucas was killed in a duel with future U.S. Senator **Thomas Hart Benton**. Thomas Biddle and Spencer Pettis, in August of 1823, killed each other in a **duel that was fought**

211

from the unbelievable distance of a mere five paces. It seems that Biddle was badly nearsighted. Thousands of St. Louisans watched the duel from the St. Louis levee and riverfront roof tops. Political quarrels were the cause of all of the deadly duels fought on Bloody Island. It has been said that boat gamblers, late at night, sometimes hear what sounds like shrieks and moans. They might merely be creaks and groans from moorings, but some think it's the voices of the dead, searching for eternal peace.

The St. Louis side of the river has plenty of cause for hapless spirits to be walking around. Steamboat workers by the scores have been killed in wharf fires, boiler explosions and in the 1896 tornado that raked the area. Some claim to have seen phantom lights from ghost ships during fog-laden nights. Both the *Mississippi Queen* and the *Iron Mountain* were boats that departed from St. Louis and then **mysteriously disappeared without a trace**. Are those strange sounds emanating from the river front at the midnight hour ghostly voices of the passengers who were on board, crying out for help?

Mark Twain, in *Life on the Mississippi*, tells of a psychic experience he once had. He dreamed that he saw his brother lying dead in a metal coffin, dressed in one of Twain's suits, with a bouquet of flowers on his chest. In the middle of the whitish flowers was a single red rose.

Not long after, Twain's brother was killed when the boiler on his steamboat, the *Pennsylvania*, exploded. When Twain went to the large room where all the deceased were laid out, he noticed that Henry's coffin was made of metal and all the others were of pine. He was even more startled when he saw his brother was dressed in one of Twain's suits. But the real shocker came when an elderly woman walked up beside him and placed a bouquet of roses on Henry's chest. Lo and behold, there was a red rose smack dab in the middle of the white ones.

Samuel Clemens was born in 1835 at **Florida**, Missouri. It was the same year that Haley's Comet appeared in the heavens. Mark Twain died in 1910, the exact year that Haley's comet, absent for 75 years, came around for another visit.

The art of **body snatching** was first started in St. Louis by an odd duck physician named Joseph McDowell. He built a medical training school at Ninth and Gratiot, near Chouteau's Pond. He had an extreme prejudice against newly arriving immigrants, coloreds, and Catholics. McDowell was noted for passing out hateful tracts that espoused his beliefs. Fearing that he had made quite a few enemies, he often wore a metal breastplate under his clothes for protection from attack. His building had a large tower with a deck walk that went around it. **The tower was outfitted with six cannon,** in order to defend it from possible attack by his enemies. One of the cannons was said to have once graced the deck of pirate Jean Lafitte's ship.

The eccentric doctor insisted that his students learn anatomy. Dissection of bodies was against the law, back then, so **McDowell resorted to snatching the dead from potter's field where few would object**.

McDowell once stole the body of a German girl who had died from an unusual disease. When local residents learned of the theft they angrily armed themselves and marched off to the medical facility. McDowell hid the body in the attic but then panicked as several from the crowd broke inside to look for the body. Not knowing where to hide, McDowell was astonished to see his dead mother beckoning to him. She pointed to the table where the girl's corpse had been. He quickly lay on the table and pulled a sheet over him, **pretending to be dead**.

As several men searched the room, they pulled down the sheets from various corpses far enough to see their faces. "Here's a fellow with his boots sticking out from the end of the sheet," one of the intruders commented. "He must be a fresh one," another one commented. The men departed without finding the girl or discovering the hoax.

Dr. McDowell had been a strict Calvinist, deriding others who believed in ghosts. But after his dead mother saved his life, he became a spiritualist.

During the Civil War, Dr. McDowell was a secessionist and his facility was commandeered by Union officials and turned into a prison. After the war, McDowell resumed his activities and kept a rattlesnake, a crocodile and a gallows with Abe Lincoln hanged in effigy. Various people in the neighborhood reported seeing ghostly faces of men in tattered prison uniforms staring out the windows of the old Gratiot Street Prison. Cries, wailing and blood curdling screams could also occasionally be heard by those who walked past the building late at night.

The cave in the *Adventures of Tom Sawyer* actually exists just outside of **Hannibal**. It is a dangerous maze cut by nature into the rock beneath the ground. Mark Twain noted in the novel that no man "knew" the cave. It was called McDowell's Cave for the St. Louis physician who owned it.

McDowell had a macabre plan for the cave. He had hung a glass lined copper cylinder **containing the corpse of a teenage girl in an alcohol solution in one of the cave's recesses**. He wanted to see if the cave would reduce the corpse to bones. Sam Clemens was one of the girl's regular visitors. With the mix of danger and secrecy, the cave always seemed to Clemens (Mark Twain) a combination of sex and death.

McDowell died from pneumonia in 1868. His building was razed in 1882 and the St. Louis property is now part of the Ralston Purina Company complex.

THE ST. LOUIS GATEWAY ARCH

The Jefferson National Expansion Memorial consists of a 91 acre park near the Mississippi River at St. Louis. It was established to commemorate American westward expansion, the Lewis and Clark journey, the Dred Scott case and the first civil government west of the Mississippi. It is one of the leading national attractions, **drawing roughly four million visitors annually**. It is also **the tallest U.S. manmade monument**.

The arch was designed by Finnish-American architect Eero Saarinen and structural engineer Hannskark Bandel. It stands 630 ft. tall and is 630 ft wide at the base. The only building in Missouri that is taller is One Kansas City Place in Kansas City. The lower half consists of a stainless steel skin covering reinforced concrete and the upper level has carbon steel and rebar under the stainless exterior. The interior is hollow and has a tram that takes visitors to a small observation area at the top.

Underneath the Arch is a visitor's center, accessed from a descending outdoor ramp starting at either base. Within the center is the **Museum of Westward Expansion** with exhibits and a gift shop. It also contains the loading areas for the tram. The Tucker Theater, finished in 1968 and refurbished thirty years later, has 285 seats and shows a documentary, *Monument to the Dream*, on the Arch's construction.

Arch topping-out ceremony

Eero Saarinen died from a brain tumor before the arch was completed. Before his death, **he hired a college dropout, Richard Bowser, to design the tram system**. Elevator companies failed to come up with a workable design, but in two weeks Bowser came up with a system that combined an elevator cable lift system with gimbaled, egg-shaped cars that functioned similar to Ferris wheel gondolas.

The top of the arch can sway up to eighteen inches in high winds. The park grounds are maintained by the National Park Service and the tram is run by Bi-State Development Agency. Leonor K. Sullivan Boulevard is named for the St. Louis congresswoman who helped secure federal funds for the Arch. Sullivan was the **first woman from Missouri to serve in the U.S. House of Representatives**.

On July 21, 2007, **nearly two hundred people were trapped** in the two trams at the top of the arch due to a power failure. Those who were ambulatory made it down a set of stairs to a service elevator. Others had to wait for the power to be restored. From the top of the arch one can see for 30 miles on a clear day.

Plans for the Arch went back to 1947 when civic leaders held a national competition for the design. Saarinen modified his original design by extending its length 40 feet. In layman's terms, the shape of the arch is similar to that of an inverted hanging chain.

Based on previous con-struction experience, it was estimated that two or three workers would die from falls during the Arch construction. However, there were no deaths related to the project from beginning to end.

Construction began February 12, 1963, and was completed October 28, 1965.

Each leg went sixty feet deep into the ground. The base of each leg at ground level had **an engineering tolerance of one-sixty-fourth of an inch** or the two legs would not mate at the top. Some of the excavated rock and dirt was hauled across the river to East St. Louis to fill in low spots left over from the 1890 street raising project. As each half of the arch moved closer to completion, the weight caused the legs to tilt inward. A brace was inserted near the top to keep them apart until construction was finished. Pittsburgh-DesMoines, the construction company, placed their name on the strut but the government considered it advertising and forced them to remove the name. The letters PDM were allowed on the cranes on each leg of the Arch.

On the day the final piece was to be inserted, it was discovered that there was insufficient room so jackscrews were used to force the two legs apart. It was a bright, sunny day and the south leg heated up and began to expand. **Firemen used a long hose to spray water on that leg to keep it from expanding too much.** The Boy Scouts organization attached a large U.S. flag to the last triangular keystone piece and the "topping out" process was successfully completed. Vice President Hubert Humphrey and Secretary of the Interior Stewart Udall attended the dedication ceremonies in May of 1968.

The total cost was approximately $15 million. In 1984, monies were set aside by Congress for expansion of the Memorial on the east side, but a moratorium was placed on this when the Casino Queen gambling facility was built in East St. Louis on the riverfront.

Eleven small aircraft have successfully piloted through the Arch, even though it is illegal. In 1980, Kenneth Sawyers tried to parachute onto the top of the Arch, planning to jump back off again with a smaller chute to land on the ground below. Instead, he slid all the way down one leg to his death. In 1984, David Adcock of Houston, Texas, began to scale the Arch using suction cups on his hands and feet, but he was talked out of it after having climbed only 20 feet. The next day he successfully scaled the nearby 21-story Equitable Building in downtown St. Louis.

On 14 September, 1992, John C. Vincent (of New Orleans) was lowered from a helicopter onto the top of the Arch, from which he parachuted to the ground below. A judge gave him three months in jail for the stunt.

The only president or former president to go to the top of the arch was Dwight D. Eisenhower who was responsible for allocating federal funds for the project.

Sometimes those of us who live in the area take the arch for granted. We should all remember the words of Barringer Fifield who said in *Seeing St. Louis*, **"The Arch is where everything comes together. The improbably stainless steel flourish unites not only earth and sky, land and water, east and west, but also St. Louis's past and present, its challenges and responses. Here is where the city begins . . . ."**

BASEBALL CARDINAL MEMORIES

In the days of my youth I had fond memories of listening to hyperbolic Harry

Caray describe the heroics of my favorite team. Yes, folks, I bleed Cardinal Red. I was born in September of 1939, and during my three score plus ten on the planet the mighty Redbirds have given me plenty to cheer about, including seven of their ten World Series victories in my lifetime.

The latest improbable story to unfold is the heartwarming saga of **Rick Ankiel**. Back in 2000, he had the best curve in baseball and won eleven games as a rookie. But, in the playoffs against Atlanta, the pressure got to him and he threw something like six wild pitches and was yanked from the game. **He spent the next five years in the minors trying to regain his form**, but in the history of baseball, no pitcher has ever recovered from such an extreme streak of wildness. However, his athletic prowess enabled him to try a comeback as an outfielder, but injuries slowed his progress. Ankiel showed signs of promise in 2007 spring training, but was sent to the minors for seasoning where he led the AAA league with 32 homers.

In early August, the Cardinals brought him up to replace Scott Spezio who went to substance abuse rehab. To paraphrase a *Post-Dispatch* writer: "In a script right from a Hollywood movie, Roy Hobbs, er, Rick Ankiel, beat the Dodgers with a late inning home run that resulted in a spine-tingling standing ovation and a tip-of-the-hat curtain call." Ankiel hit two more homers on Saturday, and on Sunday he smacked a double in a 10-2 rout of the Dodgers. When Ankiel hit that first four-bagger, he became **only the second player since Babe Ruth to accomplish the feat of hitting a homer as a pitcher and then hit another one later in his career while playing another position**. His heroics were pure baseball nirvana, and once again Cardinal fans had hopes for a pennant run down the stretch.

Announcer Jack Buck

It's the stuff of which dreams were made.

On August 31, Ankiel pounded a grand slam home run to beat the Reds (8-5) and to enable Tony LaRussa to replace Red Schoendinst as the winningest manager in Cardinal history.

Yes, this writer has witnessed dozens of great Cardinal moments throughout the years. Thank you, God, for the wonderful gift of memory. I have memories, when I was a climber of birch trees, of my dad and uncles excitedly talking about Rogers Hornsby hitting .426 and Grover Cleveland

Rick Ankiel

Alexander pitching the Cards to a World Series win. I sat there wide-eyed, eating a Moon pie, as they reminisced about the glory days of the Dean brothers and the Gas House Gang of the 1930s. I hardly believed my ears when they talked about third baseman "Pepper" Martin, the "Wild Horse of the Osage," **stopping hot smashes with his chest, and then picking up the ball to throw out hitters**.

The Cardinals have the proudest tradition in the entire National League, **leading the Senior Circuit with ten World Series victories**. Yes, folks, it's not the Dodgers, not the Giants, not the Reds, not the Phillies – it's the Cards. The Redbirds have won two out of three against the Red Sox, two out of three against the Tigers, and three out of five against the mighty Bronx Bombers. What makes it even sweeter is that **we beat the pin-stripers in 1926 when they had Ruth, in 1942 when they were led by Joe Dimaggio and in 1964 when they sported the dynamic duo of Mickey Mantle and Roger Maris**. **Awesome!**

What follows is a list of some of my other favorite Cardinal moments. Stan Musial is the only player to hit 475 home runs or more and never once lead the league in round-trippers. I was listening to the game on KMOX radio when

Albert Pujols

Stan hit five homers in a double-header against the Giants at Sportsman's Park.

Stan won seven batting percentage titles, but one of my favorite moments occurred when he was a pitcher. Back in the early 1950s, he was locked in a tight batting title race with Frank Baumholtz of the Cubs. It came down to the last day in a game in St. Louis. Musial got a couple of early hits in that game and had the title locked up. The next time Baumholtz came to bat, **Musial came in from right field to pitch to him**. Baumholtz hit a screaming liner to Red Schoendinst, who couldn't handle it. The official scorer gave the redhead an error. Musial waved from the mound to try to get it changed to a hit, but the arbiter was adamant.

Other great memories: The first two extra-inning All-Star games were won when Stan Musial and Red Schoendinst (from **Germantown**, IL) slugged home runs; Enos Slaughter winning the 1946 Series v. the Red Sox by scoring all the way from first base on a single by Harry Walker; Wally Moon and Bill Virdon winning back-to-back Rookie of the Year honors; Bob Gibson setting a Series strikeout record against Detroit in 1968; Bob Gibson pitching a no-hitter against Pittsburgh; Joe Torre winning the MVP in 1971; Willie McGee making two spectacular catches and hitting a home run in a Series game at Milwaukee in 1982; Bruce Sutter striking out the last batter to win the 1982 Series; light hitting Tommy Herr leading the league in RBIs at the All-Star game break in 1985; **Jack Clark hitting that dramatic homer** off Tom Niedenfur at Dodger Stadium (1985); Ozzie Smith hitting a game-winning homer off Niedenfur the next game at Busch Stadium; Ozzie Smith doing his patented back flip; Gary

Templeton getting 100 hits left-handed and 100 hits right-handed in a single season; Ritchie Allen becoming the first Cardinal since Stan Musial retired (1963) to hit 30 homers in a season; Mark McGuire breaking the home run mark of 61 set by Roger Maris in 1961; slow-footed, third string catcher Glen Brummer stealing home in the 12th inning against the Giants in August of 1982, giving the Cardinals a much-needed win by the score of 5-4; Fernando Tatis hitting two grand slams in one inning (1999); Mark Whiten hitting four homers in one game (1993); Albert Pujols winning three MVPs and Bob Carpenter winning the Cy Young Award in the same year; Jim Edmonds' dramatic homer in the playoffs in 2004 against Houston; Anthony Reyes setting a record in the 2006 by becoming the pitcher with the fewest regular season wins (5) to ever start game one of the World Series, and then winning that game; the Cards setting the record four years ago for winning the World Series with the fewest regular season wins (83), and, finally, beating the Cubbies – anytime!

There was a second baseman named **Bo Hart** a few years back. Like Ankiel, he was brought up from the minors in the second half of the season and injected new life into the team with his spirited play and timely hits. Probably the most dramatic moment came when he struck out instead of getting a hit. Appreciative fans, the best in baseball, gave him a standing ovation. Can you imagine that? A standing ovation for whiffing at the plate! Infielders on the opposing team probably looked at each other in amazement thinking, *I want to play here in front of these fans.*

Have there been any heartbreaks? Yep, the agony goes along with the ecstasy for diehard fans. I cried when that bum Frank Lane traded my hero, young and cocky outfielder Jackie Brandt to the Giants. In 1956, he hit .298 and led NL outfielders in fielding with a .990 percentage. Lane broke my heart again when he traded future Hall of Famer Enos "Country" Slaughter to the

Yankees. Enos also cried when he learned that he had been traded. I get this sick feeling in the pit of my stomach when I think about losing the World Series to the Tigers and Twins, both in game seven. Against the Twins, we won all three games at home, but couldn't get a single win in their nightmarish monstrosity of a domed stadium. Then there was the 1985 loss to Kansas City when umpire **Don Denkinger made the worst call in baseball history**, costing the Birds a Series-winning sixth game.

Yet, over the years, the pluses far outweigh minuses. Stand tall, Cardinal fans, the only team in baseball with a

Marty Marion 1944 NL MVP

more glorious and historic tradition is the Yankees. **In Series play, however, we are the only National League team that has dominated them (three or more confrontations). The Cards are 3-2 against the Yanks in World Series** play. No brag, just fact!

THE NFL's BIGGEST CINDERELLA STORY

When the football Cardinals left for Arizona, St. Louis was left without a team. Despite the Rams being one of the storied NFL franchises, they had fallen on hard times in Los Angeles and attendance was down. This set the stage for a move to St. Louis.

The Rams first began playing in Cleveland in 1937. The team moved to Los Angeles in 1946 and played their games at the Coliseum, built for the 1924 Olympics. The 1950 L.A. Rams held the single season team scoring mark until it was broken by the 2007 New England Patriots. From 1980 to 1994 they played their home games at Anaheim Stadium in Orange County, but they kept the name L.A. Rams.

Kurt Warner (author's collection)

The NFL owners wanted the team to go to Baltimore but owner Georgia Frontiere preferred St. Louis. They relented only after Frontiere agreed to share PSL (Permanent Seat License) money with them. Rich Brooks coached the Rams in the 1995 and 1996 seasons and then former Philadelphia Eagles coach Dick Vermeil was hired. He coached them to a Super Bowl win in 2000 and then announced his retirement. Offensive coordinator "Mad" Mike Martz was hired to take over the reins.

Going into the 1999-2000 season, the Rams had the worst record of any NFL team for the decade. They sent fumbling QB Tony Banks to Baltimore and signed former local high school star Trent Green as a free agent. **In pre-season Green was electric with an incredible 28 completions in 32 attempts.** Rams' hopes were crushed when Green's leg was broken in a preseason game and they were left with a little-known backup quarterback from Arena Football, Kurt Warner. After playing in college for Northern Iowa, he was drafted and cut by Green Bay. Then he went to work in a supermarket for $5.50 an hour. The next year he signed with the Iowa Barnstarmers. Then he played a year for the Amsterdam Admirals in NFL Europe, while connected to the Rams by a contract. Not much of a resumé. **But this was to be a season of miracles and Warner would have a stellar season in the most fantastic Cinderella story in the history of the NFL.** The Rams ran roughshod over practically everybody and ended at 13-3. The last loss was a meaningless game at Philadelphia where all the regulars were pulled after the first quarter.

In Warner's first playoff game against the Minnesota Vikings, he threw for

395 yards and 5 touchdowns. The Rams won the game 49-37 with former Illinois QB Jeff George throwing for 423 yards and 4 touchdowns.

The Rams made it to the Super Bowl by coming from behind to defeat Tampa Bay in the NFC Championship Game. The high-powered Rams, stymied by a stout Buccaneer defense, led by a scant 5-3 baseball score at the end of the first half. Tampa Bay took the lead 6-5 with a third quarter field goal, but Warner put the Rams ahead 12-6 near the end of the game with a long throw down the sideline that **Ricky Proehl** hauled in for "the catch."

In the 2000 Super Bowl in Atlanta, the Rams played the Tennessee Titans, one of only three teams that defeated them in the regular season. The Titans barely made it to the Super Bowl, thanks to the last-minute trick lateral play on the kickoff known as the "Music City Miracle" in NFL lore.

Dick Vermeil (author's collection)

The Rams, **led by the lowest paid starting quarterback in the NFL**, started fast and had four first half drives that made it to the Red Zone, but then the Titans stiffened and the Rams could only muster three field goals for a 9-0 halftime lead.

In the third quarter Kurt Warner threw a 9 yard touchdown pass to **Torry Holt** and the Rams went up 16-0. The Titans, led by quarterback Steve McNair and running back Eddie George, made a furious comeback and tied the score late in the fourth quarter. This was the **largest deficit ever erased in a Super Bowl game**. On the first play of the ensuing drive, Warner threw a deep pass to **Isaac Bruce,** but Jevon Kearse hit his arm just as he let go of the ball. Bruce came back for the ball and then dodged his way 73 yards past defenders into the end zone. With 1:54 left in the game, McNair drove the Titans from their own ten yard line to the Rams ten yard line with six seconds left, enough time for one more play. McNair completed a pass to Kevin Dyson who turned to dive into the end zone but **was miraculously stopped inches short** by Mike Jones who made what is known as "**the tackle**." The ending is considered the **most exciting in Super Bowl history**.

Other Ram stars on this team were tight end Ernie Conwell, RB **Marshal Faulk**, receiver Az Akim, offensive end Orlando Pace and defensive Pro Bowlers Grant Wistrom and Kevin Carter (17 sacks). Punt returner Tony Horne had a league-leading 29.7 return average. Warner was Super Bowl MVP, passing for 414 yards and **breaking Joe Montana's previous record**. Warner is a Christian and never fails to give credit to God for his success in life. He wears the number 13 to show that he does not believe in superstitions. Warner retired at the end of the 2009 season.

HOW TO FIND WATER WITH DOUSING STICKS

Dowsing has traditionally been a way to find something that is hidden. It dates all the way back to Germany in 1500. Martin Luther criticized the practice as a tool of the devil. Now this practice has never been scientifically proven, but if you grew up on a farm you've probably seen it done. Dowsing rods were traditionally made from forked hazel branches. Just read my Christian brother-in-law's story and you'll see how dowsing is done. Try it yourself and see if you have any luck.

Early use of dowsing rod

"I grew up on a farm during the Depression (1930s). When I was a young teen, I helped my brother Dale dig a well on the family farm. Unlike digging for oil, you don't have to worry much about looking for a specific terrain. You mostly decide upon the approximate location where you want it, usually close to a house or barn.

"Next we used the services of a reputable man good at 'dowsing.' He used an apple tree branch, stripped of extraneous growth, with a fork in it – much like a large Thanksgiving turkey wishbone. The dowser held each branch of the fork in his hands and pointed the remaining piece up in the air in front of him at a 45 degree angle. Then he started slowly walking toward the area where we wanted the well. When he came to the spot where he was perpendicular to an underground stream, the pointer section moved downward, as if propelled by some magnetic force. Now there are those who claim dousers are secretly responsible for the downward turn of the stick. Yet I was once witness to a well hunt where the dowser held tightly to the stick and this strange force was so strong it twisted the bark off the branches.

"He then marked the spot with a stake and then walked away from it at a 90 degree angle. Then he slowly walked toward it again, now looking for a place where two separate underground streams crossed. Again, the dowsing stick bent downward to indicate the presence of water.

"Now this process tells you where the water is, but it doesn't tell you how deep it is. For that the man took a six foot long fruit tree branch and held it horizontal to the earth at the spot where the two streams crossed. My brother and I stood in amazement as the branch moved up and down in his hand thirty times. We asked him what that meant, and he said that we would hit water around 30 feet down. 'Had it gone up and down forty times,' he explained, 'that would have indicated a depth of 40 feet.'

"After the man left, we set about digging the well. It was about three feet in diameter. My brother Dale dug with a shovel and when he got down about four feet we built a frame over the hole to support a winch with a bucket at the end of the rope. Dale would fill the bucket, and I would haul it to the top and empty it. Because digging was the hardest, we regularly switched positions.

"We were digging the well in late summer, and we ran into some blue clay that was as hard as concrete. As the going got tougher we went to a nearby rock quarry and bought a case of dynamite with appropriate fuses and blasting caps. We put a stick of dynamite in the hole and set it off. All it did was blow the winch off the top and create a very wide crater. We later learned that what we should have done was cut the stick of dynamite into three pieces and placed them around the perimeter equidistant. Done in that fashion, and set off electronically in simultaneous fashion, the blast would have gone inward instead of outward. We finished digging the well by hand. The dynamite came in handy later when we needed to remove some tree stumps. We also used it a few times for 4th of July celebrations and occasionally to go fishing.

"We struck water about 29 feet deep, and then we pumped the trickling water out and dug down another eight feet to make sure there would be a reservoir of water in the well during dry spells. We knew of other farmers who dug wells on their property and had to go down only nine feet because they encountered a spring.

"When we got to the bottom, my brother and I switched places. Dale sent bricks down in the bucket and I started laying them in circular fashion. No mortar was used because this method allowed for water to seep in through the cracks. About four feet from the top, we used mortar on the joints to keep out groundwater, which is more easily contaminated. Nowadays the EPA requires mortar to be used ten feet from ground level.

"After reaching ground level we went up another foot and capped the well with a solid piece of cast concrete that had a ready-made hole. A pipe was inserted down in the hole and connected to the metal hand pump. The pump had a rubber or leather gasket inside to insure proper suction. But you first had to 'prime' the pump by pouring some water into the pump shaft to create the proper suction.

"Some farmers would continue the mortared brick another three feet above the ground. Then they built a wooden A-frame roof with shake wood shingles and support beams to hold the winch, rope, and drinking bucket.

"When I was married and teaching in **Rolla**, Missouri, during the early 1960s, we needed to drill a well where we were living. We hired a company and they brought in a truck with a drilling rig. The man said there was no need for dowsing in the area. 'There's water anywhere you drill in Missouri, as long as you go deep enough.'

"The first 20 feet down was all gravel, which required casing. But after that it was all rock which required no casing. They used a rotating hammer drill with a diamond bit, and in the middle of the drill was a pipe that sent down air and water. The compressed air and water forced the ground up rock to the top. It took eight hours to drill 350 feet deep.

"For modern three foot diameter wells, installers use concrete tiles instead of bricks. If they drill an eight inch hole they use perforated plastic PVC pipe.

"Nowadays dowsers often use two bronze brazing rods or metal coat hangers as "rods." The two metal rods are bent 90 degrees into an L shape and they grab hold of one end of the rod in each hand while the other piece sticks out horizontally. If they come across a stream the rods will line up parallel to the stream. In recent years dowsers were not needed to locate pipes in the ground because metal detectors could be used. But metal pipes rust and corrode and for several decades PVC pipe has usually been used instead of metal. Today, dowsers are sometimes used to find where these plastic pipes are buried.

"I recently discovered a new and unique use for a dowser. I was doing genealogy research on my family, and I found my great, great, grandmother's grave. I figured my great, great, grandfather was probably buried next to her, but there was no marker for him. I heard about a man who was known for dowsing graves. At first, I didn't believe it, but reliable sources told me the man could actually do graves. He uses two metal wires bent at a 90 degree angle with wooden handles. When he searched a vacant spot next to my grand-mother's grave, the two rods began to bend inward. 'There's a man in that grave; probably your great, great grandfather.' He explained that if a woman had been in the grave the rods would have moved off to the side. If a grave site is empty, the rods don't move.

"I was very skeptical about this 'grave dowsing' until I blind tested him with graves where I already knew who was in them. Do I believe in dowsing or divining rods? Yep. Seeing is believing!"

HOW TO MEASURE A STORM

Storyteller **Marilyn Kinsella of Fairview Heights**, Illinois relates this fascinating tale.

The knock-knocks happened on stormy nights. I hated storms, especially at night. We had two huge elm trees that died, but their skeletal arms reached menacingly over the roof of our house. I was convinced they acted as the perfect conductors for any and all electricity that a terrible storm could muster.

When I was small, I would jump into grandpa's bed and hide under the covers. After all, his bedroom was right next to mine. In fact, the only thing that separated my bed from his was the wall. But, as I got older, even I had to agree that it seemed a tad childish, so I stuck it out and trembled in my own bed.

Sometimes, I could hear the rumbling thunder miles away before it ever reached our home. Grandpa Joe taught me how to figure out how close a storm was. You just counted how many times you could say Mississippi between the flash of lightning and the clap of thunder. So, if I saw a flash of blue-white light, I started counting "One Mississippi, two Mississippi, three Mississippi – boom!" The storm was three miles away. I restarted counting again and again until "One" and boom! The storm was overhead. I resisted running into grandpa's room like a scaredy cat. I didn't want to be a baby.

Then I heard the knock-knock. It's the universal call and response. Knock-knock, knock-knock. I answered back with my own knock-knock. Grandpa was saying, "Are you okay over there?" And I was answering, "I'm fine." The strange thing was, I actually was fine because after that, the storms always subsided.

Lightning occurs when water droplets collide with each other inside storm clouds causing electrons to move so quickly that a large electrical spark is created. As the lightning moves quickly toward the ground its path is heated so intensely and expands so much that it creates a loud noise we call thunder.

While lightning and thunder occur together, we see the lightning some time before the boom of thunder reaches our ears. That is because the speed of light is about a million times faster than the speed of sound.

Since we know this it becomes possible to estimate how many miles away a storm is by counting the number of seconds between the lightning flash and the clap of thunder. Divide that number by 5 and that will give you the approximate distance in miles.

THE GREAT 1925 TORNADO

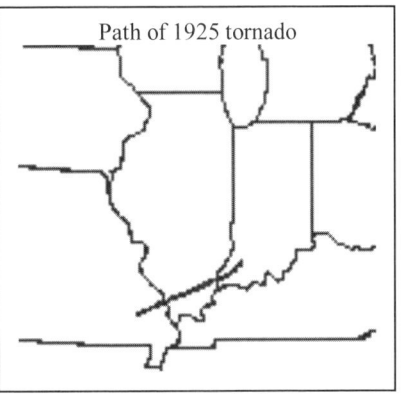
Path of 1925 tornado

Mother Nature flexed her muscles around 1 P.M. on March 18, 1925, and created a record-breaking tornado that started in southeast Missouri, crossed into Illinois and, three hours later, it was wreaking havoc in Indiana. It remains the **deadliest storm in U.S. history**.

The storm originated just north of **Ellington** and it began snapping trees along its destructive path. Fortunately, most of the Missouri landscape that it ravaged was sparsely settled. However, as the storm continued along at a speed of about 55 mph, it hit the Missouri town of **Annapolis**, destroying about 90 percent of the structures. Annapolis is 111 miles south of St. Louis and is located on the Missouri Pacific Railroad. The entire lead industry of that town was devastated as two citizens were killed and 50 were injured. Brick buildings crumbled as easily as if they had been log cabins. In the area just north of **Cape Girardeau**, there were reports of 12 dead and fifty injured. The storm then continued to **Biehle** where it killed ten residents. After hitting Biehle, the storm crossed the Mississippi and devastated the Illinois town of **Desoto**. It roared all the way across southern Illinois and proceeded to wreck towns in Indiana.

Doctors from **Poplar Bluff** and surrounding areas made haste for **Annapolis** to treat the injured, many of whom were taken by train to **St. Louis** hospitals. The Missouri Pacific Railroad brought in Pullman cars to house the homeless. Damage to the Annapolis Lead Company was estimated to be $200,000 and total damage to the town was $800,000. Of the 300 structures there, only three were left standing. A brick schoolhouse, on the edge of town, survived because it was not in the tornado's path.

Strangest of all, a residence in the middle of town, housing a bed-ridden woman and her family, was surrounded by other destroyed buildings, but was left untouched. However, it was eventually devoured by flames from fires that started because of the storm.

It is estimated that the storm stayed on the ground for 219 miles, a new record. This deadly tri-state tornado killed over 1,000 people and injured over 2,000.

The 1925 storm, in today's terms, would probably be described as an F-5 as measured on a scale developed by University of Chicago scientist Theodore Fujita. The cyclonic winds within the storm might have varied between 200 and 250 miles per hour.

A wrecked building in Missouri

Historian Wallace Akin says that one reason the devastation was so widespread was that the U.S. Weather Bureau had no tornado warning system in place. **In 1925, government meteorologists were forbidden to use the word "tornado,"** **fearing the term might scare people** and ruin commerce for that day.

The terrain of Midwest geography played a significant part in the story since the vast expanse of flat land between the Rockies and the Appalachians allows storms to ravage the area, unimpeded by mountains. The Great Tornado was spawned when moist air coming up from the Gulf of Mexico clashed with a cold front, brought down from the north by the Jet Stream. In 1925, scientists were not yet aware of the Jet Stream. **The Jet Stream was first discovered by Japanese scientists during World War II when they sent incendiary balloons aloft in an attempt to set fire to the woods of the Pacific Northwest.** The southernmost tip of the Jet Stream path pretty well coincided with the path of the 1925 storm through Missouri and Illinois.

The parent storm actually started out in Montana and Wyoming two days earlier. As the two air masses collided and moved east, the warm air began to override the cold air and it then shifted counterclockwise, producing a cyclonic wind and a super cell thunderstorm.

The swirling death wind, which swept over the southern part of three states, caused property damage in excess of ten million dollars. The death and injured figures were based on bodies recovered from the stricken area, and upon the number of persons still unaccounted for in the storm-ridden territory. The original figures were revised upward daily.

Nine were killed in an 1871 St. Louis tornado. Four more were dead after an 1890 storm. Three were killed and 100 injured in a 1904 cataclysm. Yet another tornado hit St. Louis and **Granite City**, Illinois in 1927, leaving 79 dead and 550 injured. Finally, in 1959, 21 more St. Louisans were killed and another 345 injured. The 1927 tornado now ranks as the **second deadliest storm in U.S. history**. This storm touched down in **Maplewood** and traveled in a northeasterly direction, barely missing most of downtown St. Louis.

Since big cities are not usually hit by tornadoes (because of their relatively small area geographically), **this makes St. Louis the deadliest large city in America – weather wise**.

THE GREATEST INDIAN PAINTING

Along the bluffs of the Mississippi, north of **West Alton**, is the painting (a reproduction of an Indian pictograph) of the legendary **Piasa Bird**, known by Native Americans as the Bird of Evil Spirit. The fiendish looking creature, first seen by Marquette and Jolliet in 1673, and first sketched in 1826, had the

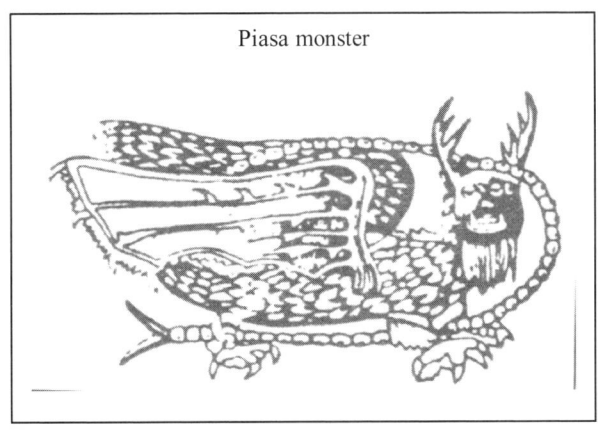

Piasa monster

body of an alligator and feet with talons, pointed teeth, enormous wings, and the face of a man with antlers on its head. It originally was painted red, green, and black. It is generally regarded as the **greatest Native American painting in North America**.

Named for a local creek, the bird was presumably the thunder-bird or storm spirit of the Iliniwek. The monster pictograph was seen and recorded by explorers Marquette and Jolliet in their early voyage down the Illinois and Mississippi rivers.

The creature was said to have **lived in a cave and feasted on local natives**, swooping down and carrying them away to be devoured in its lair. Finally, the brave young chief of the Illini, Wassatoga, took twenty armed warriors with him and stood brazenly on a rock to defy the monster. The evil one swooped down to kill its intended victim, and at the last second, the hidden warriors emerged and **killed the beast with their poisoned arrows.**

The original painting was quarried away for railroad ballast in 1847. Local Boy Scout groups erected a metal replica of the terrifying creature on the bluff face in the 1980s.

INDIAN CURSE PUTS KASKASKIA IN MISSOURI!

Do you believe in curses? Did you know that **14,000 acres of Illinois land are physically in the state of Missouri**? How is that possible, you ask? It's enough to make you scratch your head and say, "gee whiz!" Here's what happened.

Kaskaskia before the 1881 flood

In 1703, the French village of Kaskaskia was established by Jesuit priests who came down from the Starved Rock area (on the Illinois River) where they had founded the Immaculate Conception Church in 1675. A new Immaculate Conception Church in Kaskaskia was constructed (of logs with a thatched roof) that same year. Kaskaskia thus became one of the oldest, and possibly the oldest town in Illinois. The settlement was named for the Kaskaskias, one of the five tribes of the Illinois Native-American confederacy.

The town that grew around the church was located on a peninsula between the Mississippi and Kaskaskia rivers. A new church, made of stone, was built in 1714 at the expense of the French government. The stone church was enlarged in 1737. Yet a third church of vertical palisade posts was built around 1775. It was torn

British Union Jack

down in 1838 and a new brick church was constructed. It lasted until the 1881 flood, and the materials were used to build a new church farther west and south at the site of New Kaskaskia, Illinois.

Kaskaskia, with a population that quickly swelled to about 7,000 inhabitants, was the **largest town in Illinois at its zenith**. It ruled as the social and commercial center of "Upper Louisiana" for more than a century. French inhabitants in Canada were attracted to Kaskaskia due to its warm climate and rich soil. The site was so prosperous that the gay social life earned it the title, **"The Versailles of the West."**

The French government decided to protect the settlement of Kaskaskia and strengthen its hold on Illinois by building a fort near the town. In 1718, Pierre du Boisbriant, the French military commander of Illinois, built **Fort de Chartres**, located 18 miles north of Kaskaskia. Wood was taken from the virgin forest and stone was secured from the nearby bluffs. The star-shaped fort was similar in outline to the more famous Fort Ticonderoga, captured by Ethan Allen and Benedict Arnold in the Revolutionary War. The fort was named in honor of the Duc de Chartres, the French regent's son. In 1753, it was refurbished by Jean B. Saucier and Richard McCarty. McCarty was an Irishman who later became the fort's commander. The wooden walls were replaced with stone, over a three year period, at an astounding cost of one million dollars. The sum nearly bankrupted the French government. **This largest and best-built French fort in North America**, covering four acres, protected settlers from the nearby Chicasaws, Piankashaws, Kickapoo and the fierce Fox who made periodic raids from the north. By 1771, Fort de Chartres was officially abandoned because it was in a state of neglect.

If you visit the site today there is a partially reconstructed fort, a museum, and a research library.

Britain took control of Illinois after winning the French and Indian War (1756-63). In 1766, just before the British took possession, the French burned **Fort Kaskaskia**, which was near the town and much smaller than Fort Chartres, but up on the bluffs. It was the only bluff overlooking Kaskaskia where a fort might be built to protect the town. When Fort Kaskaskia was completed, the garrison at Fort Chartres abandoned the place and occupied the new fort. After the British took over, they built **Fort Gage** near the town and located on the flood plain.

Liberty Bell of the West at Kaskaskia

It was from Kaskaskia that **George Rogers Clark** launched his intrepid campaign to evict the British from Illinois during the Revolutionary War (1776-1783).

In 1741, King Louis XV presented the parish at Kaskaskia with a 650-pound cast bronze bell. The bell, which is still preserved and on display, bears the inscription (in French): "For the church of the Illinois, with the compliments of the King from beyond the sea." In time, new bells (1878) were procured from St. Louis and the old one was placed in storage. When George Rogers Clark took control of the territory, French citizens retrieved the old bell and rang it loudly to proclaim their new freedom from the hated British. This historic Illinois "**Liberty Bell of the West**" is actually **11 years older than the more famous Liberty Bell** in Philadelphia. It took about four months for men to tow the bell up the Mississippi from New Orleans with the bell sitting on a raft.

Yet Kaskaskia, so proud and so prosperous, was doomed. According to legend, a curse was placed on the town by an Algonquin Indian who was not allowed to marry a French maiden that he loved. The Indians around Kaskaskia were friendly, with many of them having been converted to Christianity. A good number of natives lived on the fringe of town. This particular Indian brave, educated by French missionaries, worked at a house and plantation owned by an affluent man named Bernard. No one knows for sure how it happened, but the handsome native met and fell in love with Marie, the man's daughter.

Now Marie was the beautiful "**Belle of Kaskaskia**," with numerous hot blooded suitors, but she loved only the Indian. It was quite common, back then, for French men to marry Indian maidens, but almost unheard of for a white woman to marry a native. When the Indian asked the father for his daughter's hand in marriage, he was refused. The Red Man simply wasn't suitable. Not long after that, the couple ran away to begin a new life together. Outraged, the father and some of his close friends chased after them. The lovers were tracked down and finally apprehended near **Cahokia**. The Indian was beaten and tied to a pirogue, and then banished from the community. As the log moved down the river, the Indian turned and cursed the father. He said that Bernard would be dead within a year and that Kaskaskia was damned with even the dead of the town being disturbed from their graves. Then he looked up to the sky and prayed to the Great Spirit that the girl's father would one day be killed by his own people. Next, he implored that the town of Kaskaskia would be destroyed by the Mighty River. The river then swallowed the Indian beneath the muddy water.

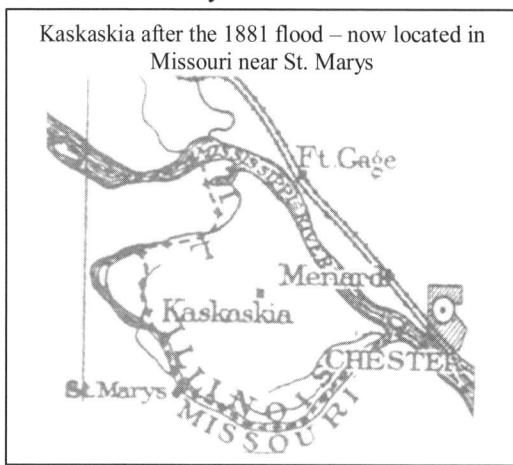
Kaskaskia after the 1881 flood – now located in Missouri near St. Marys

The damning words were quickly forgotten. But as time went on the curse seemed prophetic because the economic fortunes of the town declined as French inhabitants, unhappy with Americanization of the settlement, moved away and went to **Ste. Genevieve**, Old Mines (near **Potosi**), St. Louis and New Orleans. The population would eventually shrink to less than a thousand. In 1881, the dark curse dramatically worked its magic. In April, after weeks of rain, the raging Mississippi overflowed its banks. The big river was about to change its course and unearth dead bodies in the local cemetery. The swollen flow of the river current fed into the Kaskaskia River that was not capable of carrying such a volume. Since the eastern bank of the Kaskaskia River was composed of limestone rock, the additional riverbed needed to handle the huge volume of water was gouged out when the Mississippi savagely cut through the earthen neck of the peninsula and **placed most of the town on the Missouri side of the river**.

Thanks to the Indian's curse, much of Kaskaskia was now on the other side of the river, within the boundaries of Missouri. The Church of Immaculate Conception survived, but was also on the west side of the river. The Kaskaskia cemetery was washed away and the bodies of those buried there were disgorged into the raging waters. The old and impressive Menard House (the "Mount Vernon of the West") remained with what was left of old Kaskaskia, eventually becoming a popular tourist attraction. The forgotten "Liberty Bell of the West" was recovered from an old building and transferred to Kaskaskia Island. In

1948, the state of Illinois erected a new brick structure to house the historic bell.

With old Kaskaskia now on the west side of the Mississippi River, those sly rogues in the state of Missouri tried to claim it. There was a huge legal battle that the U.S. Supreme Court finally settled in favor of Illinois. It ruled that Kaskaskia had historically been part of Illinois and that a whimsical act of nature should not change its attachment to that state.

And **what, you ask, ever happened to old man Bernard? He got into a quarrel with a local man and was killed in the ensuing fight. Now do you believe in curses?**

THE NATION'S SMALLEST NATIONAL MONUMENT

Tower Rock is a large chunk of limestone jutting up from the Mississippi River in southern Missouri near **Altenburg**. Its location in the river presented a hazard to steamboats, and in earlier days legends of romance, mystery and evil were associated with the swirling waters surrounding its base. Just below the island of Tower Rock there is a dangerous eddy of water that early boatmen labeled the "**Devil's Whirlpool**."

How did Mother Nature create this unique and interesting piece of geology? During the great Ice Age, popularly known as the Liman Advance, a great glacier came down from Canada and pushed the bed of the Mississippi westward. This radical change forced the river to flow over a bed of limestone. Eventually, the relentless eroding waters created its present bed and left the rock in its present location. It has existed for eons, undisturbed by the scouring waters of the Mississippi which have swept its base. Prior to the glacier that changed its course, the river was between a massive rocky ridge and a large hill now known as Fountain Bluff.

In 1679, Henri de Tonti (LaSalle's faithful lieutenant) and several missionaries placed a large wooden cross at the top of Tower Rock in the Mississippi River. They called it Le Cap de Croix, **Rock of the Cross**. The Indians called Tonti "Iron Hand" and marveled at his metal claw in place of a hand. Tonti, an Italian, had previously lost his hand in a European battle.

In 1699, a French explorer by the name St. Cosme traveled down the Mississippi and confirmed the Marquette/Jolliet sighting of the one acre landmark known as Tower Rock. St. Cosme was another one of those ubiquitous Jesuit missionaries who came down from Canada to convert the "heathens." Tonti's cross had been stolen so St. Cosme was determined to erect another one to prove to the natives that the Christian god was more powerful than the Indian Manitou.

Over the years the place took on a number of names including Tower Rock, La Roche de la Croix (rock of the cross), Castle Rock, Devil's Tower, Rock of St. Cosme, and Passage of the Cross.

During the Ulysses Grant Administration (1870), the Army Corps of Engineers cleared the area around it of other rocks that might have proved dangerous to navigation. This created a nice clear channel between Tower

Rock and the Missouri shore. There were plans to dynamite the rock and eliminate the shipping hazard completely, but it was left standing because Grant thought it to be a suitable support for a future bridge.

Just north of the rock there was a ferry business that took passengers to the Missouri town of **Wittenberg**, a place originally founded by German Lutherans. It was this group that later became the nucleus of the current Lutheran Church-Missouri Synod.

The difficult passage past the rock made it a natural site for river pirates. Around 1800 there was a notorious band of renegades who thrived by attacking and pillaging boats that went past. After committing their heinous acts of murder and rob-bery, they retreated to a hideout that came to be known as **"Sinner's Har-bor."** It took a detachment of U.S. cavalry to clean up the problem.

Mark Twain, in his riverboat pilot days, knew Tower Rock quite well and noted that it was the site of many a steamboat wreckage. James B. Eads, of future bridge fame, spent many hours on the bottom of the river near the rock salvaging cargoes in his specially made diving bell. The waters around Tower Rock were a veritable treasure trove for salvage operations.

THE LEGENDARY MIKE FINK

What famed "King of the Keelboats" claimed to be half horse and half alli-gator? The outrageous Mike Fink. Fink is one of those characters known as an anti-hero. Although he had some heroic qualities, he was not the type of person you want to emulate because he had serious flaws in his character. He used foul language, drank heavily, and was a womanizer. Though he has developed a mythology to rival that of Paul Bunyan, Fink was not a figment of anyone's imagination. He was the most famous of the keelboat men who plied the Mississippi and other rivers for two decades until they and their watercraft were displaced by steamboats as the preferred means of moving goods in the early 1800s.

The keelboat men were the original American anti-heroes -- hard-living, hard-drinking hulks who used their tremendous strength to pole and pull their boats upriver against the current before floating back down.

Born around 1780 in a log cabin near Pittsburgh, Miche Phinck, as he learned to spell it from his French Canadian parents, gained notoriety as a

231

marksman and an Indian scout (in the Ohio River Valley) before settling into keelboating.

His superior physique -– he stood 6-foot, 3 and weighed 180 pounds -– and flair for self-aggrandizement -– he claimed he could "outrun, outshoot, throw down, drag out and lick any man in the country" -- transformed him into an icon for storytellers of the day.

Some of the tales they swapped had him riding a moose like a horse, **wrestling alligators and drowning wolves with his bare hands**.

Fink apparently drifted west after the demise of the keelboats and, by one unconfirmed account, died during a drunken altercation with a trapper friend.

After Walt Disney scored a huge success with his three-part television series about frontiersman Davy Crockett, he searched for another story that would

Mike Fink (University of Nebraska Press)

have Crockett in it. He found his story in 1955 and titled it *Davy Crockett's Keelboat Race.* Crockett's opponent in the race was none other than that scalawag, Mike Fink. Davy and his pal George Russell want to travel down the Ohio River to New Orleans, but they bristle when Mike Fink charges them $1,000 for a ride on his keelboat. Our heroes hire another boat captained by a crusty river man, thereby sparking a race between Crockett and Fink, with a valuable shipment of furs as the prize. Naturally, Fink pulls all sorts of underhanded tricks to keep Davy's boat from finishing the race, but good sportsmanship wins out, and Davy and Mike become friends.

Mike Fink, that notorious visitor of St. Louis saloons, had some interesting things to say about aquatic life and the food chain in the Mississippi. "I've seen trout swallow a perch, and a catfish would come along and swallow the trout, and . . . the alligators use up the cat . . ." He also said there was so much dirt and dust in the Mississippi that you could occasionally see a catfish come up to the surface to sneeze.

Although Mike Fink was a real person, the stories about him are mostly tall tales. What was one of Fink's favorite drinking games? After guzzling down several cups of grog, Mike would have a friend of his stand about twenty paces away and he would aim his rifle and shoot the container off the man's head.

What were some of Fink's alleged exploits? It was said he could bite the head off of a live rattlesnake. There was also the time he went to the doctor,

232

complaining of stomach pain. After an examination, the man told Fink that he had ruined the lining of his stomach by drinking so much hard liquor over the years. Sadly, there was nothing he could do for him. Fink went away and pondered his problem. Then he went out and wrestled a bear, strangling him to death. He then skinned the bear, swallowed the fur, and the new lining for his stomach enabled him to continue his hard drinking.

A legendary feat was accomplished by Mike Fink. He has title to the **longest jump on record**. He once boasted that he could jump across the Mississippi. When put to the test, he saw that he was going to fall short by about ten feet, so he changed course in midair and landed safely back at his starting point.

THE PONY EXPRESS

The Pony Express flourished eighteen months (1860-61) at **St. Joseph**, Missouri. It began there because railroad construction had not progressed beyond that point. The invention of the telegraph eventually killed off the service. The 1,996 mile route from St. Joe to Sacramento had 190 relay stations spaced about ten miles apart. **An average trip took ten days**. The young riders received $100 a month as pay, if they lived long enough to collect it. The job was so hazardous handbills stated that **orphans were preferred as riders**. Riders could weigh no more than 125 pounds. A rider usually traveled about 75 miles before passing his leather pouch to another rider. The riders were generally lightly armed because they discovered that a fast horse was their best defense against Indians. The route followed the Oregon Trail, then headed south along the Mormon trail, then went the rest of the way along the California Trail. The Pony Express grossed $90,000 and had expenses of about $200,000. After the Civil War, the assets were sold to Wells Fargo for well over a million dollars.

Donuts were invented when the girl friend of rider Johnny Fry passed them to him as he rode by.

THE DOOLITTLE RAID: APRIL 1942

Former St. Louisan Colonel James Doolittle was a great hero. After Pearl Harbor, Americans were desperate to get a few licks in against Japan. On April 1, 1942, following two months of extensive training, 16 highly modified B-25 medium bombers, with five man crews, were loaded onto the *USS Hornet* at Alameda, Calif. Each plane carried four 500 pound bombs and extra fuel tanks. Dummy guns were mounted in the tail section to discourage attacks from the rear. The *Hornet* joined up with a protective task force led by the *Enterprise*. The two carriers proceeded under radio silence toward their intended launch points in enemy waters near Japan. The group was sighted by a small Japanese ship so Captain Mark Mitscher launched the planes immediately, 200 miles farther from Japan than intended. The pilots were led by **Jimmy Doolittle**. None of them had ever taken off from a carrier but all 16 planes were launched successfully. They flew single file at wavetop level to avoid detection. They arrived at their targets around noon on the 18th of April. Their targets were Tokyo, Yokohama, Kobe, Osaka and Nagoya. No bomber was shot down or severely damaged.

After releasing their bombs the planes headed for landing fields in unoccupied China. Low on fuel and in rapidly deteriorating weather, most crash landed in China. Doolittle and his crew received assistance from an American missionary in China, John Birch, who later became the namesake of the conservative **John Birch Society**. The Japanese captured eight airmen and shot three of them. One died in captivity and the other four were freed by American troops in August of 1945.

Jimmy Doolittle

Since Doolittle lost all 16 planes with only light damage done to Japan (50 dead, 400 injured), he told his men he expected to be court martialed. Instead, the raid bolstered American morale so greatly he was given the Medal of Honor and promoted two grades to Brigadier General. As of March of 2010, only 8 of the original raiders remained alive. The raid was the subject of two films, *Thirty Seconds Over Tokyo* and *Purple Heart*. Doolittle Raid memorabilia is on display at the Air Force Museum in Dayton, Ohio. (Talk your dad into taking the family there for a visit. I've been there and it's magnificent.)

The 2001 film, *Pearl Harbor*, with Josh Hartnett, Kate Beckinsale and Ben Affleck, ends with scenes of B-25 Mitchells taking off from the *Hornet* and heading for Japan. Say what you will about the love story, the special effects during the attack on Pearl Harbor are spectacular in this film.

As it became evident that the war in Europe was going to be won by the Allies, Hollywood shifted its focus to the Pacific Theater. Spencer Tracy portrayed Lieutenant Colonel James Doolittle in *Thirty Seconds Over Tokyo*, a film that showed Americans paying Japan back for the treacherous raid at Pearl Harbor. Van Johnson, Robert Walker and Robert Mitchum were additional cast members.

SOLDIER IN GREASE PAINT

We often overlook the significant role that women play in our history. Here is an amazing story of one woman's devotion to her patriotic cause. Historian Bob Priddy gave the above title to Jane Froman. She was born in St. Louis and attended Christian College in Columbia, where her mother taught music. After graduating, she enrolled at the University of Missouri to study journalism. In 1927, she saw her name in lights for the first time when she grabbed the lead in a musical production. That landed her a contract with a week-long show in St. Louis where she shared a dressing room with a very young Betty Grable. Jane obtained a contract to sing on WLW in Cincinnati, and that led to a contract in **Chicago** with Paul Whiteman and NBC. Within six months she had her own show. She sang on five different occasions for President Roosevelt.

After the Japanese attacked Pearl Harbor, **she was the first entertainer to go overseas with USO troupes**. Early in 1943, she was on a plane with other entertainers headed to Europe to entertain the troops. The plane crashed in the Tagus River in Lisbon, Portugal and she suffered severe injuries. Her left leg was fractured, her right leg was nearly severed, she had several cracked ribs, and there were multiple fractures of her right arm. It took 25 operations to keep her leg intact. Her hospital bills amounted to $350,000.

Jane Froman

Later, in 1943, still in great pain, with her leg in a 35 pound cast, the 85 pound Froman sang for 3,500 soldiers in Boston. They gave her a standing ovation. In 1944, she was named to the **Philco Radio Hall of Fame**. After the war, she had recovered enough to go back to Europe and entertain the occupation troops. Congress appropriated $200,000 to help pay her bills. In 1952, she was given her own television show, "Jane Froman's USA Canteen." Actress Susan Hayward portrayed her in a 1952 film biography, *With A Song in My Heart*. Hayward did the acting and Froman did the song voice-overs.

November 10, 2007, the 100th anniversary of Froman's birth, was declared **Jane Froman Day** at Columbia, Missouri. For further reading see Barbara Seuling's recent biography of Jane Froman.

TROLLEY CARS AND BUSES

I grew up in East St. Louis, Illinois during the 1940s and 1950s. By then the trolleys in that town had been replaced by buses, but I frequently visited relatives in St. Louis and streetcars were still in service there, so I have great memories from a bygone era.

One of the most interesting aspects of trolley cars was that when they reached the end of the line there was often no turn around. Passengers climbing aboard faced the uneasy prospect of riding in a car that would be going backwards. Vera Niemann (German) of **Fairview Heights**, Illinois wrote a memoir in which she described what happened next.

"Presto! The car stopped. The motorman picked up his detachable seat and moved to the rear, which now became the front of the car. The passengers stood up and flipped over the backs of the seats, which now faced the opposite direction. The entire process took only about two minutes. Streetcars were designed so that the front and rear of the car were identical."

Most St. Louis streetcars did not have this feature. Loops were built as turnarounds at the end of the line. The most famous loop was at the end of Washington Avenue near the Eads Bridge. The earliest St. Louis streetcars had

no loops so there were poles that could be attached to either end for horse hookup.

Although streetcars were often built by the same companies that made coaches pulled by steam engines, the ride was decidedly different. Instead of a chuffing sound of the engine and a jerking noise being made by knuckle couplers as the train lurched forward, trolley riders heard only the strange low roar of the electric motor revving up with a hum that progressively grew higher in pitch, but leveled off as the car attained its top speed. There was also that distinctive and unforgettable metallic groaning sound as the metal wheels crushed down on the ribbons of steel rails.

St. Louis streetcars were built to broad gauge specifications of four feet ten inches. Standard gauge of railroads and trolleys was 4 feet, eight and ½ inches. According to tradition, this width was arrived at by engineers because **it was said to be the same width as the distance between the wheels on a Roman chariot**.

Streetcars were subject to pranks, especially on Halloween. Sometimes there was a steep grade that streetcars had to negotiate. Puckish youths sometimes obtained some grease from a local restaurant and smeared it on the tracks. The first car to hit the slick spot would stall and ten minutes later the next eastbound car came along and interurbans would back up until the grease was cleaned off.

Another common prank was committed when a trolley car made a stop to pick up a passenger. A mischievous youth would run up to the car and disconnect the overhead trolley mechanism from the power cable with a long clothes prop. The motorman, in his sharp navy blue uniform, cheered on by the passengers, had to go outside and reattach the mechanism to restore power.

WHY GEORGE ROGERS CLARK IS A HERO

In 1778 the American Revolution was now three years old. George Rogers Clark, under orders from Governor Patrick Henry of Virginia, was assigned the task of wresting control of the western frontier from the British. Virginia laid claim to Illinois Territory on the basis of an original sea-to-sea charter, granted to the Jamestown settlers in 1607. Clark and his men set out from Corn Island, in the Ohio River near Louisville, and floated down the river to Fort Massac at Metropolis. He raised the American flag, and this was the only day he ever spent at the fort. Then they marched overland from there, led by a man named John Duff, to **Kaskaskia**. For the most part, they followed the Le Grand Trace, an old French military road. With a meager force of 175 men, they took the fort by surprise and captured it without firing a shot. Clark next captured **Cahokia, St. Philippe, and Prairie du Rocher** without a struggle. At Cahokia, Francois Trottier, the commandant, prepared for a spirited defense, but when he saw his friends and relatives from Kaskaskia among the invaders, he surrendered the town and joined the American cause. At this point, Illinois became a county of Virginia.

Clark held a powwow and smoked the peace pipe with the leaders of local Indian tribes. They called him **Long Knife**. His skillful diplomacy won them over. Clark then sent emissaries to Vincennes and told the authorities that he and his men, allied with the French and Indians in southern Illinois, were now in control and that they should throw in with him. They promptly did so.

In 1780 George Rogers Clark, along with Richard McCarty and a force of 170 men, began the "**Impossible March**" of about 200 miles to recapture Fort Sackville at Vincennes, on the Illinois/Indiana border along the Wabash River. The twenty-two day trek through swampy marshland was exhausting, and **they were near starving, having run out of provisions**. Henry Hamilton was reluctant to surrender the fort, but Clark tricked him into thinking he was being attacked by a superior force. Clark and his men captured a raiding party coming back to the fort with American scalps. **Clark had them dispatched with tomahawks** in full view of Hamilton and his men who were inside the fort. Fearful for their lives, they surrendered.

Clark was asked by President Jefferson to lead the 1804 Lewis and Clark exploration of the Louisiana Purchase, but he recommended his younger brother, **William Clark,**. There is a statue of George Rogers Clark in the rotunda of a memorial to Clark on the site of old Fort Sackville at Vincennes. Seven murals there depict his heroic exploits.

Clark retired and lived out the rest of his life in a house overlooking the Ohio River.

Theodore Roosevelt wrote in *The Winning of the West* that Clark's only reward for his heroism was the sword given him by the Virginia legislature. After the war he fell upon hard times and died in near poverty. **Clark is remembered as the Father of the Northwest Territory.**

When the war was over, Clark's men carried back good reports of the country they had seen, which caused many emigrants to come seeking new homes. After the war, new settlers (largely Scotch-Irish and English) poured into Illinois Country from North Carolina, Kentucky, Tennessee and Virginia. From these migrants the great majority of "Egyptians" have descended, and their and cultural traditions, Southern in character, prevail generally in the region of Southern Illinois.

In 1783 the British signed the Treaty of Paris granting Americans their independence. The American negotiators were ready to give up claims to Illinois country in exchange for fishing rights off the coast of Newfoundland near the Grand Banks. But the British Prime Minister, Lord Shelburne, offered Illinois Country to Ben Franklin in hopes of drawing the Americans toward Britain and away from France. (Illinois should have named a county after this man.)

In 1929 the U.S. Postal Service issued a stamp to honor George Rogers Clark. It was physically **our largest stamp ever issued prior to that date**.

THE PIRATES OF CAVE-IN-ROCK

There is a place in southern Illinois known as Cave-In-Rock. Located in Hardin County, about twenty miles below Shawneetown, on the Ohio River, the natural limestone formation became a notorious den for riverboat highwaymen in the late 17th century.

The opening of the cave is in a limestone bluff overlooking the Ohio River, not many miles from where the river joins the Mississippi at Cairo. The first written record of its discovery by French explorers is dated 1744. The cave was formed in some remote geological age and was possibly the drainage for one of the many sinkholes in the area. Almost directly in front of the cave is the lower end of Cave-In-Rock Island, which becomes submerged during high water. A stone carving of a sitting man, unearthed in 1918, suggests that prehistoric natives may have used the cave for religious rituals. Henry Schoolcraft, the man who gave us a gazetteer of Southern Illinois, visited the cave in 1818.

The elliptical opening at the mouth of the cave is about 55 feet wide. The cavern extends to the rear about 160 feet at a uniform width of about 40 feet. The floor and ceiling are smooth and contain no stalagmites or stalactites. There is a gradual incline as one walks from the front of the cave to the back.

As flatboats made their way down the river, the pirates had a confederate hail a passing boat, yelling out to occupants that they were stranded. When the boat came ashore for rescue, the crew was attacked and the boat was robbed of its supplies and provisions. Sometimes the crew and boat would be released but often the people were killed and their bodies, weighted down with rocks, were thrown into the river.

One group of cutthroats turned the cave into a pleasant-looking inn and by this deception ensnared weary travelers. Another ingenious band of robbers used the treacherous serpentine river channel at that point to good advantage. They stationed a confederate about ten miles above the cave near Battery Rock. He would pose as an experienced pilot and offer to steer the boat safely past the sandbars for a fee of one dollar. He would then proceed to run the boat aground so that it could be attacked by his partners. The fact that the West (as this part of the country was known) was so sparsely settled at this time made these outlaw attacks on the citizenry possible.

Probably the most brutal persons to occupy the cave were the Harp(e) brothers. They seemed to have had a lust for blood. They were a couple of backwoodsmen, native to North Carolina. One dubious account of their life reported that they fought against the British at the battle of King's Mountain in North Carolina during the Revolution.

The oldest, Micajah "Big" Harpe, a big-boned man with huge limbs, curly hair, and a weather-beaten face, claimed two women as his wives - Betsy and Susan. His brother, the red-haired Wiley "Little" Harpe was married to a woman named Sally Rice. They left a trail of murder, arson and thievery in the frontier areas of Tennessee and Kentucky. Big Harpe was known for splitting people's skulls open with a big tomahawk that he carried in his belt.

The whole clan was once arrested for killing a man named Thomas Langford. While they were in the Danville, Kentucky jail, all three of their only children were born. But the two brothers eventually escaped from the jail, leaving their wives and babies behind.

The court and townsfolk took pity on the abandoned women and released them, thinking they would seek a fresh start in life. But instead they made their way to Cave-In-Rock where they rejoined their murderous husbands. There were other outlaws at the cave while the Harpes were there, but most of them left and went elsewhere, fearing that too many of them would bring in the authorities.

One day a flatboat came down the river and stopped about a mile north of the cave to make some repairs. Two passengers, a young man and his sweetheart, decided to go for a walk to the top of the bluff where they sat down to take in the view. The Harpe brothers rushed from the woods and pushed them off the cliff above the cave. The man and woman fell forty feet but miraculously landed on a sandy beach below, and neither was seriously hurt.

The Harpe family left Cave-In-Rock and continued their killing spree in Kentucky and Tennessee. The Harpes even killed several children who came upon them by chance, seemingly for the sport of it. There was one instance where Big Harpe grabbed his own young infant from the arms of his wife and bashed its brains out against a tree.

Finally, after the Harpes had been responsible for the brutal murders of more than twenty people, a vigilante group took out after them. In a desperate shoot-out, Big Harpe was mortally wounded but managed to lead his pursuers on a short chase until they finally caught up with him. After giving him a chance to make his peace with God, which he ignored, they shot him again and killed him. Then one of the men named Steigal cut off his head as a trophy. The decapitated body was left to be devoured by animals.

Little Harpe managed to escape and continued his criminal ways in other

states. The women, seemingly glad to be free of their polecat husbands, and the recipients of much sympathy, were not charged.

The severed head of Big Harpe was placed in the fork of a tree near a public road in rural Kentucky as a grisly reminder to all monstrous outlaws. Today, it is known as Harpe's Head Road.

There was one wily fellow by the name of Samuel Mason who made Cave-In-Rock his headquarters around 1797 and stayed there for nearly a year. After a while, Mason gave that up and continued to make a disreputable living by robbing travelers on the Natchez Trace in Mississippi.

There was a large reward on his head, and that ultimately was the cause of his demise. One night in 1804, by a campfire, he was counting his loot when one of his associates buried a tomahawk in his brain. The head was then taken to the governor of Mississippi by two men, James May and John Setton, who tried to collect the reward. Someone recognized Setton and claimed that he was really "Little" Harpe. Setton denied that he was Little Harpe, but a mole on his neck and certain body scars, left authorities in Greenville, Mississippi, convinced it was Harpe. Both men were tried and found guilty of various charges. They were taken to a field where a log was placed horizontally so that it rested in the forks of two different trees. Two nooses were tied to the pole. The men were led from the jail and made to climb ladders to reach their hangman's rope. Then the ladders were kicked out from under them. After their execution, their heads were placed on poles, on opposite sides of the road, along the Natchez Trace.

The Harpe brothers have the notorious distinction of having been **America's first serial killers.** Their activities were depicted in the 1962 Cinerama (large screen) film, *How the West Was Won*.

SLAVERY IN THE FREE STATE OF ILLINOIS

French settlers in the area extracted salt from the Half Moon Salt Lick as early as 1735. When Illinois attained statehood in 1818 the federal government retained ownership of the lands around the salt works. They then signed leases with individuals who then operated the saltworks. In 1834 John Hart Crenshaw built a three story structure with colonnaded porches on Hickory Hill, near **Equality in Gallatin County**. The house overlooks the Saline river valley. It has been a landmark for over a century and is called "The Old Slave House." The third floor has many small windowless rooms where slaves were kept. There were metal rings attached to the floor in some rooms to prevent the slaves from escaping. Crenshaw employed a good deal of slave labor and Negro indentured servants at his extensive salt works on the Saline River. He probably engaged in the practice of kidnapping free Negroes because Jon Musgrave has uncovered court records in Shawneetown showing him charged with this offense. Crenshaw owned 30,000 acres of land plus three of the nine furnaces that reduced the salt water to crystals.

There is a plaque near the Saline River that marks the road to "Nigger Spring." At this spring brine would slowly ooze to the surface, giving off an unpleasant, pungent odor of salt and sulfur. This liquid was placed in iron kettles that were heated to hasten the evaporation process. Salt making, **Illinois' oldest industry**, was so important that the Illinois Constitution of 1818 exempted the works near Shawneetown from the antislavery clause and Crenshaw was allowed to lease slaves from Kentucky. Slaves were used extensively in the manufacture of the salt. A census of Gallatin County in 1820 listed 239 slaves or servants. **This was the only place in the entire state of Illinois where slavery was allowed to exist**. The surrounding forest was cut to provide fuel for the process that made 500 bushels of "white gold" (salt) daily.

There is a place near Equality called Half Moon Lick. This was a crescent-shaped depression in the earth that was caused by numerous animals over the years coming to the spot and licking away at the earth to gain access to the salt it contained. Salt is a necessary mineral needed to sustain the life of mammals. Half Moon Lick became the site of a large facility where salt furnaces were built. The brine was brought from the spring to the furnaces by a pipeline, consisting of large logs that were hollowed out. It was then heated in huge kettles until all the water evaporated, leaving nothing but salt. Much of the Midwest's supply of salt in our nation's early history came from these Gallatin salines.

When treaties were signed with Native Americans (in 1803) to gain access to these salt licks, they contained provisions that monthly allotments of salt would be given to tribes that lived in the surrounding areas.

Salt is important to sustain life. Farmers with hogs, cattle, and horses on their land have traditionally bought blocks of salt for the animals to lick.

The site of the U.S. Salines declined as other sources of salt were found, and it was finally abandoned in 1875.

Abe Lincoln once visited the place and spent a night in the Crenshaw home.

THE KLAN COMES TO SOUTHERN ILLINOIS

The KKK isn't much of a force currently, largely due to its racist beliefs and extremist views on politics. But there was a time in America when that wasn't always the case. What follows is a description of a Klan meeting. See how many extremist positions you can detect.

It was one of those typically hot, humid days in late June of 1923 – the kind of day where you can hear the corn growing in the fields and the heat shimmers off the highway in undulating waves, giving drivers a false perception of a desert mirage.

A great gathering of oddly dressed people clustered around the base of one of the lesser mounds that was just west of the **Great Cahokia Mound** that stood an impressive 100 feet tall, on the outskirts of **Collinsville, Illinois**, on Route 40. The Cahokia Mound, colloquially known as Monk's Mound, was an historic bit of architecture that had been built by Native-Americans who had once inhabited the area in the anthropological era known as the Mississippi Period. The natives had carried basket after basket of rich alluvial soil to create an impressive oblong structure that **contained a volume of dirt that was larger than the Great Pyramid of Cheops in ancient Egypt. It is the most significant archeological Native-American site in all of the USA or Canada**. Anthropologists speculated that at one point in time the natives there had

Human sacrifice at the Great Cahokia Mound (*St. Louis Globe-Democrat*)

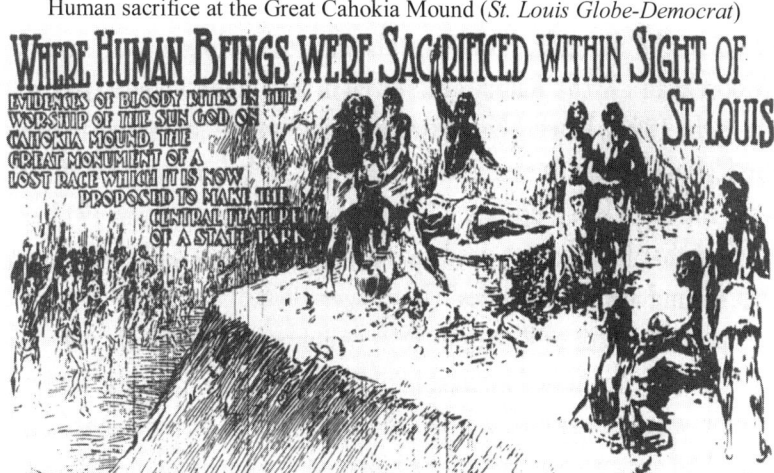

practiced the blood ritual of human sacrifice.

Lewis and Clark had spent time in the area in 1804 before launching their expedition to explore the Louisiana Purchase of 1803. Oddly, there is no evidence that they ever saw the Mound, even though their campsite was just a few miles north in **Wood River**.

But on this day the eager crowd that was waiting in white satin robes was expectant, their eyes searching the cobalt blue sky. Suddenly they began to cheer. They had seen a tiny speck in the sky, a speck that grew into an airplane. As it came closer, the Curtiss "Jenny" glistened in the bright sunlight, and they could see that it was gilded all over. The plane circled the level field, a spot that had been freshly mowed, and slowly see-sawed in for a bumpety-bump landing, its engine sputtering as it coughed to a stop.

A bulky man in a robe and hood of purple silk hoisted himself up from the rear seat of the plane. As he lowered himself to the ground a new surge of applause filled the air. White-robed figures bobbed up and down on tippy-toes; small children were hoisted up on their father's shoulders for a view. A small

242

delegation of dignitaries filed out toward the airplane, stopping at a respectful distance.

The man in royal purple stepped forward.

"Kigy," he said. In Klanspeak he just uttered, "Klansmen, I greet you."

"Itsub," they eagerly replied.

He went forward to greet each member of the small group. Klasping left hands, showed Klan loyalty and greeting.

With the newcomer in the lead, the group made its way to a raised wooden platform, decked out in bunting and flags, and especially built for the occasion.

"My worthy subjects, citizens of the Invisible Empire, Klansmen all, greetings. It grieves me to arrive late. I have just come from Washington, D.C. where we held a glorious parade down Pennsylvania Avenue, attended by thousands. The President of the United States kept me unduly long, counseling upon matters of importance to the state. He assured me that immigration bills would be passed and enforced to keep out godless radicals who would come to this country to toss bombs and stir up hatred toward Americanism." The crowd buzzed.

"Here in this uplifted hand, for all to see, I bear an official document addressed to the Grand Dragon, Hydras, Great Titans, Furies, Kleagles, Exalted Cyclops and all citizens of the Invisible Empire of the Realm of Illinois. It is signed by His Lordship, the Exalted Hiram Wesley Evans, Imperial Wizard."

The Grand Dragon paused, inviting cheers and clapping that thundered about him. Then he launched into a speech. He urged members of the audience to fight for 100 percent Americanism and against corrupting foreign influence. He warned about miscegenation – the mixing of Negro blood with that of the white race. He exhorted the crowd to ignore the slanderous writings of the liberal press that professed the innocence of those two murderous holdup men, Sacco and Vanzetti. He called them anarchist vermin that justly deserved to be exterminated. He warned about the growing influence of Catholicism in this country and urged supporters to write their congressmen, urging their support for an end to foreign immigration that was filling the land with Romanists, Jews and those who believed in godless communism.

Someone in the crowd raised a placard. It read: "The Pope Will Never Enter the White House." There had been disturbing rumors that New York Governor Al Smith, a "wet" (pro-liquor) and a Catholic, was the growing favorite for the presidential nominee of the Democratic Party in the upcoming 1924 election.

(Note: In the 1924 convention, the Klan used its influence to prevent "wet" Catholic Al Smith from getting the nomination. It was a tough battle, taking a record 103 ballots before the Protestant John W. Davis secured the nomination over Smith and his Tammany Hall political machine.)

The portly speaker went on to denounce the Knights of Columbus as a secret organization plotting to kill Protestants and install the Pope in the White House. It was no accident, he said, that the lofty spires of the wealthy Catholic churches commanded he highest view in most towns. The Knights had their guns in the basements of Catholic churches and, when the time was ripe, guns fired from the high belfries could dominate the streets.

After the leader finished his speech and stepped back, people began tossing coins, gold rings, dollar bills, bracelet charms, and anything else that was valuable, onto the platform. When the tribute slackened, officials on the platform began to gather up the treasure.

Finally, a local reverend gave an invocation and a twenty-five piece band played "America" and "The Star Spangled Banner." The meeting ended with a pledge of allegiance to Old Glory. Then the man in purple strode off to a near-by pavilion to counsel with his attendant Kleagles, Cyclopses and Titans.

The crowd dispersed and then wandered off to various sites close by and spread blankets to consume the goodies in their picnic baskets. This was an all day affair. Later that evening, there would be another message given by a lesser official. Those in the crowd who were not yet members would be invited to join the crusade. The membership fee was six dollars. Robes were sold to newcomers at a cost of $6.75. The affiliated Gate City Manufacturing Company of Atlanta made them at a cost of $3.28. Local Klaverns were supported by dues of a dollar a month. Finally, there would be blood oaths and an elaborate ceremony, followed by a nighttime cross burning.

Meetings similar to this took place in towns all over the state as the Klan had particular appeal in the lower southern tier of the state known as Little Egypt. They held numerous rallies in **Herrin, Marion, Benton, West Frankfort, Harrisburg, Carbondale, Sparta, Mount Vernon, Pinckneyville and Cairo.**

Collinsville newsman Karl Monroe had this to say about the event. "There was one summer when they were pretty big. They held parades. My father wrote articles in the newspaper against them and they didn't like that much and threatened him. But nothing ever happened. They had a tremendous event down at Cahokia Mounds. On one of those small mounds on the south side of Route 40, they set up a huge cross and had lots of speeches and big crowds. And my father took me down there. I remember it was one of the few times I ever had hot dogs in those early days, picnic style. They were selling hot dogs and other refreshments.

"That night I wasn't there, but I was told they burned this huge cross on the mound. And that was one of the high water marks of the Klan around here."

If you've never visited this site, beg your parents to take you there. The mounds site has a large, modern museum directly across from the great mound. And just a bit farther north and west, 15 minutes away, is the fabulous Lewis and Clark museum on Route 3. Besides numerous artifacts, it has a cut-away replica of their boat and a full-size replica of their fort. And then you'll only be twenty minutes away from the St. Louis Arch.

WHEN SOUTHERN ILLINOIS DOMINATED PREP BASKETBALL

One would think that Illinois would have always been dominated in high school basketball by big city schools from cities such as Chicago, Waukegan, Rockford, Joliet and Peoria. But from the 1930s to the mid-1960s, this wasn't the case. It was a time when there was just one division - schools with 200 students competed against schools with 3,000 students. Despite these odds, numerous titles were won by small schools like **Taylorville, Granite City, Herrin, Pinckneyville, Mount Vernon, Centralia and Collinsville**. Big time Chicago schools did not win their first title until 1963.

My wife, Lorna, was a 1958 Collinsville High graduate. We married in 1960 and rented an apartment in Collinsville. That year the 1960-61 Kahoks, led by Bogie Redmon and Fred Riddle, won the state tournament. The team was so dominant they won their four games at the state tournament by an average score of 27 points. I started teaching social studies at Collinsville in 1964 and their 1964-65 team won state again, led by Dennis Pace and Harry Parker.

COLLINSVILLE'S BOGIE REDMOND REMEMBERS

The first thing people usually ask me is about my unusual name. My Irish great grandmother's maiden name was Lulubelle Bogie. Her son was Charles Bogie Redmon. I was named for him.

The first I can remember about basketball is being invited by Coach John Finnan of Webster School to play in the sixth grade league. I was only in the fourth grade at Jefferson, so this was a big deal to me. Every Saturday morning I would throw my high top Converse All-Stars around my neck and ride my bike up to Webster.

Next came the sixth grade at Webster and playing on the eighth grade team. What was interesting is that one of the teams on our schedule was from Madison, and this was the first time I played against Fred Riddle and Bob Simpson. They both later moved to Collinsville when they were juniors and joined the Kahok team.

Junior high would introduce me to quite a few players that I later competed against during my high school years. When I was a freshman at Collinsville High, I was six feet tall. By the end of the year I had added six inches. During that year Coach Fletcher started to take me under his wing. He was not new to me since my big brother Gant had played football and basketball under "Fletch." I knew Coach Fletcher was tough but that was fine with me. I was used to my dad, Gant, being a real taskmaster. One Saturday my dad told me to stack a load of firewood that someone had dropped off at our house. I unwisely said that I had basketball practice to get ready for that night. His reply was, "You are a son first, a student second, and a basketball player third. If that wood is not stacked this afternoon you will not be playing in that game tonight!" I knew he meant it. That wood took me three hours to stack but I got the job done.

During the ninth grade I played on the freshman team, the sophomore games, the junior varsity games, and varsity games. Since the freshman and sopho-more games were played during the week, I would play those games after practicing with the varsity. Needless to say that freshman year gave me a lot of playing time and experience. I just found out this year from assistant coach **Bert Weber** that the IHSA now has a rule that players are allowed to play only 96 quarters a season. Bert said this new rule may have been adopted as a result of my playing in so many games that year. Who knows?

Coach Fletcher let me start one varsity game that year when we played Robinson at Robinson. I was so excited because my sister Kay was a varsity cheerleader.

My sophomore year began with football and one play in practice occurred that would affect my athletic career for the rest of my life. I caught a pass and was hit on the inside of my left knee by the tackler's helmet. When I went back to the huddle my left knee felt "funny" but I didn't think much about it. Well, that knee has always bothered me. I guess that is why I have such an unusual way of walking since that knee injury affected my gait.

Basketball came right after football and it was a tough year. I think we were something like 16-12. Coach Fletcher was so upset with us after some away game losses that he would hold another practice after we got back to Collinsville. That was a year that I was glad to see end but it also made many of us underclassmen never want to go through another season like that again.

Junior year was exciting. I had to forget about football because of my knee,

Collinsville Kahoks – State Champs 1961 (Redmon #54)

but Fred Riddle and Bob Simpson transferred from Madison and we were all pumped up for basketball season to start. Our starting five that year was **Gary Dolzadelli, Pat Darling, Bob Simpson, Fred Riddle** and myself. We had a very good year finishing 25-3. All the teams in the Southwest Conference were loaded with talent. Granite City had Rich Williams and Bob Price. Madison had Ed Walker and Don Freeman, Belleville had Mel Patton, Edwardsville had Tony Penelton, and East St. Louis had Don Brooks. All of these guys knew how to score and, like I said earlier, had been my opponents since the sixth grade. Collinsville won the conference title but trying to get out of our regional would be our downfall. We played Granite City in the regional final on March 5, 1960. They beat us and that was the third year in a row that we had lost on my sister's birthday!!!

My senior year started off real good. We had an excellent football season in

246

which we only lost one game and that loss was to powerhouse East St. Louis by a single touchdown. Basketball practice started on Saturday morning, the day after our loss to the Flyers. Coach Fletcher began the meeting by saying that he wanted a Southwest Conference championship and a state championship. He said if anyone there didn't think we could accomplish that they could leave. Well, we all stayed.   Then the work began – shooting, rebounding, blocking out, shooting free throws, and whatever else coach thought was a weakness. Coach Fletcher believed that if you did things over and over again, that it would and you would not have to think about how to do something in a game – it would be second nature. He was right and it showed in the way we played our games. It didn't matter who scored or who was high point man. If the play allowed an open shot you took it. However, he generally wanted the team to take higher percentage shots close to the basket. And you knew from his coaching that if a shot was taken you had to follow up for an offensive rebound or block out so a teammate could get the ball.

Our starting five that year was **Bob Meadows, Bob Simpson, Bob Basola, Fred Riddle** and me. Bob Meadows was a half-back on the football team and was tough as nails. He had the job on defense of being the ball chaser on Coach Fletcher's ball press defense. There were always two players on the opponent with the ball. Bob Simpson was a shooter and ball handler. His Madison background in both areas proved to be invaluable the entire year. Bob Basola was also a shooter and an excellent rebounder. He could shoot from the side exceptionally well. **Fred Riddle was an All-American quarterback** and a middle linebacker on defense. His leadership and toughness was evident on the floor when he would direct us on offense, drive in for a lay-up, or rebound. I just did what I was told and benefited from the exceptional skills of the other guys. They fed me the ball and I put it in when I could.

Only two things really stand out in detail from my senior year. The first was breaking my left ankle in practice the night before our second game. I missed nine games and **Ron Mottin** took my place, helping to keep us undefeated. The second was the last few seconds of the Super-sectional game against Centralia in the Salem gym. The score was 63-62 in our favor with ten seconds left. Centralia brought the

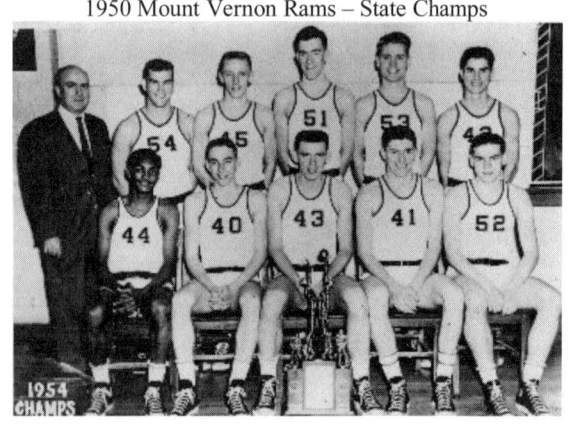

1950 Mount Vernon Rams – State Champs

ball down court and was setting up a play for the winning score. Bob Simpson stole the ball and drove in for a lay-up. I was right there behind him to put it back in case he missed. Bob was fouled on the play and sank the free throw. We let them come down and score, being careful not to foul. We won the game

247

66-64. We were going to State!!!!! (Note: Prep sports guru **Taylor Bell asserts that this was the greatest high school basketball game ever played in Illinois**.)

At Champaign we beat Rockford East, Peoria Manual, and Thornton by an average of 27 points. We held Leon Clark, an All-Stater, scoreless most of the game. He didn't make his first basket until we put the subs in near the end of the contest. Someone asked me after the championship game against Thornton if I was tired. "Are you kidding?" I replied. "Have you ever seen one of Coach Fletcher's practice sessions?"

Playing basketball at that time in history, with those great players and Coach Fletcher, and with the backing of the whole town of Collinsville, has to be the highlight of my athletic career. Every-thing I achieved I owe to Coach Fletcher, my teammates, and my parents. Coach taught me how to play and not to let down when the going got tough. **My teammates were just that – a team. You cannot do it alone. I even owe a debt to my parents for their guidance and for getting me to practice and games on time**. It has been a wonderful ride and continues to this day as I mix business with social talk about

Herrin Tigers 1957 State Champs

the glory days with customers at the insurance agency (with my son, Kai) in Collinsville!!

THE SEARCH FOR AMELIA EARHART

Amelia Mary Earhart was born in the home of her maternal grandfather at Atchison, Kansas in 1897. Amelia was more or less encouraged to be a tomboy since her mother raised her differently from other "nice little girls" in her neighborhood by allowing her to wear bloomers. In 1904 Amelia, with help from an uncle, fashioned together a wooden ramp from the top of a backyard tool shed. She got the idea from a roller coaster ride she saw while visiting St. Louis. She slid down the ramp in a produce crate and exclaimed to her sister, "It's just like flying."

Amelia also spent countless hours reading in the family library. (**It is a myth that you'll need to wear glasses if you read too much. You cannot harm your eyes simply by using them**.) Although the family received a large inheritance when her maternal grandmother died, her father's heavy drinking cost him his job and her parents' house and belongings were auctioned off to pay for debts.

Her mother took the family to Chicago where they lived with friends. Amelia graduated from Hyde Park High School in 1916 but her time there was not happy. A yearbook caption described her as the "girl in the brown dress who walks alone." As a motivation tool, she began keeping a scrapbook with pictures and stories about women who were successful working in predominantly male oriented fields.

When the Spanish flu epidemic hit in 1918, Amelia was living in Toronto and worked in a hospital as a nurse's aide. On two separate occasions she enrolled in colleges but dropped out. In 1920 she went to live with her reconciled parents in Long Beach, California. One day her father took her to an air field and for $10 she went for a ride in a plane. "As soon as that plane took off I knew I had to fly," Amelia later commented. She began taking flying lessons and eventually had 500 hours of solo flying. In October of 1922, she attained an altitude of 14,000 feet, a new record for female pilots.

In 1924 Amelia planned to enroll at MIT in Boston but had to cancel because of a lack in finances. To earn her living, she became a social worker. She continued flying and wrote an aviation newspaper column to encourage other women.

After Charles Lindbergh's solo flight across the Atlantic in 1927, people wondered who would be the first female to do it. Publisher and publicist George Putnam became involved in plans for a trans-Atlantic flight with a woman on board. When he began asking around for suggestions, Amelia's name came up. He called her and she said *yes*. The flight had two men on board; one acted as pilot and the other was co-pilot and keeper of the log book. Amelia did not do any of the flying because she had no training on instruments, which is what the pilot relied on. Nevertheless, when the plane landed in Wales, England nearly 21 hours later, all the press attention focused on Amelia.

After the flight crew returned to the U.S., they were given a ticker tape parade and were received at the White House by President Coolidge. Amelia was now famous. Trading on her resemblance to Charles Lindbergh, the press dubbed her "Lady Lindy," "Queen of the Air" and tunesmiths wrote songs about her.

Amelia Earhart (Wikipedia)

Amelia used her celebrity image to promote a clothing line, Lucky Strike cigarettes, and Amelia Earhart Luggage. In 1929 she and Charles Lindbergh promoted Transcontinental Air Transport, which evolved into Trans World Airlines. In February of 1931, Amelia married her publicist, George Putnam. To marry Amelia, George had to divorce his first wife, **whose father was one of the founders of the company that made Crayola crayons**. Later that year, Amelia set a world altitude record of 18,415 feet.

In 1932, at the age of 34, Amelia became **the first woman to solo the Atlantic** (in a Lockheed Vega), a feat that had previously claimed the lives of four other female flyers. She took off from Newfoundland and landed in Ireland. Congress awarded her the Distinguished Flying Cross. Amelia soon became friends with Eleanor Roosevelt, who also championed women's causes. Between 1930 and 1935, Amelia set seven women's speed and distance records. She then decided on one final spectacular flight, one that would circumnavigate the globe. **Little did she know that this adventure would catapult her into aviation myth**.

Amelia's 29,000 mile flight would start in Miami, hug the coastline of Central and South America, and then follow the equator. Amelia and her husband believed the flight would help promote a new book she was planning to write. She chose Fred Noonan as her navigator, an experienced pilot with Pan Am Airlines. Like her father, Tom had a drinking problem. They made it across Africa, across the Indian sub-continent, and to New Guinea in Asia. From there, the next leg of their journey was across the Pacific to tiny Howland Island for rest and refueling. Direction finding was critical for the island was only about a mile long. The U.S, Navy had a communications ship there to help guide her. Unfortunately there was a communication problem. As she drew near, the navy ship could hear her transmissions but she could not hear theirs. The Navy sent Morse Code signals, which she acknowledge receiving, but she had never bothered to master Morse Code and was unable to determine their direction. Amelia and Fred apparently missed their mark, ran out of fuel, and drowned in the ocean.

The U.S. military sent a dozen ships and spent two weeks looking for Amelia, (at a cost of $4 million), but no trace of her, or her plane, were ever found. There were all sorts of wild speculation. Some believed she and Noonan crash landed on some remote Pacific isle and spent the rest of their lives living with natives. Others thought she might have accidentally flown over a Japanese naval installation and discovered that they were cheating on naval limitation treaties they had previously signed. They sent planes up and shot her down to keep their secret undiscovered. Earhart was declared legally dead two years later.

A 1943 movie, *Flight for Freedom*, starring Rosalind Russell and Fred MacMurray, suggested that Earhart made the ill-fated flight at the request of President Roosevelt to spy on the Japanese. Jackie Cochran, famed female aviatrix and friend of Amelia's, searched American and Japanese records after the war and found no evidence of this.

In 1990, the NBC-TV series *Unsolved Mysteries* broadcast an interview with a Saipanese woman who claimed to have witnessed Earhart and Noonan's execution by Japanese soldiers.

In November 2006, the National Geographic Channel aired episode two of the *Undiscovered History* series about a claim that Earhart survived the world flight, moved to New Jersey, changed her name, remarried and became Irene Craigmile Bolam.

In 2009, a movie titled *Amelia* was released, retracing the notable events in the life of the gutsy aviatrix who defied the impossible and lived the dream. The movie stars Hillary Swank as Amelia and Richard Gere as George Putnam.

Amelia Earhart was a widely known international celebrity during her lifetime. Her shyly charismatic appeal, independence, persistence, coolness under pressure, courage and goal-oriented career, along with the circumstances of her disappearance at a young age, have given her lasting fame in popular culture. Hundreds of articles and scores of books have been written about her life which is often cited as a motivational tale, especially for girls. Earhart is generally regarded as a feminist icon.

THE GREAT CRABAPPLE WAR OF 1956
By Marilyn Kinsella of **Fairview Heights**

Although this story takes place in the Metro East, if you grew up anywhere in the St. Louis area you can probably identify with it. It's one of those classic stories of pre-teen angst that nearly all of us have experienced in one form or another.

Baby Ruth was made in by Curtiss Candy Co. in Chicago

"Sometimes I think that I lived in the greatest neighborhood in old Fairview that there ever was. First of all, you have to under-stand the layout. **Fairview Heights**, Illinois is between Collinsville and Belleville on Route 50. The main street, the one I lived on, was called St. Clair Rd. It led back off an old highway called Old Lincoln Trail, purportedly named because Abe Lincoln once stayed in one of the houses along that road. There were many off-shoots on St. Clair Rd. – North Rd., South Rd., Judith Ann Place and Center, Dog-wood and Deppe Lanes. These roads always dead ended in the woods that provided a backdrop for my neighborhood. It was the perfect place for me and my wild imagination to soar.

"For my 10th birthday I got my first bicycle – a sky blue **Western Flyer**. It was big and bulky, but it was my ticket to freedom. It had such character with white hand grips and colored plastic streamers coming out the end of them. It had a white leather seat and gleaming chrome trim. I called her "Ol' Blue." Every evening Ol' Blue and I took a ride up and down the streets of my neighborhood. I knew every house and tree and almost every person. As I sailed by, I waved at my neighbors and they waved back. When I got back home, Ol' Blue shone with the evening dew clinging to her chrome flanks. I always helped her up the front porch and put her away for the night.

"Other times Ol' Blue and I rode up to Grant School that faced Old Lincoln Trail. Even though I went to St. Albert the Great School, a lot of my friends from the neighborhood went to Grant School. Oftentimes, the school had some event going on. So, the kids from St. Albert's from my class in the neighborhood met up with the Grant School kids. We just went along and made ourselves at home. On Saturdays, they showed old black and white movies. We could buy a bag of popcorn and a small soda for ten cents. Our group sat there in the darkened gym and laughed at the antics of the Our Gang movies.

"Close to the school Mr. Randle had a tiny little house where he served root beer in icy mugs. There was a small counter with only four stools with puckered red leather seats. Ol' Blue waited patiently outside while I plopped down fifteen cents. Mr. Randle went to the freezer and took out a frosty mug. Then, he poured the dark brown liquid until a foamy head formed on top. He

Tootsie Rolls

gave me a wink and slid the root beer down to where I was sitting. On hot summer days with no air-conditioning anywhere, there was nothin' better than to sip that root beer and let those icy crystals slip down my face and hands. After I was refreshed, I hopped back on Ol' Blue and headed for the corner store.

"Now, even though it was already the Fifties, we still had a country store called the Fairview IGA. It was unbelievably small, but it had everything you could possibly want. Every inch was taken up with various sundries – seed potatoes, a dairy case, and even a butcher who cut fresh meat right there in the store. One of my favorite places in the store was a chest freezer where they kept their goodies – Popsicles, Fudgesicles and Dreamsicles. They also had malted milk bars, Eskimo pies, ice cream sandwiches and little flavored Dixie Cups with their very own distinctive wooden spoons. Since we didn't have an air conditioner at home, sometimes I opened the glass lid of the freezer and took in huge gulps of frozen air. I breathed in till my nose hairs felt like sharp needles and I thought surely my lungs would burst. Then I closed the case and, since I didn't have enough money, pretended as if nothing in the case really appealed to me. I then walked over to the candy counter and began my perusal of the chocolates. If I do say so myself, I was quite a connoisseur of candy – Milky Ways, Oh Henrys, Baby Ruths, Fifth Avenues and **Clark Bars**. I loved them all equally and with passion. But, sometimes I couldn't cough up even a nickel for a candy bar. So, I had to settle for a piece of gum. Back then you could buy a piece of gum for the pricey sum of one whole penny. I didn't have to think about it either because there was only one brand of kids gum to choose from back then and that was **Double Bubble Gum**. Childhood doesn't get any better than chewing a piece of Double Bubble and blowing massive bubbles while riding Ol' Blue down the back roads of my old neighborhood.

"It's true. Sometimes I liked to be by myself, but other times I liked to be with my gang of friends. When we put our creative minds together, we had very imaginative, if not downright wild, adventures. In the woods we had a clubhouse. It was just a dugout old ditch with a big piece of tarpaper over it. We used that as a home base for our excursions into the vast woods. Other times we played war with our little plastic army men. They were small green men cast in different poses; there was one with his carbine rifle positioned to shoot, another with his bayonet ready to charge, but my favorite was the little green man with a bazooka on his shoulder – boy, what power!

"We dug out elaborate catacomb foxhole passages into the sides of our clubhouse for our troops. Eventually, someone would call out, "To arms!" and we delighted in either flooding or destroying the enemy. By *destroying* I mean that every once in a while one of us would come up with an old firecracker left over from the Fourth of July. Now, you have to remember that this was a long time ago when firecrackers were actually legal. I'm surprised we didn't injure a hand or put out an eye in those battles, but we managed to get out of harm's way just in the nick of time. I remember this one time when someone came up with a cherry bomb. Needless to say – there wasn't much left of the catacomb, much less the fort, after that thing went off. But really, there was no finer childhood memory than finding your enemy's little green men making a hasty retreat as they slid down an avalanche of mud and rock after a surprise attack.

"But, even though we had a good time together, we all quivered and shook in the presence of the true kings of my neighborhood – a group of bigger, older, and stronger boys aptly named 'the super cool.' You know, I never actually saw the 'super cool' play together. They just sort of hung-out . . . looking cool. They actually congregated outside the front of my corner store leaning against the plate glass window, taking swigs of Coke from a bottle. Make no mistake, that storefront was staked out as their territory and they never let anyone pass without dishing out an armload of insults and then laughing uncontrollably.

"You can understand why sometimes going to the corner market could be a chore. And, I found myself going to that store almost daily. My family was spoiled by having that store so close. Inevitably, we'd be ready to sit down and eat, when I'd have to run out at the last minute and get a loaf of bread or a bottle of milk. And, of course, I'd run into the super-cool gang. There they'd be . . . sucking on those Coke bottles, lookin' cool.

"I always parked Ol' Blue well away from their bikes. They even had super cool bikes. They all rode an expensive Schwinn bike called "The Phantom" – a jet black bike with a silver racing stripe. I knew better than to leave Ol' Blue anywhere near the Phantoms. After I parked (around back), I tried to act nonchalant as I walked up to the front door, but I was always so intimidated that I usually stumbled all over the place. Even inside I could hear their jeers all the way down the dairy aisle.

"And, if the super cool acted as if they owned the store front, they did likewise with the streets. My gang and I were, to cop a term from today's vernacular, referred to as 'geeks.' And the geeks – I mean our gang – were allowed on the streets anytime, as long as the super cool weren't around. It was as if they feared some of our geekiness would rub off on their royal highnesses, if they should stoop to share the streets. If we were riding down the street and the super-cools came around the corner, it was expected that we would have to move over to the other side to give them all the room they wanted. Some unwritten laws of the streets were just naturally understood by one and all. So, we blindly abided by it.

"But, then there was that fateful day in August. I was taking Ol' Blue out for her morning ride, when a whole slew of Phantoms came into view. I politely got over to the other side of the street but that wasn't good enough. Oh, no. There was too many of them and they kept coming closer. Worse, they acted as if they didn't even see me. Like I was some sort of invisible . . . nothing. I knew Ol' Blue and I were going to have to cut our losses so I headed for the ditch. The next thing I knew, Ol' Blue was on top of me and the super cool were having a laughing fit. Now, I don't mind getting a couple of scratches or bruises, but Ol' Blue didn't come out too well. Her handlebars were all twisted around and several spokes were bent. That did it. This could only mean one thing – WAR!

Making radio sound effects

"However, when the enemy is bigger and older and stronger, it does pose a problem. But, the line had been drawn in the tar across St. Clair Road and there was no turning back. There was only one way to retaliate for such a breach in neighborhood etiquette, and that was to catch the enemy unaware, to seize the moment, to stage a surprise attack.

"First, I gathered my troops. When I told them what had happened they were more than happy to enlist. We scouted around for the perfect natural fort from which to execute our strategic maneuvers. There was only one such site. On the corner of North Road and St. Clair there was an empty lot owned by Aunt Josie and Uncle Blainey. Growing around the corner were large lilac and snowball bushes that had long since lost their blossoms. Now they were just a massive tangle of greenery that would provide us with an impenetrable walled fortress. Growing behind the bushes was our ammo supply – a line of crab apple trees just full of tiny green apples – perfect for flinging with our wooden school rulers.

"Being a child with a flair for the dramatic, I ran home and got a handful of coal chips from the coal bin in the basement, and all the old head scarves I could find. When I got back to my troops we streaked our faces with the coal dust and wrapped the scarves around our heads like bandanas. The last scarf we tied to the end of a long stick. It would make the perfect inspirational

254

ensign – a flag to wave as we went into battle. Next, we picked all the crab apples off the trees that we could reach. We virtually denuded the whole bottom half of the trees. We stored our ammo in orange crates requisitioned from our garages. With our powder kegs full we were ready for action. We didn't have to wait long. Through our hand-made periscope we could see the jet black Phantoms coming over the rise. We loaded up our rulers and cocked them. Then we waited. At just the right moment someone shouted, "To arms."

"In an instant, crab apples began catapulting across the ramparts and toward our designated targets. Like V-1 rockets our crab apples hit their marks time and again – arms, heads, butts – anything was fair game. Ha-ha-ha! They were caught completely off guard. The Phantoms began to wobble. Soon they went out of control and headed straight for the ditches. The super cool were down . . . but certainly not out. They began scrounging around for stray missiles and counterattacked by throwing them back toward the bushes. Hah! Very few missiles could penetrate our fortress.

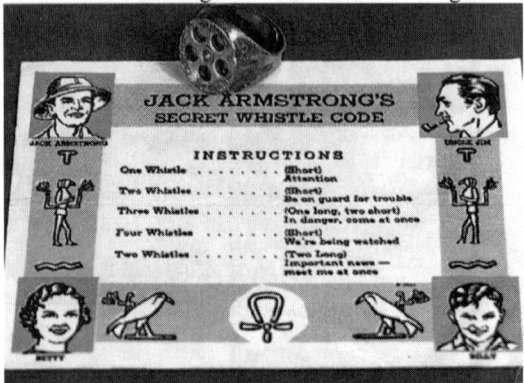

Jack Armstrong Secret Whistle Code Ring

"According to plan we were ready for phase two of the battle. And, this was crucial. To run now would be to run for the rest of our lives. So with our pockets filled with crab apples, we charged out of our fortress and met the enemy head on.

"What happened next went down in the annals of neighborhood lore as stuff from which legends are born. With our ensign flying high, bandanas on our heads, faces menacingly streaked with black war paint, and crab apples in hand, we ambushed 'em! Oh, they tried a feeble counter-attack, but they were actually awestruck and apple struck. They hurriedly retreated to their bikes and rode off with a barrage of crab apples pelting their backs.

"We won! We couldn't believe it. We won! The mighty store front gods had Achilles' heels after all.

"Well, things changed after that. Oh, not drastically. The cool ones still never talked to me or anything as civil as that. But now when I rode Ol' Blue down the street the Phantoms didn't try to crowd me off the road. And, when I went to the corner store, I parked right up front and nary a word was said. I suppose they could have pounded the daylight out of me or wrecked my bike, but I guess they had a grudging respect for my spunk.

"That fall my Aunt Josie and Uncle Blainey began harvesting their fruit trees. Unfortunately, there wouldn't be any of their famous crab apple jelly that year. There just wasn't enough to make it worthwhile. They 'sposed the squirrels got to them. Although they did think it a bit odd that the squirrels stopped precisely halfway up the trees. Hmmm.

"I never told them what actually happened. After all, they were half right. A squirrelly bunch of kids *did* rob their trees.

"A couple of months ago I went for a walk down my old neighborhood streets. The people had changed but I nodded 'hello' to the familiar homes and trees. Then, I came to that hallowed ground where the Great Crab Apple War of '56 took place. Gone were the bushes; gone were the crab apple trees. But the memory lingered on like a thick fog. I closed my eyes and I heard once again the echo of a far off, rallying cry, 'To arms!' And I thought – childhood memories . . . they just don't get any better than this!"

For more of Marilyn's great memories, go to her website at www.marilynkinsella.org.

HOW TO GET AN EGG INSIDE A BOTTLE

Hard boil an egg and then carefully peel it after you cool it down by placing it in cold water. Now find a plastic or glass bottle with a mouth that is slightly smaller than the egg at its widest point. Preheat the bottle by filling it with hot water. Pour out the water and quickly place the egg, pointed side down, in the bottle opening. As the air inside the bottle cools, the egg will slowly get sucked into the bottle.

To get the egg back out, hold the bottle upside down so that the egg is near the opening. Blow hard into the bottle with your mouth firmly against the opening. The egg will begin to vibrate, but then act as a seal, trapping the air inside. Point the bottle away from yourself and watch the egg pop out.

WORLD GEOGRAPHY

The Nile is the longest river in the world.
Mt. Everest in Nepal is the tallest mountain in the world.
American Samoa gets 198 inches of rain a year.
The Dead Sea is the lowest spot on Earth.
The Caspian Sea is the largest lake in the world.
Lake Baikal, in the Russian Federation, is the deepest lake in the world.
The Amazon River carries the most water by sheer volume.
Mt. Aconcagua (Argentina) is the highest mountain in South America.
Mt. McKinley (Alaska) is the tallest mountain in North America.
Mt. Kilimanjaro, in Tanzania, is the tallest mountain in Africa.
Mt. Elbrus (in Russia's Caucasus Mts.) is the tallest mountain in Europe.
Mandarin Chinese is the language spoken by the most people on earth.
Australia and Canada average only 3 people per square mile.
The Prime Meridian (zero degrees) originates at Greenwich, England.
The Mariana Trench, in the Pacific, is the deepest spot in any ocean.
Angel Falls in Venezuela is the highest waterfall in the world.
Much of Europe is directly east of Canada, not east of the USA.
Reno, Nevada is farther west than Los Angeles, California.
Our flattest state, topographically, is Florida.
A portion of Minnesota is farther north than the top of Maine.

Austin, Texas is our southernmost state capital.

Cannes, France, on the Mediterranean, is farther north than Milwaukee, WI.

The country of England is smaller than the state of Louisiana.

Rome, Italy is on the same latitude as Chicago, Illinois.

89 percent of the world's population lives in the northern hemisphere. The highest waterfall in Africa is Victoria Falls.

The seasons are reversed in the Southern Hemisphere. When it's spring in Missouri, it's fall in Australia.

Lake Victoria is the largest lake in Africa.

Sugarloaf Mountain is at the harbor of Rio de Janeiro, Brazil.

Ayers Rock, in central Australia, is the most famous rock in Australia.

The Galapagos Islands are owned by Ecuador.

Venezuela translated means Little Venice.

Ecuador translated means Equator.

Sudan is the largest country in Africa.

Most of South America is east of Miami, Florida.

The tip of Africa is called the Cape of Good Hope.

The tip of South America is called Cape Horn.

Mt. Aconcagua

PAPER AND TAPE BALL

Here is a game for a party group. It is a game that can be played indoors or outdoors. To make your ball, take a sheet of newspaper and crumple it up into a ball about the size of a baseball. Take some painter's tape and loosely wrap it around the newspaper to complete the ball. Arrange everyone in a circle. The object is for one person to throw it to another on the other side of the circle. The throw should be catchable – from the waist to the head and within the frame of the span of their elbows. If the person drops the throw they are out of the game. If the throw was too difficult to catch, the person making the throw is out of the game. Judging is done by group consensus. If the group can't agree, disregard the throw and do it over again. After each throw and catch, the next person to throw is the one directly to the right of the last thrower. The last person to survive wins the game.

Another interesting possibility is to play the game with two balls. You can also appoint a referee to watch the action and make the calls. With two balls, you cannot throw both balls at one person at the same time.

MASTERING THE YO YO

257

Get hold of a Duncan yo yo and let's get started. Take the end of the string with a loop and push some string inside it to form a slip knot. Loop it around the first joint in your middle finger and you're ready to go. To determine the correct length for you, let the string dangle to the ground. From that point it should reach your belly button. If it is too long, snip and re-tie.

To do the **power throw,** wind up the yo yo to the starting position. Raise your hand up toward your ear and then thrust your hand down in front of you, palm up. Stop your hand at about your waist and then turn it over so the palm is now face down. When the yo yo gets to the bottom of the string, give it a quick jerk and it will come back up in your hand.

In order to do the **hand jumper,** do the power throw and the jerk, but as the yo yo comes back up, instead of catching it allow the yo yo to jump over your hand and go back down again.

The most common problem with the yo yo is a twisted string. To prevent this, after each trick let the yo yo hang down and unwind itself. If you somehow get a bad knot in your string, use a sewing needle to separate the knot so you can untie it.

To do the **sleeper,** throw your yo yo down and instead of jerking it back up, see how long you can leave it spin at the bottom and still come back up when you jerk it.

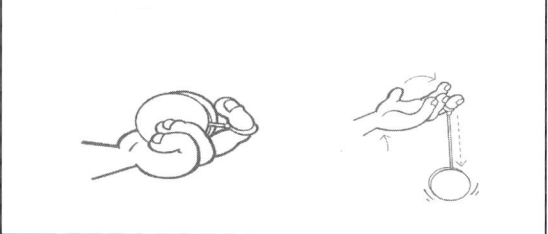

To **walk the dog,** proceed to do the sleeper trick but instead of letting the yo yo spin at the bottom, let it rest on the ground where it will roll away until you jerk it back up.

To do the **forward pass,** toss the yo yo in front of you as if you were throwing a bowling ball. It should go quickly forward and then snap back to your hand.

To do the inside loop, throw the yo yo in a forward pass but when it comes back to you use your wrist to throw it out in front of you again.

To do **around the world** (a real string twister), make sure you are either outside or in a room with a high ceiling. Start with a forward pass and keep your arm moving up and around, over your head in a circular pattern until the yo yo returns in front of you. Then give it a jerk and reel it in.

There is another move called **rock the cradle** but you need to be really good at all the others before attempting to do this. It should come with your instruction sheet or you can Google it for step-by-step instructions.

RIDDLES

A Sam wrote the name of a certain state on a sheet of paper in capital letters. He then turned the page upside down and looked at it in a mirror. He was stunned to see it read exactly as he had written it. What is the name of the state?

B The 22nd and 24th presidents of the U.S. had the same mother and father but they were not brothers. How is that possible?

C   If the doctor gave you 3 pills and told you to take 1 every half hour, how long would it take for you to run out of pills?

D   You are in quite a pickle. You are trapped in a house that has a room full of hungry crocodiles, another room filled with angry gorillas, and a third room occupied by lions that haven't eaten in over a year. Which room is safest to enter?

E   I have holes in my top, bottom, left, and right. Even with all those holes I can still hold water. What am I?

F   What are the only two days of the year that no professional baseball, football, basketball, or hockey games are played?

G   Try to name three days that come right after another without saying Monday, Tuesday, Wednesday, Thursday, Friday, Saturday, or Sunday.

H   If a butcher is 6 feet tall, wears size 10 shoes, and has black hair, what does he weigh?

I   Look at a dollar bill. How many heads are there on both sides?

J   I am light as a feather yet the strongest man can't hold me for more than a minute. What am I?

K   A young man and his elderly father are seriously injured in an auto accident. By the time the two get to the hospital the father is dead. When the doctor sees the injured young man, the doctor cries out in disbelief, "That's my son!" How is this possible?

L   I can turn out the lights and get into bed before the room is dark. The light switch and the bed are 12 feet apart. How is this possible?

M   There are 10 white socks and 10 black socks in a drawer. How many socks can you take out at random, one at a time, before you have a matching pair?

N   A canoe carries only 200 pounds. How can a mother, weighing 200 pounds, cross the lake with two sons who weigh 100 pounds each?

O   During a certain season this is a common occurrence. A man leaves home, turns left three times, and comes home to see two masked men. Who are they? HINT: It's not Halloween.

P   There is a strange South Pacific island where the law says your hair must be cut once a week but you cannot cut your own hair. There are no mirrors and only 2 barbers on Haircut Island who are identical twins. One barber is lousy at cutting hair but the other one is very good. The locals refuse to tell you which one is good and which one isn't. How do you know which barber to pick?

Q   There is only one place where the American flag flies 24-7, 365 days a year and is never taken down or flown at half mast. Where is it?

R   A sports car traveled 5 miles at high speeds with a flat tire but the driver was unaware of this. No, he didn't have 'run flat' tires. How is this possible?

S   A woman decided she needed a pet so she went to a store that sold parrots. "Will this parrot talk?" she said, pointing to one of the birds. I guarantee this bird will repeat every word it hears. The woman bought the bird. A week later she brought the bird back claiming it hadn't said a single word. The man refused to give her the refund. He said his guarantee still held, though. How is this possible?

T   A starving wolf came upon a flock of sheep. They were behind a tall metal fence too high to jump. However, the bars were spaced so that he could barely squeeze through them. Unfortunately, if he went through and ate one of the sheep he would be too fat to get back through the bars again. A little lamb noticed his predicament and said, "Mr. Wolf, I know how to solve your problem." The rest of the sheep told the lamb to shut up. What was he going to say?

President Grover Cleveland

U   A man builds a four sided home with each side having a southern exposure. A bear walks by. What color is the bear?

V   A donkey is tied to a 10 foot rope. There is a pile of hay 30 feet away. Somehow the donkey is able to eat the hay without breaking or stretching the rope. How does he do this?

W   Tim went to the movies with his only sister's husband's mother-in-law's only daughter-in-law. Who did he go to the movies with?

X   What gets wetter and wetter the more it dries?

Y   There was a serious road crash that involved 2 trucks and 6 cars. All the vehicles were severely damaged. Police and emergency workers found the two truck drivers and took them to the hospital. Strangely, no drivers of any of the cars could be found but the police didn't seem to care? Why not?

Z   A man drives his truck under an overpass and his truck is slightly too high and it gets stuck. He can't go backward or forward. What is the easiest way to free the truck?

AA   Is it legal for a man to marry his widow's sister?

BB   Is it cheaper to take two friends to the movies once or one friend to the movies twice?

CC   A man has a dollar and a dime. He uses all his money to buy a dog and a collar. The dog is a dollar more than the collar. How much is the collar?

DD   How could all of your cousins have an aunt who is not your aunt?

EE   Johnny's mother had four children. The first was named April, the second, May, the third June. What was the name of her fourth child?

FF You are driving a bus. Four people get on and two get off. Then ten people get on and five get off. Then three get on and four get off. What color are the bus driver's eyes?

GG   There was an airplane crash. Every single person died in the crash yet two survived. How is this possible?

HH   The peacock is a bird that does not lay eggs. If the peacock doesn't lay

260

eggs, how do they get baby peacocks?

II   Why did the chicken cross the road?

JJ   If 3 dogs can catch 3 cats in 3 minutes, how many dogs do you need to catch 100 cats in 100 minutes?

ANSWERS

A – OHIO

B - Grover Cleveland was the 22nd and 24th president; he was the only man to serve two non-consecutive terms.

C – One hour – you take one at noon, another at 12:30 and another at 1 p.m.

D - Open the door with the lions; if they haven't eaten for a year they're dead.

E - A sponge

F – The day before and the day after the baseball All-Star Game

G – Yesterday, today, and tomorrow

H - A butcher weighs meat

I – Fifteen; 1 Washington, 1 eagle and 13 arrowheads

J – Breath

K – The doctor is the boy's mother

L – I go to bed during the day.

M – Three

N – The two boys go across first. One comes back for the mother and he stays while she crosses the river. Then the other boy comes back for his brother.

O – The man has hit a home run and the masked men are the catcher & umpire.

P – You pick the man with the bad haircut

Q – The moon

R – It was the spare tire

S – The parrot was deaf

T – Come inside the fence and kill one of the sheep by tearing it apart. Next, carry each part back through the fence and then finish your meal.

U – A white bear; they're at the North Pole

V – The rope wasn't tied to anything

W –His wife

X – A towel

Y – The cars were all being transported by one of the trucks

Z – Let some air out of the tires

AA – If he has a widow he's dead

BB – It's cheaper to take two friends once (3 tickets), if he takes one friend twice he buys four tickets

CC – 5 cents; the dog cost $1.05

DD – Their aunt is your mother

EE - Johnny

FF – Whatever color your eyes are since you are the driver

GG –They were married

HH – The peahen lays the eggs

II – To prove to coons and skunks that it can be done

JJ - Three

261

PUT THE THUG BACK IN JAIL

This is an optical illusion. In the drawing on 264 a criminal has escaped from jail and you can put him back behind bars. All you have to do is place your nose in the middle of the dotted line that separates the criminal from the jail cell. Let your eyes relax out of focus and the man will instantly be behind bars. Granted, he's a bit fuzzy, but he's back in jail.

UNUSUAL DEATHS

The French scientist **Antoine Lavoisier** fell victim to the Reign of Terror and was sentenced to die by the guillotine. He told his friends he wanted to conduct one final experiment. "When the executioner holds up my severed head to show the crowd, I want you to count how many times I can blink. His friends said they saw him blink 11 times!

Manfred Von Richthofen was the leader of a World War I German flying group called the "Flying Circus." He racked up 80 "kills" in aerial combat and had a Berlin jeweler inscribe a small silver cup for him with the date of each victory and the type of enemy plane he shot down. Shortly after his 80th victory, he was mortally wounded in combat by the Canadian RAF pilot, Roy Brown. Von Richthofen managed to land his plane but his mates found him dead in the cockpit. Von Richthofen was succeeded by Herman Goering, who later became the head of Hitler's Air Force.

The Greek playwright **Aeschylus** was killed when a **turtle fell out of the sky** and struck him on the noggin.' Now what was a turtle doing flying around in the sky? Most likely, it had been captured by an eagle which then dropped it from a great height to break open its shell to gain access to the meat inside.

Archimedes was the greatest mathematician of antiquity and was known for discovering the principal of the lever. He had drawn a math problem in the sand and was contemplating it when a Roman soldier, during the siege of Syracuse, came up to him and killed him.

In 1943 British actor **Leslie Howard** was flying to England from Portugal and was killed when a German Junkers shot down his flight over the Bay of Biscay. Howard's manager bore a striking resemblance to Winston Churchill, and the Germans shot down the plane thinking they had killed the British Prime Minister.

Isadora Duncan was a popular American dancer during the Roaring Twenties. She performed all over Europe entertaining audiences with her Bohemian style of interpretative dancing. Known for living a scandalous lifestyle, Duncan was killed in 1927 at Nice, France due to her fondness for long scarves. She was riding in an open roadster when one end of her scarf became wrapped around the car's rear tire, **snapping her neck**.

Clement Vallandigham, a political opponent of Abe Lincoln, fatally injured himself while trying to make a point in a courtroom trial. He was representing a client in a murder case and was trying to show the jury how the victim accidentally shot himself. He did not realize the gun was loaded and died from a self-inflicted wound.

Robert Wadlow

Robert Wadlow of Alton, Illinois, **the world's tallest man** (8 ft.,11.1 inches), died in 1940 from an infected blister. His frame grew so large that he required special metal braces on his legs to enable him to walk. The braces rubbed a blister that became infected and he died of blood poisoning. Penicillin had been invented but it wasn't yet available to doctors for general use.

Wild Bill Hickok, of Troy Grove, Illinois was a noted gunfighter, scout and lawman of the Old West. He was always cautious and when playing cards in a saloon he would be sure to sit with his back to a wall. In August of 1876 Hickok was playing cards in a saloon in Dakota Territory. His back was not against a wall. A man named Jack McCall walked up and shot him from behind. At the time, Hickok was holding two pair – aces and eights in spades and clubs. It is now known as the **Dead Man's Hand in poker**.

Tennessee whiskey distiller **Jack Daniel** died in 1911 from blood poisoning. The infection started when he injured his toe by kicking his safe. He lost his temper when he had difficulty opening the safe.

John Erik Hexum, a ruggedly handsome actor, was killed in 1984 on the set of *Cover Up*. During a break in filming, Hexum began playing a game of Russian roulette with a .44 Magnum gun that was loaded with a single blank cartridge. He placed the gun to his head and pulled the trigger. He apparently was unaware that blanks propel wadding out the barrel when fired. He died from injuries sustained to his brain caused by the wadding.

In 2005 a South Korean video game junkie named Lee Seop collapsed and died at a Seattle Internet Café after **50 straight hours of playing Starcraft**. In 2006 Crocodile Hunter and TV personality **Steve Irwin** was killed in an untimely manner. He was filming a documentary titled *The Ocean's Deadliest* when a stingray lashed out and pierced Irwin's heart, killing him instantly.

Escape Artist Harry Houdini

In 2007, Jennifer Strange, a Sacramento, California woman**, died of water intoxication.** She was participating in a radio station contest in an effort to win a Nintendo video game set. The goal was to see which contestant could consume the most water without urinating.

In 1926: Harry Houdini, a famous American escape artist, **was punched in the stomach** by an amateur boxer who had heard Houdini brag that he could withstand any blow to his body above his waist, excluding his head. Though this had been done with Houdini's permission, complications from this injury caused him to die days later, on October 31, 1926. It was later determined that Houdini died of a ruptured appendix. The boxer struck Houdini in the stomach before he had time to flex his muscles down there, which previously had prevented injury.

1941: **Sherwood Anderson**, novelist and short story writer from Ohio, swallowed a toothpick at a party and then died of peritonitis. He accidentally swallowed a piece of a toothpick embedded in a martini olive at a party. He was buried at Round Hill Cemetery in Marion, Virginia. His epitaph reads, "Life, Not Death, is the Great Adventure."

In 1955: **Margo Jones**, very well known and popular theater director, was **killed by exposure to carbon tetrachloride fumes** from her newly cleaned carpet. Carbon tetrachloride, a clear liquid, was subsequently banned for use as a cleaning agent.

In 1983 American author **Tennessee Williams** died when he **choked on an eyedrop bottle cap** in his room at the Hotel Elysee in New York. He would routinely place the cap in his mouth, lean back, and place his eyedrops in each eye. Williams' lack of gag response may have been due to the effects of drugs and alcohol abuse, and it is highly likely that Williams was high when the cap ended up in his throat as drugs and alcohol were found in his room and inside his body.

In 1972, **Luigi Greco**, the **Mafia** boss of the Sicilian faction of **Montreal**, died from an incident occurring while renovating a family pizzeria. He used a **mop dipped in gasoline** and a metal scraper to remove the filth on the floor.

However, the combination provoked an explosion and flash fire, and Greco died four days later at the Sacré-Cœur Hospital.

John Bowen, a 20-year-old of Nashua, New Hampshire was attending a halftime show at a football game at Shea Stadium on December 9, 1979. During an event which featured novelty and custom-made remote control flying machines, **a 40-pound model plane shaped like a lawnmower accidentally dived into the stands** with its sharp blades striking Bowen and another spectator and causing severe head injuries. While the other spectator survived, Bowen died in hospital four days later.

Tennessee Williams

David Allen Kirwan a 24-year-old, attempted to rescue a friend's dog after it fell into Celestine Pool, a hot spring at Yellowstone National Park on July 20, 1981. Kirwan dove into the pool but was unable to save the dog. After swimming back to shore, his injuries became apparent - the exposure to the 200°F water of the hot spring resulted in third-degree burns to 100% of his body and had also blinded him. He died the next day at a Salt Lake City hospital. Although there have been at least 19 deaths due to scalding at Yellowstone, this was the only known case where someone died after deliberately jumping into one of the park's hot springs.

In 1982 **Vic Morrow**, actor, was **decapitated by a helicopter blade** during filming of *Twilight Zone: The Movie*. Two child actors, Myca Dinh Le (who was decapitated) and Renee Shin-Yi Chen (who was crushed), also died.

Actor **Brandon Lee**, son of Bruce Lee, was shot and killed by Michael Massee using a prop gun while filming the movie *The Crow*. A cartridge with only a primer and a bullet was fired in the pistol before the fatal scene; this caused a squib load, in which the primer provided enough force to push the bullet out of the cartridge and into the barrel of the revolver, where it became stuck. The malfunction went unnoticed by the crew, and the same gun was used again later to shoot the death scene. His death was not instantly recognized by the crew or other actors; they believed he was still acting.

1993: **Michael A. Shingledecker Jr.** was killed almost instantly when he and a friend were **struck by a pickup truck while lying flat on the yellow dividing line of a two-lane highway** in Polk, Pennsylvania. They were copying a daredevil stunt from the movie *The Program*. Marco Birkhimer died of a similar accident while performing the same stunt on Route 206 of Bordentown, New Jersey.

In 1995 a 14 year old girl, **Ryan Bielby**, plummeted to her death while riding the rollercoaster the Timber Wolf at Kansas City's Worlds of Fun amusement park. She had unbuckled her seatbelt and maneuvered herself free from the lap bar and restraint devices in an attempt to switch seats with a friend. She fell about 25 feet to her death.

In 2003 **Dr. Hitoshi Nikaidoh**, a surgical doctor, was decapitated as he stepped on to an elevator at Christus St. Joseph Hospital in Houston, Texas on August 16, 2003. According to a witness inside the elevator, the elevator doors closed as Nikaidoh entered, trapping his head inside the elevator with the remainder of his body still outside. His body was later found at the bottom of the elevator shaft while the upper portion of his head, severed just above the lower jaw, was found in the elevator. A subsequent investigation revealed that improper electrical wiring installed by a maintenance company several days earlier had effectively bypassed all of the safeguards.

Brandon Lee

One of the most dangerous foods you can eat is the hot dog. Because of its unique shape and texture, it presents a unique choking risk compared to all other foods. **An average of 77 children choke to death each year** in the USA while trying to consume this All-American product. Families who have lost children are pressuring the FDA to cause hot dogs to be manufactured in a different shape with a mushier texture to the meat. Failing that, they want warning labels placed on hot dogs similar to those placed on packages of cigarettes. **The best way to avoid the hazard is to chew all of your food thoroughly before trying to swallow**.

JOHN COLTER'S RACE FOR LIFE

John Colter, a tall Virginian, became known for his skills as an outdoorsman. In October of 1803, Meriwether Lewis, of the Lewis and Clark Expedition accepted Colter into the group with the rank of private and a pay of $5 a month.

While Lewis and Clark were away from the base camp at **Wood River, Illinois**, securing supplies, Colter and several other men were court martialed for disobeying the orders of Sergeant John Ordway. Colter spent ten days in the brig and was only reinstated after issuing an apology and promising to reform.

During the expedition Colter was considered the best hunter in the group and was routinely sent out to scout for game meat. He was also instrumental in helping the group find passes through the Rocky Mountains to gain access to the Pacific shore.

Rather than complete the mission with the rest of the expedition, Colter was discharged on the return trip in North Dakota so he could lead a group of fur traders back to the region he had just helped explore. In 1807 Colter became the first white man to explore Jackson Hole, and what later became Yellowstone and Grand Teton National Parks. He reported seeing geysers and other geothermal activity. These reports were ridiculed and the land referred to as "Coulter's Hell."

In 1809 Colter was captured by the Blackfoot Indians. The natives decided to make sport of his death. They stripped him of his clothing and told him to run for his life. Fortunately, Colter was a fast runner. He managed to outdistance his pursuers, except for one brave. Colter turned his head and saw the savage not 20 yards from him. Colter surprised the Indian by quickly turning to face him. The native threw his spear at Colter but, exhausted with running, threw the spear into the ground. Coulter grabbed the pointed end and used it to stab his pursuer to death.

Colter finally returned to St. Louis in 1810 after having lived in the wilderness for six years. **Colter is generally regarded as the first Mountain Man.**

In 1966 Cornel Wild made a movie titled *The Naked Prey*, and used Colter's story as the basis for much of the movie.

AMERICA'S GREATEST NAVAL HERO: JOHN PAUL JONES

Born in Scotland, he began life with the name John Paul. He took to the sea at the tender age of 13 and gained valuable skills in tactics and navigation. In 1768 his career received an unexpected boost. The captain and first mate on his ship took suddenly ill and died of yellow fever. Despite his youth, John Paul managed to bring the ship to port and deliver the cargo. The grateful owners made him master of the ship and crew.

John Paul's many voyages included various trips to the North American colonies. He added the name Jones to honor a man he knew from Halifax, North Carolina. When the Revolutionary War broke out, Jones offered his services to the American cause. Historians are unsure what motivated him to throw in his lot with what appeared to be a hopeless cause. Even the mighty French had lost their North American empire to the British in the Seven Years War (1756-1763). The Americans had a few ships but they would have to be content with making raids on British merchant shipping, not engaging the British Navy in grand sea battles.

Jones commanded first the *Alfred* and then the *Ranger* and saw a fair amount of success attacking British shipping and by making raids on British coastal towns. Jones went to Paris and met with our ambassadors, John Adams and Ben Franklin. In 1778, Jones engaged the British warship *Drake* in battle and captured it after an hour long struggle.

Jones was now given command of a 42 gun ship called the *Bonhomme Richard*. This was only a medium sized warship since a class known as a ship-of-the-line carried 72 guns. The ship was donated by a Frenchman who greatly admired Ben Franklin. *Bonhomme Richard* translates to "Poor Richard," the name Franklin gave to an almanac he published.

In 1779, Jones led a squadron of five ships to make raids on the British coast. The British sent a squadron after him and an engagement took place off Flamborough Head, near Scotland. Jones was attacked by the 50 gun British warship, the *Serapis*. After an hour long battle, Jones' ship was sinking and on fire. The British commander yelled and asked if Jones was ready to surrender. The British commander was dumbstruck when he heard Jones reply, "**I have not yet begun to fight.**" Incredibly, Jones and his men maneuvered their ship next to the *Serapis* and boarded it. What followed was some serious hand-to-hand combat in which Jones and his men prevailed. Incredibly, Jones had managed to snatch victory from the jaws of defeat. The *Bonhomme Richard* was unsalvageable and sank the next day. Jones sailed the *Serapis* to neutral (but pro-American) Holland. He was honored by the French and given the title Chevalier. Congress later struck a gold medal in his honor.

John Paul Jones

Jones died in 1792 from a severe brain tumor, and he was buried in a small cemetery in Paris, where he was living at the time. For over a century Jones was largely forgotten and the cemetery he was buried in fell into disrepair. In 1905 the American Ambassador to France began painstaking research to discover the whereabouts of Jones' body. Five coffins were unearthed and the third one searched yielded the body of our sacred hero. The face in the coffin was compared to a bust of Jones that had been executed by the sculptor Jean Houdon. Jones body was ceremoniously brought back to America aboard the *U.S.S. Brooklyn*, escorted by three other cruisers. **As the ships neared the eastern coast, they were joined by seven U.S. battleships**. Jones body was re-interred in a magnificent sarcophagus at the Chapel of the U.S. Naval Academy at Annapolis.

THE GAME OF CHARLIE

This is a party game that can be played by anywhere from five to twelve people. Arrange the necessary number of chairs in a semi-circle. The person designated as Charlie has the first seat. The game begins as Charlie leads the group by establishing a rhythm. The rhythm begins as everyone pats their thighs twice, then they snap their fingers on their left hand and then snap their fingers on their right hand.   Maintaining the cadence, Charlie now says "Charlie, Charlene." Charlie has just called out the name of another person in the group. The rhythm and cadence continues with the patting of thighs twice and the snapping of fingers twice. Since Charlene was called out by Charlie, she must maintain the cadence by saying "Charlene, Susan," after the snapping of the fingers. The established routine continues, and Susan must now say her name and call out another person. It could be Frank, or she might go back to Charlie in an effort to trip that person up.

If any person gets called out and then messes up the rhythm and cadence, the game temporarily stops, and the person who goofed has to go to the end of the line. Everyone behind that person now gets to move up a seat. What makes the game more difficult is that **each seat is named for the original person sitting there at the beginning of the game**. Thus anytime a player changes seats he must ask the person in the seat what his/her name was. That is the name he must respond to once the game continues – not his own name.

Another way to goof up is by calling out the wrong person. If, let's say, Sally calls out the name associated with your seat then you must respond in cadence. You may call out any person's name except the one associated with your seat or the person who just called you out. You must go to someone else; you cannot go directly back to them.

The object of the game is to keep moving up until you are finally the one to replace Charlie and then you maintain that spot without goofing up.

One way of tripping someone up is to look at them directly in the face as if you are going to call out their name, but then you call out someone totally different.

Set a time limit on the game of 30 minutes and the person who is Charlie after time runs out is declared the winner.

THE MAN WITHOUT A COUNTRY

"The Man Without a Country" is a short story by American writer Edward Everett Hale, first published anonymously in the *Atlantic Monthly* in December 1863. The novel is the story of American army lieutenant Philip Nolan, who renounces his country during a trial for treason and is consequently sentenced to spend the rest of his days at sea without so much as a word of news about the United States. Although the story is set in the early 1800s, the story is an allegory about upheaval of the American Civil War and was intended to promote the Union

The protagonist of the story is a young United States Army lieutenant named Philip Nolan, who develops a friendship with the visiting Aaron Burr. When Burr is tried for treason (historically this occurred in 1807), Nolan is tried as an accomplice. During his testimony, Nolan bitterly renounces his nation, angrily shouting "Damn the United States! I wish I may never hear of the United States again!" Upon conviction, the judge icily grants Nolan his wish; he is to spend the rest of his life on warships of the United States Navy, in exile, with no right to ever again set foot on U.S. soil, and with explicit orders that no one shall ever mention his country to him again.

The sentence is carried out to the letter. For the rest of his life, Nolan is transported from ship to ship, living out his life as a prisoner on the high seas, never once being allowed back in a home port. None of the sailors in whose custody Nolan remains are allowed to speak to him about the U.S., and his newspapers are censored. Nolan is unrepentant at first, but over the years becomes sadder and wiser, and desperate for news. One day, as he is being rowed over to another ship on which he is to be held, he beseeches a young sailor never to make the same mistake he made: "Remember, boy, that behind all these men....behind officers and government, and people even, there is the Country Herself, your Country, and that you belong to her as you belong to your own mother. Stand by her, boy, as you would stand by your mother!"

Deprived of a homeland, Nolan slowly and painfully learns the true worth of his country. He misses it more than his friends or family, more than art or music or love or nature. Without it, he is nothing. Dying, he shows his room to an officer named Danforth; it is "a little shrine" of patriotism. The Stars and Stripes are draped around a picture of George Washington. Over his bed, Nolan has painted an eagle, with lightning "blazing from his beak" and claws grasping the globe. At the foot of his bed is a dated map of the old territories. Nolan smiles, "Here, you see, I have a country!" Nolan dies content after Danforth finally tells him all that has happened to the U.S. since his sentence was imposed. Nolan asks him to have them bury him in the sea and have a gravestone placed in memory of him, at Fort Adams at Orleans.

In 1973, a made-for-television movie titled *The Man Without a Country* was directed by Delbert Mann and written by Sidney Carroll. It featured Cliff Robertson as Philip Nolan, Beau Bridges as Frederick Ingham, Peter Strauss as Arthur Danforth, Robert Ryan as Lt. Cmdr. Vaughn, John Cullum as Aaron Burr and Patricia Elliott as Mrs. Graff.

HOW TO CHANGE YOUR CAR'S OIL

Ask your father if he would be willing to show you how to change the oil on the family car. When I was younger I changed my own oil for years and when my son became a teenager I showed him how to do it.

The first thing you need is a set of ramps. Make sure they are sturdy and well-made because they must support a lot of weight. My ramps are made of 8x8 solid oak and they came from a mill. Go to a dealer or to a place such as Auto Zone and buy the correct oil filter for your car. You will also need 5-6 quarts of oil. Check your car's manual to determine exactly how much. Synthetic oil costs a bit more to begin with but it is a superior oil. Most motorists won't use synthetic oil because they don't even know what it is. They think maybe it comes from soybeans. Here's the scoop. Regular oil that you buy for your car is made up of molecules and every molecule is slightly different from the next one. This difference produces a slight friction, thus decreasing performance. To get synthetic oil, the companies take the regular oil and remanufacture it making every molecule exactly the same. This reduces friction resulting in longer engine life and better gas mileage.

You also want to use an oil with the correct viscosity. **Viscosity** is an internal property of a fluid that offers resistance to flow. Thus in wintertime you want oil with a low resistance to flow because cold weather causes oil to thicken. Heat tends to thin out oil during the hot summer months so you want oil that has a higher viscosity than what you use in the winter. The oil companies have largely solved this problem for you by coming up with 10 W 30. This means that when your engine is cold when you first start it up, the oil is thin. As the engine heats up and needs more protection, the oil gets thicker. Check with your dealer or the car manual to see what viscosity is recommended.

Place the ramps directly against the front tires of your car. Do this on a level spot in your driveway, not in your garage. The concrete on your garage floor has been finished to a polish, and this causes the ramps to skid forward as the tires make contact. Driveways are not finished in this manner. Your dad can pull the car forward while you wait to signal him when he reaches the top of the ramp. He should now place the car in the "park" position. If the car is a stick shift, leave it in gear and set the emergency brake.

Use a "creepy crawler" to go under the car and locate the drain plug on the oil pan. Use a ratchet wrench to loosen the plug. Turn it counterclockwise to loosen. Make sure you have a bucket or pan in place to catch the oil as it comes out. Try not to let the plug and washer fall into the pan when it comes totally free. While this is draining find the oil filter. Use a special oil filter wrench to loosen. Again, you should be turning it counterclockwise to get it off. When it comes free, make sure the rubber gasket comes off with it. Place the old filter in the box the new one came in. Take your finger and rub a very light coating of oil over the gasket on the new filter. Screw on the new filter, being careful to make sure you are not forcing anything and stripping the threads. Tighten as much as possible by hand, then use the filter wrench to tighten it by about a ¾ turn.

When the oil pan stops dripping, you can replace the washer and the drain plug. Use the ratchet socket wrench to tighten the plug. It should be snug but not too tight. Now remove the cap from the engine crankcase so you can add the new oil. Add the recommended amount and replace the cap. Now find the dipstick to see if the oil comes up to the full mark. Start up the car engine and let it run a few minutes while you make sure there are no leaks from the filter or the drain plug.

AMERICA'S GREATEST HEROES

Todd Morgan Beamer **(November 24, 1968 – September 11, 2001) was a passenger aboard United Airlines Flight 93 who has been called a hero for his actions in the September 11, 2001 attacks.**

Beamer attended Los Gatos High School, Wheaton Academy, DePaul University (Chicago), California State University, Fresno and Wheaton College. Todd and Lisa, both age 32, met while they were attending Wheaton

College in Chicagoland. In September 2001, he was an account manager for Oracle and resided in Cranbury, New Jersey, with his wife, Lisa Beamer, and two sons, David and Drew. His daughter, Morgan Kay, was born January 9, 2002, approximately four months after his death.

After United Airlines Flight 93 was hijacked, Beamer and other passengers communicated with people on the ground via in-plane and cell phones, and learned that the World Trade Center had been attacked using hijacked airplanes. Beamer tried to place a credit card call through a phone located on the back of a plane seat but was routed to a customer-service representative instead, who passed him on to GTE supervisor Lisa Jefferson. Beamer reported that one passenger was killed and, later, that a flight attendant had told him the pilot and co-pilot had been forced from the cockpit and may have been wounded. He was also on the phone when the plane made its turn in a southeasterly direction, a move that had him briefly panicking. Later, he told the operator that some of the plane's passengers were planning to "jump on" the hijackers. According to Jefferson, Beamer's last audible words were "**Are you guys ready? Let's roll**."

Beamer's phrase "Let's roll" was widely cited and later became a battle cry for those fighting Al-Qaeda in Afghanistan.

Todd M. Beamer

At least four facilities have been named for Beamer: a post office in Cranbury, New Jersey, Todd Beamer High School in Federal Way, Washington, the Todd M. Beamer Student Center at Wheaton College, and a neighborhood park in Fresno, California.

The Cranbury Post Office was dedicated to Todd Beamer on May 4, 2002 as a result of an Act of Congress authored by Congressman Rush D. Holt, Jr..

The bill was signed into law by President George W. Bush.

Beamer was posthumously awarded with the ESPY Arthur Ashe Courage Award in 2002. He is survived by his wife, Lisa Beamer, two sons, David and Drew, and a daughter, Morgan Kay, who was born on January 9, 2002, nearly four months after her father's death.

On 9-11-01, Muslim terrorists hijacked four flights. Two of them crashed into the twin towers of the World Trade Center in NYC. A third crashed into the Pentagon Building in Washington, D.C., and Beamer's flight was headed for the Capitol Building in D.C. Beamer and several other men rushed the three hijackers in the cockpit of flight #93. **Other heroes of the day included Tom Burnett and Jeremy Glick**. Beamer and his cohorts were unarmed while the hijackers had boxcutters with sharp blades. Beamer and the guys were able to overpower the hijackers and the plane crashed on a Pennsylvania farm, killing all on board. They sacrificed their lives but saved the nation's Capitol Building.

Beamer and his wife were active Christians and members of Princeton Alliance Church in Plainsboro, New Jersey. Todd taught a high school level Sunday school class.

PAT TILLMAN JOINS THE WAR ON TERROR

Patrick Daniel "Pat" Tillman **(November 6, 1976 – April 22, 2004) was an American football player who left his professional sports career and enlisted in the United States Army in May 2002 in the aftermath of the September 11 attacks. He joined the United States Army Rangers and served multiple tours in combat before he was killed by friendly fire in the mountains of Afghanistan. He was awarded the Silver Star.**

Pat Tillman was born in San Jose, California. He started his college career as a linebacker for Arizona State University in 1994, when he secured the last remaining scholarship for the team. Tillman excelled as a linebacker at Arizona State, despite being relatively small for the position at five-feet eleven-inches tall. As a senior, he was voted the Pac-10 Defensive Player of the Year. Academically, Tillman majored in marketing and graduated in three and a half years with a 3.84 GPA.

In the 1998 NFL Draft, Tillman was selected as the 226th pick by the Arizona Cardinals. Tillman moved over to play the safety position in the NFL and started ten of sixteen games in his rookie season.

Pat Tillman

At one point in his NFL career, Tillman turned down An astounding five-year, $9 million contract offer from the St. Louis Rams out of loyalty to the Cardinals.

Sports Illustrated football writer Paul Zimmerman (Dr. Z) named Tillman to his 2000 NFL All-Pro team after Tillman finished with 155 tackles (120 solo), 1.5 sacks, 2 forced fumbles, 2 fumble recoveries, 9 pass deflections and 1 interception for 30 yards.

Tillman finished his career with totals of 238 tackles, 2.5 sacks, 3 interceptions for 37 yards, 3 forced fumbles, 2 pass deflections, and 3 fumble recoveries in 60 career games. In addition he also had 1 rush attempt for 4 yards and returned 3 kickoffs for 33 yards.

In May 2002, eight months after the September 11, 2001, attacks and after completing the fifteen remaining games of the 2001 season which

273

followed the attacks (at a salary of $512,000 per year), Tillman turned down a contract offer of $3.6 million over three years from the Cardinals to enlist in the U.S. Army. In 2003 the brothers were awarded the Walter Ashe (tennis star) award for courage at the annual ESPY awards. Senator John McCain said Pat Tillman was the quintessential definition of a patriot.

Pat enlisted, along with his brother Kevin, who gave up the chance of a career in professional baseball. The two brothers completed the Ranger Indoctrination Program in late 2002 and were assigned to the second battalion of the 75th Ranger Regiment in Fort Lewis, Washington. He resided in University Place with his wife before being deployed to Iraq. After participating in the initial invasion of Operation Iraqi Freedom, he graduated from Ranger School.

After his death, the Pat Tillman Foundation was established to carry forward its view of Tillman's legacy by inspiring and supporting those striving for positive change in themselves and the world around them.

A highway bypass around the Hoover Dam will have a bridge bearing Tillman's name. When completed in September 2010, the Mike O'Callaghan-Pat Tillman Memorial Bridge will span the Colorado River between Nevada and Arizona.

Lincoln Law School of San Jose has established the Pat Tillman Scholarship in honor of Tillman. Tillman's father, Patrick Kevin Tillman, earned his Juris Doctor from Lincoln in 1983.

On Sunday, September 19, 2004, all teams of the NFL wore a memorial decal on their helmets in honor of Pat Tillman. The Arizona Cardinals continued to wear this decal throughout the 2004 season. Former Cardinals quarterback Jake Plummer requested to also wear the decal for the entire season but the NFL turned him down saying his helmet would not be uniform with the rest of the Denver Broncos. Plummer would later grow a full beard and his hair long in honor of Tillman, who had such a style in the NFL before cutting his hair and shaving his beard off to fit military uniform guidelines. Plummer, now retired from the NFL, has since gone back to cutting his hair short but maintains the beard.

The Cardinals retired his number 40, and Arizona State did the same for the number 42 he wore with the Sun Devils. The Cardinals have named the plaza surrounding their University of Phoenix Stadium in Glendale, Pat Tillman Freedom Plaza. Later, on November 12, 2006, during a Cardinals game versus the Cowboys, a bronze statue was revealed in his honor. ASU also named the entryway to Sun Devil Stadium the "Pat Tillman Memorial Tunnel" and made a "PT-42" patch that they placed on the neck of their uniforms a permanent feature.

Pat Tillman's high school, Leland High School, in San Jose, California, renamed its football field after him. A memorial to Pat Tillman was created at Sun Devil Stadium, where he played football for the Sun Devils and the Cardinals.

In 2004, the NFL donated $250,000 to the United Service Organizations to build a USO center in memory of Tillman. The Pat Tillman USO Center, the first USO center in Afghanistan, opened on Bagram Air Base on April 1, 2005.

Forward Operating Base Tillman is close to the Pakistan border, near the village of Lwara in Paktia Province, Afghanistan.

On Saturday, April 15, 2006, more than 10,000 participants turned out for Pat's Run in Tempe, Arizona. The racers traveled along the 4.2-mile (6.8 km) course around Tempe Town Lake to the finish line, on the 42-yard line of Sun Devil Stadium in order to commemorate the number which he wore as a Sun Devil and was later retired in his honor. A second race took place in San Jose. Sponsored by the Pat Tillman Foundation, a total of 14,000 runners took part. In 2005, about 6,000 took part in a single race in Tempe.

LEARNING ABOUT ELECTRONICS

Circuit symbols are used in circuit diagrams which show how a circuit is connected together. The actual layout of the components is usually quite different from the circuit diagram. To build a circuit you need a different diagram showing the layout of the parts on stripboard or printed circuit board. (Symbols courtesy of the Electronics Club.)

Wires and connections

Component	Circuit Symbol	Function of Component
Wire	———————	To pass current very easily from one part of a circuit to another.
Wires joined	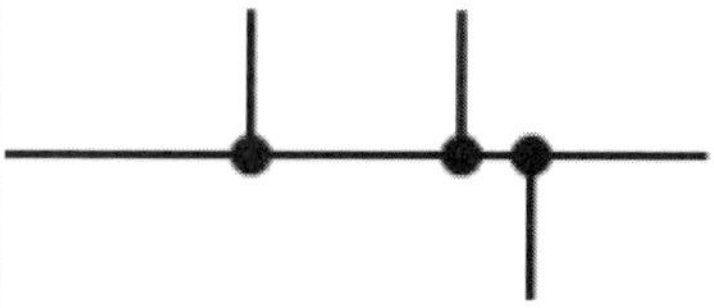	A 'blob' should be drawn where wires are connected (joined), but it is sometimes omitted. Wires connected at 'crossroads' should be staggered slightly to form two T-junctions, as shown on the right.

Wires not joined	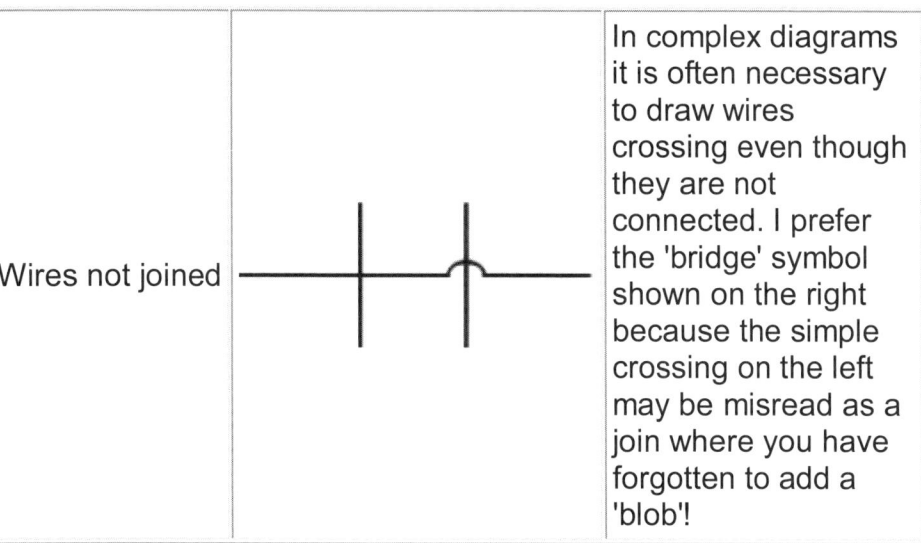	In complex diagrams it is often necessary to draw wires crossing even though they are not connected. I prefer the 'bridge' symbol shown on the right because the simple crossing on the left may be misread as a join where you have forgotten to add a 'blob'!

Power Supplies

Component	Circuit Symbol	Function of Component
Cell		Supplies electrical energy. The larger terminal (on the left) is positive (+). A single cell is often called a battery, but strictly a battery is two or more cells joined together.
Battery		Supplies electrical energy. A battery is more than one cell. The larger terminal (on the left) is positive (+).
DC supply		Supplies electrical energy. DC = Direct Current, always flowing in one direction.
AC supply		Supplies electrical

Component	Circuit Symbol	Function of Component
		energy. AC = Alternating Current, continually changing direction.
Fuse		A safety device which will 'blow' (melt) if the current flowing through it exceeds a specified value.
Transformer		Two coils of wire linked by an iron core. Transformers are used to step up (increase) and step down (decrease) AC voltages. Energy is transferred between the coils by the magnetic field in the core. There is no electrical connection between the coils.
Earth (Ground)		A connection to earth. For many electronic circuits this is the 0V (zero volts) of the power supply, but for mains electricity and some radio circuits it really means the earth. It is also known as ground.

Output Devices: Lamps, Heater, Motor, etc.

Component	Circuit Symbol	Function of Component
Lamp (lighting)		A transducer which converts electrical energy to light. This

		symbol is used for a lamp providing illumination, for example a car headlamp or torch bulb.
Lamp (indicator)		A transducer which converts electrical energy to light. This symbol is used for a lamp which is an indicator, for example a warning light on a car dashboard.
Heater		A transducer which converts electrical energy to heat.
Motor		A transducer which converts electrical energy to kinetic energy (motion).
Bell		A transducer which converts electrical energy to sound.
Buzzer		A transducer which converts electrical energy to sound.
Inductor (Coil, Solenoid)		A coil of wire which creates a magnetic field when current passes through it. It may have an iron core inside the coil. It can be used as a transducer converting electrical energy to

Component	Circuit Symbol	Function of Component
		mechanical energy by pulling on something.

Switches

Component	Circuit Symbol	Function of Component
Push Switch (push-to-make)		A push switch allows current to flow only when the button is pressed. This is the switch used to operate a doorbell.
Push-to-Break Switch		This type of push switch is normally closed (on), it is open (off) only when the button is pressed.
On-Off Switch (SPST)		SPST = Single Pole, Single Throw. An on-off switch allows current to flow only when it is in the closed (on) position.
2-way Switch (SPDT)		SPDT = Single Pole, Double Throw. A 2-way changeover switch directs the flow of current to one of two routes according to its position. Some SPDT switches

		have a central off position and are described as 'on-off-on'.
Dual On-Off Switch (DPST)		DPST = Double Pole, Single Throw. A dual on-off switch which is often used to switch mains electricity because it can isolate both the live and neutral connections.
Reversing Switch (DPDT)		DPDT = Double Pole, Double Throw. This switch can be wired up as a reversing switch for a motor. Some DPDT switches have a central off position.
Relay		An electrically operated switch, for example a 9V battery circuit connected to the coil can switch a 230V AC mains circuit. NO = Normally Open, COM = Common, NC = Normally Closed.

Resistors

Component	Circuit Symbol	Function of

		Component
Resistor		A resistor restricts the flow of current, for example to limit the current passing through an LED. A resistor is used with a capacitor in a timing circuit. Some publications still use the old resistor symbol:
Variable Resistor (Rheostat)		This type of variable resistor with 2 contacts (a rheostat) is usually used to control current. Examples include: adjusting lamp brightness, adjusting motor speed, and adjusting the rate of flow of charge into a capacitor in a timing circuit.
Variable Resistor (Potentiometer)		This type of variable resistor with 3 contacts (a potentiometer) is usually used to control voltage. It can be used like this as a transducer converting position (angle of the control spindle) to an electrical signal.

Variable Resistor (Preset)		This type of variable resistor (a preset) is operated with a small screwdriver or similar tool. It is designed to be set when the circuit is made and then left without further adjustment. Presets are cheaper than normal variable resistors so they are often used in projects to reduce the cost.

Capacitors

Component	Circuit Symbol	Function of Component
Capacitor		A capacitor stores electric charge. A capacitor is used with a resistor in a timing circuit. It can also be used as a filter, to block DC signals but pass AC signals.
Capacitor, polarised		A capacitor stores electric charge. This type must be connected the correct way round. A capacitor is used with a resistor in a timing circuit. It can also be used as a filter, to block DC signals but pass

		AC signals.
<u>Variable Capacitor</u>		A variable capacitor is used in a radio tuner.
<u>Trimmer Capacitor</u>		This type of variable capacitor (a trimmer) is operated with a small screwdriver or similar tool. It is designed to be set when the circuit is made and then left without further adjustment.

Diodes

Component	Circuit Symbol	Function of Component
<u>Diode</u>		A device which only allows current to flow in one direction.
<u>LED</u> <u>Light Emitting Diode</u>		A transducer which converts electrical energy to light.
<u>Zener Diode</u>		A special diode which is used to maintain a fixed voltage across its terminals.
Photodiode		A light-sensitive diode.

Transistors

Component	Circuit Symbol	Function of Component

Transistor NPN		A transistor amplifies current. It can be used with other components to make an amplifier or switching circuit.
Transistor PNP		A transistor amplifies current. It can be used with other components to make an amplifier or switching circuit.
Phototransistor		A light-sensitive transistor.

Audio and Radio Devices

Component	Circuit Symbol	Function of Component
Microphone		A transducer which converts sound to electrical energy.
Earphone		A transducer which converts electrical energy to sound.
Loudspeaker		A transducer which converts electrical energy to sound.
Piezo Transducer		A transducer which converts electrical energy to sound.

Amplifier (general symbol)		An amplifier circuit with one input. Really it is a block diagram symbol because it represents a circuit rather than just one component.
Aerial (Antenna)		A device which is designed to receive or transmit radio signals. It is also known as an antenna.

FRANK SELVY SCORES 100 POINTS

Franklin Delano "Frank" Selvy (born November 9, 1932 in Corbin, Kentucky) is a former collegiate and NBA basketball player. Selvy was an All-State basketball player at Corbin High School and was a teammate of College Football Hall of Fame inductee Roy Kidd.

Nicknamed *The Corbin Comet*, Selvy is best remembered for scoring 100 points in a college game for South Carolina's Furman University against Newberry College on February 13th, 1954, **the only NCAA Division I player ever to do so.** "Bevo" Francis, playing for Rio Grande College (Ohio), scored 113 points against Hillsdale College in 1954. He is the only Division II (small college) player to score over 100 points in a game.

The game was played towards the end of Selvy's final collegiate season, and Furman coach Lyles Alley had designated the game "Frank Selvy Night" in order to garner recognition for the player who was already certain to finish the season leading the nation in scoring and earn first-team All-American honors, two accomplishments he had already attained the year before. The game was the first to be broadcast live on television in South Carolina and a large contingent from Selvy's hometown, including his family, had made the six-hour trek just for the occasion. The instructions from Coach Alley were simply to get the ball to Selvy so he can score as much as possible. Selvy obliged, hitting 41 of 66 field goals and 18 of 22 free throws, his last two points coming on a desperate heave near midcourt at the buzzer. (The game was played well before the introduction of the three-point line; Selvy would later estimate that about a dozen of his shots that day would have been three-pointers today.)

The only other player to score 100 points was Wilt Chamberlain. He did it in a 1962 NBA game against the New York Knicks while playing for the Philadelphia Athletics. At 7 foot 1 inch tall, he towered over other NBA players and many of his points were mere dunk shots where he just dropped the ball in the basket.

HOW TO PLAY THE GAME OF HORSE

This is a shooting basketball game for two or three players. Each player is out to win the game for himself. To determine the order of play, each player steps to the free throw line and keeps shooting until he misses. The person who makes the most goes first and the one with the least goes last. The first person can then try to make any shot he wishes. If he misses, it now is the second person's turn. If the second player makes the shot, then person number three must make the exact same shot. If he makes it there is no penalty and player number one now gets another turn. If player two misses the shot, he is given the first letter (H) in the spelling of the word **H-O-R-S-E**. The first player to receive all five letters – H-O-R-S-E – is out of the game and the contest is finished by the two remaining players.

Different parts of the country have different rules for this game, so players should agree in advance on the rules. In most cases, if a player says in advance that he is going to bank the shot in off the backboard and does so, the next player must also bank his shot for it to count.

HOW TO PLAY 21 BASKETBALL

Twenty-one, also called **21**, **hustle**, **American cutthroat**, **roughhouse** or **crunch**, is a popular variation of street basketball. The game is played most often with three to five players on a half court, typically when not enough players are available to at least play three-on-three. However it is possible to play twenty-one with only two players, or more than five players. Twenty-one is an individual game that does not utilize team play.

1. Have player 1 shoot an uncontested shot from the players choice (depending on skill), while players 2 and 3 position themselves for a possible rebound.
2. Allow player 1 to shoot uncontested free throws, up to three in a row or until he/she misses, if the initial shot was made.
3. Award player 1 possession of the ball at the top of the key if he/she makes all three free throws.
4. Understand that the ball goes "live" if player 1 misses a free-throw. Whoever rebounds the ball may shoot the ball.
5. Note that once a player has cleared the ball, he/she then tries to score a basket against the opposing players.

6. Know that when a player scores, he/she shoots uncontested free throws, up to three in a row or until he/she misses, at which point the play is "live" once more. Again, all rebounds must be taken back to the 3-point arc.
7. Have each player keep a mental count of their points: Free throws earn 1 point, baskets in "live" play are worth 2 points, and the initial shot of the entire game is worth 3 points.
8. Understand that the winner is the first player to reach 21 points exactly. If a player is at 20 and misses a free throw, that player's score is reduced to 13

Common additional rules include:

- A player can attempt a 3-pointer in lieu of attempting three free throws.
- Note that if you attempt a 3 point range freethrow, it's only worth 2 points, as each freethrow is worth 1 point each.
- If a player who has 13 points misses the next shot, regardless of
- whether it is a free throw, then that player's points revert to 0. This is
- referred to as "poison points".
- Whoever wins the game must shoot a 3-pointer in order to start with the ball at the beginning of the next game, and upon success receives the 3 points in the new game, does not get the free throws, but does have the
- ball and may shoot again.
- Players with fewer than 13 points at the end of a game keep their points into the next game (a sort of handicapping system for when there is a wide variation in skill between the players).
- "Tips" or "Taps" is an addition to Twenty-One. With these rules, if a player jumps up, gets a rebound in the air and makes a shot before touching the ground, the player who initially shot the ball is said to have been "tipped." In this situation, the tipper is awarded 3 points and resumes to shoot their post-goal free throws, and the one being tipped reverts to 0 if their score is under 14, otherwise they will revert to 14. If a player gets tipped 3 times, they are out of the game. All free throws in tips must at least hit the rim, or the shot must be retried. In addition, on a free throw the ball must hit the rim before the shooting player may charge the lane.
- Another variation of the Tips rule is thus: a two-handed tip knocks the original shooter's score to 0, but if his score is already 0, he or she is out of the game. Additionally, if a player makes a tip with one hand, the original shooter is automatically out and must wait for the next airball. Also, if a player is "dunk-tipped", the last player to touch the ball is automatically out and must also wait for the next airball.

Players should read all these rules in advance and agree on which ones will be followed before the game begins.

ST. LOUIS HAWKS DEFEAT THE MIGHTY CELTICS

Ben Kerner was the owner of the Milwaukee Hawks, a struggling NBA franchise. In 1953 the Hawks drafted 6-10 LSU star Bob Pettit, but they remained one of the worst teams in the NBA. In 1955 Kerner left Milwaukee and moved the franchise to St. Louis. In 1956 the Hawks had the second pick in the draft and they chose All-American Bill Russell. Kerner quickly traded him to Boston for two great players he knew would help the team immediately, **Cliff (Lil' Abner) Hagen of Kentucky and "Easy" Ed Macauley from St. Louis University**. That trade ranks as one of the most significant in sports history. Kerner, years later, said if he had it to do all over again he would still make the trade. It took the Hawks to several championship finals and made them a serious contender for a decade. In 1957

Bob Pettit

they barely made the playoffs but suddenly caught fire and made it to the finals against the vaunted Celtics. With Bob Pettit playing with a cast on one wrist, the Hawks lost a seventh game heartbreaker in double overtime to the Boston Celtics.

The next year they faced the same Celtics, **but this time they won the World Championship in a scintillating game six at St. Louis**. Bob Pettit set a record by scoring 50 points in that contest. I still have fond memories of that game because at the last minute, two of my buddies and I decided to drive over to Kiel Auditorium and find last-minute tickets. We must have been the last three people admitted because our seats were in the last row of the balcony, up near the pigeons. The thing I remember most about that exciting one-point nail biter was Pettit scoring 50 and Ed Macauley throwing the ball high up in the air as time ran out so the Celtics couldn't steal the ball. The Hawks had defeated a Celtics team that consisted of Bob Cousey, Bill Russell, Bill Sharman, Tom Heinson, and Sam Jones. From 1957 through 1966 the Red Auerbach-coached Celtics won nine world championships in ten years. Their only miss was the loss to the St. Louis Hawks in 1958. Their record will probably never be broken because expansion has added many more teams. Free agency also makes it difficult for winning teams to stay together very long. Finally, the draft process gives bad teams a chance to improve themselves by giving them the first crack at the best college players.

A Boston spurt in the opening moments of the final period gave the Celts an 86-84 lead, and the gloom was so thick in the arena one could practically cut it with a knife. That's when Pettit took charge. Before a cheering, stomping crowd of 10,218 at St. Louis, Pettit put on a show perhaps unmatched by any individual in NBA playoff history. Despite double and triple-teaming by the Celtics, the Hawk star sank basket after basket, free throw after free throw, singlehandedly keeping St. Louis in a game they otherwise would have lost, and preventing a dreaded return trip to Boston for a seventh game.

Pettit scored 18 of the team's last 21 points in that storied game that ended with a score of 110 to 109.

Bob Pettit went on to be named one of the NBA's 50 greatest players of all-time. At one of the All-Star games he pulled down a record 27 rebounds, a feat that not even the great Wilt Chamberlain was able to match.

THE BOSTON MOLASSES DISASTER

The awful disaster occurred at the Purity Distilling Company facility on January 15, 1919, an unusually warm day. At the time, molasses was the standard sweetener in the United States. Molasses can also be fermented to produce rum and ethyl alcohol, the active ingredient in other alcoholic beverages and a key component in the manufacturing of munitions at the time. The stored molasses was awaiting transfer to the Purity plant situated between Willow Street and what is now named Evereteze Way in Cambridge. near Keany Square. At 529 Commercial Street, a huge molasses tank 50 ft tall, 90 ft in diameter, and containing as much as 2,300,000 US galllons collapsed. Witnesses stated that as it collapsed, there was a loud rumbling sound, like a machine gun as the rivets shot out of the tank, and that the ground shook as if a train were passing by.

The collapse unleashed an immense wave of molasses between 8 and 15 ft high, moving at 35 mph, and exerting a pressure of 2 ton/ft. The molasses wave was of sufficient force to break the girders of the adjacent Boston Elevated Railway's Atlantic Avenue structure and lift a train off the tracks. Nearby, buildings were swept off their foundations and crushed. Several blocks were flooded to a depth of 2 to 3 feet (60 to 90 cm). As described by author Stephen Puleo:

Molasses, waist deep, covered the street and swirled and bubbled about the wreckage. Here and there struggled a form — whether it was animal or human being was impossible to tell. Only an upheaval, a thrashing about in the sticky mass, showed where any life was. Horses died like so many flies on sticky fly-paper. The more they struggled, the deeper in the mess they were ensnared. Human beings — men and women — suffered likewise.

The Boston Globe reported that people "were picked up by a rush of air and hurled many feet." Others had debris hurled at them from the rush of sweet-smelling air. A truck was picked up and hurled into Boston Harbor. Approximately 150 were injured; 21 people and several horses were killed — some were crushed and drowned by the molasses. The wounded included people, horses, and dogs; coughing fits became one of the most common ailments after the initial blast.

Anthony di Stasio, walking homeward with his sisters from the Michelangelo School, was picked up by the wave and carried, tumbling on its crest, almost as though he were surfing. Then he grounded and the molasses rolled him like a pebble as the wave diminished. He heard his mother call his name and couldn't answer, his throat was so clogged with the smothering goo. He passed out, then opened his eyes to find three of his sisters staring at him.

Rescuers found it difficult to make their way through the syrup to help the victims. It took four days before they stopped searching for victims; many dead were so glazed over in molasses, they were hard to recognize. Two found on the fourth day were never identified.

YOUR LANGUAGE AND YOUR VOCABULARY

President Nixon secretly taped many of his conversations that were held in the Oval Office. When the Watergate scandal broke a judge ruled that he had to turn the tapes over to federal prosecutors. When the tapes became public, Americans were shocked to learn that President Nixon routinely used vulgar langage during the course of his private conversations.

In March of 2010, citizens were shocked once again when Vice-president Joe Biden was caught by an open mike using the F word.

As a young man growing into maturity, you will need to make a decision about the type of language you use. A lot of this will be determined by the household you grow up in. If you live with a family where curse words aren't used, chances are this will greatly affect the way you talk and express yourself. However, if you go away to college and become friends with others who routinely use curse words, you might feel the need to fit in and start talking the way they do.

My wife had a cousin who grew up in a family that did not smoke, drink, curse or gamble. Despite all those years of training, when he went away to college he fell in with a crowd of smokers, and he soon developed a nicotine habit. He died in his fifties from mouth cancer.

Back in 1939, Hollywood had a strict production code that forbade nudity, excessive violence and curse words in films. When the film *Gone With the Wind* came out that year, audiences were shocked to hear the Clark Gable character of Rhett Butler utter the line, "Frankly, my dear, I don't give a damn." The film's producer was fined $5,000 for that lapse in judgment and curse words did not start creeping into films again until around 1959. At first, all you heard in the movies were a few hells and damns. But once the floodgates were opened just about any word or expression was eventually permitted. To deal with this problem the industry implemented a rating system in 1968 to give viewers in advance an idea about the content of the film. The letters G, PG, R and X were used as rating guides. Nowadays, if you go see an R-rated film, it is quite likely that you will hear every curse word in the book, including numerous violations of the Third Commandment about taking the Lord's name in vain.

290

Our son and daughter were raised in a Christian environment and at age 40 they still don't drink, gamble, smoke, use drugs, or use curse words. Because society increasingly refuses to make judgments about bad behavior, our grandchildren rub elbows every day with other children who use crude language when the teachers are not around. Our daughter must continually remind her children that certain words are not acceptable. It has even gotten to the point where my grandchildren are not allowed to watch Bart Simpson, because he is such a poor role model.

Generally speaking, the more educated you are the less likely you are to use curse words in your conversation. If you grow up in a conservative Protestant church, it is quite likely that you will not drink, smoke, cuss or gamble. The upside to all of this is that people who attend church regularly and don't smoke, drink, cuss, or gamble live longer and happier lives than those with different lifestyles.

THE JOHNSTOWN FLOOD

The **Johnstown Flood** occurred on May 31, 1889. It was the result of the failure of the South Fork Dam situated 14 miles upstream of the town of Johnstown, Pennsylvania, made worse by several days of extremely heavy rainfall. The dam's failure unleashed a torrent of 20 million tons of water (4.8 billion U.S. gallons). The flood killed over 2,200 people and caused $17 million of damage. It was the first major disaster relief effort handled by the new American Red Cross, led by Clara Barton. Support for victims came from all over the United States and 18 foreign countries. After the flood, victims suffered a series of legal defeats in their attempt to recover damages from the dam's

Johnstown, Pennsylvania Flood

owners. Who were the owners? Henry Clay Frick led a group of speculators to purchase the abandoned reservoir, modify it, and convert it into a private resort lake for the wealthy of Pittsburgh, many of whom were closely associated with Carnegie Steel.

On May 28, 1889, a storm formed over Nebraska and Kansas, moving east. When the storm struck the Johnstown-South Fork area two days later it was the worst downpour that had ever been recorded in that part of the country. The U.S. Army Signal Corps estimated that 6 to 10 inches of rain fell in 24 hours over the entire region. During the night, small creeks became roaring torrents, ripping out trees and debris. Telegraph lines were downed, and rail lines were washed away. Before daybreak the Conemaugh River that ran through Johnstown was about to burst its banks.

On the morning of May 31, 1889, in a farmhouse on a hill just above the South Fork Dam, Elias Unger, the president of the South Fork Fishing and Hunting Club at the time, awoke to the sight of Lake Conemaugh swollen after a night-long heavy rainfall. Unger ran outside in the still-pouring rain to assess the situation and saw that the water was nearly cresting the earthen dam. Unger quickly assembled a group of men to try to save the face of the dam by trying to unclog the spillway which was blocked by the broken fish trap and debris caused by the swollen waterline. Other men tried digging another spillway at the other end of the dam to relieve the pressure but without success. Most remained on top of the dam, some plowing earth to raise it, while others tried to pile mud and rock on the face to save the eroding wall.

John Parke, an engineer for the South Fork Club, briefly considered cutting through the dam's end, where the pressure would be less, but decided against it. Twice, under orders from Unger, Parke rode on horseback to the nearby town of South Fork to the telegraph office to send warnings to Johnstown explaining the critical nature of the eroding dam. But the warnings were not passed onto the authorities in town since there had been many false alarms in the past of the South Fork Dam not holding against flooding, but which it did. Unger, Parke, and the rest of the men continued working to save the face of the dam until they were exhausted in which they abandoned their efforts at around 1:30 p.m. when they felt that their work was futile and the dam would collapse at any minute. Unger ordered all of his men to fall back to high ground on both sides of the dam where they could do nothing but wait. During the day in Johnstown, the situation worsened as water rose to as much as 10 feet in the streets of Johnstown.

At around 3:10 p.m., the South Fork Dam burst, allowing the 20 million tons of Lake Conemaugh to cascade down the Little Conemaugh River. It took about 40 minutes for the entire lake to drain of the water. The first town to be hit by the flood was the small town of South Fork. Fortunately, the town was on high ground and most of the people ran farther up the nearby hills when they saw the dam literally spill over. Despite 20 to 30 houses being destroyed or washed away, only four people were killed.

On its way downstream towards Johnstown, the crest picked up debris, such as trees, houses, and animals. At the Conemaugh Viaduct, a 78-foot high railroad bridge, the flood temporarily was stopped when debris jammed against the stone bridge's arch. But after around seven minutes, the viaduct collapsed, allowing the flood to resume its course. Because of this, the force of the surge gained renewed impetus, resulting in a stronger force hitting Johnstown than otherwise would have been expected. The small town of Mineral Point, one mile below the Conemaugh Viaduct, was hit with this renewed force. About 30 families lived on the village's single street. After the flood, only bare rock remained. About 16 people were killed.

The village of East Conemaugh was next to be hit by the flood. One witness on high ground near the town described the water as almost obscured by debris, resembling "a huge hill rolling over and over". Train engineer John Hess, sitting in his locomotive engine, heard the rumbling of the flood and, correctly assuming what it was, tried to warn people by tying down the train whistle and racing toward the town by riding backwards to warn the residents ahead of the wave. His warning saved many people who were able to get to high ground. But at least 50 people died, including about 25 passengers stranded on trains in the town. Hess himself miraculously survived despite the flood picking up his locomotive and tossing it aside.

Just before hitting the main part of the city, the flood surge hit the Cambria Iron Works at the town of Woodvale, taking with it railroad cars and barbed wire. Of Woodvale's 1,100 residents, 314 died in the flood. Boilers exploded when the flood hit the Gauliter Wire Works, causing black smoke seen by the Johnstown residents.

Some 57 minutes after the South Fork Dam collapsed, the flood hit Johnstown. The inhabitants of Johnstown were caught by surprise as the wall of water and debris bore down on the village, traveling at 40 miles per hour and reaching a height of 60 feet in places. Some, realizing the danger, tried to escape by running towards high ground. But most people were hit by the surging floodwater. Many people were crushed by pieces of debris, and others became caught in barbed wire from the wire factory upstream. Those who sought safety in attics, or managed to stay afloat on pieces of floating debris, waited hours for help to arrive.

At Johnstown, the Stone Bridge, which was a substantial arched structure, carried the Pennsylvania Railroad across the Conemaugh River. The debris that was carried by the flood formed a temporary dam, stopping further progress of the water. The flood surge rolled upstream along the Stoney Creek River. Eventually, gravity caused the surge to return to the dam, causing a second wave to hit the city, but from a different direction Some people who had been washed downstream became trapped in an inferno as debris that had piled up against the Stone Bridge caught fire, killing at least 80 people. The fire at the Stone Bridge burned for three days. Afterwards, the pile of debris there covered 30 acres, and reached 70 feet in height. The mass of debris took three months to remove, because of the masses of steel wire from the ironworks binding it. Dynamite was eventually used to clear it. As of 2010, the Stone Bridge is still standing, and is often portrayed as one of the images of the flood.

For decades and decades after the flood it was quite common to see this sign in saloons all around the nation: **Don't Spit on the Floor – Remember the Johnstown Flood!**

THE GREAT GALVESTON HURRICANE KILLS 8,000

At the end of the 19th century, the city of Galveston, Texas was a booming town with a population of 42,000 residents. Its position on the natural harbor of Galveston Bay along the Gulf of Mexico made it the center of trade and **the biggest city in the state of Texas**. With this prosperity came a sense of complacency.

A quarter of a century earlier, the nearby town of Indianola on Matagorda

Aftermath of Galveston Hurricane

Bay was undergoing its own boom and was second to Galveston among Texas port cities. Then in 1875, a powerful hurricane blew through, nearly destroying the town. Indianola was rebuilt, though a second hurricane in 1886 caused residents to simply give up and move elsewhere. Many Galveston residents took the destruction of Indianola as an object lesson on the threat posed by hurricanes. Galveston was a low, flat island, little more than a large sandbar along the Gulf Coast. They proposed a seawall be constructed to protect the city, but their concerns were dismissed by the majority of the population and the city's government.

Since its formal founding in 1839, the city of Galveston had weathered numerous storms, all of which the city survived with ease. Residents believed any future storms would be no worse than previous events. In order to provide an official meteorological statement on the threat of hurricanes, Galveston Weather Bureau section director Isaac Cline wrote an 1891 article in the *Galveston Daily News* in which he argued not only that a seawall was *not* needed to protect the city, but also that it would be impossible for a hurricane of significant strength to strike the island. The seawall was not built, and development activities on the island actively increased its vulnerability to storms. Sand dunes along the shore were cut down to fill low areas in the city, removing what little barrier there was to the Gulf of Mexico.

On September 4, the Galveston office of the U.S. Weather Bureau began receiving warnings from the Bureau's central office in Washington, D.C. that a "tropical storm" had moved northward over Cuba. The Weather Bureau forecasters had no way of knowing where the storm was or where it was going. **At the time, the Weather Bureau discouraged the use of terms such as** *tornado* **or** *hurricane* **to avoid panicking residents in the path of any storm event.** Conditions in the Gulf of Mexico were ripe for further strengthening of the storm. The Gulf had seen little cloud cover for several weeks, and the seas were as warm as bathwater, according to one report. For a storm system that feeds off moisture, the Gulf of Mexico was enough to boost the storm from a tropical storm to a hurricane in a matter of days, with further strengthening likely.

Weather Bureau forecasters believed the storm would travel northeast and affect the mid-Atlantic coast. "To them, the storm appeared to have begun a long turn or 'recurve' that would take it first into Florida, then drive it northeast toward an eventual exit into the Atlantic." Cuban forecasters disagreed, saying the hurricane would continue west. One Cuban forecaster predicted the hurricane would continue into central Texas near San Antonio. Early the next morning, the swells continued despite only partly cloudy skies. Largely because of the unremarkable weather, few residents heeded the warning. Few people evacuated across Galveston's bridges to the mainland, and the majority of the population was unconcerned by the rain clouds that had begun rolling in by midmorning.

At the time of the 1900 storm the highest point in the city of Galveston was only 8.7 feet above sea level. The hurricane had brought with it a storm surge of over 15 feet, which washed over the entire island. The surge knocked buildings off their foundations and the surf pounded them to pieces. Over 3,600 homes were destroyed and a wall of debris faced the ocean. The few buildings which survived, mostly solidly built mansions and houses along the Strand District, are today maintained as tourist attractions.

The highest measured wind speed was 100 miles per hour (160 km/h) just after 6 p.m., but the Weather Bureau's anemometer (measures wind speed) was blown off the building shortly after that measurement was recorded. The eye passed over the city around 8 p.m. Maximum winds were estimated at 120 mph at the time, though later estimates placed the hurricane at the higher Category 4 classification on the Saffir-Simpson Scale. The lowest recorded barometric pressure was 28.48 inHg, considered at the time to be so low as to be obviously in error. Modern estimates later placed the storm's central pressure at 27.49 inHg, but this was subsequently adjusted to the storm's official lowest measured central pressure of 27.63 inHg.

As severe as the damage to the city's buildings was, the human toll was even greater. Because of the destruction of the bridges to the mainland and the telegraph lines, no word of the city's destruction was able to reach the mainland. At 11 a.m. on September 9, one of the few ships at the Galveston wharfs to survive the storm, the *Pherabe*, arrived in Texas City on the western side of Galveston Bay. It carried six messengers from the city. When they reached the telegraph office in Houston at 3 a.m. on September 10, a short message was sent to Texas Governor Joseph D. Sayers and U.S. President William McKinley: "I have been deputized by the mayor and Citizen's Committee of Galveston to inform you that the city of Galveston is in ruins." The messengers reported an estimated five hundred dead; this was considered to be an exaggeration at the time.

The citizens of Houston knew a powerful storm had blown through and had made ready to provide assistance. Workers set out by rail and ship for the island almost immediately. Rescuers arrived to find the city completely destroyed. It is believed 8,000 people—20% of the island's population—had lost their lives. Most had drowned or been crushed as the waves pounded the debris that had been their homes hours earlier. Many survived the storm itself but died after several days trapped under the wreckage of the city, with rescuers unable to reach them. The rescuers could hear the screams of the survivors as they walked on the debris trying to rescue those they could. A further 30,000 were left homeless.

So many died that corpses were piled onto carts for burial at sea. The bodies were so numerous that burying them all was not possible. The dead were initially dumped at sea; the gulf currents washed the bodies back onto the beach so a new solution was needed. Funeral pyres were set up wherever the dead were found and burned for weeks after the storm. Authorities passed out free whiskey to work crews that were having to **throw the bodies of their wives and children on the burn piles**. More people were killed in this single storm than the total of those killed in all the tropical cyclones that have struck the United States since. This count is greater than 300 cyclones, as of 2009. The Galveston Hurricane of 1900 remains the deadliest natural disaster in U.S. history.

For many people who attended the 1904 World's Fair at St. Louis, the scariest exhibit was a mechanical recreation of the Galveston Flood which was a frighteningly **realistic simulation of the tidal wave that killed eight thousand people in 1900**. Raging waters and mournful winds convinced many that they were in real danger.

THE HINDENBURG AIR DISASTER

The *Hindenburg* **disaster** took place on Thursday, May 6, 1937, as the German passenger airship LZ 129 Hindenburg caught fire and was destroyed as it was attempting to dock with its mooring mast at the Lakehurst Naval Air Station, which is located adjacent to the borough of Lakehurst, New Jersey. The Hindenburg was named for Paul Von Hindenburg, the great German general of World War I and president of Germany in the early 1930s. Of the 97 people on board, 35 people died in addition to one fatality on the ground. The disaster was the subject of spectacular newsreel coverage, photographs, and Herbert Morrison's recorded radio eyewitness report from the landing field, which was broadcast the next day. The actual cause of the fire remains unknown, although a variety of theories have been put forward for both the cause of ignition and the initial fuel for the ensuing fire.

The accident served to shatter public confidence in the giant, passenger-carrying rigid airship, and marked the end of the airship era.

The first of 10 scheduled round trips between Europe and the United States to be made by the Hindenburg in the 1937 season departed Frankfurt for Lakehurst on the evening of May 3 and except for strong headwinds which slowed the passage the crossing was uneventful. The airship was only half full with 36 passengers (capacity 70) and 61 crew members (including 21 training crew members), but the return flight was fully booked by people planning to attend the festivities for the coronation of King George VI in London the following week.

The airship was hours behind schedule when it passed over Boston on the morning of 6 May, and its landing at Lakehurst was ex-pected to be further delayed because of afternoon thunder-storms. Advised of the poor weather conditions at Lakehurst, Captain Max Pruss charted a course over Manhattan, causing a public spectacle as people rushed out into the street to catch sight of the airship. After passing over the field at 4 p.m., Captain Max Pruss took passengers on a tour over the seasides of New Jersey while waiting for the weather to clear. After finally being notified at 6:22 p.m. that the storms had passed, the airship headed back to Lakehurst to make its landing almost half a day late. However, as this would leave much less time than anticipated to service and prepare the airship for its scheduled departure back to Europe, the public was informed that they could not be permitted at the mooring location or be able to visit aboard the *"Hindenburg"* during its stay in port.

Around 7:00 p.m. local daylight saving time, at an altitude of 650 feet, the *Hindenburg* approached the Lakehurst Naval Air Station. This was to be a high landing, known as a *flying moor*, because the airship would be moored to a high mooring point, and then winched down to ground level. This type of landing maneuver would reduce the number of ground crew, but would require more time.

7:09: The airship made a sharp full speed left turn to the west around the landing field because the ground crew was not ready.

7:11: The airship turned back toward the landing field and valved gas. All engines idled ahead and the airship began to slow.

7:14: At altitude 394 feet, Captain Pruss ordered all engines full astern to try to brake the airship.

7:17: The wind shifted direction to southwest, and Captain Pruss was forced to make a second, sweeping sharp turn, this time towards starboard.

7:19: The airship made another sharp turn and dropped 300, 300 and 500 kg of water ballast in successive drops because the airship was stern heavy. Six men were also sent to the bow to trim the airship. These methods worked and the airship was on even keel as it stopped.

7:21: At altitude 295 feet, the mooring lines were dropped from the bow, the starboard line being dropped first, followed by the port line. The port line was overtightened as it was connected to the post of the ground winch; the starboard line had still not been connected.

At 7:25, a few witnesses saw the fabric ahead of the upper fin flutter as if gas were leaking. Witnesses also reported seeing blue discharges, possibly static electricity, moments before the fire on top and in the back of the ship near the point where the flames first appeared. Commander Rosendahl testified to the flames being "mushroom-shaped" and knew at once that the airship was doomed. One witness on the starboard side reported a fire beginning lower and behind the rudder on that side. On board, people heard a muffled explosion and those in the front of the ship felt a shock as the port trail rope overtightened; the officers in the control car initially thought the shock was due to a broken rope.

At 7:25 p.m. local time, the *Hindenburg* caught fire and quickly became engulfed in flames. Where the fire started is controversial; several witnesses on the port side saw yellow-red flames first just forward of the top fin, around the vent of cell 4. One, with views of the starboard side, saw flames beginning lower and farther aft, near cell 1. No. 2 Helmsman Helmut Lau also testified seeing the flames spreading from cell 4 into starboard. Although there were four newsreel cameramen and at least one spectator known to be filming the landing, they were all recording the actions of the ground crew when the fire started and therefore there is no motion picture record of where it first broke out at the instant of ignition.

Wherever it started, the flames quickly spread forward. Almost instantly, a water tank and a fuel tank burst out of the hull due to the shock of the blast. This shock also caused a crack behind the passenger decks, and the rear of the structure imploded. The buoyancy was lost on the stern of the ship, and the bow lurched upwards as the falling stern stayed in trim.

As the *Hindenburg's* tail crashed into the ground, a burst of flame came out of the nose, killing nine of the 12 crew members in the bow. As the airship kept falling with the bow facing upwards (because there was more lifting gas still in the nose), part of the port side directly behind the passenger deck collapsed inward (where a crack formed during the initial blast), and the gas cell there exploded, erasing the scarlet lettering "Hindenburg" while the airship's bow lowered. The airship's gondola wheel touched the ground, causing the airship to bounce up once more. At this point, most of the fabric had burned away. At last, the airship went crashing on the ground, bow first. The ship was completely destroyed. Although the hydrogen had finished burning, the Hindenburg's diesel fuel burned for a few more hours.

Hindenburg Disaster 1937

The time it took for the airship to be completely destroyed has been disputed. Some observers believe it took 34 seconds, others say it took 32 or 37 seconds. Since none of the newsreel cameras were filming the airship when the fire started, the time of the start of the fire can only be estimated from various eyewitness accounts, and will never be known accurately. The duralumin framework of the airship was salvaged and shipped back to Germany where it was recycled and used in the construction of military aircraft for the Luftwaffe as were the frames of the *LZ 127 Graf Zeppelin* and *LZ 130 Graf Zeppelin II* as well when both were scrapped in 1940.

Also contributing to the Zeppelins' downfall was the arrival of international passenger air travel and Pan American Airlines. Aircraft regularly crossed the Atlantic and Pacific oceans much faster than the 80 mph of the Hindenburg. The one advantage that the *Hindenburg* had over aircraft was the comfort it afforded its passengers, much like that of an ocean liner.

Although some researchers believe the Hindenburg was the victim of sabotage by Jews, all of the evidence pointing in that direction is circumstantial. Most historians believe that a spark of static electricity doomed the airship.

HOW TO PLAY CROQUET

Croquet (crow-kay) is a fun yard game that has a moderate level of difficulty. Croquet equipment consists of 9 wire wickets, 2 posts (stakes), mallets, and balls. Each mallet is colored to match its corresponding ball. Each post has colored rings which indicate the order of play, the color on top goes first.

Set up for play according to the following directions.

1. The 2 Posts 72 feet apart.
2. Wicket #1 7 feet in front of the Starting Post.
3. Wicket #2 7 feet in front of #1
4. Wicket #3 14 feet to the right of and 1 foot in advance of #2.
5. Wicket #4 22 feet in advance of #2 and in direct line with #1 & #2 and the post.
6. Wickets #5,6,7,8 &9 at the same relative distances.
7. Wickets #1,2,4,6,&7 should be in line with the 2 Posts.
   Wickets #3,5,8,&9 are called the Wing Wickets.

Definitions

8. Croquet
   When a Player's ball is touching a Roqueted ball, the player is allowed to put his hand or foot on his own ball and strike it with the mallet, sending the roqueted ball in any direction, leaving the Players ball stationary.
9. Rover
   After completing the entire course, through wickets 1-9 and 2&1 again, if the player does not strike the Starting Post, he may make his ball a Rover and continue play.
10. Roquet
    A ball is Roqueted if the Players ball comes in contact with it after the Player's ball is driven with the mallet. The Player is entitled to 2 additional strokes. Or, he may elect to Croquet or Roquet-Croquet the roqueted ball and only take 1 additional stoke.
11. Roquet-Croquet
    The Player's ball is placed in contact with a roqueted ball and the Player strikes his ball with the mallet, driving both balls in any direction.

TO BEGIN PLAY

12. Players start their tour by placing their ball 1/3 the way between the
13. Starting Post and Wicket #1, when it is their turn.
14. To complete their TOUR, a player must get his/her ball through wickets #1,2,3,4,5,6,&7 , stike the Turning Post, and then return through wickets #7,6,8,4,9,2,&1 , in that order, to strike the Starting Post(unless the Player opts to be a ROVER).
15. The ball must always be struck with the full face of the mallet tip, never pushed.
16. A Player's turn, or tour, lasts as long as it passes through a wicket, stikes another ball, or strikes a post.
17. A Player receives 1 additional shot for each wicket they pass through or post they strike, in the correct order.
18. The ball is played from where it comes to rest after striking a Post.
19. A Player receives 2 additional strokes for striking (roqueting) another ball. He may place his ball a mallet's head length from the other ball to take his 2 stokes. He also has the option of croqueting or roquet-croqueting the struck ball.
20. A stroke is counted if the ball is struck and moves AT ALL. Even if it returns to its original position.
21. If a player plays out of turn, all balls are returned to their original position, and play continues as normal.
22. If the wrong ball is played, the offending player loses his turn, and the ball is returned to its original position.
23. If a Player passes through a wicket after striking another ball, he must
24. replay that wicket and follow the rules of roqueting.
25. A Player (except a rover) cannot roquet the same ball twice in a row
26. unless it passes through a wicket, roquets another ball or strikes a post first.
27. If both the roqueted and the croqueted balls pass through the proper
28. wicket on one stroke, only the croqueted ball gets the extra stroke.
29. If more than one ball is roqueted, play is taken from the first ball roqueted. Play off the other balls is permissible.
30. If a Rover ball strikes a post, it is eliminated from play, immediately. It cannot be roqueted-croqueted or croqueted once eliminated.
31. Opponents alternate turns in Partnership play.
32. If a ball goes out of bounds, it is replaced at the edge of the playing area, where it went off.
33. A ball is "bridged," not through a wicket, if the ball touches the handle
34. of the mallet when laid across the wicket on the side from which the ball was struck.
35. A player's mallet must not contact the wicket when striking a Bridged ball. The ball must be returned and the turn forfeited if the wicket is struck.
36. If a player strikes a bridged ball while passing through that wicket, it does not count as a roquet. The Player may then proceed to roquet the ball with his gained stroke

If you find that allowing a player to become a rover in team play sort of ruins the fun for everyone else, simply eliminate this aspect of play.

The best way to hold a croquet mallet for striking your ball is to stand a bit behind the ball and adopt a wide stance. Grasp the mallet handle near the top with your left hand and hold the handle closer to the mallet head with your right hand. This enables you to line up your mallet head with the ball. Before you push the mallet with your right hand, go into a bit of a squatting stance and this will help with your accuracy.

HEROISM AT THE ALAMO

The **Battle of the Alamo** (February 23 – March 6, 1836) was a pivotal event in the Texas Revolution. Following a 13-day siege, Mexican troops under President General Santa Anna launched an assault on the Alamo Mission near San Antonio de Béxar (modern-day San Antonio, Texas). All but two of the Texian defenders were killed. Santa Anna's perceived cruelty during the battle inspired many Texians—both Texas settlers and adventurers from the United States—to join the Texian Army. Buoyed by a desire for revenge, the Texians defeated the Mexican Army at the Battle of San Jacinto, on April 21, 1836, ending the revolution.

Jim Bowie (Library of Congress)

Several months previously, Texians had driven all Mexican troops out of Mexican Texas. Approximately 100 Texians were then garrisoned at the Alamo. The Texian force grew slightly with the arrival of reinforcements led by eventual Alamo co-commanders James Bowie and William B. Travis. On February 23, approximately 1,500 Mexican troops marched into Béxar as the first step in a campaign to retake Texas. For the next 12 days the two armies engaged in several skirmishes with minimal casualties. Aware that his garrison could not withstand an attack by such a large force, Travis wrote multiple letters pleading for more men and supplies, but fewer than 100 reinforcements arrived.

In the early morning hours of March 6, the Mexican Army advanced on the Alamo. After repulsing two attacks, Texians were unable to fend off a third. As Mexican soldiers scaled the walls, most of the Texian soldiers withdrew into interior buildings. Defenders unable to reach these points were slain by the Mexican cavalry as they attempted to escape. Between five and seven Texians may have surrendered; if so, they were quickly executed. Most eyewitness accounts reported between 182 and 257 Texians dead, while most historians of the Alamo agree that 400–600 Mexicans were killed or wounded. Several noncombatants were sent to Gonzales to spread word of the Texian defeat. The news sparked a panic and the Texian army, most settlers, and the new Republic of Texas government fled from the advancing Mexican Army.

Within Mexico, the battle has often been overshadowed by events from the Mexican-American War of 1846–48. In 19th-century Texas, the Alamo complex gradually became known as a battle site rather than a former mission. The Texas Legis-lature purchased the land and buildings in the early part of the 20th century and designated the Alamo chapel as an official Texas State Shrine. The Alamo is now "the most popular tourist site in Texas". The Alamo has been the subject of numerous non-fiction works beginning in 1843. Most Americans, however, are more familiar with the myths spread by many of the movie and television adaptations, including the 1950s Disney miniseries *Davy Crockett* and John Wayne's 1960 film *The Alamo*.

David Crockett (August 17, 1786 – March 6, 1836) was a celebrated 19th-century American folk hero, frontiersman, soldier and politician. He was elected U.S. Congressman from Tennessee in 1832 and actively opposed many of President Andrew Jackson's policies. This led to his defeat in the 1834 election. A disgruntled Crockett soon left Tennessee and headed for Texas. A former slave and a cook for Santa Anna's army later testified that Davy Crockett's body was found surrounded by 16 Mexican corpses.

Jim Bowie spent most of his early life in Louisiana where he gained a

The Alamo in San Antonio (Wikipedia)

reputation as a fearless fighter with a specially-made knife that became known far and wide as the **Bowie Knife**. In 1830 he moved to Texas and soon became involved in the fight for Texas independence. Illness and an injured back placed him on a cot in a small room at the time Santa Anna's troops overwhelmed the defenders of the Alamo. Bowie fought off his attackers with a brace of pistols and his knife until he was fatally bayonetted. Bowie's death at the Alamo only served to enhance his legend and increase the popularity of his Bowie Knife. Knife collectors worldwide continue to currently push a large demand for the Bowie Knife.

The significance of the Alamo is that its defenders, by holding Santa Anna's army at bay for nearly two weeks, gave General Sam Houston precious extra time to organize his army for the battle of San Jacinto, where the Mexican army was defeated and Santa Anna was captured. The men who died at the Alamo played a huge role in Texas winning its independence.

HOW TO PLAY TENNIS

I didn't learn how to play tennis until I was about 26 years old. I began by playing one of my high school students who was the number one singles player on Collinsville High's team. I found tennis to be good exercise and the one-on-one competition challenging. Unlike golf, tennis is a cheap sport to play since a raquet and balls are quite reasonable. Tennis is also more wide open as a high school sport since fewer fathers take their sons out on the courts compared to the number of fathers who teach their sons how to play golf.

Choosing a raquet: When looking to buy a raquet you should figure out the level of play you are at. Beginners might want to choose a head that is wider, which reduces the chance of missing the ball. More experienced players might want to choose a narrower head which has more power and accuracy.

Tennis Grip: In order to understand the grips, it is important to know that the handle of a racquet always consists of 8 sides, or in other words, has an octagonal shape. A square shape would hurt the hand, while a round shape would not give enough friction to gain a firm grip. The grip on your raquet is an important aspect in your tennis play. You should grip the tennis raquet loosely between strokes, but when you are about to swing, it is better to tighten your hold.

The following is the **Eastern Grip**. Note that the eastern grip is popular with beginners and is widely used with forehands because of its comfort. The **Eastern Backhand Grip**, is obtained when placing the hand such that the base knuckle of the index finger is right on the 1st bevel. This is essentially the same as the Western [forehand] grip and allows for significant spin and control.

The **Continental Grip** is obtained when placing the hand such that the base knuckle of the index finger is right on the 2nd bevel. It is naturally obtained when holding the racket as if it were an axe, for chopping. Hence the second name "Chopper grip". The Continental grip does not allow for much topspin on groundstrokes. Since modern tennis, especially clay court tennis, has shown an evolution towards topspin, the Continental grip has gone out of fashion with professional players for hitting groundstrokes. It is still the preferred grip for serves and volleys. The rest of the grips strike a balance between high spin capacity on one hand, and variety and control on the other hand.

The **Eastern Forehand Grip** is obtained when placing the hand such that the base knuckle of the index finger is right on the 3rd bevel. It is naturally obtained when picking up a racquet lying on the ground, or "shaking hands" with a perpendicularly held racquet. The Eastern Forehand grip allows for more topspin on the forehand while keeping control, because the shift along the handle is only 45 degrees (from the multi-purpose Continental grip).

The **Western Grip** is secured when placing the hand such that the base knuckle of the index finger is right on the 5th bevel. Compared to the Continental grip, the blade has rotated 135 degrees. This forces the wrist in an uncomfortable twist but allows for the greatest possible spin. This is basically equivalent to the Eastern Backhand grip, except that the SAME face of the racquet is used to strike the ball.

The western grip generates maximum topspin and power. Because of the angle of your tennis racquet when you use the western forehand grip, you should make contact with the ball a bit earlier than you would with the eastern forehand grip.

Forehand Stroke: The forehand stroke is usually the most powerful and the stroke most users want to use. Of course it has to be on the right side of the person to get the forehand stroke. The forehand in tennis is a shot made by swinging the racquet across one's body in the direction of where the player wants to place the shot.

Backhand Stroke: The backhand stroke is when the ball is on the opposite side of you. It is the opposite of the forehand. There are two types of back hands. There is the two-handed back hand and there is also the one handed back hand which are primarily the same thing, except you are using different amounts of hands.

Volleys: Net play is an important aspect to playing tennis. At the net, the player will primarily use a volley to hit the ball. The volley is when the ball does not hit the ground before you hit it. It is out of the air pretty much. You want to get yourself about 3 feet away from the net. Make sure you keep your feet shoulder width apart.

Tennis champion John McEnroe (noted for throwing temper tantrums)

The Serve: The serve in tennis is a shot to start a point. The serve is usually initiated by tossing the ball into the air and hitting it (usually near the apex of its trajectory) into the diagonally opposite service box without touching the net. It may be performed underhand or overhead. The serve is the only shot where a player can take his time to set up. Your foot must not touch the service line before hitting the ball. If this happens a foot fault is called and the server loses the point.

Scoring the game: A game consists of a sequence of *points* played with the same player serving, and is won by the first player to have won at least four points, and at least two points more than his or her opponent. The half of the court used for service alternates between sides, beginning with the right-hand half, known as the *deuce court,* and continuing with the left-hand side, known as the *advantage court*. In other words, in the first point the server serves from the right-hand side of the court into the left-hand side (from his or her point of view) of the opponents' court.

The server's score is always given first. If he wins the first point the score is 15-love. The word love is substituted for zero. If he loses the point it would be love 15. If the server wins the first two points the score is 30 love. If the other player wins the next point the score is 30-15. If the server wins the first 3 points in a row the score would be 40 love. If each player has won three points, the score is described as **"deuce"** (from French *deux* meaning two [more points]) rather than "40-all". From this point on, whenever the score is tied, it is described as "deuce" regardless of how many points have been played. The player who wins the next point after deuce is said to have the **advantage**. If the player with advantage loses the next point, the score is again deuce, since the score is tied. If the player with the advantage wins the next point, that player has won the game, since the player now leads by two points. When the server is the player with the advantage, the score may be stated by him before the next point as "advantage in." When the server's opponent has the advantage, the server may state the score as "advantage out." These phrases are sometimes shortened to "ad in" and "ad out." Alternatively, the server may simply use players' names; in professional tournaments the umpire announces the score in this format (e.g., "advantage McEnroe" or "advantage Borg").

Thus the numbers used in scoring tennis are 15, 30, and 40. A match consists of three sets with a player being required to win 7 games to complete a set. To win a set a player must have an advantage of at least two games over his opponent. Thus a score of 7 games to 5 wins the set. If each player has won 6 games in a set, the use of a tiebreaker comes into play.

At a score of 6–6, a set is often determined by one more game called a "seven point tiebreak." Points are counted using ordinary numbering. The set is decided by the player who wins at least seven points in the tiebreak but also has two points more than his opponent. For example, if the score is 6 points to 5 points and the player with 6 points wins the next point, he wins the tiebreak and the set. If the player with 5 points wins the point, the tiebreak continues and cannot be won on the next point, since no player will be two points better than his opponent.

The player who would normally be serving after 6–6 is the one to serve first in the tiebreak, and the tiebreak is considered a service game for this player. The server begins his service from the deuce court and serves one point. After the first point, the serve changes to the first server's opponent. Each player then serves two consecutive points for the remainder of the tiebreak. The first of each two-point service starts from the server's advantage court and the second starts from the deuce court. In this way, the sum of the scores is even when the server serves from the deuce court. After every six points, the players switch ends of the court.

If you are having difficulty understanding the scoring in tennis, watch a few professional matches on television, and you'll get the hang of it.

HOW TO PLAY BADMINTON

This is a comparatively easy backyard game for two or four people. A net, rackets and birdies can be purchased reasonably at most sporting goods stores. This is also a good activity for couples who are dating because the speed of the shuttlecock is much slower than a tennis ball.

When the British colonized India they noticed the children there playing a game with a paddle and a ball that had feathers in it. The Duke of Beaufort introduced the game at his estate where he served tea and cucumber sandwiches. His guests started calling the game badminton, which was the name of his estate.

Begin play by tossing a coin. The player winning the toss chooses between serving or receiving first.

Start service from the right side (always) and serve to the diagonal service box.

Serve underhand only.

Count scored points only on your serve.

Gain control of the serve by winning the point when your opponent is serving.

Rally by hitting the shuttle (sometimes called a birdie) over the net, trying to land it on your opponent's court to score a point.

Score a point also when your opponent hits the shuttle out of your court, into the net, hits the shuttle with his body or clothing, or hits it before it crossed the net.

Win the game by scoring 15 points first.

Play a match based on the best two out of three.

SERGEANT ALVIN C. YORK

Alvin Cullum York (December 13, 1887 – September 2, 1964) was an American soldier who is renowned as a World War I hero. He was awarded the Medal of Honor for leading an attack on a German machine gun nest, taking 32 machine guns, killing 28 German soldiers and capturing 600 others. This action took place during the U.S.-led portion of the Meuse-Argonne Offensive in France, which was part of a broader Allied offensive masterminded by Marshal Ferdinand Foch to breach the Hindenburg line and ultimately force the opposing German forces to capitulate.

Alvin C. York was born in a two-room log cabin near Pall Mall, Tennessee, on December 13, 1887, the third of eleven children born to Mary Elizabeth Brooks and William Uriah York. The York family resided in the Indian Creek area of Fentress County. The family was impoverished, with William York working as a blacksmith, by which he supplemented the family income. The father and sons of the York family would gather and harvest their own food, while the mother knitted all family clothing. The York sons only attended nine months of schooling, and withdrew from education because William York wanted his sons to assist him in tending to the family farm.

When William York died in November 1911, his son Alvin assisted his mother in raising his younger siblings. Alvin was the oldest living sibling that was then residing in the county, as his two older brothers had married and moved into different areas. In order to supplement the family income, York first held employment as a community laborer in Harriman, Tennessee. By all accounts he was very devoted to his family. However, in the few years before the war, York was a violent alcoholic and prone to fighting in saloons. His mother, a member of a pacifist Protestant denomination, tried to persuade York to change his ways because she worried he would "amount to nothin'", however to no avail. In the winter of 1914, he and his friend engaged in a fight with other saloon patrons during a night of heavy drinking. The incident resulted in his friend Everett Delk being beaten to death inside a saloon in Clinton County, Kentucky. The event was profound enough that York finally followed his mother's advice and became a pacifist, and stopped drinking alcohol. York was baptized as a born again Christian in the Wolf River, with the baptism being conducted by Reverend H.H. Russell in early 1915.

On June 5, 1917, at the age of 29, Alvin York registered for the draft as all men between 21 and 31 years of age did on that day. When he registered for the draft, he answered the question "Do you claim exemption from draft (specify grounds)?" by writing "Yes. Don't Want To Fight." When his initial claim for conscientious objector status was denied, he appealed.

In World War I, conscientious objector status did not exempt one from military duty. Such individuals could still be drafted and were given assignments that did not conflict with their anti-war principles. In November 1917, while York's application was considered, he was drafted and began his army service at Camp Gordon in Georgia. There, extensive conversations with Major George Buxton challenged his pacifism and its Biblical basis until York decided he could and would serve.

York enlisted in the United States Army and served in Company G, 328th Infantry Regiment, 82nd Infantry Division at Camp Gordon, Georgia. Discussion of the Biblical stance on war with his company commander, Captain Edward Courtney Bullock Danforth (1894–1974) of Augusta, Georgia and his battalion commander, Major Gonzalo Edward Buxton (1880–1949) of Providence, Rhode Island, eventually convinced York that warfare could be justified.

Sergeant York (National Archives)

During an attack by his battalion to secure German positions along the Decauville rail-line north of Chatel-Chehery, France, on October 8, 1918, York's actions in the Argonne Forest sector earned him the Medal of Honor. He recalled:

"The Germans got us, and they got us right smart. They just stopped us dead in our tracks. Their machine guns were up there on the heights overlooking us and well hidden, and we couldn't tell for certain where the terrible heavy fire was coming from... And I'm telling you they were shooting straight. Our boys just went down like the long grass before the mowing machine at home. Our attack just faded out... And there we were, lying down, about halfway across [the valley] and those German machine guns and big shells getting us hard."

Four non-commissioned officers and thirteen privates under the command of Sergeant Bernard Early (which included York) were ordered to infiltrate behind the German lines to take out the machine guns. The group worked their way behind the Germans and overran the headquarters of a German unit, capturing a large group of German soldiers who were preparing a counter-attack against the U.S. troops. Early's men were contending with the prisoners when machine gun fire suddenly peppered the area, killing six Americans and wounding three others, The fire came from German machine guns on the ridge, which turned their weapons on the U.S. soldiers. The loss of the nine put Corporal York in charge of the seven remaining U.S. soldiers. As his men remained under cover, and guarding the prisoners, York worked his way into position

307

to silence the German machine guns. York recalled:

"And those machine guns were spitting fire and cutting down the undergrowth all around me something awful. And the Germans were yelling orders. You never heard such a racket in all of your life. I didn't have time to dodge behind a tree or dive into the brush... As soon as the machine guns opened fire on me, I began to exchange shots with them. There were over thirty of them in continuous action, and all I could do was touch the Germans off just as fast as I could. I was sharp shooting... All the time I kept yelling at them to come down. I didn't want to kill any more than I had to. But it was they or I. And I was giving them the best I had."

During the assault, a group of eight German soldiers in a trench near York were ordered to charge him with fixed bayonets. York had fired all the rounds in his rifle, but drew out his pistol and shot all eight of the soldiers before they could reach him.

One of York's prisoners, German First Lieutenant Paul Jürgen Vollmer (who spoke fluent English) of 1st Battalion, 120th Württemberg Landwehr Regiment, emptied his pistol trying to kill York while he was contending with the machine guns. Failing to injure York, and seeing his mounting losses, he offered to surrender the unit to York, who gladly accepted. By the end of the engagement, **York and his seven men marched 132 German prisoners back to the American lines**. His actions silenced the German machine guns and were responsible for enabling the 328th Infantry to renew its attack to capture the Decauville Railroad.

York was awarded the Distinguished Service Cross for his heroism, but this was upgraded to the Medal of Honor, which was presented to York by the commanding general of the American Expeditionary Force, General John J. Pershing. The French Republic awarded him the Croix de Guerre and Legion of Honor. Italy and Montenegro awarded him the Croce di Guerra and War Medal, respectively.

York was a corporal during the action. His promotion to sergeant was part of the honor for his valor. Of his deeds, York said to his division commander, General George B. Duncan, in 1919: "A higher power than man power guided and watched over me and told me what to do."

Sergeant York is a 1941 biographical film about the life of Alvin York, the most-decorated American soldier of World War I. It was directed by Howard Hawks and was the highest-grossing film of the year. Gary Cooper won the "Best Actor" Oscar for his portrayal of the hillbilly hero.

THE MOST DECORATED SOLDIER OF WORLD WAR II

Audie Leon Murphy (June 20, 1925 – May 28, 1971) was the most decorated American soldier of World War II and a celebrated movie star for many years in the post-war era, appearing in 44 films. He also found some success as a country music composer.

Murphy became the most decorated United States soldier of the war during his twenty-seven months in action in the European Theatre. He received the Medal of Honor, the U.S. military's highest award for valor, along with 32 additional U.S. and foreign medals and citations.

Murphy's successful movie career included the biographical *To Hell and Back* (1955), based on his book of the same title (1949). The film grossed almost ten million dollars during its initial theatrical release, and at the time became Universal's biggest hit of the studio's 43-year history. This movie held the record as the company's highest-grossing motion picture until 1975, when it was finally surpassed by Steven Spielberg's *Jaws*. Murphy also starred in 39 Hollywood films. For his contribution to the motion picture industry, Audie Murphy has a star on the Hollywood Walk of Fame at 1601 Vine Street. He died in a plane crash in 1971 and was interred, with full military honors, in Arlington National Cemetery. Audie **Murphy's grave site is the second-most visited grave at Arlington, after that of President John F. Kennedy.**

Murphy was born in Texas, to Emmett Berry and Josie Bell Murphy who was of Irish descent, poor sharecroppers, and grew up on farms between Farmersville and Greenville, as well as near Celeste, Texas (Hunt County). Murphy was the sixth of twelve children, nine of whom survived until the age of eighteen. He went to school in Celeste until the eighth grade, when he dropped out to help support his family (his father deserted them in 1936), working for a dollar a day, plowing and picking cotton on any farm that would hire him. He became very skilled with a rifle, hunting small game to help feed the family. One of his favorite hunting companions was neighbor Dial Henley. When he commented that Murphy never missed when he shot at squirrels, rabbits, and birds, Murphy replied, *"Well, Dial, if I don't hit what I shoot at, my family won't eat today."* During the 1930s Murphy worked at a combination general store/garage and filling station in Greenville, Texas. At fifteen he was working in a radio repair shop when his mother died on May 23, 1941. Later that year, in agreement with his older sister, Corrinne, Murphy placed his three youngest siblings in an

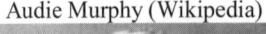
Audie Murphy (Wikipedia)

orphanage to ensure their care (he reclaimed them after World War II).

After the attack on Pearl Harbor on December 7, 1941, Murphy tried to enlist in the military, but the services rejected him for being under age. In June 1942, shortly after his 17th birthday, his sister Corrine adjusted his birth date so he appeared to be 18 and legally allowed to enlist. Murphy was accepted into the United States Army, at Greenville, after being turned down by the Marines and the paratroopers for being too short (5 feet 5.5 inches) and of slight build (145 pounds). He was also turned down by the Navy for being slight of build. He was sent to Camp Wolters, Texas, for basic training and during a session of close order drill, passed out. His company commander tried to have him transferred to a cook and bakers' school because of his baby-faced youthfulness, but Murphy insisted on becoming a combat soldier. His wish was granted: after 13 weeks of basic training, he was sent to Fort Meade, Maryland for advanced infantry training.

Murphy's combat initiation finally came when he took part in the invasion of Sicily on July 10, 1943. Shortly after arriving, Murphy was promoted to corporal after killing two Italian officers as they tried to escape on horseback. He contracted malaria while in Sicily, an illness which put him in the hospital several times during his Army years.

After Sicily was secured from Axis forces, the 3rd Division invaded the Italian mainland, landing near **Salerno** in September 1943. While leading a night patrol, Murphy and his men ran into German soldiers but fought their way out of an ambush, taking cover in a rock quarry. The German command sent a squad of soldiers in, but they were stopped by intense machine-gun and rifle fire. Three German soldiers were killed and several others captured. As a result of his actions at Salerno, Murphy was promoted to sergeant.

Murphy distinguished himself in action on many occasions while in Italy, fighting at the Volturno River, at the **Anzio** beachhead, and in the cold, wet Italian mountains. While in Italy, his skills as a combat infantryman earned him promotions and decorations for valor.

Following its participation in the Italian campaign, the 3rd Division landed in Southern France on August 15, 1944 as part of Operation Anvil-Dragoon. Shortly thereafter, Murphy's best friend, Lattie Tipton was killed by a German soldier in a machine gun nest who was feigning surrender. Murphy went into a rage, and single-handedly wiped out the German machine gun crew which had just killed his friend. He then used the German machine gun and grenades to destroy several other nearby enemy positions. For this act, Murphy received the Distinguished Service Cross (second only to the Medal of Honor). During seven weeks of fighting in that campaign in France, Murphy's division suffered 4,500 casualties.

Just weeks later, he received two Silver Stars for further heroic actions. Murphy, by now a staff sergeant and holding the position of Platoon Sergeant, was eventually awarded a battlefield commission to second lieutenant, which elevated him to the Platoon Leader position. He was wounded in the hip by a sniper's ricocheting bullet 12 days after the promotion and spent ten weeks recuperating. Within days of returning to his unit, and still bandaged, he became company commander (January 25, 1945), and suffered further wounds from a mortar round which killed two others nearby.

The next day, January 26 (the temperature was 14 F with 24 inches of snow on the ground), the battle at Holtzwihr (France) began with Murphy's unit at an effective strength of 19 out of 128. Murphy sent all of his men to the rear while he took pot-shots at the Germans until out of ammunition. He then proceeded to use an abandoned, burning tank destroyer's .50 caliber machine gun to cut into the German infantry at a distance, including one full squad of German infantry that had crawled in a ditch to within 100 feet of his position. Wounded in the leg during heavy fire, he continued this nearly single-handed battle for almost an hour. His focus on the battle before him stopped only when his telephone line to the artillery fire direction center was cut by either U.S. or German artillery. As his remaining men came forward, he quickly organized them to conduct a counter attack, which ultimately drove the enemy away from Holtzwihr. For these actions Murphy was awarded the Medal of Honor.

Murphy was then removed from the front lines and made a liaison officer; he was promoted to 1st lieutenant on February 22, 1945. On June 2, 1945, Lt. Gen. Alexander Patch, commander of the US Seventh Army, presented him with the Medal of Honor and Legion of Merit. The Legion of Merit was awarded for meritorious service with the 3rd Infantry Division during January 22, 1944 to February 18, 1945. On June 10, Murphy left Paris by plane, arriving in San Antonio, Texas four days later.

Audie Murphy received 33 US medals, plus five medals from France and one from

Belgium. It has been said that **he received every US medal available at the time; 5 of them awarded more than once**.

In 2000, Audie Murphy was honored with his portrait on a thirty-three cent United States postage stamp.

CARD TRICK

Lay out eleven cards and ask a volunteer from the audience to move several cards from the right side to the left side – anywhere from zero to as many as six cards. While he does this, turn around so you can't possibly see how many cards were moved. When the volunteer is finished, turn around and announce that you will guess, using the powers of your perception, exactly how many cards were moved.

Set up: Take eleven cards from a deck. Take a Joker, an ace and one each of numbers 2-10. Plan for the trick by laying the cards face down in this order – 6,5,4,3,2, ace, joker, 10, 9, 8. 7. Invite the volunteer to come up and move the cards. When the volunteer has finished count five cards from the right and pick up the fifth card. That card will always tell you the number of cards moved. If it's the ace, then one card was moved. If it's the Joker, then no cards were moved.

This trick always works because of the way the cards are laid out. You can try it yourself for practice. Spread out the cards and then move four from the right side to the left side. Now count over five cards from the right, turn the fifth card over and it is the number four.

MIRACLE ON ICE 1980

The "**Miracle on Ice**" was a medal-round men's ice hockey game during the 1980 Winter Olympics at Lake Placid, New York, on February 22. The United States team, made up of amateur and collegiate players and led by coach Herb Brooks, defeated the Soviet team, which was considered the best hockey team in the world.

Team USA went on to win the gold medal by winning their final match over Finland, which finished 4th. The Soviet Union took the silver medal by beating Sweden in their final game. As part of its 100th anniversary celebrations in 2008, the International Ice Hockey Federation (IIHF) chose the Miracle on Ice as the number-one international hockey story of the century.

The Soviet Union entered the Olympic tournament as heavy favorites, having won the ice hockey gold medal in 1956 and every year since 1964. In the four Olympics after the Soviet squad was upset by Team USA at Squaw Valley in 1960, Soviet teams had gone 27-1-1 and outscored the opposition 175-44. In head-to-head matchups against the United States the cumulative score over that period was 28-7. The Soviet players were classed as amateurs, but soft jobs provided by the Brezhnev government (some were active-duty military) allowed them to essentially play professionally in a well-developed league with world class training facilities. They were led by legendary players in world ice hockey, such as Boris Mikhailov (a top line right winger and team captain), Vladislav Tretiak (considered by many to be the best ice hockey goaltender in the world at the time), the speedy and skilled Valeri Kharlamov, as well as talented, young, and dynamic players such as defenseman Viacheslav Fetisov and forwards Vladimir Krutov and Sergei Makarov. From that team, Tretiak, Kharlamov, and Fetisov would eventually be enshrined in the Hockey Hall of Fame.

Herb Brooks conducted tryouts in Colorado Springs in the summer of 1979. Of the 20 players who eventually made the final Olympic roster, Buzz Schneider was the only one left over from the 1976 Olympic team. Nine players had played under Herb Brooks at the University of Minnesota. Four more were from Boston University. Assistant coach Craig Patrick had played with Brooks on the 1967 U.S. national team.

The Soviet and American teams were natural rivals due to the decades-old Cold War. In addition, President Jimmy Carter was at the time considering a U.S. boycott of the 1980 Summer Olympics, to be held in Moscow, in protest of the Soviet invasion of Afghanistan, which had begun just weeks before. On February 9, the same day that the American and Soviet teams met in an exhibition in New York City, U.S. Secretary of State Cyrus Vance denounced the impending Moscow games at a meeting of the IOC. President Carter eventually decided in favor of the boycott.

In exhibitions that year, Soviet club teams had gone 5–3–1 against National Hockey League (NHL) teams, and a year earlier **the Soviet national team had routed the NHL All-Stars 6–0** to win the Challenge Cup. In 1979–80, virtually all the top North American players were Canadians, although the number of U.S.-born professional players had been on the rise throughout the 1970s. The 1980 U.S. Olympic team featured several young players who were regarded as highly promising, and some had signed contracts to play in the NHL immediately after the tournament.

In September the American team started exhibition play, playing 61 games in five months against teams from Europe and America. The last exhibition game was against the Soviets in Madison Square Garden on February 9, 1980. **The Soviets crushed the Americans 10-3**. Viktor Tikhonov later said that this victory "turned out to be a very big problem" by causing the Soviets to under-estimate the American team.

In Olympic group play, the United States surprised many observers with their physical, cohesive play. In their first game against favored Sweden, Team USA earned a dramatic 2–2 draw by scoring with 27 seconds left after pulling goalie Jim Craig for an extra attacker. Then came a stunning 7–3 victory over Czechoslovakia, considered by many to be the second-best team after the Soviet Union and a favorite for the silver medal. With their two toughest games in the group phase out of the way, the U.S. team reeled off three more wins, beating Norway 5–1, Romania 7–2, and West Germany 4–2 to go 4–0–1 and advance to the medal round from their group, along with the Swedes.

In the other group, the Soviets stormed through their opposition undefeated, often by grossly lopsided scores – knocking off Japan 16–0, the Netherlands 17–4, Poland 8–1, Finland 4–2, and Canada 6–4; easily qualifying for the next round, although both the Finns and the Canadians gave the Soviets tough games for two periods. In the end, the Soviet Union and Finland (who overcame a disastrous start after sensationally losing to Poland in their opening game of the tournament, but then rallied to upset Canada) advanced from their group.

Preparing for the medal round

The U.S. and Soviet teams prepared for the medal round in different ways. Soviet coach Viktor Tikhonov rested most of his best players, preferring to let them study plays rather than actually skate. U.S. coach Herb Brooks, however, continued with his tough, confrontational style, skating "hard" practices and berating his players for perceived weaknesses.

The day before the match, columnist Dave Anderson wrote in the *New York Times*, "Unless the ice melts, or unless the United States team or another team performs a miracle, as did the American squad in 1960, the Russians are expected to easily win the Olympic gold medal for the sixth time in the last seven tournaments."

"Do you believe in miracles?"

The Field House (capacity 8500) was packed. The home crowd waved American flags and sang patriotic songs such as "God Bless America." The rest of the United States (except those who watched the game live on Canadian television) had to wait to see the game. After the Soviets refused to consent to moving the game from 5 p.m. to 8 p.m. for American television (this would have meant a 4 a.m. start in Moscow for Soviet viewers), ABC decided to broadcast the late-afternoon game on tape delay in prime time. Before the game, Brooks read his players a statement he'd written out on a piece of paper, telling them that "You were born to be a player. You were meant to be here. This moment is yours."

First period

As in several previous games, the U.S. team fell behind early. Vladimir Krutov deflected a slap shot by Aleksei Kasatonov past U.S. netminder Jim Craig to give the Soviets a 1–0 lead, and after Buzz Schneider scored for the United States to tie the game, the Soviets struck again with a Sergei Makarov goal. Down 2–1, Craig improved his play, turning away many Soviet shots before the U.S. team had another shot on goal **(the Soviet team had 39 shots on goal in the game, the Americans 16)**.

In the waning seconds of the first period, Dave Christian fired a slap shot on Tretiak from 100 feet away. The Soviet goalie saved the shot but misplayed the rebound, which bounced out some 20 feet in front of him. The Soviet defensemen, Pervukhin and Bilyaletdinov, quit playing and watched the clock tick off the last few seconds. Tretiak started to move out of goal. Mark Johnson sliced between the two defensemen, **found the loose puck and fired it past a diving Tretiak to tie the score with one second left in the period.** The Soviet team played the final second of the period with just three players on the ice, as the rest of the team had retired to their dressing room for the first intermission. Unbelievably, the first period ended with the game tied 2-2.

Second period

Tikhonov replaced Tretiak with backup goaltender Vladimir Myshkin immediately after Johnson's tying goal, a move which shocked players on both teams. Fetisov later identified this as the "turning point of the game." Later Tikhonov called the decision "the biggest mistake of my career". Myshkin allowed no goals in the second period. The Soviets dominated play in the second period, outshooting the Americans 12-2, but scored only once, on a power play goal by Aleksandr Maltsev. After two periods the Soviet Union led 3-2.

Third period

Vladimir Krutov was sent to the penalty box at the 6:47 mark of the third period for high-sticking. The Americans, who had managed only two shots on Myshkin in 27 minutes, had a power play and a rare offensive opportunity. Myshkin stopped a Ramsey shot, then Eruzione fired a shot wide. Late in the power play, Dave Silk was advancing into the Soviet zone when Vasilev knocked him to the ice. The puck slid to Mark Johnson. Johnson fired off a shot that went under Myshkin and into the net at the 8:39 mark, as the power play was ending, tying the game 3-3. Only a couple shifts later, Mark Pavelich passed to U.S. captain Mike Eruzione, who was left undefended in the high slot. Eruzione, who had just come into the game, fired a shot past Myshkin, who was screened by Pervukhin. This goal gave Team USA a 4–3 lead, its first of the game, with exactly 10 minutes left.

The Soviets attacked furiously. Moments after Eruzione's goal, Maltzev fired off a shot which ricocheted off the right goal post. As the minutes wound down, Brooks kept

Mike Eruzione – team captain

313

repeating "Play your game. Play your game." Instead of going into a defensive crouch, the United States continued to play offense, even getting off a few more shots on goal. The Soviets began to shoot wildly, and Starikov admitted that "we were panicking." As the clock ticked down below a minute the Soviets got the puck back into the American zone, and Mikhailov passed to Petrov, who shot wide. The Soviets never pulled Myshkin for an extra attacker, much to the disbelief of the Americans. Starikov later explained that "We never did six-on-five", not even in practice, because "Tikhonov just didn't believe in it." Craig kicked away a Petrov slap shot with 33 seconds left. Kharlamov fired the puck back in as the clock ticked below 20 seconds. A wild scramble for the puck ensued, ending when Johnson found it and passed to Morrow. As the U.S. team tried to clear the zone (move the puck over the blue line, which they did with seven seconds remaining), the crowd began to count down the seconds left. Sportscaster Al Michaels, who was calling the game on ABC along with former Montreal Canadiens goalie Ken Dryden, picked up on the countdown in his broadcast, and delivered his famous call: Eleven seconds, you've got ten seconds, the countdown going on right now! Five seconds left in the game. **Do you believe in miracles? Yes!!!**

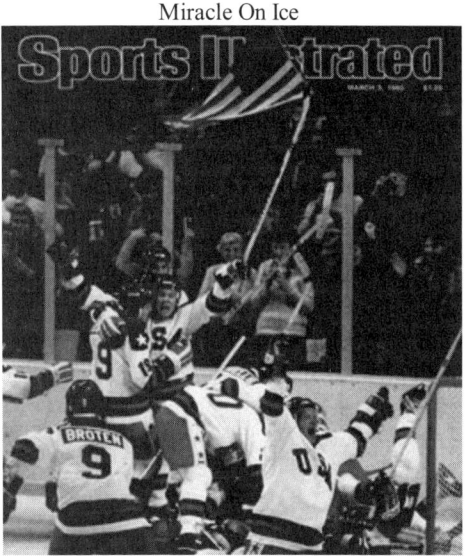
Miracle On Ice

In the locker room afterwards, players spontaneously broke into a chorus of "God Bless America". As his team ran all over the ice in celebration, Herb Brooks sprinted back to the locker room and cried.

For its March 3, 1980 issue, *Sports Illustrated* ran a cover with just a photograph by Heinz Kluetmeier, without any accompanying caption or headline. Kluetmeir said, "It didn't need (any cover language). Everyone in America knew what happened."

The victory was voted the greatest sports moment of the twentieth century by *Sports Illustrated*.

HOW TO PLAY SLAP JACK

Slapjack can get crazy as players around the table smack and whack their opponents in this simple but energetic game. The goal is slap every Jack card that turns face up before your opponents. The winner is the person with the quickest hands and the largest pile of won cards. This game is meant for two or more players. Increase the number of card decks if you have more than four players. Add to the energy of the game by yelling "Slap Jack!" as you slap the card. This is also a fun way to psych out your opponents.

Things You'll Need:

Standard deck of 52 cards
Second deck of cards if more than 4 players

Deal out all cards face down to all the players as evenly as possible. Do not look at

314

your cards. Use one deck for less than four players and two decks if you have more than four.

Turn up one card in the center of the table, starting with the player to the left of the dealer.

Slap the pile of cards if a Jack is turned up, regardless of suit. The first person to notice the Jack slaps their hand down on the pile of cards therefore winning the whole pile.

Place the cards won on the winner's face down pile. The player to the left of the winner turns up the next card in the center of the table, starting the next play.

Rotate to the next player, allowing them to place a card face up. Continue through all the players, slapping Jacks as the game progresses.

Continue play. If a player has run out of cards, but still has face up cards in play, they may continue to slap Jacks, winning cards in order to stay in the game. If they are entirely out of cards, they are disqualified and the game continues.

Forfeit two cards if you accidentally slap something other than a Jack. You must give one card from your face down pile to the person whose card you slapped.

Win the game by collecting all the cards from the other players. Make sure each person playing a card does so quickly so as not to give them an unfair advantage over the rest of the players if a Jack comes up. They should also turn loose of the card while it is high enough from the playing pile so as not to give them an unfair advantage. After playing several practice games it shouldn't be difficult to understand these two instructions.

THE GAME OF WAR

Shuffle a standard 52 card deck and deal the cards so that each player gets 26 cards. Players keep their cards in front of them, face down. Each player simultaneously turns over their top card. The higher card wins the pair; the winning player takes both cards and puts them at the bottom of their face-down pile. (Ace is high card; 2 is low card.)

In the event of a tie, the players have a "war." Each player places three cards face down in the middle of the table and then turns a fourth card face up. The player with the higher of these cards takes all 10 cards which are now in the middle. If these two cards are also a tie, additional cards are turned face up, one at a time, until one player wins; that player takes the entire set of cards.

The first player to win the entire deck of cards is the winner. Alternatively, because winning the entire deck can take a long time, the first player to win three wars is the winner.

You might want to try this alternative way of playing War. This simple variant, designed by Erik Arneson, adds some decision-making to the game.

After the cards are dealt, each player draws the top three from his pile and holds them in his hand. On each turn, he chooses one card to play and then draws a new card to refresh his hand to three cards. When a tie occurs, each player takes three cards from his face down pile and puts them in the middle, still face down. He then chooses a card from his hand to play as the face-up fourth card. The player who plays the higher card takes all six of the face-down cards plus the two "fourth" cards. The player who plays the lower card takes the two cards which caused the war to take place.

CRAZY EIGHTS

This game uses a standard 52-card deck. The goal is to be the first person to discard all of your cards. In a two-player game, each player is dealt seven cards. In a game with three or four players, each player is dealt five cards. The remaining cards are placed face down in the center of the table, forming a draw pile. The top card of the draw pile is turned face up to start the discard pile. The player to the left of the dealer goes first. Play moves clockwise.

On a turn, each player adds to the discard pile by playing one card that matches the top card on the discard pile either by suit or by rank (i.e. club, 6, jack, ace, etc.). A player who cannot match the top card on the discard pile by suit or rank must draw cards until he can play one. When the draw pile is empty, a player who cannot add to the discard pile passes on his turn.

All eights are wild and can be played on any card during a player's turn. When a player discards an eight, he chooses which suit is now in play. The next player must play either a card of that suit or another eight. The first player to discard all of his cards wins.

With four players, it is possible to play partnership. If you do this, the game ends when both members of a partnership discard all their cards. To play multiple games, add up the cards remaining in the losers' hands and give the points to the winner: 10 points for each face card, 1 point for each ace, 50 points for each eight, and 5 points each for the other number cards. Play to a set number, such as 150 or 200.

HOW TO PLAY RUMMY

This is a game for two or three players. One standard deck of 52 cards is used. Cards in each suit rank from low to high:

Ace 2 3 4 5 6 7 8 9 10 Jack Queen King.

The cards have values as follows:

    Face cards (K,Q,J)   10 points
    Ace   1 point
    Number cards are worth 5 points each.

The first dealer is chosen randomly, and the turn to deal alternates between the players. Each player is dealt ten cards, one at a time. The next card is turned face up to start the discard pile and the remainder of the deck is placed face down beside it to form the stock. The players look at and sort their cards.

The object of the game is to collect a hand where most or all of the cards can be combined into sets and runs and the point value of the remaining unmatched cards in your hand is low.

A **run** or **sequence** consists of three or more cards of the same suit in consecutive order, such as ♣4, ♣5, ♣6 or ♥8, ♥9, ♥10, ♥J.

A **set** or **group** is three or four cards of the same rank, such as ♦7, ♥7, ♠7.

A card can belong to only one combination at a time - you cannot use the same card as part of both a set of equal cards and a sequence of consecutive cards. Note that in Rummy the **Ace is always low**. A-2-3 is a valid sequence but **A-K-Q** is not.

A normal turn consists of two parts:

The Draw. You **must** begin by taking one card from either the top of the stock pile or the top card on the discard pile, and adding it to your hand. The discard pile is face up, so you can see in advance what you are getting. The stock is face down, so if you choose to draw from the stock you do not see the card until after you have committed yourself to take it. If you draw from the stock, you add the card to your hand without showing it to the other players.

The Discard. To complete your turn, one card **must** be discarded from your hand and placed on top of the discard pile face up.

Instead of piling cards on top of each other in the discard pile, the cards are fanned out so that each card can still be seen. Let's say the discarded cards, in order, are: ace, seven, jack, four, nine, ten and a five. On a player's turn he notices that he has two jacks in his hand. He can pick up the jack and every card after the jack as long as he uses that jack to lay down three of a kind or a run of three in a row. Having extra cards in one's hand is usually an advantage because it makes it easier to form three of a kind or a run of three consecutive numbers of the same suit. These extra cards become a liability if someone goes out and you get stuck with them.

A player goes out by playing all the cards in their hand by forming them into three of a kind or a run of three or more consecutive numbers of the same suit. The player who goes out must have no cards in his/her hand and must always have a card to discard on their last play.

To score the hand each player counts the total value of the cards they still have in their hands. This total is then subtracted from the value of the cards that they have played in front of them to form combinations of runs and three or four of a kind. The cards have values as follows:

Play the game to end at a set number such as 200 or 300 points.

HE DIED SO THAT ENGLAND MIGHT LIVE

William Meade "Billy" Fiske III (4 June 1911 – 17 August 1940) was the 1928 and 1932 Olympic champion bobsled driver and was the first American pilot killed in action in World War II. At the time **Fiske** was serving in the Royal Air Force. Billy Fiske was born in New York in 1911, the son of Beulah and William Fiske, a New England banking magnate. He attended school in **Chicago**, and then went to school in France in 1924, where he discovered the sport of bobsled at the age of 16. Fiske attended Trinity Hall, Cambridge in 1928 where he studied Economics and History.

He then worked at the London office of Dillon, Reed & Co, the New York bankers. On 8 September 1938, Fiske married Rose, Countess of Warwick, in Maidenhead. Shortly before the outbreak of World War II, Fiske was recalled to the New York offices of Dillon, Reed & Co, but returned to England with a bank colleague who was also a member of No. 601 Auxiliary Air Force Squadron, aboard the *Aquitania* on September 1, 1939, the day author Bill Nunes was born..

As driver of the first five-man U.S. Bobsled team to win the Olympics, **Fiske became the youngest gold medalist in the sport, aged just 16 years,** at the 1928 Winter Olympics in St. Moritz, Switzerland. He remained the youngest person in Olympic history to win a gold medal until his record was broken by 15 year-old figure skater, Sonja Henie. He was an exceptional all-around athlete having driven a Stutz Bearcat at the Le Mans 24 hour race, and competed in skiing events. **It was largely through his efforts that Aspen, Colorado became a mecca for skiers**. He regularly participated in Cresta competions in Switzerland and is considered **the greatest Cresta sportsman of all time**. The Cresta is a one-man sled event where the participant races hownhill head first. **He captured the Grand National Title in 1936.** Fisk was a man of many talents for he also made a Hollywood movie (*White Heat*), starring Virginia Cherill, the future wife of Cary Grant.

Fiske competed again at the 1932 Winter Olympics at Lake Placid, New York, USA, where **he was given the honor of carrying the flag for the United States at the opening ceremony**. The format of the race was altered to a four-man team, but again Fiske and his teammates, Clifford Gray, Eddie Eagan, and Jay O'Brien took gold. He was invited, but declined to lead the bobsled team in the 1936 Winter Olympics in Garmisch-Partenkirchen in Germany. It is believed by some that this decision was due to his hatred for Adolph Hitler and vehemently disagreeing with the politics in Germany at the time, which may also explain his later decision to join the war effort in 1940.

Fiske was the first American to join the RAF and became one of 10 US pilots who fought in the Battle of Britain, although due to the neutrality of the United States, he pretended to be a Canadian. He joined the Royal Air Force Volunteer Reserve and was promoted to the rank of Pilot Officer on 23 March 1940. He undertook his flying training at No 10. Elementary Flying Training School at RAF Yatesbury, Wiltshire before moving to RAF Brize Norton, Oxfordshire, for advanced flying training. He joined No. 601 Squadron RAF at RAF Tangmere, West Sussex, the so-called *Millionaire's Squadron* on the 12 July 1940.

On August 16, 1940, in the midst of the Battle of Britain, No. 601 Squadron were scrambled to intercept a squadron of German Stuka dive-bombers. Fiske was flying a Hurricane - code number P3358. After just 15 minutes of flight, a German gunner put a bullet through Fiske's fuel tank. The Squadron destroyed eight Stukas, but Fiske's aircraft was badly damaged and his hands and ankles were burnt. Fiske knew that England was in desperate need for aircraft. Instead of bailing out, Fiske nursed his Hurricane fighter home, gliding over a hedgerow to the airfield. Although Fiske landed his aircraft safely back at Tangmere, he had to be extracted from the aircraft by ambulance attendants. Shortly after his fuel tank exploded. Fiske was taken to Royal West Sussex Hospital in Chichester for treatment, but he died 48 hours later from burns and surgical shock. He was 29 years old.

Billy Fiske

Of Fiske's role in the Battle of Britain, Bill Bond, founder of the Battle of Britain Historical Society, wrote: "*although Billy made several sorties he didn't shoot anything down, so that his impact on the battle in that respect was negligible, but he is most definitely still very much a hero in our book.*"

Fiske's Flight Commander, Sir Archibald Hope, added:

"*Unquestionably* **Billy Fiske was the best pilot I've ever known**. *He was absolutely fearless. It was unbelievable how good he was. He picked up so fast it wasn't true. He'd flown a bit before, but he was a natural as a fighter pilot. He was also terribly nice and extraordinarily modest, and fitted into the squadron very well.*"

Fiske is buried in St Mary and St Blaise churchyard in Boxgrove, Sussex. The inscription on his gravestone reads simply: *He died for England*. A memorial stained glass window was dedicated to him on 17 September 2008 at Boxgrove Priory. At the dedication service, a number of former colleagues of Fiske attended and his green Bentley was on display.

On July 4, 1941, **a plaque was unveiled in the crypt of St Paul's Cathedral, London. The inscription reads:** *An American citizen who died that England might live.* The decision to unveil this plaque on American Independence Day was probably a political one; the United States had not officially joined the war and the British Prime Minister, Winston Churchill, was anxious to popularize Fiske's story. The plaque was unveiled by Sir Archibald Sinclair, the Secretary of State for Air. He said at the ceremony:

"Here was a young man for whom life held much. Under no kind of compulsion he came to fight for Britain. He came and he fought and he died."

A memorial tablet was dedicated to him in the crypt of the Cathedral of Saint John the Divine, New York. Fiske is listed on the Battle of Britain Monument in London and the Battle of Britain Memorial, Capel-le-Ferne.

The United States Bobsled and Skeleton Federation created the ***Billy Fiske Memorial Trophy* as a posthumous tribute to him.** The trophy is awarded to the national champion four-man bobsled team each year.

It is true that Fiske's overall contribution to the Battle of Britain was unremarkable. However, we honor him because in the greater context, Fiske went to great lengths to procure the chance to fight to protect the liberty of countrymen that were not his own.

"I DOUBT IT" CARD GAME

This game for three to six people requires one or two standard 52-card decks. With two decks, it's best to have identical backs so that the players cannot tell them apart. The goal is to be the first to get rid of all your cards.

Shuffle all the cards together. Deal them out as evenly as possible. (It's fine if some players have one card more than other players.)

The first player plays one or more cards from his hand, face down, starting a discard pile in the middle of the table. He says, "One Ace," or whatever number is appropriate (i.e. the number of cards he played).

The second player plays one or more cards from his hand, face down, on top of the discard pile. He says, "Two Kings," or whatever number is appropriate (i.e. the number of cards he played).

This continues with each subsequent player moving down one rank -- so the third player would say "Queens," the fourth "Jacks," the fifth "10s," and so on. After a player discards (or claims to discard) 2s, the next player will discard (or claim to discard) Aces.

It is perfectly legal, and in fact necessary, for players to sometimes play cards that are not what they say. For example, a player might play a 10 and a 9 but say, "two Queens." The only penalty comes if such a player is caught (see "Doubting," below). If a player names the wrong rank (i.e. says "Two 5s" when he should have said "Two 8s"), that player must take all of the cards from the discard pile and add them to his hand.

After each discard, any other player can say, "I doubt it."

The last player's discarded cards are then turned face up. If any card in that set is not of the stated rank, the player who discarded them must take the entire discard pile into his hand. If all of the cards in that set are of the stated rank, the doubter must take the entire discard pile into his hand.

NOTE: The first player to say "I doubt it" is the official doubter.
The first player to get rid of all his cards wins. The last play is always made face up, because other players will inevitably doubt it.

"OH, HECK!" CARD GAME

This is an easy to learn strategy game for three to five players. Shuffle and cut a standard deck of 52 playing cards. Leave out the Jokers. Deal clockwise, five cards face down to each player. Turn up the top card on the remaining deck. The suit of this card is trump. Let's say for this round or trick it is a heart. The dealer should now tell everyone to check his/her cards to make sure they have the correct number. This should be done at the end of each deal. There is nothing more disheartening than to get near the end of a round only to discover that a player has one too many or one too few cards. If that happens you simply have to do a "do over" and redeal.

Bid on how many tricks you think you will take. Usually this is based on the number of high cards and trumps you have in your hand. Bidding starts with the person to the left of the dealer and proceeds clockwise once around the table.

End bidding with the dealer, who must ensure that someone will lose. He looks at the total cards bid by the other players. Let's say the total bid so far is four tricks. Thus he can bid zero, two, three, four or five. He cannot bid one because that would make the total bid five and five cards were dealt. Remember, at least one person must always goof in any given round.

Record bids on a score pad as they are made. Once the bidding is finished play begins with the player to the left of the dealer playing the first card. Let's say he plays an 8 of spades. Each player in clockwise fashion lays down a card. You must follow suit if you have a spade in your hand. High spade wins and aces are the high cards. If a player is out of spades he has the option of "sloughing off" by playing a different suit. If he plays a card of a different suit, he cannot possibly win the "trick." However, if he plays a heart trump and it ends up being the high card, he captures the first trick. Remember, you must be out of the suit of the first card played before you have the option of playing a trump.

The person who captures the trick is the person who plays the first card for the next trick. After all tricks in that round have been captured, the dealer writes down the score for each person. You get 10 points for doing what you said you were going to do. You also get 1 point for each trick captured. Thus a person who bid 2 and captured 2 tricks gets a score of 12. Another person might have bid zero and captured no tricks. His score is 10. If a third player bid 1 but captured no tricks his score for that round is zero.

For the next round, each player is given 6 cards. After that they get 7 cards. The next round goes up to 8, then 9 and, finally, 10. After you reach ten then it starts going down until it reaches five and after the last hand of five the game ends and high score wins. If there is a tie, then one hand of 8 cards is played to break the tie.

For my wife and I, this is our favorite card game. Here's why! There is some luck involved in this game, but good players generally prevail. Some card games are so intense you can't talk or socialize during rounds of play. You have to pay attention in this game but, not to the point of absolute silence.

Perhaps the game's best attribute is, unlike poker or pinochle, you don't need a bunch of high cards to win. If you get dealt a poor hand then just bid zero or one. If you bid just one and make it you get 11 points. The fellow who bid 4, but only made 3, gets a mere 3 points.

WARNING! Don't get started playing in card games where money is involved. This is called gambling and it is also called a vice. Gambling, like so many other things, can become addictive. When riverboat gambling was first permitted in the St. Louis area there was a Collinsville woman who went during the day without her husband and became addicted. It got so bad that she even started losing money that had been set aside to make their mortgage payments on their house. One day the husband was astounded when he learned that the bank was going to foreclose on the house. The guilt ridden and depressed wife committed suicide. The games at Casinos are fixed so that they make money at the expense of the gullible gamblers.

No matter how good a card player you become, there is always someone better. On top of that there is the element of luck or chance. I have been in many a card game where I played a king thinking about how impossible the odds would be for the person following my play to have the ace. Then I am dumbfounded when that person plays the ace to win!

HE CHANGED THE GAME OF BASKETBALL

Peter "Pistol Pete" Maravich (June 22, 1947 – January 5, 1988) was born and raised in Pennsylvania. Maravich starred in college at Louisiana State University (LSU) and for three NBA teams. **He is still the all-time leading NCAA Division I scorer with 3,667 points scored and an average of 44.2 points per game.** Maravich died suddenly at age 40 during a pick-up game as a consequence of a previously undetected congenital heart defect. One of the youngest players ever inducted into the Basketball Hall of Fame, Maravich was cited as **"perhaps the greatest creative offensive talent in history."**

Pete Maravich, of Serbian descent, was born in Aliquippa, Pennsylvania, a small steel town in the Pittsburgh metropolitan area. Maravich amazed his family and friends with his basketball abilities from an early age. His father, Press Maravich, a former professional player-turned-coach, showed Maravich the fundamentals starting when he was seven years old. Obsessively, Maravich spent 10,000 hours practicing ball control tricks, passes, head fakes, and long range shots by the time he was in the 8th grade.

Maravich got his nickname "Pistol" in high school. He would shoot the ball from the side like a western-style gunfighter. Maravich attended and played basketball at Daniel High School in Central, South Carolina from 1961 to 1963 while his father was the head basketball coach at Clemson University. His father joined the coaching staff at North Carolina State, and the family moved to Raleigh, North Carolina, where Pete attended and played for Needham B. Broughton High School.

While Maravich would tell friends later in life he always desired to play basketball for West Virginia University and was all set to be a Mountaineer, his father was the varsity coach at LSU, and his father offered the "Pistol" a spot at LSU. In his first game on the LSU freshman team, Maravich put up 50 points, 14 rebounds, and 11 assists against Southeastern Louisiana College.

In only three years playing for his father at LSU, Maravich scored 3,667 points —
1,138 points in 1968, 1,148 points in 1969 and 1,381 points in 1970 while averaging 43.8, 44.2 and 44.5 points per game. In his collegiate career, the 6' 5" guard averaged an incredible 44.2 points per game in 83 contests and led the NCAA in scoring in each of his three seasons.

Maravich's longstanding collegiate scoring record is particularly impressive when two other factors are taken into account. First, **Maravich played before the advent of three-point line**. His long-distance shooting skill thus produced far fewer points than would have been the case in a later era. Years later former

LSU head basketball coach Dale Brown charted every college game Maravich played, taking into consideration all shots he took. Brown calculated that at the NCAA rule of a three-point line at 19-foot, 9-inches from the rim, Maravich would have averaged thirteen 3-point scores per game, **lifting the player's career average to 57 points per game**. Second, NCAA rules at the time of Maravich's collegiate career prohibited freshmen from taking place in varsity competition, preventing Maravich from adding to his career record for a full quarter of his time at LSU. During this first year, Maravich scored 741 points in freshmen competition.

More than 35 years later, many of his NCAA and LSU records still stand. **Maravich was a three-time All-American**. Though he never appeared in the NCAA tournament, Maravich played a key role in turning around a lackluster program that had posted a 3–20 record in the season prior to his arrival.

After departing LSU in 1970 (he left after the NIT tournament and did not graduate, and therefore, can never be inducted to the LSU Hall of Fame), Maravich was the third selection in the first round of that year's NBA player draft and made league history when he signed a $1.9 million contract — one of the highest salaries at the time — with the Atlanta Hawks. He wasted little time becoming a prime time player by averaging 23.2 points per game his rookie season and being named to the **NBA All-Rookie Team**. After spending four seasons in Atlanta, Maravich was traded to the New Orleans Jazz for 8 players, where he peaked as an NBA showman and superstar. He made the All-NBA

Pete Maravich

First Team in 1976 and 1977 and the All-NBA Second Team in 1973 and 1978. He led the NBA in scoring in the 1976–77 season with 31.1 points per game. Prior to the 1979–80 season, Maravich moved with the team to Utah. He was waived by the Jazz on January 18, 1980, and was quickly picked up by the Boston Celtics where he played the rest of the season alongside Larry Bird.

A leg injury suffered during the 1977–78 NBA season ultimately prompted his retirement two years later in 1980. Pete Maravich was **inducted into the Basketball Hall of Fame in May, 1987** at age 39.

After the injury forced him to leave basketball in the fall of 1980, Maravich became a recluse for two years. Through it all, Maravich said he was searching "for life." He tried the practices of yoga and Hinduism, read Trappist monk literature and took an interest in the field of ufology, the study of unidentified flying objects. He also explored vegetarianism and macro-biotics. **Eventually, he embraced evangelical Christianity.** A few years before his death, Maravich said, "I want to be remembered as a Christian, a person who serves Him to the utmost, not as a basketball player."

On January 5, 1988, Pete Maravich collapsed and died, at age 40, of a heart attack while playing in a pickup basketball game in the gym at the First Church of the Nazarene in Pasadena with a group that included Focus on the Family head James Dobson. (Maravich had flown out from his home in Louisiana to tape a segment for Dobson's radio show that aired later that day.) An autopsy revealed the cause of death to be a rare congenital defect; he had been born with a missing left coronary artery, a vessel which supplies blood to the muscle fibers of the heart. His right coronary artery was grossly enlarged and had been compensating for the defect.

"He'll be remembered always", former LSU head basketball coach Dale Brown said on hearing the news of Maravich's death. Maravich is buried at Resthaven Gardens of Memory and Mausoleum in Baton Rouge, Louisiana.

In addition to his wife, Jackie, Pete Maravich was survived by his two sons Jaeson, who was 8 years old, and Josh, aged 5.

After Maravich's death, Louisiana Governor Buddy Roemer signed a proclamation officially renaming the LSU home court the Pete Maravich Assembly Center.

In 1991, a biographical film dramatizing his 8th grade season entitled, *The Pistol: The Birth of a Legend*, was released. In 1996, he was named **one of the 50 Greatest Players in NBA History** by a panel made up of NBA historians, and coaches. He was the only deceased player on the list.

In 2001, a comprehensive 90-minute documentary film debuted on CBS entitled, *Pistol Pete: The Life and Times of Pete Maravich*.

In 2005, ESPN named Maravich **the greatest college basketball player of all-time.**

AMERICA'S TOUGHEST COP

It was 1945 and this author was in the first grade over in the Washington Park section of East St. Louis, a town of 70,000. Located next to St. Louis, over a million people in the metro area did business in East St. Louis, more than any other city in Illinois except Chicago.

Robert Sweeney started out in the 1920s doing park patrol on an Indian brand motorcycle. He switched over to the police force as soon as he became of age and gained a reputation for being a savvy, tough, no-nonsense cop. During the course of his eventful career **he killed 12 men in the line of duty. That equals the number of men killed by outlaws Frank and Jesse James combined.**

During the 1920s and 1930s, the dreaded Shelton Gang was in control of bootlegging and gambling operations in East St. Louis and Southern Illinois. In 1934 Carl Shelton, the leader of the outfit, and his attorney filed a lawsuit against the city of East St. Louis and Officer Bob Sweeney. Sweeney hated the Sheltons, and when he found out that Carl was in St. Mary's Hospital, he dragged him out of his bed and arrested him on some trumped up minor charge.

323

The lawsuit was later dropped.

But on this day the thing that bothered twenty year veteran Sweeney and his partner Jerry Sullivan was the prospect of a serial robber who was preying on servicemen from nearby Scott Air Base by taking their money at knifepoint when they left an entertainment hot spot with their dates.

After the second such robbery, rookie officer Rich Mackin was the first to arrive on the scene and found a knife that had inadvertently been dropped by the robber. There seemed to be a pattern to all this because the holdups took place within two blocks of each other in the areas of St. Louis and Missouri Avenues. Sweeney was afraid the robberies might escalate to murder. The 200 pound "Tree" Sweeney and his partner came up with a plan. They would set a trap to catch this robber. Officer Mackin was extraordinarily good looking. It was decided that he would dress up as a woman and Sweeney would don a soldier's uniform and together stroll the area where the other robberies had taken place. Sweeney knew that a lot was riding on this gambit. City Hall wanted East St. Louis to be known as a safe town where people could come to play the ponies, go dancing and attend various venues of popular entertainment. If this failed, he would be known as a buffoon and laughed off the force.

The "real" Rich Mackin

They decided to stroll the robbery area between 10:30 p.m. and 1:30 a.m. Since the previous robberies had taken place after the couples had left taverns, the 40-year-old Sweeney and his partner frequented one tavern after another. East St. Louis was a blue collar all-night town so there were plenty of places from which to choose.

In bright daylight one could guess that the 135 pound Mackin was a man dressed like a girl but in the dark the ruse worked just fine. His outfit consisted of scuffed saddle oxford shoes, nylons, a dress, plenty of make-up, and a scarf over the head and tied under the chin.

According to what Sweeney's son told this author, the pair strolled the area at night for weeks before they hit pay dirt. When Sweeney showed his gun and said "You're under arrest," the man pulled his weapon and got off a couple of shots, one of them whizzing by Mackin's head. Sweeney wasn't carrying his trusty .38 that night because its bulk was hard to hide under the uniform. Instead, he had a snub nosed .32. Sweeney drilled five shots into the guy's stomach. His name was Scott, and he was big - 280 pounds hung on a massive 6'- 6" frame. Dr. Matthew Eisele operated on him and took the slugs out. He told Sweeney that most of the bullets barely penetrated the muscle tissue, and only two of them did any serious damage. This was the only time in his career Sweeney pumped that many shots into vital areas with the perpetrator living to tell about it. Sweeney contacted a lawyer and made plans to sue Olin-Winchester at East Alton, for making defective bullets. The guy died of complications about six months later.

Sweeney quit the police force in 1954 when ordered by his superiors to "lay

Sweeney, Mackin, and Sullivan (Note the blood on Sweeney's tie and pants.)

off" hoodlums who were "home town boys." Three of the Shelton brothers had been killed and Frank "Buster" Wortman was their successor in East St. Louis. Sweeney had the same hatred for Wortman as he did for the Sheltons. Sweeney was a member of the department for over 30 years. He was noted for having run Ben "Bugsy" Siegel and Ma Barker's nephew out of town on separate occasions.

Mackin lived at 1104 College Avenue, a mere block from East St. Louis High School. Right after the incident, **Mackin quit the force** because he came so close to being killed when that bullet whizzed by his head. The brave hero Mackin took a bit of teasing after that and Bill Jacobus said that the guys called

325

him Pauline because he had dressed like a woman. Mackin's father worked as a pipefitter. He used to brag about his wages. He said, "We're number 2 in the nation! New York City leads the nation in steamfitter and pipefitter salaries and East St. Louis is always right behind them."

(Information provided by **Carol Hinson of O'Fallon** & *Detective Magazine*)

MARTIAN INVASION PANICS USA

The War of the Worlds was an episode of the American radio drama anthology series *Mercury Theatre on the Air*. It was performed as a Halloween episode of the series on October 30, 1938, and aired over the Columbia Broadcasting System radio network. Directed and narrated by Orson Welles, the episode was an adaptation of H. G. Wells' novel *The War of the Worlds*.

The first two thirds of the 60-minute broadcast was presented as a series of simulated news bulletins, **which suggested to many listeners that an actual Martian invasion was in progress**. Compounding the issue was the fact that the *Mercury Theatre on the Air* was a 'sustaining show' (it ran without commercial breaks), thus adding to the dramatic effect. There were sensationalist accounts in the press about a panic in response to the broadcast, the precise extent of which has never been determined. In the days following the adaptation, however, there was widespread outrage. The program's news-bulletin format was decried as cruelly deceptive by some newspapers and public figures, leading to an outcry against the perpetrators of the broadcast, but **the episode launched Orson Welles to fame**.

The program, broadcast from the 20th floor at 485 Madison Avenue in New York City, starts with an introduction from the novel, describing the intentions of the aliens and noting that the adaptation was set in 1939, a year ahead of the actual broadcast date. The program continues as a weather report, then as an ordinary dance band remote featuring "Ramon Raquello and His Orchestra" (actually the CBS orchestra under the direction of Bernard Herrmann) that is interrupted by news flashes about strange explosions on Mars. Welles makes his first appearance as (the fictional) famous astronomer and Princeton professor Richard Pierson, who refutes speculation about life on Mars.

The news grows more frequent and increasingly ominous as a cylindrical meteorite lands in Grover's Mill, New Jersey. A crowd gathers at the site and events are related by reporter Carl Phillips (portrayed by Frank Readick). The meteorite unscrews, revealing itself as a rocket machine, and onlookers catch a glimpse of a tentacled, pulsating, barely mobile Martian before **it incinerates the crowd with Heat-Rays**. Phillips' shouts about incoming flames are cut off in mid-sentence. (Later surveys indicate that many listeners heard only this portion of the show before contacting neighbors or family to inquire about the broadcast. Many contacted others in turn, leading to rumors and confusion.)

Regular programming breaks down as the studio struggles to keep up with casualty updates, fire-fighting developments and the like. A shaken Pierson speculates about Martian technology. The New Jersey state militia declares martial law and attacks the cylinder; a message from their field headquarters goes on about the overwhelming force of properly equipped infantry and the helplessness of the Martians in Earth's gravity until a tripod alien fighting machine rears up from the pit.

The studio returns to establish the Martians as an invading army with the obliteration of the militia force. Emergency response bulletins give way to damage reports and evacuation instructions while millions of refugees clog the roads. Three Martian tripods from the cylinder destroy power stations and uproot bridges and railroads, reinforced by three others from a second cylinder as gas explosions continue. An unnamed Secretary of the Interior advises the nation. The secretary sounded like President Roosevelt as the result of directions to actor Kenny Delmar by Welles.)

A live connection is established to a field artillery battery. Its gun crew reports damaging one machine and a release of black smoke/poison gas before fading in to the sound of coughing. The lead plane of a wing of bombers broadcasts its approach and remains on the air as their engines are burned by the Heat-Ray and the plane dives on the invaders. Radio operators go active and fall silent, right after reporting the approach of the black smoke. The planes destroyed one machine, but cylinders are falling all across the country.

Orson Welles

This section ends famously: a news reporter (played by Ray Collins), broadcasting from atop the CBS building, describes the Martian invasion of New York City — "five great machines" wading across the Hudson River, poison smoke drifting over the city, people running and diving into the East River "like rats", others "falling like flies" — until he, too, succumbs to the poison gas. Finally, a despairing ham radio operator is heard calling, "2X2L calling CQ. Isn't there anyone on the air? Isn't there anyone on the air? Isn't there.... anyone?"

After an intermission for station identification, in which announcer Dan Seymour mentions the show is merely fiction, the last third is a monolog and dialog, with Welles returning as Professor Pierson, describing the aftermath of the attacks. The story ends, as does the novel, with the Martians falling victim to earthly germs and bacteria.

After the play, Welles informally breaks character to remind listeners that the broadcast was a Halloween story (the equivalent, as he puts it, "of dressing up in a sheet and saying, 'Boo!'").

Some listeners heard only a portion of the broadcast, and in the atmosphere of tension and anxiety just prior to World War II, took it to be a news

327

broadcast. Newspapers reported that panic ensued, people fleeing the area, others thinking they could smell poison gas or could see flashes of lightning.

Richard J. Hand cites studies by historians who "calculated that some six million heard the CBS broadcast; 1.7 million believed it to be true, and 1.2 million were 'genuinely frightened". While Welles and company were heard by a comparatively small audience, the uproar was anything but small: within a month, there were 12,500 newspaper articles about the broadcast or its impact, while **Adolf Hitler cited the panic as "evidence of the decadence and corrupt condition of democracy."**

Seattle CBS affiliate stations KIRO and KVI broadcast Orson Welles' radio drama. While this broadcast was heard around the country, it made a deep impact in Concrete, Washington. At the point where the Martian invaders were invading towns and the countryside with flashes of light and poison gases and the lights were going down, there was a loud explosion and a power failure plunged the entire town of 1,000 into darkness. Some listeners fainted while others grabbed their families to head into the mountains. Others headed for the hills to guard their moonshine stills. One was said to have jumped up out of his chair and, in bare feet, run two miles to the center of town. Some men grabbed their guns, and one Catholic businessman got his wife into the car, drove to the nearest service station and demanded gasoline. Without paying the attendant, he rushed to Bellingham, Washington (50 miles away) to see his priest for a last-minute prayer. He reportedly told the gas-station attendant that paying for the gas "wouldn't make any difference; everyone is going to die!"

THE BATTLE OF NEW ORLEANS

The battle of New Orleans was America's greatest victory in the War of 1812, sometimes referred to as the Second War For Independence. Its main cause was the British practice of impressment. England was in a war of survival against Napoleon and this led that country to take desperate measures. British warships began to violate international law by using the threat of force to stop American ships and look for deserters from their

Battle of New Orleans

navy. Desperately in need of manpower, they frequently seized American sailors and "pressed" them into service on their ships. America declared war when the British refused to stop engaging in this practice.

The war did not go well for America. We didn't have much of a naval force and our army consisted mostly of state militia units. The Americans invaded

British Canada for the purpose of adding that territory to the continental United States. The invasion was a failure. The British invaded the Chesapeake area and captured Washington D.C., burning nearly every public building in our nation's capital, including the White House.

It was learned in November of 1814, that the British were sending a huge flotilla of ships to capture New Orleans and wrest control of the recently acquired Louisiana Territory from the United States. General Andrew Jackson arrived in New Orleans on December 1. He was discouraged to learn that the city had only about 1,000 armed defenders and had yet to take any defensive measures. Jackson sent out recruiters and hundreds of volunteers poured into the city from all over America. Realizing he could use every man he could get, **Jackson made a deal with the famed pirate of the region, Jean Lafitte**. Dozens of Lafitte's men had been imprisoned for their various crimes. In exchange for their release, Lafitte promised that he and his men would help defend the city.

The British outnumbered the Americans by more than four to one. However, they were going up against a brilliant military commander whose hatred for the British was unequaled. Jackson bore a scar on his face administered to him by a British officer's sword when he was just a youth. Young Jackson was given the gash after he refused to polish the officer's boots. The British also killed several members of Jackson's family during the Revolutionary War (1775-1783).

Jean Lafitte

The British commander, Edward Packenham, was supremely confident that his seasoned troops would crush the rag tag Americans and New Orleans would be his. But Jackson and his men established a strong defensive perimeter behind cotton bales and earthenworks. Also, they had just enough artillery pieces to get the job done.

Early on January 8, under cover of fog, Packenham led his forces in a major assault on Jackson's entrenched forces. Fortunately for the Americans, the fog lifted, exposing the British to withering fire from Jackson's defenders. **Packenham and many of his senior officers fell, mortally wounded**. The British suffered about 2,000 casualties while only 13 Americans were killed. It was a stunning turn of events.

The British had such an overwhelming numerical superiority that Americans nationwide had feared the worst – another military disaster. The news of this incredible victory spread like wildfire and came upon the country like a clap of thunder. This victory would propel Andrew Jackson into the White House.

Towns and parks were named for Jean Lafitte. Instead of emerging from this war with heads bowed and their tails between their legs, Americans noisily celebrated this victory annually and faced the future with renewed confidence.

The battle of New Orleans was depicted in the film *The Bucaneer*, starring Illinoisan Charlton Heston and Yul Brynner as Jean Lafitte. In 1959 pop singer Johnny Horton released "The Battle of New Orleans" which became a huge hit. In 1965 a postage stamp commemorated the 150th anniversary of the conflict.

There is much confusion surrounding the death of Jean Lafitte in 1823. **According to one version, Lafitte is buried at Alton, Illinois** near the Mississippi River. Rumors abound that Lafitte buried treasure in many places in the Gulf region and along the banks of the Mississippi near Alton. Happy hunting you sons of Illinois!

THE PRIDE OF THE MARINES

Al Schmid grew up a cheerful, freckle-faced kid in a Philadelphia neighborhood. After his mother died, Schmid was on his own. He worked on farms and other odd jobs. In 1940, he became an apprentice burner at the Dodge Steel Company in northeast Philadelphia, near the Delaware River.

Since he could not afford his own place, Schmid lived with fellow Dodge Steel worker Jim Merchant and his wife, Ella Mae. While living with the Merchants, Schmid met Ruth Hartley, a friend of the family, who worked at a Sears department store in Philadelphia. In time, Schmid fell in love with Ruth.

Al Schmidt receiving his medal

On Sunday, December 7, 1941, Schmid was sprawled out on the floor of Jim Merchant's house, looking at the paper and trying to get up the energy to get dressed for a date he had with Ruth that night. All of a sudden, the radio stopped playing dance music; a voice relayed the startling news that the Japanese had attacked Pearl Harbor.

For a day or so, Schmid could not see how the war affected him. Then things changed. He talked to Ruth about enlisting in the Marines, but she didn't take him seriously; he was always talking big. On December 9, 1941, he told her, "I'm in. I went down to the Custom House and signed up."

After recruit training at Parris Island, S.C., and further training at New River, North Carolina, Schmidt returned to Philadelphia on a short leave before heading for "destination unknown." He collected a bonus from Dodge Steel for his work during 1941 and used the money to buy an engagement ring for Ruth.

Soon afterward, Schmid boarded a troop transport as part of the 11th Machine Gun Squad, Company H, 2nd Battalion, 1st Regiment, 1st Marine

Division. On August 7, 1942, the 10,000 men of the 1st Marine Division assaulted Guadalcanal, **beginning the first American offensive against the Japanese.**

The Marines encountered no real opposition during their first two weeks. Then the Japanese sent a crack army regiment commanded by Colonel Kiyono Ichiki from Rabaul to retake Guadalcanal. Ichiki landed his elite troops on Guadalcanal on August 18, then marched west toward Marine positions along the Ilu River.

H Company's machine-gun squad was there waiting for them. Schmid and Corporal Leroy Diamond and Pfc John Rivers, manned a .30-caliber water-cooled machine gun inside a camouflaged sandbag-and-log emplacement.

At 3 a.m., August 21, 1942, Ichiki, confident of victory, attacked by the sickly green light of flares. The Japanese yelled, jabbered and fired machine guns, trying to force the Marines to reveal their positions. The Marines held their fire.

Across the river from their nest, Schmid saw a dark, bobbing mass at the edge of the water. "It looked like a herd of cattle coming down to drink," he remembered. Fifty Japanese crossed the river yelling, **"Marine, tonight you die,"** and "Banzai," firing their rifles as they came.

Johnny Rivers opened up on them, and the mass broke up. Screams of rage and pain came from the other side as the Japanese concentrated everything they had on Schmid's position and on another machine-gun position 150 yards downstream. Bullets whined past the Marines' heads, throwing mud and wood chips around them. Schmid's heart pounded rapidly.

The machine gun on their right stopped firing, put out of action. Then a dozen bullets tore into Rivers' face, killing him. His finger froze on the trigger, sending 200 rounds into the darkness. Cold rage rising in him, Schmid shoved Rivers' body out of the way and took over the gun. Corporal Diamond got in position to load it for him. Every time Schmid raked the attacking Japanese he heard them yelling as bullets ripped into them. He heard one particular Japanese officer "screeching and barking commands at the others; he had a nasty shrill voice that stood out over the others." Schmid fired a burst at the voice, but failed to silence it. It would haunt him for years.

Diamond then was hit in the arm, the bullet knocking him partially across Schmid's feet. He could not load anymore, but while Schmid fired the gun, Diamond stood beside him, spotting targets. Schmid would fire across the river to the left, feel Diamond hitting him hard on the arm and pointing to the right, swing the gun and hear Japanese yelling as his bullets hit them.

Schmid now was both loading and firing the machine gun. When he got close to the end of a 300-round belt of ammunition, Diamond would punch his arm. Schmid would fire a burst, rip open the magazine, insert a new belt and resume firing. At one point a Japanese soldier put a string of bullets through the .30 caliber's water jacket. Water spurted over Schmid's lap and chest; the gun crackled and overheated but did not jam.

Schmid continued loading and firing the machine gun for more than four hours, with and without help. Somehow a Japanese soldier got through the body-choked stream and got close enough to throw a hand grenade into Schmid's position.

"There was a blinding flash and explosion," Schmid recalled. "My helmet was knocked off. Something struck me in the face." When he put his hand up, all he felt was blood and raw flesh. Then he felt pain in his left shoulder, arm and hand. He could see nothing. He collapsed on his back in the nest. "They got me in the eyes," he muttered to Diamond, who lay beside him.

The Japanese were still pouring bullets into the machine-gun position; Schmid reached around to his holster and took out his .45. Diamond heard him fussing with it and yelled, "Don't do it, Smitty, don't shoot yourself."

"Don't worry about that," Schmid said. "I'm going to get the first Jap that tries to come in here!"

"But you can't see," Diamond reminded him.

"Just tell me which way he's coming from and I'll get him," Schmid replied.

Although his sight was gone, Schmid took his position between the spread rear tripod legs of the machine gun, squeezed the trigger and, with Diamond yelling directions in his ear, resumed firing at the Japanese across the river.

Private Whitey Jacobs, one of the squad's members, braved the continuous Japanese gunfire, jumped into the nest and staunched Schmid's and Diamond's wounds. The next thing Schmid knew, they were taking him out on a blanket.

All night the Japanese continued their assaults, but the Marines' anti-tank guns, machine guns and artillery cut Ichiki's men down. At dawn, when it was clear the position would hold, Vandegrift sent a reserve battalion across the river to attack the Japanese from their flank and rear. Of the 800 Japanese who attacked across the Ilu on August 21, only 14 wounded were picked up, and one was captured unhurt. The rest were killed. Ichiki burned his regimental colors and committed suicide.The number of bodies counted within range of Al Schmid's machine gun ran into the hundreds. The other Marines who were there that night credited him with killing at least 200 Japanese.

Schmid was put on a hospital ship and sent back to the United States. He was admitted to the naval hospital at San Diego, Calif., on October 20, 1943, where he endured many operations to remove shell fragments from his face and eyes. His recovery was helped by the care and understanding of Virginia Pfeiffer, a Red Cross worker in the hospital, who wrote a four-page letter to Ruth explaining Schmid's wounds. "Today he told me he might as well let you know," she wrote. "He has lost one eye, and the other is seriously damaged. The doctors will not know for several months whether he will have any sight in that eye." Virginia encouraged Ruth to keep writing to Schmid. On February 18, 1943, **Schmid received the Navy Cross** "for extraordinary heroism and outstanding courage." He went to Washington, D.C., and was commended by President Franklin D. Roosevelt and the Joint Chiefs of Staff.

In Philadelphia, a parade was given in Schmid's honor, and the *Philadelphia Inquirer* presented him with its Hero Award and $1,000. In New Orleans, Schmid received the key to the city. Articles about him appeared in *Life* and *Cosmopolitan* magazines, and a book, *Al Schmid--Marine,* was written by Roger Butterfield. In 1944 Warner Brothers studio began production on a movie based on Butterfield's book, *Pride of the Marines,* starring John Garfield.

Before he began the movie, Garfield went to Philadelphia, met the real Al Schmid, became his friend, lived in his home, and studied him. *Pride of the Marines* was released in 1945 and became an instant hit.

Schmid never thought of himself as a hero. "When I came back I was the most disgusted man you ever saw. I didn't want to bother to do anything. I could see people looking away from my ugly scars. They wouldn't want to associate with me. I even told my girl it was all over."

Ruth would not take *no* for an answer. She and Schmid were married in April 1943. In June 1944, she gave birth to a son, Albert A. Schmid, Jr. The publicity generated by the marriage brought a flood of requests for war bond, hospital and charity appearances.

Schmid regained partial eyesight in his remaining eye and spent his years pursuing his hobbies of organ-playing, ham radio and fishing.

Al Schmid died of bone cancer on December 2, 1982, in St. Petersburg. He was buried with full military honors in Arlington National Cemetery.

AMERICA'S FIRST NATIVE BORN HERO

Although the War of 1812 was pretty much a draw, it is still nonetheless significant. The conflict produced two heroes that would later become president – Andrew Jackson and William Henry Harrison. It gave us our national anthem, written by Francis Scott Key as he watched the British attack on Fort McHenry at Baltimore. More significantly, it was now obvious to the Europeans that the American experiment in democracy was going to succeed.

Following the fall of Detroit in August 1812, the British took control of Lake Erie. In an attempt to regain naval superiority on the lake, the US Navy began construction of two 20-gun brigs at Presque Isle, PA (Erie, PA). These vessels were intended to be the foundation of the new American fleet. In March 1813, the new commander of American naval forces on Lake Erie, Commandant **Oliver H. Perry** (26 years-old), arrived at Presque Isle. Perry diligently oversaw the construction of the two 20 gun brigs, named USS *Lawrence* and USS *Niagara*, each double masted ships. Perry was the older brother of Commodore Matthew Perry, the man who sailed a fleet of warships into Tokyo Bay in 1852 and forcibly opened Japan to the Western World. Matthew was also with his older brother aboard the *Lawrence* during the Battle of Lake Erie. After reconnoitering Presque Isle, Barclay (the British commander) focused his efforts on completing the 19-gun ship HMS *Detroit* which was under construction at Amherstburg. As with his American counterpart, Barclay was hampered by a perilous supply situation. Convinced that construction of *Detroit* was on target, he departed with his fleet and began a blockade of Presque Isle. This British presence prevented Perry from moving *Niagara* and *Lawrence* over the harbor's sand bar. Finally, on July 29, Barclay was forced to depart due to low supplies. Taking advantage, Perry moved his ships out of the harbor. With his two brigs ready for service, Perry took control of the lake. From this position, he was able to prevent supplies from reaching Amherstburg. As a result, Barclay was forced to seek battle in early September. Sailing from his base, he flew his flag from the recently completed *Detroit*, and was joined by HMS *Queen Charlotte* (13 guns), HMS *Lady Prevost* (13), HMS *Hunter* (10), HMS *Little Belt* (3), and HMS *Chippawa* (1).

Perry countered with *Lawrence* (20 guns), *Niagara* (20), USS *Ariel* (4), USS *Caledonia* (3), USS *Scorpion* (2), USS *Somers* (2), USS *Porcupine* (1), USS *Tigress* (1), and USS *Trippe* (1). Commanding from *Lawrence*, Perry's ships sailed under a blue battle flag emblazoned with Captain James Lawrence's immortal command, "Don't Give Up the Ship." Departing Put-in-Bay (OH) harbor on September 10, 1813, Perry placed *Ariel* and *Scorpion* at the head of his line, followed by *Lawrence*, *Caledonia*, and *Niagara*. The remaining gunboats trailed to the rear.

As the principal armament of his brigs was short-range carronades, Perry intended to close on *Detroit* with *Lawrence* while Lieutenant Jesse Elliot, commanding *Niagara*, attacked *Queen Charlotte*. As the two fleets sighted each other, the wind favored the British. This soon changed as it began to lightly blow from the southeast benefiting Perry. With the American's slowly closing on his ships, Barclay opened the battle at 11:45 AM with a long-range shot from *Detroit*. For the next thirty minutes, the two fleets exchanged shots, with the British getting the better of the action.

Finally at 12:15, Perry was in position to open fire with *Lawrence*'s carronades. As his guns began pummeling the British ships, he was surprised to see *Niagara* slowing rather than moving to engage *Queen Charlotte*. Elliot's decision not to attack may have been the result of *Caledonia* shortening sail and blocking his path. Regardless, his delay in bringing *Niagara* allowed the British to focus their fire on *Lawrence*. Though Perry's gun crews inflicted heavy damage on the British, they were soon overwhelmed and *Lawrence* suffered 80% casualties. Most commanders would have surrendered – but not Perry.

With the battle hanging by a thread, the intrepid Perry ordered a boat lowered and transferred his flag to *Niagara*. After ordering Elliot to row back and hasten the American gunboats which had fallen behind, Perry sailed the undamaged brig in to the fray. Aboard the British ships, casualties had been heavy with most of the senior officers wounded or killed. Among those hit was Barclay who was wounded in the right arm. As *Niagara* approached, the British attempted to turn their vessels. During this manuever, *Detroit* and *Queen Charlotte* collided and became entangled. Surging through Barclay's line, Perry pounded the helpless ships. Around 3:00, aided by the arriving gunboats, *Niagara* was able to compel the British ships to surrender.

When the smoke settled, **Perry had captured the entire British squadron** and secured American control of Lake Erie. Writing to General William Henry Harrison, Perry profoundly reported "**We have met the enemy and they are ours.**" American casualties in the battle were 27 dead and 96 wounded. British losses numbered 41 dead, 93 wounded, and 306 captured. Following the victory, Perry ferried Harrison's Army of the Northwest to Detroit where it began its advance into Canada. This campaign ended in the American victory at the Battle of the Thames on October 5, 1813.

Perry's victory was astonishing because he was a novice going up against a seasoned veteran of the Napoleonic Wars - someone who had participated in the stunning British victory at Trafalgar in 1805. It was the equivalent of sending out a rookie to strike out the mighty Babe Ruth. The thing was, Perry was absolutely sure he could do it.

Were it not for Perry's bravery that day in 1813, we Americans might be filling our cars with liters instead of gallons of gasoline. Like Canada, we could be part of the British Commonwealth of Nations paying our respects to the British Queen and reading endless magazine articles about princes William and Harry.

Hopefully, young boys who read the stories in this book will come to realize that history is much more than just dates and dull facts about things that happened decades and centuries ago. These events determined our destiny, shaped our national character. These stories are integral strands in the national tapestry that tells us who we are as a people and what we are about. History is anything but dead or ancient. History is a living saga of how we have come to be, a meaningful record of those who have gone before us and a guide for those who are yet to come. As Craig Heimbuch writes, "In order to truly understand and absorb history, you have to experience it, to see for yourself the difficulties and challenges, to *use your imagination* and feel what it was like."

Oliver H. Perry

It is my hope that this book, in some small way, will challenge you to become a person of integrity and to put your best foot forward. May the numerous activities inspire your confidence. May you become a doer and not just an observer floaring along with the tide. May you no longer be a dream-addled wannabe but someone who looks at the horizon and decides to find out what's on the other side. May this book inspire you to become the best at everything!

IF YOU THINK EDUCATION IS EXPENSIVE, TRY IGNORANCE!

IF YOU THINK YOU CAN, YOU CAN!

ENTHUSIASM IS THE FUEL THAT BOOSTS YOU UP THE LADDER OF SUCCESS

LIBERTIES & FREEDOMS ARE WORTH DEFENDING AT ALL HAZARDS!

AND I'M PROUD TO BE AN AMERICAN, WHERE AT LEAST I KNOW I'M FREE. AND I WON'T FORGET THE MEN WHO DIED, WHO GAVE THAT RIGHT TO ME!   LEE GREENWOOD

IT'S NOT WHAT HAPPENS TO YOU THAT DETERMINES HOW WELL YOU WILL DO IN LIFE, IT'S HOW WELL YOU HANDLE IT!

THE TWELVE COMMANDMENTS FOR BOYS

Always try to do your best
Don't lie, cheat, or steal
Avoid liquor and illegal drugs
Don't be a verbal or physical bully
Respect your parents
Stay in shape physically
Acquire knowledge and many skills so you are employable
Control your temper
Get involved in sports and youth activities at church
Obey the laws
Be kind to animals and all God's creatures
Don't go overboard with computer and video games

THE MAN WHO BOMBED PEARL HARBOR BECOMES A CHRISTIAN

What follows is an excerpt from a historical novel I wrote about the attack on the American naval base at Pearl Harbor, causing America to enter World War II on the side of England and the Allies. Harry, the main character, is from the year 1958 and has traveled back in time to try to prevent the attack. Although the work is fiction, **the amazing story of Commander Fuchida is true**.

210 miles north of Oahu, Hawaii, December 7, 1941, 5:50 a.m.

The imperial Japanese Navy carrier *Akagi,* a converted battle cruiser, turned eastward into the wind. Standing in the cockpit of his "Kate" three-seater torpedo plane, Commander Mitsuo Fuchida braced his hands on either side of the open canopy, fearful that his trembling would be visible.

The 34,347 ton *Akagi* heeled over as it turned, pounded by towering forty-foot waves that, as their heading shifted from south to southeast and now to east, became a stomach-lurching sea, from the crests of the waves, spray sweeping over the bow with each downward plunge of the 34,000 ton aircraft carrier.

Fuchida craned his neck to see the other carriers. To his immediate right was the *Kaga*, armed with 18 Mitsubishi Zeroes, 26 Aichi Vals, and 26 Nakajima Kate torpedo bombers. The formidable Zero was agile without peer. On his left was the similarly armed *Soryu*. Behind him were the *Shokaku* and

336

Zuikaku, the newest carriers, and the *Hiryu*. The most recent carriers had been built from American scrap metal – old Fords, Chryslers, Chevrolets, Kelvinator appliances and Singer sewing machines.

But on this day, Fuchida's mind was full of excitement and anticipation as he was about to lead a strike force that would achieve the greatest victory in the history of naval warfare.

He caught the eye of his chief and nodded; the chief had given him the traditional headband that he now sported like a samurai of old, grinned, and gave a thumb's up signal that all was well. Assistants knelt under either wing, hands wrapped taut around the ropes that would pull the wheel chocks clear. In this mad, rolling sea, there'd be a disaster in the making if they were removed too early. A plane rolling backward or forward into another, since they were spaced but a few feet apart, could set off a chain reaction explosion that would sweep the deck and in an instant shatter the entire plan.

Captain Fuchida

Fuchida caught Genda's eye, salutes were exchanged between two old friends and he knew Genda was in agony, wishing to go with them and not tied to the deck command bridge. It was now a few minutes after 6:00. The tropical twilight was brightening in the east, arcing under low scudding clouds, the trailing wisps of the storm that had covered their advance across 4,000 nautical miles of the Pacific.

A bosun's pipe shrieked over the ship's public address system. He went rigid, his eyes focused just to the aft of the bridge to the string of signal flags, heart pounding. There it was, the legendary Z flag, the flag that had reverently been brought out from its honored place aboard the old flagship *Mikusa*. It was the very flag that Admiral Togo had raised in 1905 to signal the commencement of actions against the Russians.

Another shrill from the bosun's pipe and the flag that was at half mast rose ever so sharply to the top of the signal mast. At the sight of it thus, a wild shout went up. The years of training now came to the fore.

Fuchida slipped down into the cockpit, quickly buckling his harness, pulling the shoulder straps tight. Now seated, he could not see straight ahead and could only catch a glimpse of the Kate in front and to the port side. With a dramatic gesture the crew chief pointed to the crews holding the chocks in place, telling them to pull on the ropes. The heavy Kate began to roll forward, the launch chief, up on the bridge, pointing to the moment the deck was pitching up, thus by the time they reached the end of the great deck, it would be heaving downward. Fuchida's plane sailed off the deck and began to climb skyward. Fuchida could see the Zeroes beginning to circle into formation. He looked down at his chronometer. It was 6:20 a.m. In Japan it was already December 8. Pearl Harbor and Battleship Row were one hour and twenty minutes away.

Harry rushed over to Laura. Please excuse me but there's someone I saw that I need to speak with before I leave. She nodded an okay. Harry made his way over to Captain Fuchida and touched him on the arm. "Excuse me, sir, but there's something very important I need to talk with you about."

Fuchida looked at him with a puzzled expression. "I'm sorry, but until you gave that speech I had never before laid eyes on you."

"I know, but trust me; it's very important and will only take five minutes."

Fuchida's shoulders sagged in resignation. "All right," he pointed, "there's a room over there."

"What is it?" Fuchida impatiently asked after they closed the door behind them.

"Don't ask me how I know this, but here's what the future has in store for you. There will probably be a war between America and Japan; you will play a signi-

7:55 a.m. Pearl Harbor under attack (notice the bomb splashes)

ficant part and become a big hero. You will survive the war but Japan will be defeated. About fifteen of your military leaders will be hanged after the war, most of them for allowing soldiers under their command to commit atrocities similar to what has already happened at Nanking."

Fuchida stared at Harry incredulously. "That is the most outrageous thing I have ever heard."

"Please, hear me out. I'm almost finished. You'll be outraged at these trials, convinced they are unfair and nothing more than 'victor's justice.' As Japanese prisoners of war are released and returned home, you are stunned to discover that they were all treated well by their American captors. One particular group tells you they were cared for by a woman whose parents were mis-sionaries that were beheaded in the Philippines. You become curious why such a woman would treat her enemies with love and compassion rather than mimic the Bushido code and seek revenge. Discovering that she was a Christian, you begin reading a copy of the Bible and become a Christian and an evangelist preacher. In 1951 you will become an American citizen."

338

"Fuchida became angry as he stood there with clenched fists. "No one has the power to foretell the future. Why would you make up such a ridiculous story and then waste my time with this fairy tale?"

"I tell you this in hopes that men of influence in Japan will come to their senses and choose peace rather than war. Millions of lives could be saved. Talk to Rear Admiral Nagumo, he vehemently opposes a war with America. Talk to Admiral Yamamoto. He will tell you that Japan has no chance of winning a protracted war with America. He went to Harvard. Perhaps no man in Japan knows America better than Yamamoto."

"I suppose Yamamoto and Nagumo will also become big heroes," Fuchida said with a sneer.

"Yes, but Yamamoto will not survive the war; he will be killed. And Nagumo will commit suicide."

Fuchida, with a disgusted look on his face, pivoted and walked out of the room.

I dared not tell him more about Pearl Harbor, Harry thought. To do so would have put my life in danger. I can only hope he remembers what I told him when Yamamoto admits to other top officers he is skeptical about Japan winning a protracted war with America.

HOW TO SOLDER

First a few safety precautions: Do not attempt to solder on your own. Have your father or a responsible adult work with you on this.

Never touch the element or tip of the soldering iron. They are very hot (about 400°C) and will give you a nasty burn.

Take great care to avoid touching the mains flex with the tip of the iron. The iron should have a heatproof flex for extra protection. An ordinary plastic flex will melt immediately if touched by a hot iron and there is a serious risk of burns and electric shock.

Always return the soldering iron to its stand when not in use. Never put it down on your workbench, even for a moment!

Work in a well-ventilated area. The smoke formed as you melt solder is mostly from the flux and quite irritating. Avoid breathing it by keeping your head to the side of, not above, your work.

Wash your hands after using solder. Solder contains lead which is a poisonous metal.

Preparing the soldering iron:

Place the soldering iron in its stand and plug in. The iron will take a few minutes to reach its operating temperature of about 400°C.

Dampen the sponge in the stand. The best way to do this is to lift it out of the stand and hold it under a cold tap for a moment, then squeeze to remove excess water. It should be damp, not dripping wet.

Wait a few minutes for the soldering iron to warm up. You can check if it is ready by trying to melt a little solder on the tip.

Wipe the tip of the iron on the damp sponge. This will clean the tip.

Melt a little solder on the tip of the iron. This is called 'tinning' and it will help the heat to flow from the iron's tip to the joint. It only needs to be done when you plug in the iron, and occasionally while soldering if you need to wipe the tip clean on the sponge. You are now ready to start soldering: Hold the soldering iron like a pen, near the base of the handle. Imagine you are going to write your name. Remember to **never touch the hot element or tip**. Touch the soldering iron onto the joint to be made. Make sure it touches both the component lead and the track. Hold the tip there for a few seconds and feed a little solder onto the joint. It should flow smoothly onto the lead and track to form a volcano shape as shown in the diagram. Apply the solder to the joint, not the iron.

Remove the solder, then the iron, while keeping the joint still. Allow the joint a few seconds to cool before you move the circuit board.

Inspect the joint closely. It should look shiny and have a 'volcano' shape. If not, you will need to reheat it and feed in a little more solder. This time ensure that **both** the lead and track are heated fully before applying solder.

FIRST AID Most soldering burns are likely to be minor and treatment is simple:

Immediately cool the affected area under gently running cold water. Keep the burn in the cold water for at least 5 minutes (15 minutes is recommended). If ice is readily available this can be helpful too, but do not delay the initial cooling with cold water.

Do not apply any creams or ointments. The burn will heal better without them. A dry dressing, such as a clean handkerchief, may be applied if you wish to protect the area from dirt.

Seek medical attention if the burn covers an area bigger than 1 inch square.

WHEN OPPORTUNITY KNOCKS

Da, da, da dum! The dramatic first four notes of Beethoven's 5th Symphony – fate knocking at the door. There are times in life when opportunity knocks and you have to be ready to take advantage of it. In the movie *You Light up my Life*, Kacey Cisyk, an unknown, sings the title song. She was offered the chance to record and release it as a single but turned down that opportunity, believing the song to be a dud. Instead, Debby Boone recorded the song on the Warner label and in 1977 it became the #1 song for an unheard of fifteen weeks, transforming Boone into a millionaire and making it **the #1 song of the entire decade**.

A big thanks to Wikipedia for supplying pictures and information for portions of this book.

HOW TO FIND YOUR BLIND SPOT

Everyone has a blind spot. Place your left hand over your left eye and hold this book in your other hand. Stare at the black circle below. Slowly move the book closer to your face while continuing to stare at the circle. At a certain distance you will notice that the heart on the right side will disappear. Bingo! That's your blind spot. This effect is caused by a lack of light-detecting receptor cells on part of your retina.

●   ♥